State Board of Education, California

History of the United States

State Board of Education, California

History of the United States

ISBN/EAN: 9783744704618

Printed in Europe, USA, Canada, Australia, Japan

Cover: Foto ©ninafisch / pixelio.de

More available books at **www.hansebooks.com**

COLUMBUS BEFORE ISABELLA.

(From Group of Statuary in State Capitol at Sacramento, presented to State of California by D. O. Mills.)

CALIFORNIA STATE SERIES OF SCHOOL TEXT-BOOKS.

HISTORY

OF THE

UNITED STATES.

COMPILED UNDER THE DIRECTION

OF THE

STATE BOARD OF EDUCATION.

SACRAMENTO, CALIFORNIA.
Printed at the State Printing Office.

PREFACE.

In this book it has been the aim to emphasize the political and social aspects of national life rather than to enlarge upon its wars. Much work for the pupil in connection with the study of the narrative has been suggested. It is largely comprised in the models of abstracts, or outlines, introduced at the head of chapters and the blank forms of review given at the end of them. The teacher must judge in each case to what extent the work so suggested can be performed, but it is earnestly recommended that enough be done to give the pupil facility in the use of these methods of study.

The chapters on the History of California will be recognized as a necessity of this publication. The space given to an account of measures in behalf of Public Education will be remarked as a new feature, and its uniform approval by the excellent and able teachers to whom it has been submitted for advice and criticism, gives assurance that it will be cordially welcomed. Indeed, whatever merit the features peculiar to this book may have, is largely due to the interest taken in it by the many eminent men and women who have been consulted in its preparation, and whose services and suggestions are here gratefully acknowledged.

Especial mention should be made of the opportunity to consult the admirable manuscript charts prepared by Mr. S. A. Espy and used by him in his school at Alleghany City, Pennsylvania, which were kindly forwarded to the Board for its use.

If the study of this work shall give the youth of the state a deeper interest in the welfare of their country, and contribute in some degree to establish its permanence through their love for it, its purpose will be well attained.

CONTENTS.

I. COLONIAL PERIOD.

	PAGE.
CHAPTER I.—*Introduction*.	7
CHAPTER II. *Columbus and his Voyage.*	12
CHAPTER III.—*The People of the New Land.*	16
CHAPTER IV.—*Later Discoveries.*	20
1. Spain.	
2. France.	
3. England.	
4. Portugal.	
CHAPTER V.—*Beginning of Settlement.*	29
1. France.	
2. Spain.	
3. England.	
CHAPTER VI.—*Plymouth and Massachusetts Bay.*	36
1. Plymouth.	
2. Massachusetts Bay.	
CHAPTER VII.—*Other New England Colonies.*	43
1. Rhode Island.	
2. Connecticut.	
3. New Hampshire.	
CHAPTER VIII.—*New England.*	47
CHAPTER IX.—*Virginia and Maryland.*	56
1. Virginia.	
2. Maryland.	
CHAPTER X.—*Southern Colonies.*	63
1. North Carolina.	
2. South Carolina.	
3. Georgia.	
4. The Southern Group.	
CHAPTER XI.—*Middle Colonies.*	71
1. New York.	
2. New Jersey.	
3. Pennsylvania.	
4. Delaware.	
CHAPTER XII.—*The Thirteen Colonies in 1750.*	81
CHAPTER XIII.—*Canada and Louisiana.*	91
1. French Exploration of the Interior.	
2. Wars between French and English.	
3. Growth of New France to 1750.	

	PAGE.
CHAPTER XIV.—*The Struggle for the Interior.*	98
CHAPTER XV.—*The Birth of the Nation.*	111

II. TRANSITION TO NATIONAL LIFE.

CHAPTER XVI.—*War for Independence.* 130
       1. First Hostilities.
       2. Invasion of Canada.
       3. State Governments.
       4. Along the Coast.
       5. Independence.
       6. Washington's Campaigns.
       7. Burgoyne's Defeat and the French Alliance.
       8. On the Frontier.
       9. Naval Affairs.
      10. Arnold's Treason.
      11. War in the South.
      12. The Last Campaign.
      13. The Close of the War.
CHAPTER XVII.—*The Formation of a National Government.* 179

III. NATIONAL LIFE WITH A DIVIDED LABOR SYSTEM.

CHAPTER XVIII.—*The United States Government Established.* . . . 190
       1. Work of the First Congress.
       2. The President and the Country.
       3. The Indians.
       4. Excise and the Whisky Insurrection.
       5. United States Bank.
       6. Foreign Affairs and Political Parties.
       7. Immigration and Western Development.
       8. Washington Retires.
CHAPTER XIX.—*Government by the Federalists.* 206
       1. The New Administration.
       2. "Adams and Liberty."
       3. Downfall of the Federalists.
CHAPTER XX.—*New Ideas and a New Party.* 211
CHAPTER XXI.—*Young America and the War of 1812.* 219
       1. Beginning of Hostilities.
       2. War of 1812.
CHAPTER XXII.—*North and South set a Dividing Line.* 233
CHAPTER XXIII.—*A Protective Tariff and New Political Parties.* . . 240
CHAPTER XXIV.—*Jackson and the People.* 246
       1. Political Affairs.
       2. Domestic Affairs.
CHAPTER XXV.—*Speculation and Panic.* 259
CHAPTER XXVI.—"*Tippecanoe and Tyler, too.*" 264

	PAGE.
CHAPTER XXVII.—*Texas and Mexico.*	272
CHAPTER XXVIII.—*El Dorado, the Land of Gold.*	280
CHAPTER XXIX.—*The Struggle for Kansas, and a New Party.*	288
CHAPTER XXX.—*From the Dred Scott Decision to Secession.*	296
CHAPTER XXXI.—*War of Secession.*	303

    1. Beginning of War.
    2. Around Washington and Richmond.
    3. The War in the West.
    4. Along the Coast.
    5. Around Vicksburg.
    6. Around Chattanooga.
    7. Sherman's Advance into Georgia.
    8. Final Campaign in Virginia.
    9. Finances of the War.
    10. The Final Tragedy.

IV. NATIONAL LIFE WITH A UNITED LABOR SYSTEM.

CHAPTER XXXII.—*The Constitution Amended.*	337
CHAPTER XXXIII.—*The Nation One.*	343
CHAPTER XXXIV.—*The Beginning of a New Age.*	353
CHAPTER XXXV.—*Education and Science.*	367
CHAPTER XXXVI.—*Settlement of California.*	378

    1. Exploration and Early Settlement.
    2. Under Mexican Rule.
    3. American Conquest.

CHAPTER XXXVII.—*Our State.*	388

LIST OF MAPS.

	BETWEEN PAGES.
1. *Explorations and Discoveries.*	16–17
2. *French and English Territory 1750.*	96–97
3. *Territory of 1783.*	192–193
4. *United States in 1830.*	256–257
5. *Areas of Secession.*	304–305
6. *Territorial Map of 1876.*	352–353

APPENDIX.

	PAGE.
1. *Explanation of Terms.*	400
2. *Pronunciations.*	407
3. *Books of Reference.*	409
4. *Declaration of Independence.*	412
5. *Constitution of United States.*	415
6. *General Index.*	426

A HISTORY

OF

THE UNITED STATES.

CHAPTER I.

INTRODUCTION.

For Explanation.—Celtic; crusades; pagans; Mohammedans; lore; Jaffa; Constantine; de Medici; astrolabe; Hercules; Aristotle; Alexander; Oriental; Venetian; blazoned; state; turquoises; cloth of gold; ermine; sable; Khan.

To be Pronounced.—Teū-tŏn'ic; Är'yan; Eū-ro-pē'an; Elbe (elb); Ptolemy (tŏl'e-my); Cā'diz; Mo-hăm'me-dans; Christendom (krĭs'n-dum); Asia (ā'she-a); Ganges (găn'jĕz); Är'is-tŏt-le; Cŏn'stan'tine; Bŏs'pō-rus; Medici (mĕd'e-chee); ăs'trō-lābe; Khän; Cipango (sē-pang'o); Cam-ba-lu'; Cath-ay'.

1. **We are to study** the history of the people living in the country now known as the United States of America. Travel and the study of maps give a knowledge of this land and its people as they now are. But not even the land has always been what we see at the present time. Its mountains, rivers, and plains, which seem to us unchanging, had their beginning and gradual growth. In like manner the character and condition of the inhabitants have also changed. Only 400 years ago there was not one white man living in all America. How the part of America which is now the territory of the United States has been settled by white men; how cities have been built and the country brought under cultivation; how governments have been established and maintained, we are now to learn. Nature made this land beautiful and rich, and our forefathers by establishing liberty and justice have left to us and to all the world a noble record for study and imitation.

2. Beginning of United States History.—Of the whole present population of the United States about thirteen per cent were born in foreign countries, mostly in Europe. The forefathers of all the white people born in this country came also from Europe. Therefore the history of the United States takes its beginning from that of Europe. England, of all European countries, has had the greatest influence upon the United States. From England came the great majority of the first settlers, the language that we use, our common law, and forms of government.

3. [**Early England.**—The people of England belong to what is called the Teutonic race, one member of a great family known as the Aryan or Indo-European. Under the names of Angles and Saxons, tribes of warriors sailed from the country around the mouth of the river Elbe across the North Sea to the island of Britain; and between the years 450 and 600 they gradually conquered the land, driving the Celtic inhabitants into the mountains of Wales and Scotland. The Angles and Saxons were pagans when they came into Britain. Missionaries sent from Rome introduced Christianity. The southern part of the island received the name of England, which means the land of the Angles. The English lived for a time under separate kingdoms, but these were united in 827. The king did not have all power. He was surrounded by a body of advisers, a council of the great and wise men, which afterwards grew to be the English Parliament (42).]

4. The Dark Ages.—This name is sometimes given to the time from the end of the fifth century to the beginning of the fifteenth, because in that time the people of Europe made but little progress in knowledge and civilization and forgot a great deal of the learning of the ancient Greeks and Romans. Before the fifteenth century no one in Europe knew anything about Southern Africa, Australia, or America. Ships were small and hardly able to endure the storms of ocean. Only the boldest sailors dared trust themselves out of sight of land. Many learned men had thought of the earth as a globe, but the common people all believed it to be flat.

5. [**End of the Dark Ages and the Revival of Ancient Learning.**—"According to Ptolemy, the best recognized authority, whose geography

had stood the test of thirteen hundred years, the then known world was a strip of some seventy degrees wide, mostly north of the equator, with Cadiz on the west, and farthest India, or Cathay, on the east, lying between the frozen and burning zones, both impassable by man. The inhabitants, as far as known in Europe, were Christians and Mohammedans, the one sect about half the age of the other. Christendom, the elder, that once held considerable portions of Asia and Africa, had been driven back inch by inch, in spite of the Crusades, even from the Holy Land, the place of its birth, up into the northwest corner of Europe; and both in lands and people was outnumbered six to one by the followers of Mohammed. For seven hundred years the fairest provinces of Spain acknowledged the sway of the Moors, and the Mediterranean from Jaffa to the Gates of Hercules (Straits of Gibraltar), was under their control. . . . India beyond the Ganges, from the days of Moses, Alexander, and Aristotle . . . was deemed the land of promise, the abode of luxury, the source of wealth, and the home of the spices; but the routes of commerce thither . . . were one by one being closed to the Christians. . . . Finally, in 1453, Constantinople, the Christian city of Constantine, fell into the hands of the Turks, and with it the commerce of the Black Sea and the Bosporus, the last of the old trading routes from the East to the West. . . . The learned Christians of Constantinople, with nothing but their heads and their books, fled in exile into Italy, and became its schoolmasters. At once began there the *revival of learning*, which soon extended throughout the West. The Medici family of Italy at Venice and Florence welcomed these learned Greeks, and bought their precious manuscripts of ancient lore. . . . On the Rhine the young printing press was just giving forth its first sheets. (See Lesson 115, Second Reader.) The compass and the astrolabe, recent inventions, began now to give confidence to mariners, and teach them that, though the old paths of trade overland were closed, they might venture on new ones over sea. . . . . The manuscript travels of Marco Polo and Sir John Mandeville had found their way into the hands of thinking men. . . . Soon after the date of the fall of Constantinople, Italy and Portugal had reached that turn for adventure and enterprise which spread like wildfire throughout the other states of Europe, and caused the entire revolution in the commerce of the world."—*Stevens*.]

6. [**Marco Polo,** the Venetian wanderer, and first European to visit China, told of the rich realm ruled over by the Great Khan. His provinces covered southern and eastern Asia, including the great island of Cipango—Japan. "At the city of Cambalu (now Peking), on the northeast of Cathay, where the Khan resided for three winter months, his palace was of marble with a roof of gold, so blazoned in many colors that nothing but gold and imagery met the eye. . . . In another city, the Khan made his residence for three of the summer months, and

there also was 'a marvelous palace of marble and other stones' in an inclosure of sixteen miles. So large was the banquet hall of this royal residence, that the Khan's table in the center was eighty yards high. ... The Khan's army was almost like the sands of the sea for numbers, and so magnificent was the state of its many generals that they sat in chairs of solid silver. ... In one province a mountain of turquoises pierced the clouds; in a valley of another nestled a lake where pearls were so plentiful that had there been freedom to gather them, pearls would have been so common as to be of little worth. There were many mines of silver, many rivers whose beds were spangled with gold. The beasts and birds were various and wonderful. ... Spices grew everywhere; and of fruit there were nuts as large as a child's head, filled with a delicious milk, pears that weighed ten pounds, peaches two pounds each. ... The people of this favored region clothed themselves in cloth of gold, in silks, in lawns, and cambrics of the finest fabric, in furs of ermine and of sable."—*Bryant*.]

7. Value of Oriental Trade.—In the middle of the fifteenth century the rising nations of Western Europe were all eager to gain control of oriental trade. A nation's wealth was then counted in the gold, silver, jewels, silks, and fine robes of the sovereign and his court. Palaces for the nobles were grand things; but nobody thought of comfortable homes for laborers. A spice island was a far greater prize than a valley that would yield wheat. All riches were to be sought for in the distant East.

QUESTIONS.—*Where is the Elbe? Name the divisions of Great Britain. What is a mariner's compass? Where is the Holy Land? In what year did the 5th century begin? The 15th? Where is Jaffa located?* (**Jaffa is ancient Joppa.**) *Gibraltar? Cadiz? Farthest India? Constantinople? The Black Sea? The Bosporus? The Rhine? About how old was Christianity at this time? Mohammedanism?*

OUTLINE, OR ABSTRACT.

[**To the Pupil.**—*The outline of five paragraphs given below is designed to furnish a suggestion, or model, for work to be done in preparing a lesson for recitation. It will be found helpful to make a similar outline, before coming into class, of each paragraph to be recited.*]

1. *U. S. History*—land and people. *Land*—not unchanging, has its growth. *People*—Studied in settlements, growth of cities, establishment

---

7. *Name the nations of Western Europe.*

of governments. *Land*—rich by nature; liberty and justice established by forefathers; noble record.

2. Thirteen per cent present population born in Europe; forefathers of all native whites, also; therefore history begins in Europe. England influences most; gave majority of first settlers, our language, law, form of government.

3. *English*—of Teutonic race, Aryan family; *forefathers*—Angles and Saxons, pagans, from mouth of Elbe; conquered England 450 A. D. to 650 A. D.; drove out Celts. Missionaries; Christianity introduced. *England means*—land of the Angles; *consisted* of five kingdoms, united 827 A. D.; *government*—king and body of advisers.

4. *Dark Ages*—end of 5th to beginning of 15th century; little progress; ancient learning neglected; no knowledge of South Africa, Australia, America; ships small and weak; seldom sailed out of sight of land; earth generally thought to be flat.

5. Ptolemy's Geography standard for 1300 years; *taught*—world a strip E. and W. 70° wide, between Cadiz and farthest India; N. and S. between impassable frozen and burning zones. *Inhabitants known to Europe*—Christians and Mohammedans; Mohammedanism half as old as Christianity, followers six times as numerous, possessions six times as great. Jaffa to Gibraltar 700 years under the Moors (Mohammedans); Christians cut off from the finest lands of Asia; Constantinople and the trading routes to the East fall to the Turks; Christians flee to Italy; learning revives there; printing press on the Rhine; inventions increase; sea routes thought of in place of land routes closed; writings of travelers quicken thought; Italy and Portugal begin enterprises; commerce revolutionized.

[**To the Teacher.**—Should the making of abstracts be found at first burdensome to the pupils, separate single paragraphs may be given to each of them. The practice of making abstracts, however, is so great an aid to mastery of the narrative, and the ability to give, in outline, the substance of any statement, either written or oral, is so valuable, that, to *some* extent the exercise should be a part of every lesson; for though the early efforts of the pupil may yield unsatisfactory results, perseverance in them will in the end gladden both pupil and teacher by the power awakened and the facility given in mastering the text. "It is the first step that costs."]

CHAPTER II.
1453-1493.

COLUMBUS AND HIS VOYAGE.

For Explanation.—Oriental; successively; admiral: viceroy; San Salvador; pawn.

To be Pronounced.—Dä Gä'mä; Pavia (pä-vee'ä); Cäs-tile'; Pä'los; Ba-hä'ma; Hayti (hä'te); Āz'ores; Gĕn'o-ă.

8. To find a sea-road to the Indies was the problem of the age (1450–1493). All the royal power of Portugal was put forth in pushing voyages further and further southward, with the plan of sailing around Africa. This was finally accomplished by a fleet in charge of Vasco da Gama in 1498. Before this date, however, a humble Italian navigator had formed the plan of reaching the East by sailing west.

9. This navigator was Christopher Columbus, born in Genoa, Italy, about 1435. He received at the University of Pavia some instruction in geometry, geography, astronomy, and navigation; but from the age of fourteen for many years the sea was his home. In the wild life of a sailor at that time, he met with many adventures, and showed himself strong and brave. He lived several years in Portugal, marrying a Portuguese woman. He thus became acquainted with all that the Portuguese had done in exploring the Atlantic, and all that they were attempting to do to reach India.

10. Columbus concluded, from the study of modern and ancient geographers and from the reports of travelers and seamen, that Europe and Asia covered at least two thirds of the distance around the earth, and that therefore India might be reached by an easy voyage westward across the Atlantic over the remaining third. He underestimated the size of the earth, and did not know that a whole continent and another ocean kept the waves of the Atlantic from the shore of Asia. His conclusion having once been formed, his faith never weakened. He was a deeply religious man, and believed that he was the messenger of heaven appointed to carry the gospel to benighted lands.

11. Money was needed to buy an ocean ship and to hire sailors to cross the Atlantic; Columbus had none. He applied successively to King John II. of Portugal, to his native city, Genoa, and to Ferdinand and Isabella, the sovereigns of Castile and Arragon, the founders of the modern kingdom of Spain. Years and years he waited, argued, and pleaded at the Spanish Court. He had just received assurances of help from Portugal, and an encouraging letter from England, where his brother, Bartholomew Columbus, had presented his plan, and was on the point of leaving Spain forever, when a message from Isabella brought him again before her. She promised help, offering to pawn the royal jewels of Castile, if necessary. (See Frontispiece.) Money was furnished from the royal treasury for two ships. With the help of friends Columbus added a third. He was appointed Admiral and Viceroy of all new lands and seas.

12. The First Voyage.—With his fleet of three vessels and a total crew of 120 men, Columbus sailed from Palos, Spain, August 3d, 1492. His ships were all small, hardly safe for an ocean voyage, but Columbus preferred them, thinking that his voyage would be short and that small vessels would be better for exploring an unknown coast. Three weeks were spent on one of the Canary islands in making repairs. On September sixth, the westward voyage began. The wind was generally favorable; the troubles of Columbus came from the fears of his men. The magnetic needle was found to vary from the true north as observed by the north star, and this puzzled even Columbus. The sight of birds and fishes known to live near land gave hope to the sailors, and often they thought that they saw land; but found afterwards that they had been deceived by cloudbanks in the western sky. All the persuasion and all the authority of Columbus were several times required to prevent the sailors from turning homeward.

13. The Discovery.—On the night of October eleventh, Columbus saw a light moving in the distance, and early in

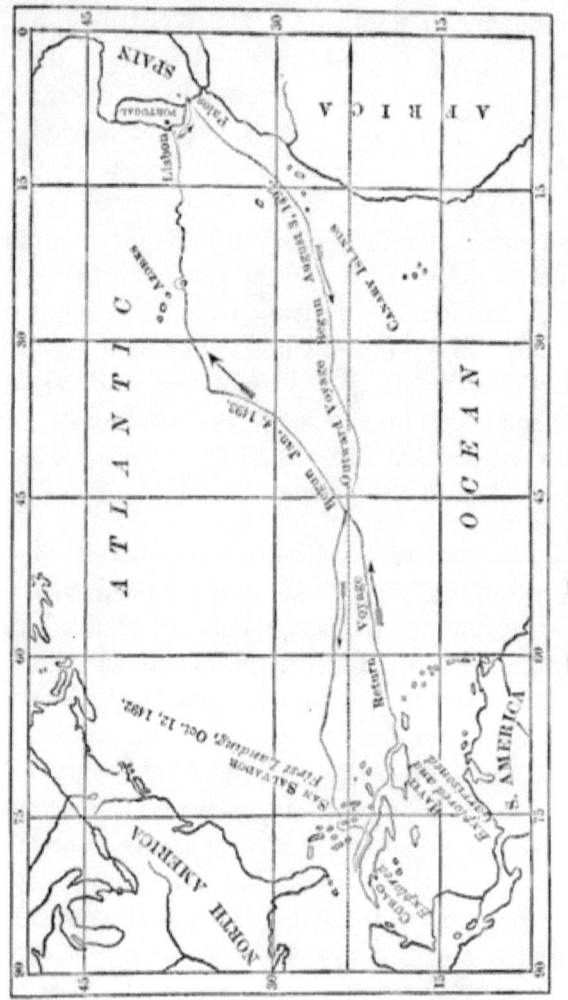

FIRST VOYAGE OF COLUMBUS.

Map Questions.—From what port did Columbus first sail? On what date? In what general direction? Where and when did he first land? What islands were explored? Near the border of what zones? On what island did he leave a garrison? On what day did he begin his return voyage? At what points did he touch?

the morning the glad shout of a watchful sailor announced that land was in sight. There was no mistake this time. On October 12th, 1492, Columbus landed upon one of the

Bahama Islands, to which he gave the name, San Salvador. He gave thanks to God for the safety of his expedition, and declared the land to be the property of the sovereigns of Spain.

14. The inhabitants of the island were naked savages, who were filled with fear and wonder at the sight of white men. Columbus called them Indians, believing that he was near the coast of India, and the name American Indians has become the general name for the native races of the continent (17).

15. Explorations.—Columbus spent several months exploring San Salvador, Cuba, Hayti, and neighboring islands, searching always for gold and tropical products. His largest ship was wrecked on the coast of Hayti. A fort was then built from the wreck, and thirty-nine men were left as a garrison and the beginning of a colony.

16. The return voyage began January 4th, 1493, with the two remaining ships. They met with violent storms, and were finally separated. After a perilous voyage, and detention by the Portuguese at one of the Azores and in the harbor of Lisbon, Columbus's ship anchored at Palos, March fifteenth. The other vessel arrived shortly afterwards, having been driven northward into the Bay of Biscay.

Questions on Map of Discoveries.—Name the explorers of the Atlantic coast of North America. Of the Gulf coast. Of the Pacific coast. What regions of the interior were penetrated? What part of South America was first explored? By whom? Name the largest rivers of North America. How many had been discovered by 1600? What are the best harbors on the Atlantic shore? On the Pacific shore? Did these early explorers find any of them? Does North America offer an opportunity for a sailing vessel to penetrate the interior? What difficulties beset land expeditions? (Read about De Soto.)

CHAPTER III.

THE PEOPLE OF THE NEW LAND.

For Explanation.—Revealed; dialects; superstitious; museum.

To be Pronounced.—Wig′wam; Iroquois (ĭr′o-quoy); Al-gŏn′quin; Pueblo (pwĕb′lo).

INDIAN VILLAGE.

17. **The Indians** of North America, frequently called *red men* on account of their tawny complexion, became known to Europeans first along the Atlantic coast. A savage people, divided into tribes, differing widely in habits, language, and character, and generally at war with one another, they never offered any serious barrier to the oc-

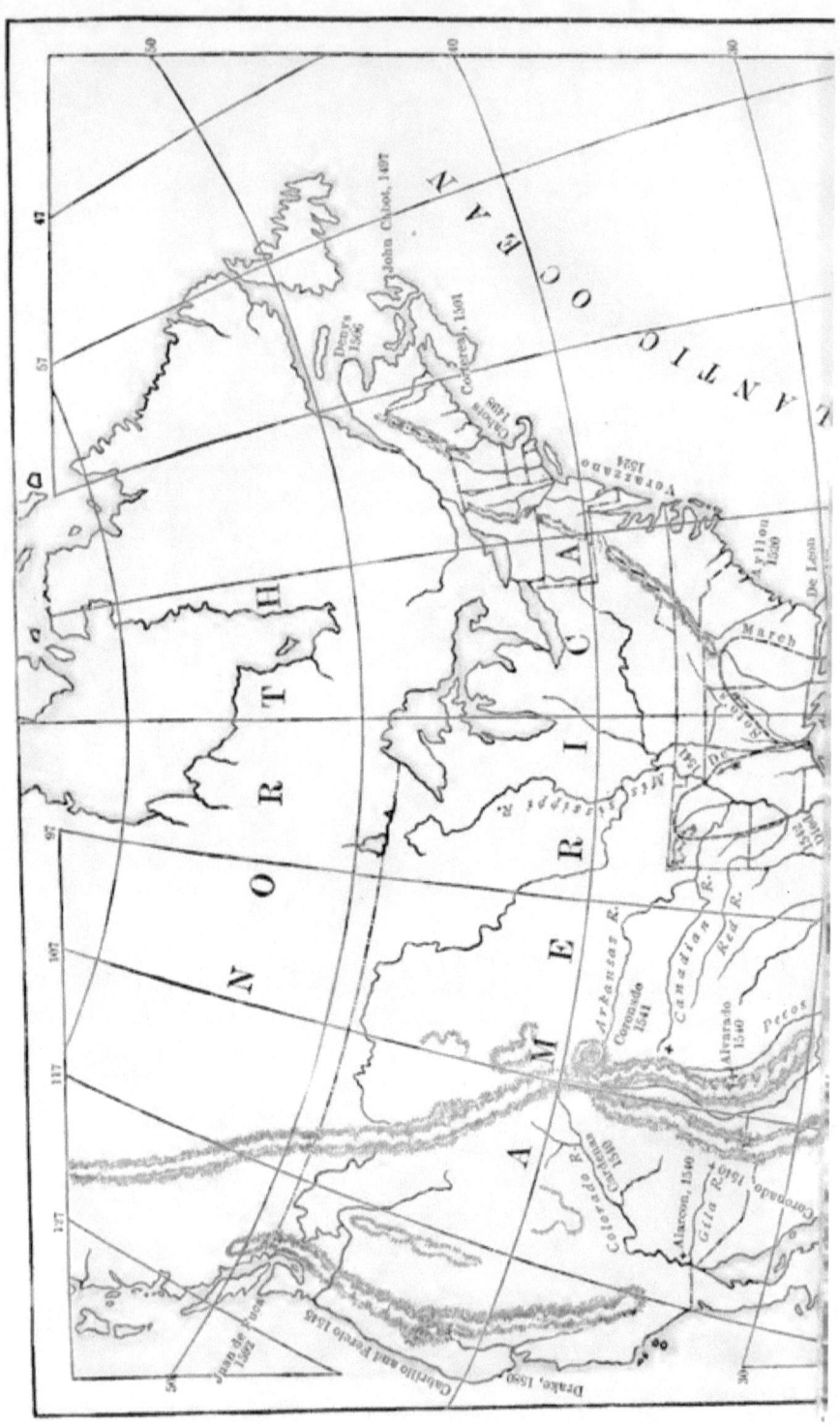

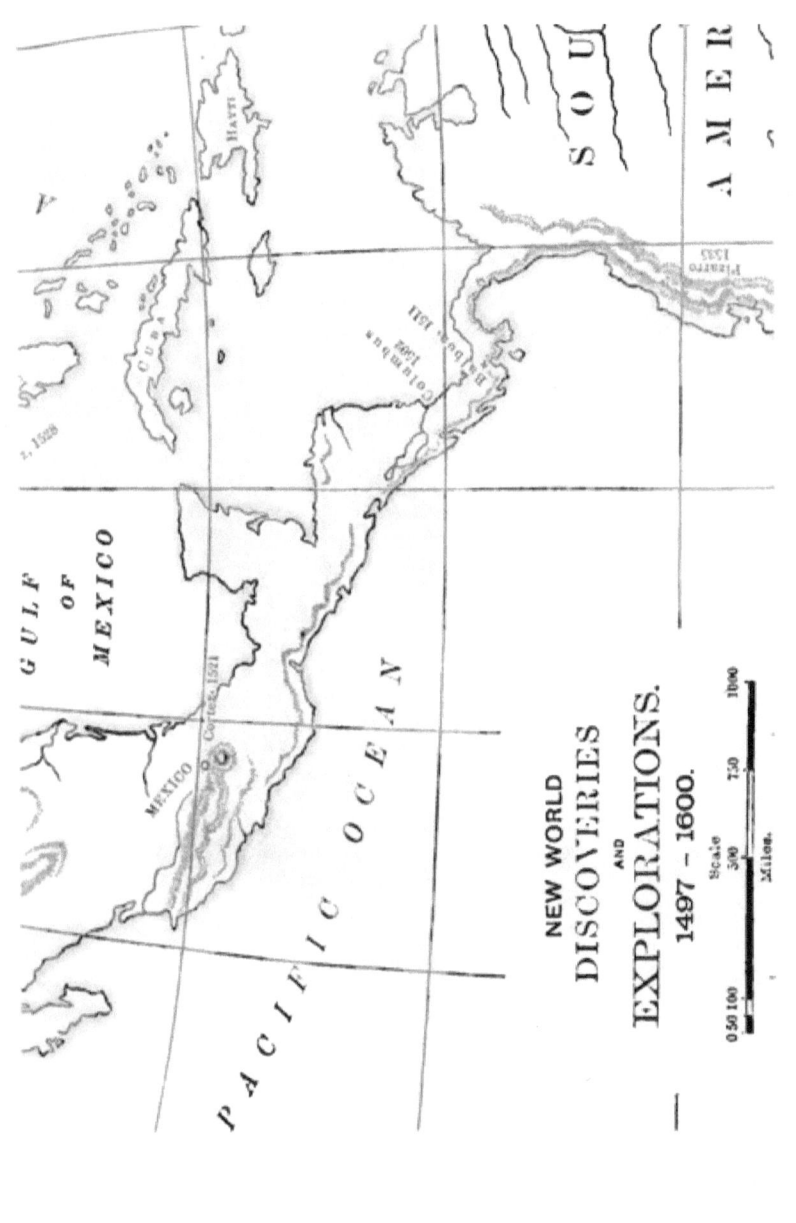

cupation of this land by civilized nations. Within the present territory of the United States the Indian population has gradually diminished. The remnants of the ancient tribes are now gathered in the Indian Territory and upon other lands reserved for them by our government. In British America they still remain numerous.

18. Indian Life.—There were wide differences among the numberless Indian tribes. Some surpassed in hunting; others in rude agriculture. Some were constantly at war; others were glad to be at peace. Some built houses of poles covered with bark or skins (*wigwams*); others dug holes, or burrows, in the earth. Every tribe obeyed some chief as a leader in war, and the customs of the tribe, handed down from its ancestors, filled the place of laws. Students of Indian life have arranged the tribes in several groups, according to the relationships revealed by the study of their dialects. The two groups with which the early settlers on the Atlantic shore came most in contact were the Algonquins and the Iroquois (**181**). The Algonquins stretched along the coast from the St. Lawrence River toward the southwest. The Iroquois were strongest in the central part of the present State of New York, stretching off to the west and south, a strong and intelligent people.

19. Indian character was marked by bravery in war and fortitude in the endurance of fatigue and pain. Cunning was a virtue. To kill a sleeping foe was to the Indian more glorious than to subdue him in open fight. An Indian never forgot nor forgave an injury. He would do anything for the sake of revenge. He had a power of oratory that could stir his companions to the fight, but no power of close thought or means of accurate expression either in speech or writing. He was extremely superstitious, believing generally in a single supreme deity, yet engaging in religious ceremonies chiefly to ward off or to appease the wrath of evil spirits. He lacked energy and perseverance, and sel-

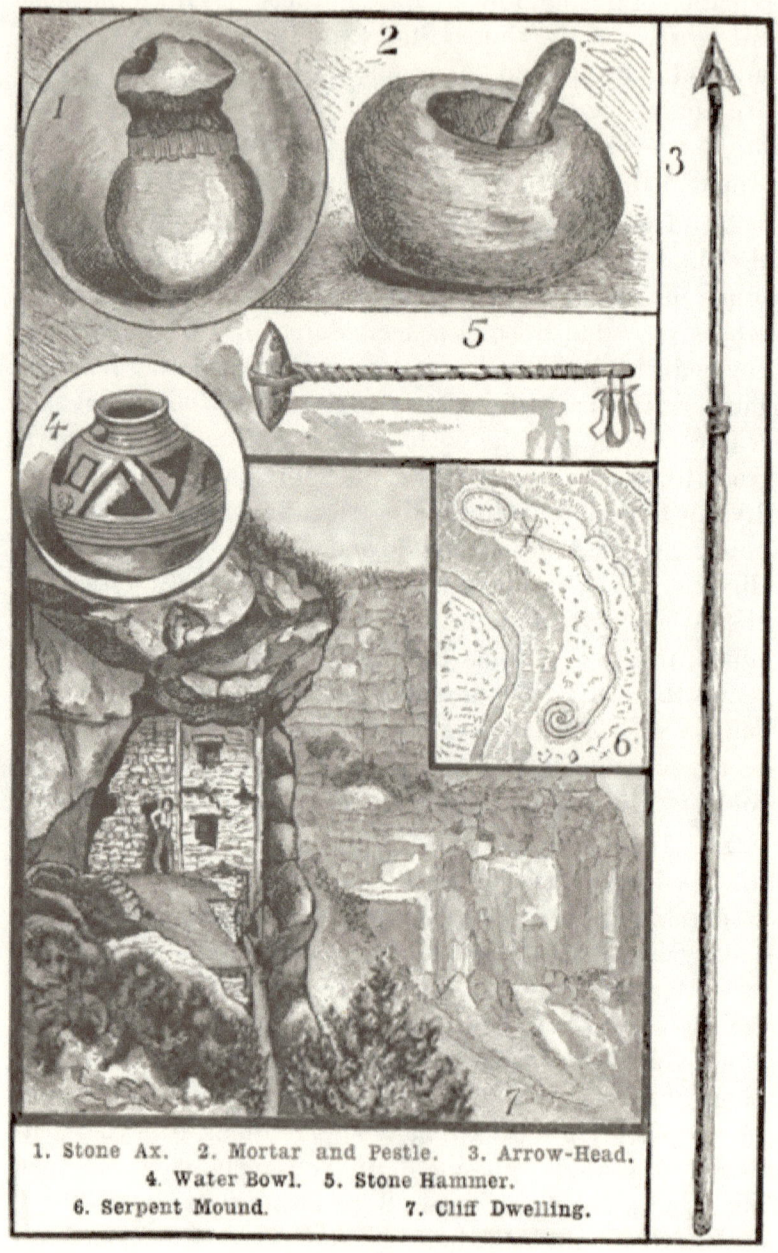

1. Stone Ax. 2. Mortar and Pestle. 3. Arrow-Head.
4. Water Bowl. 5. Stone Hammer.
6. Serpent Mound. 7. Cliff Dwelling.

dom showed capacity for hard work. With his rude tools of stone, everything that he attempted was laborious. Without the knowledge of the useful metals, especially iron, the Indian could never rise from a savage to a civilized man.

20. Indian relics are found throughout the United States. The most abundant are the stone implements in use among the inhabitants found by the Europeans. Stone arrowheads, hatchets, and mortars for grinding corn can be seen in almost any museum. In some parts of the country are found traces of an earlier and more civilized people. These traces consist chiefly in a series of earth-mounds beginning north of the Ohio and stretching toward the southwest.

21. The Mound-builders is the name given to this earlier race. The mounds are of peculiar shapes. They are most numerous in Ohio, some of them over 1,000 feet long and several feet high. Inside the mounds have been found tools of copper, ornaments of copper and silver, and excellent clay pottery, skillfully decorated, all showing workmanship superior to that of the later tribes. Quite probably the mound-builders were related to the ancestors of the present Pueblo or "village" Indians now living in New Mexico.

22. The Aztecs were people found in Mexico and Peru on arrival of the Europeans (29). In civilization they were far in advance of the tribes of the United States. They had an established government, built cities of brick and stone buildings, and were wealthy in stores of the precious metals.

23. [**The Northmen,** or ancient people of Norway, Sweden, and Denmark, were the first of Europeans to venture long voyages upon the ocean. In the tenth century they made many voyages westward and shorter excursions southward. They settled in Iceland, and from Iceland they reached Greenland, and a few visited the shore of North America (about 1000). Their discovery of America never became widely known. They did not continue their visits, and neither they nor any other people profited by the discovery.]

CHAPTER IV.
1493-1592.
Later Discoveries.

For Explanation.—Adventurer; fabled; maritime.

To be Pronounced.—Amerigo Vespucci (ah-mä-rē'go vĕs-poot'chee; Flŏr'en-tine; Cor'tĕz; Pizarro (pe-zär'o); Bäl-bō'ä; Pän-a-mä'; Ponce de Leon (pŏn'thä dä lä-ōn'); Ayllon (il-yōn'); Nar-vä'ez(eth); Mä-gĕl'lan; de Sō'to; Col-o-rä'do; Cä-brĭl'lo; Fe-re'lo; Juan de Fuca (hoo'an dä foo'kä); Denys (deh-nĕ); Verrazzano (ver-rät-sä'no); Cartier (kär-te-ä'); Cäb'ot; Bo-de'gä; Cor-te-re-äl'.

1. Spain.

24. Columbus's Report.—Though Columbus had failed to find the civilization and wealth that he expected, yet he was not discouraged. From the words and gestures of the natives in answer to his questions, he had been convinced that farther inland, or on some island to the south, lay the riches that he sought. Occasionally Indians had been seen with ornaments of gold, which they willingly bartered for trinkets. In his letter to the Spanish monarchs, "respecting the islands found in the Indies," Columbus wrote.—"Your Highnesses have become masters of a new world, where our holy faith may become much increased, and whence stores of wealth may be derived."

25. The news of the successful voyage, and the wonders of the new land, spread quickly over Europe. Adventurers of all nations were eager to go in search of the fabled wealth. The greed of nations was aroused to gain possessions in the new lands and control of the Indian trade.

26. [European Nations, 1493.—The maritime nations at the end of the fifteenth century were Spain, Portugal, France, and England. Holland had ships and sailors, but was subject to Spain, and could do nothing until she won independence (1648). Germany and Italy had no fleets and were divided into many states constantly quarreling. Sweden was too weak to compete with the great powers.]

27. Columbus's Later Voyages.—Columbus made four voyages in all. On his second voyage he took with him horses, calves, goats, sheep, fowls, and seeds of oranges, lemons, and other orchard fruits, intending to provide for permanent settlement. He found that the men he had left in his fort (15) had perished, most of them murdered by the Indians in revenge for outrages committed by the Spaniards. Columbus chose a new location, and founded a town on the Island of Hayti. He explored the interior of Hayti, and also the coast of Cuba, which he considered a part of the mainland of Asia. In a subsequent voyage (1498), he reached the coast of South America, near the mouth of the Orinoco River. At another time he touched on the coast of Honduras, but never reached the mainland of North America. He died (1506) believing that he had reached India, and that the land of riches lay only a little further to the west.

[The companions of Columbus on his first voyage continued his searches. Spanish colonies, under the control of military governors, were kept alive on the larger islands of the West Indies, and these afforded an opportunity for dispatching exploring parties to the continent, and furnished supplies to expeditions sent from Spain.]

28. [**Columbia-America.**—The western world is named from its discoverer, only in the language of poetry and song. The name, America, is derived from the first name of Amerigo Vespucci, an educated Florentine merchant and adventurer, who accompanied one of the early companions of Columbus on a voyage to South America in 1499, and made a voyage for himself in 1501. A letter, in which he gave an account of the land seen in South America, was printed in several editions, in towns of Southern Germany, where printing was advancing (5). A suggestion of one of these printers led to the application of the name America to the land visited by Amerigo, and gradually the name was extended to the whole continent.]

29. Spanish exploration had made known the Gulf coast of North America as early as 1520. Mexico was conquered by Cortez in 1520; and Peru by Pizarro in 1535. Both

---

28. *Find and commit to memory some poem or song in which this country is named Columbia.*

these lands were really rich, and their conquest brought large amounts of the precious metals to the Spanish kingdom.

[In 1511, Balboa crossed the Isthmus of Panama and saw the great ocean of the west, "the great marine sea heretofore unknown to the inhabitants of Europe, Africke, and Asia." As the land became known further north, the ocean being always seen to the south, it was for a long time known as the "South Sea." In 1512, Ponce de Leon landed on the eastern coast of Florida, giving the name because he discovered the land on Easter Sunday (in Spanish *Pascua Florida*). In 1520, Ayllon, hunting for slaves, explored the coast northward as far as South Carolina. In 1528, Narvaez attempted to gain possession of Florida, but his party was destroyed by Indians and by shipwreck. In 1520, Magellan, a Portuguese navigator in the service of Spain, sailed around South America into the ocean, which he named Pacific. He crossed the ocean and reached the East India islands. Here he was killed by savages, but his ship was brought back to Spain by the survivors of his crew. The return voyage, by way of the Cape of Good Hope, was completed in 1522, the first circumnavigation of the globe.]

30. De Soto.—The most remarkable expedition into the interior was that of Ferdinand de Soto. He landed at Tampa Bay in 1539 with a large force, perhaps a thousand men, many of them mounted and clad in armor. He took with him hogs for food, and blood-hounds to kill Indians. For three years he wandered through the land of Florida, Georgia, Alabama, and Mississippi. He came upon the great river near the southwest corner of Tennessee, crossed it and traversed a large part of Arkansas, hunting always for gold, and slaughtering and enslaving the Indians. He was "a stern man and of few words, and after he had delivered his own opinion he would not be contraried." Failing in the object of his expedition, at last, discouraged and exhausted, he died in 1542, and his companions, wishing to conceal his death from the Indians, buried him beneath the waters of the Mississippi. His surviving followers built boats on the Red River and sailed downward to the gulf. A very few succeeded in reaching the Spanish settlements on the Mexican coast.

31. [**Expeditions from Mexico (29)** went northward, both inland and along the coast. New Mexico was penetrated in 1540, and the Colorado River was discovered in the same year. Cabrillo and Ferelo, in 1543, sailed up the coast as far as Oregon; and in 1592 Juan de Fuca explored the coast northward to the strait named after him.]

2. France.

32. Early Voyages.—At an early date hardy fishermen from the north of France crossed the Atlantic and discovered the bountiful fisheries of the coast of Newfoundland. One of them, John Denys, in 1506, discovered the Gulf of St. Lawrence. Private enterprise prompted these early voyages. Finally the example of Spain and Portugal roused Francis I., king of France, to take part in exploration. He is said to have exclaimed: "Why, these princes coolly divide the New World between them! I should like to see that article of Adam's will which gives them America."

33. French Exploration.—A French fleet, commanded by Verrazzano, a Florentine, sailed in 1524. Verrazzano explored the Atlantic coast of the United States with considerable care, and sent an excellent account of his explorations to the king. Verrazzano set forth a true theory as to the size of the earth, and helped correct the error of Columbus **(10)**. In 1534 Cartier discovered the St. Lawrence River, and turned the attention of France to that region.

3. England.

34. John Cabot was probably, like Columbus, a native of Genoa. He lived for a time in Venice, married a Venetian woman, but afterwards moved with his family to Bristol, England. Like Columbus, he had accepted the new views about the roundness of the earth, and was ready to test them. The great discovery of Columbus was much talked about in the Court of Henry VII. **(41)**, and Cabot, laying his plans before the king, easily gained authority to make discoveries, and to carry on commerce with the new lands. In the early part of May, 1497, Cabot sailed from

SIR FRANCIS DRAKE.

Bristol. On June twenty-fourth, he landed probably on Cape Breton island, and took possession of the land in the name of the king of England. He returned in the early part of August, after an absence of about three months.

35. **A second voyage** was made the following year, with John Cabot as commander, but the only record is drawn from the conversation of his son Sebastian, who no doubt accompanied his father, and has been regarded as the leader of the expedition. They coasted North America from where

they encountered ice, southward to the latitude of 36° N., or the vicinity of Albemarle Sound.

36. Sir Francis Drake, a bold English navigator, having sailed around South America, in 1580 visited the shore of California. His ships passed a winter month in a bay, probably Bodega (sometimes called Drake's Bay), and, departing, he named the land New Albion, claiming it as an English possession.

4. PORTUGAL.

37. [Cortereal.—An agreement with Spain prevented Portugal from competing in the exploration of America. One voyage, however, is noteworthy. Cortereal, about 1501, explored the Atlantic coast from Maine northward, and called the country Terra de Labrador, or land of laborers, thinking the natives valuable for slaves.]

38. Result and Forecast.—With the middle of the sixteenth century the voyages in search of the lands of "great and exceeding riches" ceased. After the voyage of Magellan, the new land became known as a continent, with the vast Pacific separating it from Asia. Europeans continued seeking a route to India by a Northwest Passage around North America, and also by the northeast around Europe and Asia. The interest in the new world took the form of a desire to trade with the natives and to establish settlements for the development of the natural resources of the country.

REWRITING OF PARAGRAPH 24.

[*Frequently rewrite paragraphs of the narrative, condensing as much as practicable.*]

Columbus reported to Ferdinand and Isabella that they were masters of a new world, in which religion could be extended and from which wealth could be obtained. Though failing to find all he had hoped, he was led to this belief by the replies of the natives to his questions, and by seeing Indians with ornaments of gold.

38. Write, in one column, so much of this paragraph as is **result,** *and, in another, so much as is* **forecast.**

ABSTRACT OF THE DISCOVERIES OF A CENTURY.

Copy and complete the following Review of Discoveries—1492-1592. Refer both to the map between pages 16 and 17 and to the narrative:

	Explorer.	Region.	Time.
Spanish.	1. Columbus. 2. 3. 4. 5. 6. 7. 8. 9. 10. 11.	West Indies and shore of Caribbean Sea.	1492-9.
French.	1. 2. 3. 4.		
English.	1. 2. 3.		
Portuguese.	1.		

NOTE ON EUROPEAN HISTORY.

39. [Protestantism.—When Columbus discovered America all Europe upheld the Christian religion, and all except Russia was included in one great church, called Catholic or universal. Its center was at Rome. It had a systematic government, its chief officer being the Pope. A religious separation, however, had already commenced, which gained headway, about the year 1520, under the preaching of Martin Luther, a German monk. Luther and his followers protested against the sinfulness and impurity of the Church of Rome, and the movement begun by them spread through Europe under the name of the Protestant Reformation. In the course of a hundred years, the nations of Northern Europe became for the most part Protestant, while Southern Europe remained for the most part Catholic. Fierce religious wars between Catholics and Protestants drove many people to America.

40. Puritans.—England became a Protestant nation under Henry VIII. **(41).** For many years, however, the country was nearly equally divided between Catholics and Protestants, and the worship of the English Church did not differ very much from that of the Catholic Church. A considerable number of Englishmen desired a purer and more spiritual worship, and in the time of Queen Elizabeth **(41)** they came to be called Puritans. As they refused to comply with the requirements of the regular English Church they were also called Nonconformists. Some went so far as to organize congregations and a form of worship for themselves, and were, therefore, called Separatists.

41. English Sovereigns.—When Columbus discovered America, Henry VII. was king of England. His full name was Henry Tudor, and with him began the line of Tudor sovereigns. In 1603, James Stuart, king of Scotland, succeeded to the throne of England as James I., and England and Scotland have since had the same ruler. In 1649, at the end of a civil war, called the Puritan Revolution, Charles I. was beheaded, and there was no regular king in England until 1660, when Charles II., the son of Charles I., was placed on the throne (Stuart Restoration). In 1688, James II., successor to Charles, was deposed, and William and Mary were made joint rulers.

TABLE OF ENGLISH SOVEREIGNS.

TUDOR FAMILY.

Henry VII.	1485–1509.	Mary	1553–1558.
Henry VIII.	1509–1547.	Elizabeth	1558–1603.
Edward VI.	1547–1553.		

40. State, in your own language, the difference between Puritans and Separatists.

STUART FAMILY.		HOUSE OF BRUNSWICK.	
James I.	1603–1625.	George I.	1714–1727.
Charles I.	1625–1649.	George II.	1727–1760.
(*Beheaded in 1649.*)		George III.	1760–1820.
The Commonwealth, 1649-1660. (*Rule of Oliver Cromwell and the House of Commons.*)		George IV.	1820–1830.
		William IV.	1830–1837.
		Victoria	1837 ——.
Charles II.	1660–1685.		
(*Stuart restored.*)			
James II.	1685–1688.		
(*Deposed 1688.*)			
William and Mary	1688–1702.		
Anne	1702–1714.		

42. The English Government.—English laws are made by Parliament, which consists of two assemblies—the House of Commons and the House of Lords. The House of Commons, at the present time, represents the people of Great Britain nearly as our Congress represents the people of the United States **(358)**. Members of the House of Lords hold their positions chiefly by right of birth, the title passing from father to oldest son in the families of high rank, called the nobility. Under the Tudors, the House of Commons did not have much power, and did not represent the people so much as it does now. In that time the king's will ruled the land almost entirely. Under the Stuart kings a great change began, and by the Puritan Revolution—1642-9—(a war between the people of England, represented by the House of Commons, and King Charles I., aided by the Cavaliers, or nobility), the House of Commons gained a controlling power in the government of Great Britain. This power has increased, until now the House of Commons practically governs the British Empire. The man who has the most influence in the House of Commons is selected by the sovereign to see that the laws are executed, and is called the Premier or Prime Minister. He selects other men to assist him. They fill several high offices, having charge of departments of public affairs, as the treasury, the navy, etc. The Prime Minister and his assistants are known as the Ministry, or the Cabinet.]

CHAPTER V.
1540-1607.
BEGINNING OF SETTLEMENT.

For Explanation.—Flinch; notable; impediment; conceded; depredations; patent; dispatched; equipped; armada; compete.

To be Pronounced.—Russia (rŭsh′e-a); prē′mi-er; Ro-ber-väl′; de Monts′ (mŏng); Är′gall; Brä-zĭl′; Ribaut (re-bō′); Beaufort (bū′fort); Laudonniere (lō-don-yāre′); Saint Augustine (sĕnt au-gŭs′tin); Menendez (mā-nĕn′deth); Dŏm-i-nique′ (nēk); de (deh) Gourgues (goorj); Huguenots (hū′ge-nots); Santa Fe (sän′tä-fā); Frŏb′ish-er; Raleigh (raw′ly).

43. Many attempts to plant settlements within the present territory of the United States were made during the latter part of the sixteenth century. They were failures, because men did not know the difficulty of living in a new land, and did not come prepared. The settlers were often adventurers, not men of perseverance. There was no regular communication with the old world to furnish supplies to the young settlements, and Indians joined with famine in the work of their destruction.

1. FRANCE.

44. Exploration and Attempted Colonization.—In 1540 the king of France commissioned Roberval, a French nobleman, to build ships with which to explore the St. Lawrence River, and to lead out a company of settlers to occupy the land. Cartier, who had visited the region in 1534-5 (**33**), was appointed pilot, and sailed in 1541 with a part of Roberval's company. Roberval and the remainder waited for the completion of more ships. Cartier and party spent the winter of 1541-2 in a fort, which they built on the bank of the St. Lawrence, somewhere near Quebec. They suffered greatly from cold, and want of food. Many died. The survivors hastened to return to France early in the spring. At the mouth of the river, they met Roberval with the rest of the party, but did not turn back to the scene of their sufferings.

In a few months, Roberval and the second party followed them back to France, and this attempted colony was a failure.

45. [**Canada**, however, became a French possession. French fishermen never ceased to frequent the fisheries of Newfoundland, and French sailors opened a profitable trade in furs with the Indians along the St. Lawrence. Acadia (Nova Scotia) was settled first, a party led by De Monts gaining a permanent foothold in 1605. Quebec was founded in 1608, by Champlain, a man renowned for his explorations in the interior (**175**). In this region the sons of France flourished, free from interference, and under the care of Jesuit missionaries (**176**) and the Church of Rome (**39**). A colony located further south at Mount Desert, in 1613, was destroyed by Englishmen.]

FIRST FRENCH SETTLEMENTS.

Map Questions.—By whom and when was the first settlement made in Nova Scotia? At what point? When and by whom was the settlement of Quebec begun? What natural division of land is Nova Scotia? Bordered by what waters?

46. **French Protestants**, called Huguenots, foreseeing years of persecution that were to come upon them in France, labored to make a home in America (**39**). After a fruitless attempt in Brazil, a company led by Ribaut, in 1562, selected the harbor of Port Royal, South Carolina, and built a fort near the present site of Beaufort. At first they thought this place "the fairest, fruitfullest, and pleasantest of all the world," but when the supplies gave out, they deserted and went home. Laudonniere led the next colony, in 1564. They sailed five miles up St. John's River, Florida, and built Fort Caroline. The settlement

---

45. What lands may be approached through the St. Lawrence River? Why was the possession of the St. Lawrence valuable to France?

HUGUENOT AND SPANISH SETTLEMENTS.

Map Questions.—At what points and at what dates were settlements made by Huguenots? In which of the present United States? Tell the same of Spanish settlements. What is the character of the coast of South Carolina, Georgia, and Florida? Are there good harbors? Was progress into the interior easy? What difficulties existed? Of these settlements, which one locates a present city?

did not prosper. "The foundation stone was forgotten; there were no tillers of the soil." Visions of military conquest and gold filled the minds of the colonists. Some of them mutinied and turned pirates, attacking Spanish vessels. Troubles within the colony were enough to ruin it; it fell, however, a victim to Spanish hatred.

47. [Spanish Cruelty and its Punishment.—Philip II., king of Spain, commissioned Pedro Menendez, a man blood-thirsty and bigoted, to rid his possessions of the Protestant heretics. Menendez left Spain in the year 1565 with a large force. His fleet was scattered, however, as he reached Florida, and with only three vessels he appeared at the mouth of the St. John's. Meeting there a strong French fleet, he retired down the coast and found his missing men already at work laying out St. Augustine. The French fleet sailed to attack him, but was wrecked by a storm. Hearing this, Menendez decided to march overland upon the French fort, now poorly defended. Through a raging storm, thick forests, and marshes, he pushed his half-starved men. "This is God's war," he said, "and we must not flinch. We must wage it with blood and fire." Few were the Frenchmen that, escaping his fury, reached the small vessels left in the harbor and sailed for France. Menendez found the crew of the wrecked fleet struggling along the shore to reach their fort, and put them to death without mercy. The tidings of the massacre called forth a cry of horror from all Protestants. Three years later Dominique De Gourgues, who had sailed from France for the purpose, fell upon the fort at St. Augustine and put to death 400 Spaniards, with the same cruelty. But it was not for France to plant the banner of Protestantism in the new world, or to gain territory on the Atlantic shore of the United States. Many Huguenots, as French Protestants were called, however, subsequently found a refuge among English colonies.]

2. SPAIN.

48. Spanish Settlements.—The settlement at St. Augustine, so bloodily commenced in 1565 (47), remained a Spanish settlement until Florida became a part of the United States (456). Thus St. Augustine is our oldest city. Santa Fe, in New Mexico, our second city in point of age, was founded likewise by Spaniards, in 1582. Neither of these cities has been otherwise distinguished in the history of the United States. Spanish rule was also extended over the new world from New Mexico and California southward.

3. ENGLAND.

49. Englishmen claimed the main-land of North America from the discovery of the Cabots. They had no idea of the real value of the country, and regarded the new land simply an impediment in the road to India. The thing to do was to find a way around or through it. In 1527, Robert Thorne, a sea captain, addressed a letter to Henry VIII. (41), urging the king to gain glory and wealth by finding a northern passage. Portugal had the route around Africa, and Spain that by way of the Strait of Magellan. The northern and most direct course, he said, was left for England. But the king took no interest in the matter, and the sailors who attempted the passage were stopped by frozen seas.

50. [**Voyages** were made by Martin Frobisher, in 1576, and afterwards. In 1579 John Davis pushed his way far up the coast of Greenland, into Baffin's Bay. Frobisher's Bay and Davis Strait still keep alive the names of these bold sailors.]

51. The Gilbert and Raleigh Expeditions.—Sir Humphrey Gilbert was anxious to extend discovery into the vast land of North America, as well as to sail around it.

Gilbert was half brother of Sir Walter Raleigh, and the two engaged in the enterprise of planting settlements somewhere between the French in Canada and the Spaniards in Florida. At this time every English expedition meant depredations upon Spanish commerce, if an opportunity was offered. English sailors hated Spaniards as the enemies of mankind, and considered the plundering of Spanish ships and colonies a righteous occupation. Gilbert led an ill-fated expedition to Newfoundland in 1583. A fruitless search for precious metals, shipwreck, sickness, and desertion of the sailors, prevented any advance southward, and on the way home the little vessel carrying Sir Humphrey "was devoured and swallowed up of the sea." Queen Elizabeth gave a patent to Raleigh the next year, for "discovering and planting new lands," and he immediately dispatched two ships, well manned and equipped, and commanded by Philip Amidas and Arthur Barlow. They anchored in Pamlico Sound, made friends with the Indians, and carried home a favorable report.

BEGINNING OF ENGLISH SETTLEMENT.

Questions on the Map.—What inland water was explored by Raleigh's first expedition? In what year? In what years and where were settlements made? Jamestown was settled by a company called the London Company. When? On what river located? In which of the present States of the Union? Describe the shore of North Carolina. To what territory does Chesapeake Bay afford an entrance? Did Raleigh's colonies make good locations? What advantages had Jamestown? (Consider the necessities of fresh water, wood, game, good soil, etc.)

SIR WALTER RALEIGH.

52. **Raleigh's first colony** was composed of 101 persons, who were carried out by Sir Richard Grenville, in 1585, and left on Roanoke Island. They hunted for gold instead of raising grain, quarreled with the Indians, nearly starved, and were glad to get home the next year in the ships of Sir Francis Drake (36), who happened to visit them. A few weeks after their departure, Grenville arrived with abundant supplies, but found no colony to use them.

[The settlers were not well chosen. Many were mere hunters of gold and silver. "Others were of a nice bringing up, only of cities or townes,

BEGINNING OF SETTLEMENT. 35

or such as never had seene the world before. Because there were not to be found any English cities, nor such fair houses, nor at their owne wish any of their old accustomed dainty food, nor any soft beds of downe or feathers, the country was to them miserable, and their reports thereof according."]

53. Raleigh's Second Colony.—A second company of 150 men and women, made up by Raleigh and others, sailed in 1587, intending to settle on Chesapeake Bay. The shipmaster, however, landed them on Roanoke Island, and for three years a war between England and Spain prevented the sending of supplies. Then no trace of them could be found, and search was soon given up.

[A voyage of Bartholomew Gosnold, in 1602, gave the name to Cape Cod, and served to direct attention to that region. The first English settlement, to live, in all North America, began at Jamestown, Virginia, in 1607 (**102**).]

54. Result and Forecast.—The sixteenth century closed leaving the Spaniards the only Europeans living in America. During the next century, however, the English gain a permanent hold on all the Atlantic coast between Florida and Canada. The French maintain their hold on the St. Lawrence, and thence travel inward, while the Dutch and Swedes compete with England on the Atlantic shore.

TABULAR ABSTRACT OF THE BEGINNING OF SETTLEMENT.

Copy and complete the following review:

Nation.	Leader.	Date.	Region.	Result.
French..	1. Cartier and Roberval. 2. 3.	1540-2.	Near Quebec.	Failure. Success.
Spanish..	1. 2.			
English..	1. 2. 3.			

54. What part of this paragraph is result *and what* **forecast**?

CHAPTER VI.

1620-1643.

PLYMOUTH AND MASSACHUSETTS BAY.

For Explanation.—Revealed; incorporation; conferred; Joint Stock Companies; monopoly; resident councilors; franchise; Lincolnshire; immunity; temerity; persecution; mortgaging; emigrant; struck root; craftsmen; vanguard; propagate; satirized.

To be Pronounced.—Leyden (li'den); South-hămp'ton; lăm'ent-a-ble.

Outline of Paragraph 56.—New scheme of settlement in 1606. James I. gives to companies titles to lands, and certain rights. Territory from Cape Fear to Halifax, extending to Pacific Ocean, divided equally between Northern and Southern Colonies; Southern Colony called London Company, Northern Colony called Plymouth Company; both Joint Stock, with monopoly of fishing and trade.

[*Make a similar outline of other paragraphs.*]

55. More than a century of exploration had left the interior of North America still unknown to Europeans, but it had revealed the profits of the northern fisheries, and of fur trade with the Indians. It had spread a favorable report of the natural virtues of the land, while the old hope of mines of gold and silver still lived on.

56. The Two Companies.—A change in the manner of English settling was made in 1606, when James I. (41) gave titles to land, and charters of incorporation to two great trading and colonizing companies. The territory of North America, from Cape Fear to Halifax, and from ocean to ocean, including all the islands within 100 miles of the coast, was equally divided between the companies, which were to be known as the Northern Colony and the Southern Colony. As most of the company for the Southern Colony lived in London, the company came to be called the London Company; and from a similar cause the company for the Northern Colony received the name of Plymouth

---

56. *How did the Northern Colony come to be known as the Plymouth Company?*

Company. These were joint stock companies. Their charters conferred monopolies of fishing and trade.

[Afterwards each company was reorganized, the London Company coming to be called the Virginia Company; and the Plymouth Company being changed to the Council for New England. The territory of the six States east of New York received the name, New England, from Captain John Smith (**104**), who explored, and made an excellent map of the coast, in 1614.]

57. Colonizing was at once commenced by both companies. The London Company was fairly successful at Jamestown, in 1607 (**102**), but the efforts of the Plymouth Company were failures.

58. [**The Charters.**—" For each colony separate councils were in turn to name resident councilors for the colonies. Thirteen members constituted the resident council. They had power to choose their own president, to fill vacancies in their numbers, and, a jury being required only in capital cases, to act as a court of last resort in all other causes. Religion was established in accordance with the forms and doctrines of the Church of England. The adventurers, as the members of the company were called, had power to coin money and collect a revenue, for twenty-one years, from all vessels trading with their ports. One article alone, and only in the most general terms, provides for the liberty of the subjects, as follows: 'Who (ever) shall dwell and inhabit within every and any of said several colonies and plantations, and every of their children, shall have and enjoy all liberties, immunities, and franchises within any of our other dominions, to all intents and purposes as if they had been abiding and born in this our realm of England.'"]

PLYMOUTH.

59. Separatist Puritans.—" The history of Massachusetts begins in an obscure Lincolnshire village, among a company of plain farmers and simple rustics, who had separated from the Church of England, and paid for their temerity by bitter and unceasing persecution." They were Separatists, a branch of the great body of English Puritans (**40**), and sought outside of England for shelter from persecution A congregation gathered first at Amsterdam, then removed to Leyden, where they learned the work of tradesmen, and maintained themselves by manual labor. They dreaded the mingling of their children with the easy-

38   HISTORY OF THE UNITED STATES.

Yᵉ Puritan.

going Dutch, and, longing for a permanent home, their thoughts turned toward America.

60. Overtures for land were made to the Council for New England, and were favorably received. Money, too, was needed, and for this they made terms with London merchants, mortgaging the profits of their labor for seven years. A charter was gained, but it was not put in the names of any of the emigrants, for they had no favor with the king. This charter was left in England, and seems never to have been used.

61. The emigrants, or Pilgrims as they were called, gathered at Southampton, England, in the summer of 1620, and in August sailed with two vessels, the Mayflower and the Speedwell. After eight days they put back to Dartmouth for repairs. Again they sailed, and again they had to return, for the master of the Speedwell claimed that his ship was leaking. A third time (September eleventh), only the Mayflower put out, this

Yᵉ Easy-Going Dutch.

PLYMOUTH AND MASSACHUSETTS BAY. 39

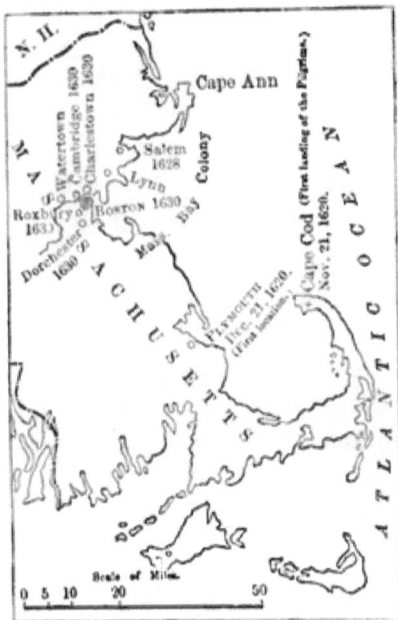

PLYMOUTH AND MASSACHUSETTS BAY COLONIES.

Map Questions.—When and where did the Pilgrims first land? When and where first locate? Where and when was the first settlement by the Massachusetts Bay Colony? Name the settlements that were made two years later. Did eastern Massachusetts offer any advantages for early settlement? Has it good harbors? Has it any rivers offering avenues to the interior? Would settlers there be in danger of disturbance by nations seeking to control the new land? Why? What is the distance between Plymouth and Boston?

time from Plymouth, carrying all the company, now reduced to 102.

[The company proper consisted of thirty-four adult males, eighteen of them accompanied by their wives. Of minor children there were twenty boys and eight girls. Besides these, there were three maid-servants, and nineteen men-servants, sailors, and craftsmen.]

62. The Location.—The plan was to settle in the north part of Virginia, and the merchants, the money-lenders, had taken out a patent from the Virginia Company. This was probably the authority under which the Pilgrims sailed. They decided, however, to search for a location somewhere near the Hudson River, in the vicinity of the Dutch (141). Worn out with the voyage, when off Cape Cod, they gained the shelter of the point and anchored, "blessing yᵉ God of heaven, who had brought them over yᵉ vast and furious ocean, and delivered them from all the perils and miseries thereof." After a thorough exploration of the coast, they decided upon a location, naming the place Plymouth, in honor of the English port. Here they landed December 21st, 1620, "the vanguard of a great column, bearing a civilization and a system of government which was destined to prevail throughout the length and breadth of a continent." On board the Mayflower, they bound themselves by a solemn agreement to make laws for the common good, promising obedience to them.

63. A fearful struggle with cold, famine, and disease followed. "That which was most sad and lamentable was, that in 2 or 3 months' time halfe their company dyed, especialy in Jan: and February, being ye depth of winter and wanting houses and other comforts." They bore up under all difficulties and the colony struck root.

64. [**The Chief Men.**—John Carver was elected governor before disembarking, but died during the first winter. His successor was William Bradford, who was reëlected year after year. He has left us an invaluable history of the colony. Miles Standish was the military leader, a small man, but renowned for his courage. "As a little chimney is soon fired, so was the Plymouth captain, a man of very little stature, yet of a hot and angry temper."]

65. The growth of Plymouth was steady but never rapid. The early years were burdened by the mortgage to the London merchants. According to the first arrangement the colonists held land in common, and all gave a portion of their time to pay the common debt. In 1626 eight of the leading men, with the help of London friends, assumed the outstanding debts, receiving a monopoly of the colony's trade as a compensation. Land was assigned to every man, and greater prosperity marked the introduction of private ownership. Several other towns in time grew from the Plymouth settlement.

MASSACHUSETTS BAY.

66. The First Settlement.—A well laid plan of Puritan colonization built the towns clustering about Massachusetts

---

63. Two hundred years ago there was little uniformity in spelling—every one seeming to follow his own taste. Write and properly spell the misspelled words in the quotation of this paragraph.

64. Read Longfellow's poem, "The Courtship of Miles Standish."

Bay. "Men of fortune and religious zeal 'offered the help of their purses to advance the glory of God' by establishing a colony of the best of their countrymen on the shores of New England." The Council for New England conveyed a belt of land, lying between the Merrimac and the Charles Rivers, from ocean to ocean, to six men, one of whom was John Endicott, and these, in 1629, obtained from Charles I. a charter incorporating them as "The Governor and Company of Massachusetts Bay in New England." The year before, Endicott, as deputy governor, with others, had gone to Salem, already inhabited by fishermen. More immigrants came in 1629, and the people of Salem organized a Puritan "Church-State," electing Mr. Francis Higginson teacher, and Mr. John Skelton pastor, both of whom were non-conformist clergymen.

67. **The Grand Plan.**—The location at Salem served as a foothold; the great achievement of the Puritans was made in 1630. The charter had been granted to men supposed to live in England; but this year the majority of the company quietly removed to America, *carrying their charter along with them*. Free from interference, they could now carry out their plan of a Puritan Church and State, and govern themselves under the authority of the English king. During the year a thousand crossed the ocean. This was not the movement of a band of adventurers, but the "migration of a people." Seven new towns around the bay were "planted" by the immigrants of 1630.

68. [**The founders** of Massachusetts Bay were Puritans, but they had not severed their fellowship with the Church of England. Higginson's farewell to his native land represents the feeling of his fellows: "We will not say as the Separatists were wont to say at their leaving of England, 'Farewell, Babylon! Farewell, Rome!' but we will say Farewell, dear England! Farewell to the Church of God in England, and all Christian friends! We do not go to New England as Separatists from the Church of England; though we cannot but separate from the corruption in it, but we go to practice the positive part of church reformation and propagate the gospel in America."]

69. Government.—The charter gave authority to the freemen of the company to elect annually a governor, deputy governor, and eighteen assistants, from their own number. Any Englishman might join the colony and own land, but to vote he must be elected a freeman by those already freemen. In 1631 the rule was made that no man should be elected a freeman unless a member in good standing in one of the regular Puritan churches. This was in accordance with the Puritan idea of a State resting upon the Church as its foundation, with the Bible as the authority for civil laws. As many who were not regular church members joined the colony, the voting power was wielded by a minority.

[This restriction caused dissatisfaction, and was one reason for the migration to Connecticut, the Connecticut settlers being men who favored more extended suffrage (78).]

70. [**Intruders.**—Building a home for themselves in their own fashion, the Puritans had no notion of any duty to share it with persons who made themselves disagreeable. They regarded as dangerous to the commonwealth all who desired to introduce variations from the belief and worship of the Puritan congregation, and accordingly employed the civil authority to expel them from the colony. There were many disturbers. Roger Williams, the minister of Salem, disagreed with the other ministers, and was banished in 1635 (**71, 72**). Mrs. Anne Hutchinson, a restless and energetic woman, got up meetings for women, in which she introduced new doctrines and satirized the ministers. She and her adherents were banished from the colony as "unfit for the society" of its citizens. Massachusetts was a strong colony, but considered freedom of opinion dangerous.]

---

59. *To what branch of the Puritans did the Plymouth Colony belong?*
40, 68. *How did the Massachusetts Bay Colony differ from these?*

CHAPTER VII.
1634-1643.
OTHER NEW ENGLAND COLONIES.

For Explanation.—Controversy; ferment; fanatics; fervor; turbulent; factious; factions; brunt; allegiance; nucleus.

To be Pronounced.—Pis-căt′a-qua; Gor′gĕṣ.

RHODE ISLAND.

71. Providence Founded, 1636.—Roger Williams, a good man, but fond of controversy, had been chosen pastor of Salem church on the death of Mr. Skelton (66). He found favor with his congregation, but raised a ferment in the Bay colony by his peculiar opinions. After his banishment (70) he retired to the southward with a few friends, and in 1636 they built homes at the head of Narragansett Bay. Williams obtained a title to the surrounding land from the Indians, and named his location Providence, in memory of his preservation from the perils of banishment.

72. [**Williams** reproved the women of Salem for going unveiled; he persuaded Endicott to cut the cross (a Catholic emblem) out of the English flag. Some believing in Williams would not follow a flag with the cross in it, while others, honoring the old flag, would not have a flag with the cross out of it. Williams claimed that the colonists received no title to land by their charter, for, he said, the King of England had no right to give away what belonged to the Indians. Williams also maintained that punishment for matters of conscience and belief was persecution, and he carried out this principle of toleration in the government afterwards established for Rhode Island. For this reason the historian, George Bancroft, says of him: "Let the name of Roger Williams be preserved in universal history as one who advanced moral and political science, and made himself a benefactor of his race."]

73. Newport, Portsmouth.—Mrs. Hutchinson (70) and some others who found living in Massachusetts impossible or unpleasant, followed Williams to the south. A settlement was made at Portsmouth in 1638, and at Newport on the island of Rhode Island in 1639. These settlements grew slowly, and had no regular government until 1644.

["The first settlers of both Providence and Newport were the extreme fanatics who always come to the surface in a period of intense religious fervor. They were men and women who could not submit to a strong and well-ordered government . . . the factious and turbulent elements of the rigid, order-loving, and strong communities of Connecticut and Massachusetts."—*Lodge*.]

74. Government.—Williams went to England, and in 1644 obtained from Parliament a charter of incorporation for the "Providence Plantation on Narragansett Bay," authorizing a representative government, which got under way in a few years. Perfect freedom of religious belief and worship was allowed, but the right of voting was limited to land owners.

[The islands towns set up a separate government in 1651, but in 1663 **(92)** the factions were united under the name of the "Governor and Company of Rhode Island and Providence Plantations."]

CONNECTICUT.

75. The first settlements in Connecticut were offshoots from Massachusetts, attracted by the good farming land along the Connecticut River **(69)**. The first regular emigration from Massachusetts to Connecticut took place in 1635 and 1636. Towns were formed, which in 1637 received the names of Wethersfield, Windsor, and Hartford. Dutch from New York **(141)** had built trading posts, and were disposed to contest the occupation of the land. The Massachusetts men strengthened their hold, established churches and towns, and became the masters of the valley.

76. [**The English title** to Connecticut land had passed from the Plymouth Company **(56)** into the hands of two noblemen (Lord Say-and-Sele, and Lord Brooke), and some others. By the authority of these men, a fort was built at the mouth of the river, and, in 1639, the town of Saybrook was commenced.]

77. [**Pequod War, 1637.**—The towns of Connecticut had to bear the brunt of the first serious Indian war. The Pequods, a fierce tribe living east of the Connecticut, were annoyed at the presence of the whites. They committed several murders, and finally, in 1637, attacked Saybrook fort. Massachusetts sent Captain Endicott and 120 men to help the men of Connecticut, and the Indians were driven to their forts. A dangerous alliance between the Pequods and the Narragansett tribe was prevented by Roger Williams, whom the Indians revered. One of the Pequod forts was surrounded and set on fire, and the Indians were shot as they tried to escape. Their warriors slain, their women and children distributed as captives, the tribe of Pequods was crushed. Indians had, as yet, no firearms, and their arrows were no match for bullets. The energy and severity displayed in punishing the Pequods prevented further Indian troubles for many years.]

ANALYSIS OF THE PEQUOD WAR.

(*Connecticut, 1637.*)

Cause.	Indians annoyed by the white people taking their land, commit murders, and attack Saybrook fort.
Events.	1. Indians driven to their forts. 2. Alliance with the Narragansetts prevented by Roger Williams. 3. Indian fort surrounded, burned, and warriors slain.
Result.	1. Tribe crushed. 2. Indians, taught to fear the whites, keep peace for many years.

(*Use the above analysis as a model in the analysis of future topics.*)

78. Government.—The towns along the Connecticut united in forming a government "with the first written constitution in America." The government was democratic. The freemen elected their governor, and representatives in the legislature. The right to vote was not limited to church members. Every freeman had to swear allegiance to the Commonwealth of Connecticut, and there was no mention of any other sovereign. The first governor was elected in 1639. Hartford was the seat of government.

79. Another Puritan colony began at New Haven in 1638, upon land obtained from the Indians. In forming a government, the colonists asserted that "the Scriptures are the only perfect rule of a commonwealth." Their church and state were one. Other towns were settled on Long

Island Sound, and New Haven became a second nucleus. For a long time the name of the Connecticut settlements was "The Colonies of Connecticut and New Haven."

NEW HAMPSHIRE.

80. The first settlement in New Hampshire was made in 1623, at the mouth of the Piscataqua River, by David Thomson, a Scotchman, who came with a patent from the Council for New England (56). Three years later Thomson moved to Boston Harbor. Another party of settlers located further up the river at Dover, probably in 1627. More settlers were sent in 1630 by Sir Ferdinando Gorges and John Mason, of the Council for New England, who had received a patent covering the territory of New Hampshire and Maine. They occupied Thomson's buildings at the mouth of the Piscataqua, and there grew the town of Portsmouth. New Hampshire was named in honor of Mason's home, the county of Hampshire, England.

81. [**Other towns** within the territory of New Hampshire grew from the Massachusetts settlements. Immigrants also came from England, and in later times from the northern part of Ireland. The towns governed themselves in the New England fashion, and some established Puritan churches. In 1641 all the people of New Hampshire were glad to come under the rule of Massachusetts, and they so continued for thirty-eight years.]

SUMMARY.

Five governments are now (1643) established in New England, independent of each other and practically independent of England.

Name.	Date of First Settlement.	Present State.
1. Plymouth	1620 (62)	Massachusetts.
2. { Massachusetts Bay	1628 (66)	Massachusetts.
{ New Hampshire	1623 (80)	New Hampshire.
3. Providence and Rhode Island	1636 (71) 1639 (73)	Rhode Island.
4. Connecticut	1635 (75)	Connecticut.
5. New Haven	1638 (79)	Connecticut.

CHAPTER VIII.
1643-1750.
NEW ENGLAND.

For Explanation.—Yeomanry; niggardly; instinct; judicial; sovereign; smuggling; forfeited; tradition; popular; dissolve; property qualification; veto; wizard; mysterious; dead letter.

To be Pronounced.—Po-ka-nō'ket; Swansey (Swŏn'ze).

82. Puritan emigration to New England was very large, until the outbreak of the civil war in England (42), in 1642, stopped the persecution that had been its cause. Twenty thousand people came here between 1629 and 1639. These people were of the purest English stock, "drawn from the country gentlemen, small farmers, and yeomanry of the mother country. Many of the emigrants were men of wealth, as the old lists show, and all of them, with few exceptions, were men of property and good standing." A small inflowing continued during the century, additions being received from French Protestants, and Scotch who had lived in the north of Ireland.

83. The land was poor for agriculture. Along the Connecticut River there was farming land of fair quality; but in general the soil was thin, and hard to cultivate. But there were noble forests, and fine rivers afforded an abundance of water power—the life of early manufactures. Furs, lumber, and fish were natural exports. The energy of the people took advantage of every help that nature gave, and quickly covered the niggardly soil with thriving villages.

84. The towns, "the glory and strength of New England," show the political instinct of the English race. The settlers of New England reproduced the local government of their Anglo-Saxon ancestors (3). As they spread out from the first locations, they went in small companies,

---

83. Why is water power "the life of early manufactures?"

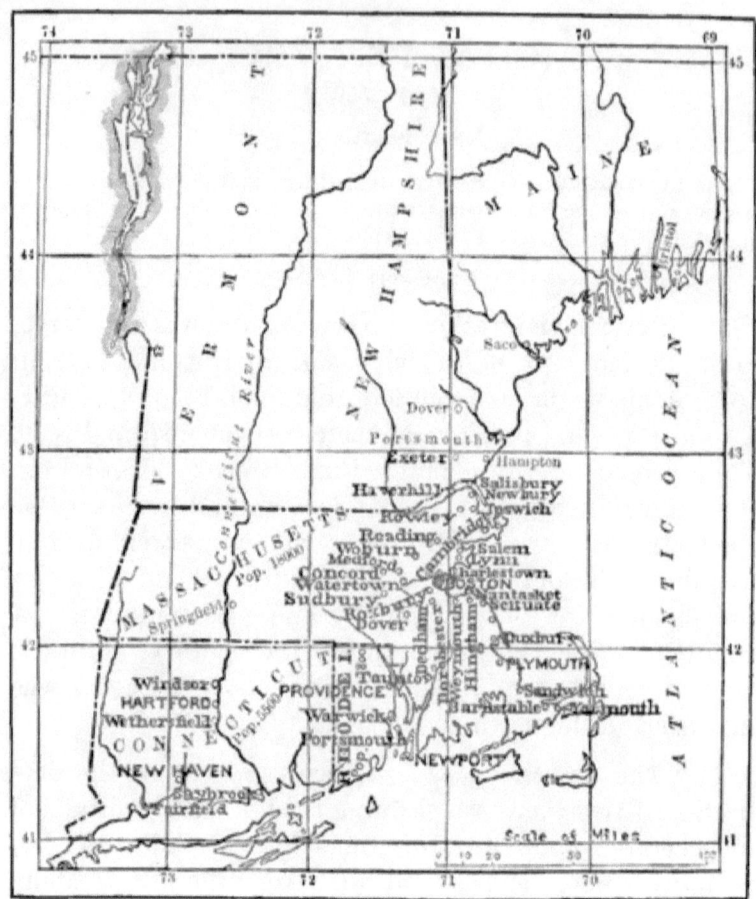

Towns of New England, 1643.

Map Questions.—Give the population of Massachusetts, Connecticut, and Rhode Island, in 1643. Name the towns of Connecticut. Of Rhode Island. Of Massachusetts. Of New Hampshire. Of Maine. How many years since the first landing at Plymouth? (See map, p. 30.)

chose a piece of land beside a stream, and built their houses near together. Every man had a small piece of farming land, but the outside land was the common pasture for the village cows. At regular times all the men assembled in "town meeting," and transacted the public business. In time, when the number of citizens became too great for this, they elected a board of "selectmen," who carried out the will of the town. Each town managed its own roads, schools, and churches, and took care of the common property. The town, therefore, was the political unit.

85. [**County and State Governments.**—In 1643 Massachusetts was divided into four counties, but this division was chiefly for judicial purposes. The next distinct political institution above the towns was the colony government. In this government the towns were directly represented, and the representatives of the people always had control of taxation. Even a royal governor had to ask a colonial assembly for his salary. In the colony government we find the outline of the present states.]

86. Union.—The common dangers from the encroachments of the Dutch, the hostility of the Indians, and the tyranny of the king, early suggested the benefits of a union. The matter was brought up by Connecticut, in 1637, immediately after the Pequod war. After thorough discussion a plan of confederation was adopted, in 1643, by representatives of the four governments of Massachusetts, Plymouth, Connecticut, and New Haven. The union was named the United Colonies of New England. Providence and Rhode Island desired membership, but were excluded, chiefly because they would not consent to be under the control of Plymouth, which had claimed their land.

[The names of the ablest and most prominent men of the colonies appear among the delegates to this convention. John Haynes was there from Connecticut, Theophilus Eaton from New Haven, Edward Winslow from Plymouth, and John Winthrop from Massachusetts, "the honored governor of the colony." The terms of agreement were very carefully considered. For managing all affairs of the whole confederation, two commissioners, in church fellowship, were to be chosen by each colony, to meet annually at Boston, Hartford, New Haven, and Plymouth, in succession. The expense of all wars was to be shared in proportion to population, but each colony was to tax itself, in its own way, and the confederation had no right to interfere in the private affairs of any colony.]

86. What is meant by "common dangers?"

87. **This confederation** is remarkable because it foreshadowed the greater Union that was to come afterward. But it did not long endure. Massachusetts sought to control it. "So long as the confederacy acted in accordance

JOHN WINTHROP.

with the wishes of Massachusetts, all went well; but when she differed from the others, she was ready to dissolve the union rather than yield." With the reign of James II. (1685) the union was abandoned.

88. **The conversion of the Indians** was always announced as one of the chief purposes in planting the colonies. The ministers of New England labored diligently. Rev. John

Eliot, known as "the apostle Eliot," learned their language, constructed an Indian grammar, and made a translation of the Bible. He was successful in persuading many Indians to profess the Christian faith and to adopt the ways of living of the white men. In all this the influence of the chiefs and of the medicine men (priests) was generally against them. Christianity never spread beyond the settlements.

89. [**King Philip's War, 1675-7.**—The Indians knew that they were being crowded out of the land of their fathers. As a race they hated the whites, and causes for a quarrel were seldom lacking. Rumors reached the English that the Indians were preparing for war. Philip, chief of the Pokanokets, who lived on Narragansett Bay, was the mover. The punishment of several Indians for the murder of a traitor brought on the conflict known as King Philip's War. It began with an attack on the town of Swansey, in 1675, and soon raged along the whole line of settlements. It lasted for two years, and is the long story of Indian massacre. No one in the outlying towns felt safe at any time. The Indians fought with the secrecy and fierceness of wild beasts. Some of them had obtained firearms from the traders, and were able to contend on more equal terms than they could do with arrows. At the end of the first year the Narragansetts joined Philip in the war. Large bands of white men sought out the Indians, and slaughtered them without mercy. Gradually the savages began to yield. Philip, deserted and friendless, was shot by a traitor Indian. The war ended in 1677, with the Pokanokets and Narragansetts nearly exterminated, and a loss to the English colonists of 600 men, and a dozen towns.]

90. England and the Colonies.—All that the colonies wanted from England was to be let alone, and to be allowed to manage their own affairs. The contest between the House of Commons and the king (42) was especially favorable, because neither party had any time to meddle with America. The sympathy of Puritan New England was naturally with the Commons. During Cromwell's time (41), New England maintained her independence. In 1652 Massachusetts even took upon herself the right of coining money, always the sign of sovereign power.

91. The Navigation Acts.—Every European nation that

---
89. Make an analysis of King Philip's War. See the form on page 45.

had colonies in America desired to gain wealth from them. When the English colonies in America became strong and productive, the British government passed laws known as the Navigation Acts, requiring the colonies to buy all their supplies in the British market, and to ship to England whatever products the English merchants cared to purchase. The first law was passed in 1651, under the management of Cromwell (41), and chiefly to ruin the trade which Holland was building up with the English colonies. The second law was made in 1660, and simply for the purpose of enriching English merchants. These commercial laws were a great burden upon the colonies, especially upon New England, where business was most active. They were evaded in all the colonies, and gradually came to be regarded as "dead letters." Smuggling was so common that it became a regular business.

92. **Changes under Charles II., King, 1660-1685.**—When the commonwealth ended and Charles II. became king of Great Britain, the colonies recognized him as their king, and acted in his name. Connecticut, in 1662, got from him a charter confirming her self-established government. Under this charter Connecticut and New Haven colonies were united. A new charter for Rhode Island (1663) established religious freedom by the words, "No person shall at any time hereafter be anyways called in question for any difference of opinion in matters of religion." The law officers of the crown having decided that Massachusetts had no jurisdiction over New Hampshire, the king made New Hampshire a royal province, in 1679, with a governor and a council appointed by him, and an assembly elected by the people.

[New Hampshire was again united with Massachusetts in 1688, and again separated in 1691.]

93. **Massachusetts** was especially hateful to many of the advisers of the king. But the colony acted carefully, and

prepared to resist any encroachments on her self-government. The people of New England, and especially of Massachusetts, were charged with aiming at independence. Charles II., a careless, good-natured, pleasure-loving king, was at last aroused. Repeated charges of disobedience on the part of Massachusetts resulted in punishment. In 1684 an English court declared the charter of Massachusetts forfeited, and her right to govern herself revoked.

94. James II., King, 1685-8, was determined to rule the colonies after his own will, regardless of charters or local governments. Sir Edmund Andros was appointed governor of all New England, and was "authorized to make laws, lay taxes, and control the militia of the country." He was instructed to tolerate no printing press, and to encourage the English Church. The charters of Connecticut and Rhode Island were suspended, and popular government was everywhere interrupted.

95. [**Charter Oak.**—Andros demanded the surrender of the Connecticut charter, first by letter and then in person. At Hartford he was met by the governor and council, and tradition tells that while a consultation was in progress in the evening, all the lights were suddenly put out. When they were relighted, the charter, which had been lying on the table, had disappeared. A hollow oak tree near by, which is said to have been the hiding place for the precious document, was long preserved and gratefully remembered as the Charter Oak.]

CHARTER OAK.

96. The Change in 1688.—James II. lost his kingdom in 1688, and Andros departed. Rhode Island and Connecticut resumed their charters and popular government. Massachusetts hoped to regain her old liberties, but her magistrates were not united. Some of them had come to fear the power of the people. William III., the new king, was no friend of democracy. The old charter was not restored, but, in 1691, a new government was formed. The king appointed the governor, his deputy, and secretary, and these appointed the higher judges. The governor could veto laws and dissolve the legislature. But his salary depended on the legislature, which managed all the taxes. The religious test (69) for voters was exchanged for a property qualification.

97. Quakers.—The narrow religious spirit of the seventeenth century, which so controlled the government of Massachusetts that a different sect could not live in the colony, found serious annoyance in the people called Quakers (146). This class began to come into New England about 1656. The first that appeared at Boston were expelled, or shipped back to England. But this treatment was only an invitation to the most fanatical of the Quaker faith to come back again. The more the authorities of Massachusetts cut off their ears, whipped them, and hanged their brethren, the more they rejoiced in the persecution, and continued their disturbances. But the people of Massachusetts did not sympathize with the severe measures of the magistrates, the Quakers began to complain to the king, and the laws were modified. When the severe treatment ceased, the Quakers gave no further trouble.

98. [Salem Witchcraft.—In 1692 there was a popular craze at the village of Salem, Massachusetts, which is known as the Salem witchcraft. A witch or a wizard is a person supposed to have made a bargain with the devil, giving a soul in exchange for some mysterious powers. Belief in witches used to be common all over the world, and the New England colonies had laws for their punishment as evil-minded persons. At Salem village, two young girls claimed that they were constantly pinched by hands that no one could see, and pricked by pins that no one could find. An old servant was accused of being the troubling witch. The affair came to be talked about. Some people said that the belief in witchcraft was foolishness; others thought that there were witches, and began themselves to have mysterious troubles.

The ministers set themselves to catch the witches, and to punish as irreligious persons all who denied that there were any witches. The jails were soon full; twenty persons were hanged, and then the people came to their senses. Like other superstitions, the belief in witches has passed away. Samuel Parris, minister of Salem, and Cotton Mather, a minister of Boston, were the most active in arresting and condemning accused persons. They seem to have used the opportunity for punishing persons whom they considered their enemies.]

99. Education.—One of the chief characteristics of the Puritan immigrants to America was their interest in general education. The public school system of the United States had its origin in New England. A law was made in 1642, for the Puritan congregations, that "none of the brethren shall suffer so much barbarism in their families as not to teach their children and apprentices so much learning as may enable them perfectly to read the English tongue." Five years later the law declared that "every township having fifty families should appoint one to teach all children to read and write;" and when any town should increase to one hundred families, it should "set up a grammar school, the master thereof being able to instruct youths so far as they may be fitted for the University."

100. [**The "University" was Harvard College**, the oldest college in America. Founded at Cambridge, Massachusetts, as a colonial school, in 1638, it was always a popular institution. It was named for the Rev. John Harvard, who bequeathed £800 and his library towards its establishment. Yale College, located at New Haven, dates from 1700. It is also named for an early benefactor, Elihu Yale, and is the third college of the United States in order of establishment.]

101. Peace and Growth.—During the reigns of George I. and George II. (1714-60), Sir Robert Walpole was most of the time the Prime Minister. His policy was peaceful, and he had no desire to interfere with the colonies. Wars with other nations occupied the English government, and the navigation acts (91) were not enforced. The children and the grandchildren of New England's settlers kept the power and the spirit of their ancestors. The hills and valleys of New England were the home of a strong and thrifty race.

CHAPTER IX.
1607-1660.
VIRGINIA AND MARYLAND.

For Explanation.—Gentlemen; libertines; dissensions; gorgeously; liveried; ostentation; nicotine; borough; burgess; royalists; feudal; representative; fashion; maize.

To be Pronounced.—Ches'a-peake; Chickahominy (chik-a-hom'e-ne;) Pow-hat-ăn'; Car-ri-bees'; Jean (zhŏn) Nicot (ne-ko'); nic'o-tine.

Outline of Paragraph 102.—Settlement of Virginia by London Company, at Jamestown, 1607; first colony, 105; three ships; Commanders, Newport, Gosnold, Ratcliffe; *one half*—gentlemen; *remainder*—laborers, tradesmen, mechanics; few workers, many adventurers.

[*Make a similar outline of other paragraphs.*]

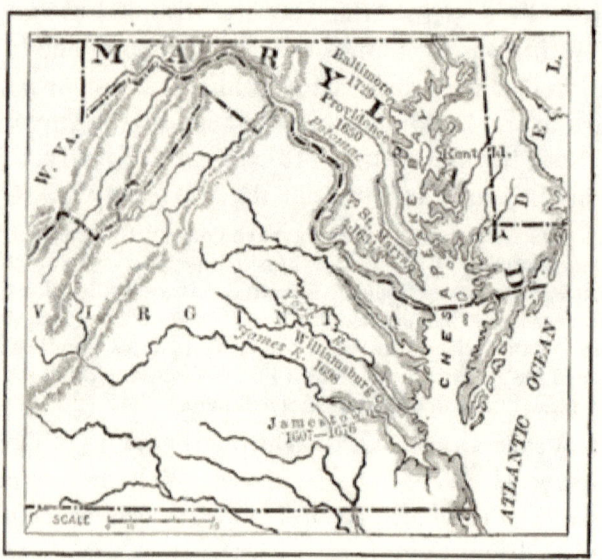

EARLY SETTLEMENTS IN VIRGINIA AND MARYLAND.

Map Questions.—What settlements were made in Virginia and Maryland between the years 1607 and 1660? Under what leaders? (See text.) Name the subsequent settlements prior to 1730, with date. Where is Kent Island? What advantage did Virginia offer to early settlers? In what part are mountains? Compare their direction with that of the coast line. Count the rivers shown here. What waters make a peninsula of the land on which Jamestown and Williamsburg stood? Find other peninsulas.

102. The colony at Virginia dates from the settlement of Jamestown, in 1607, under the management of the London Company (57). The first band of colonists, numbering 105 men, was brought to Chesapeake Bay in April, 1607, on three ships commanded by the experienced sailors, Christopher Newport, Bartholomew Gosnold (53), and John Ratcliffe. In the old list of the colonists more than half are put down as gentlemen; the remainder are classed as laborers, tradesmen, and mechanics. Captain John Smith, the most energetic man of the company, described them as "poor gentlemen, serving-men, and libertines." Genuine workers were few, and adventurers many.

103. Jamestown.—After exploring the James River, the company landed at Jamestown, May 13th, 1607, and a fort was commenced at once, but was not completed until the middle of June. The colony was poorly governed. The management had been intrusted to a board of seven councilors. There was no harmony or energy of action, and factions divided the colony. Time that should have been spent in planting corn was wasted in gold hunting. For four years the colony trusted to supplies from England, and as a consequence there was often very little to eat. By September of the first year fifty men, including Gosnold, had died. The hard times made the dissensions worse; only the courage and energy of Smith kept the colony from ruin.

104. [**Captain John Smith**, the hero of the early colony, was at that time not twenty-eight years old, but he was quick-witted, and sound of judgment. While on a voyage up the Chickahominy, in search of corn, in December, he incurred the hostility of the Indians, and was taken prisoner, but was released on the promise that he would pay a ransom of "two guns and a grindstone." On his arrival at Jamestown he found the number of colonists reduced to forty.]

105. The Colony Kept Alive.—In January supplies

were brought by Newport, who made repeated voyages across the Atlantic, bringing to America food and fresh settlers, and taking home sassafras, tar, iron ore, and anything else that would take the place of the gold expected by the company, and repay them for their outlay. Smith was elected President of the Council in 1608, and for a year he had almost the entire control. He managed wisely, planted corn, and built defenses for Jamestown.

106. Changes in Government.—Still the prospects of the colony were not encouraging. On the plea of improvement, in 1609, the company obtained an enlargement of their privileges, and appointed a governor for the colony, who had absolute authority. The first governor, Lord Delaware, did not arrive until 1610; and before his coming, Smith, the mainstay of the colony, had returned to England. Delaware met the colonists at the mouth of the river, already embarked for England, having given up in despair. Lord Delaware came with servants, gorgeously liveried. But in spite of his ostentation, his rule was beneficial. Emigration to Virginia increased. Various governors were appointed by the company until 1624. At that time King James, displeased with the independence of the company, took back their charter, and the governors were thenceforth royal appointees.

107. Indians.—The Jamestown settlement suffered an Indian attack during the first month of its existence, but got off with the loss of only one man. There was general hostility for seven years. An Indian girl was then the means of securing peace with the nearest tribes.

108. Pocahontas was the well-featured and best beloved daughter of Powhatan, the chief of the Patowomekes. In 1613 she was staying with her uncle Jopassus. With the bribe of a copper kettle, Argall, one of the colony leaders,

---

106. What is meant by "royal appointees?"

induced Jopassus to betray Pocahontas into his hands. An attempt was then made to extort from Powhatan a supply of corn, and a surrender of some English captives, in exchange for his daughter. The Indian king was defiant. His village was destroyed, and his daughter retained. A widowed colonist, John Rolf, became interested in Pocahontas; and, the attachment being mutual, they were married (April, 1614). The English thereupon enjoyed the good will of the father, Powhatan, and peace with his tribe for the rest of his life.

[Two years after her marriage, Pocahontas accompanied her husband to England, where she received much attention, and was presented at Court. Preparing to return to Virginia, in 1617, she died at the age of twenty-two. While she was in England, Captain Smith told the following story of his captivity in the first year of the colony. The savages had decided to kill him, and the executioners stood ready to beat out his brains. But "Pocahontas, Powhatan's dearest daughter, when no entreaty could prevail, took his head in her armes, and laid her own upon his to save him from death: whereat the Emperor was contented he should live to make him hatchets." This story, published by Smith in his "General Historie," in 1624, has been accepted as true, but it is rendered doubtful by other writers, as well as by the previous words of Smith himself.]

109. The culture of tobacco, commenced in 1612, became the source of wealth and prosperity in Virginia, and exerted a controlling influence in the future of the colony. Tobacco was more profitable than anything else. It was made the currency of the colony, passing at the rate of three shillings per pound for first quality, and eighteen pence for second quality. The church was supported and public officers were paid by a tax on tobacco.

[Tobacco is a native of America. Columbus found tobacco smoking common among the natives of the islands. The Carribbees called their pipes "tabak," and the Spaniards applied the name to the plant. Seeds were sent to Spain. In 1559 Jean Nicot, Minister of France in Portugal, made the plant known in France, and from his name came the word "nicotine." Tobacco was carried to England, in 1560, by Sir Francis Drake, and its use was made popular by Raleigh.]

109. How much money of United States currency is three English shillings? Eighteen pence?

110. The first Legislature in America was held in Jamestown in 1619. The settled region now extending outward from Jamestown over the broad river lands of Virginia, was divided into eleven districts or boroughs, after the fashion of the English counties; and two representatives elected from each borough, together with the governor and his council, made the first Virginia House of Burgesses. Measures were taken for the erecting of a University, and for the education of English children. The House of Burgesses remained the law-making power of Virginia. All taxpayers could vote for its members.

111. Religion was established in accordance with the Church of England by the first House of Burgesses; but there was no trouble about church parties until 1642. Then Puritans came from Massachusetts as missionaries, and raised opposition. A law was passed that "all non-conformists (40) shall be compelled to depart the colony with all convenience."

112. Puritan Rule.—Virginia was loyal to Charles I. to the end, and expressed sorrow and indignation at his "murder." Many royalists found an asylum in Virginia during the years of the Commonwealth (41). Cromwell compelled the submission of the colony, and Sir William Berkeley, the royalist governor, was superseded. The self-government of Virginia grew strong under Puritan rule.

[In 1648 the population consisted of 15,000 whites and 300 negro slaves. Domestic animals were abundant; corn, wheat, rice, hemp, flax, and many vegetables were cultivated; there were fifteen varieties of fruit, and excellent wine was made. The average export of tobacco for several years had been 1,500,000 pounds.]

MARYLAND.

113. George Calvert, Baron of Baltimore, a Catholic nobleman, was a favorite of James I., and a shrewd and wealthy man. He owned land in Newfoundland, and tried to make a settlement there, but desiring a warmer climate, he visited Virginia in 1628. Returning to England he drew up a charter, giving to himself and heirs the present territory of Maryland and Delaware. Before this charter received the signature of the king, Calvert died.

114. The Charter, however, was given to George Calvert's son Cecil, who carried out his father's plan. The charter was framed on feudal principles, and made Calvert almost an independent monarch with respect to England. Simply two Indian arrows were to be sent annually to the King of England in token of allegiance. All subjects of England were free to settle in Maryland, and the charter guaranteed them the rights of Englishmen. The people were to tax themselves, through a representative assembly like that of Virginia. Maryland was a proprietary colony, being under the control of Lord Baltimore and his heirs.

115. [**Religious toleration** was the important feature of Maryland. Calvert being a Catholic, wanted to make a home for Catholics; the English government being Protestant, would, of course, never consent to the exclusion of Protestants. The words of the charter were indefinite, simply prohibiting any interpretation "whereby God's holy and true Christian religion may in anywise suffer change, prejudice, or diminution," but the general practice of the colony allowed the free exercise of every religion.]

116. First Arrival.—In 1634 Calvert's ship arrived in the Potomac, with the two brothers of Calvert, "twenty other gentlemen of very good fashion, and three hundred laboring men, well provided with all things." Calvert had taken advantage of the experience of Virginia, and selected colonists of the right sort. The Virginians, loyal to the wishes of the king, received the new-comers courteously, and promised to provide a stock of fruit trees and domestic animals. The new-comers located near the mouth of the Potomac, and called the place St. Mary's.

117. Maryland and Virginia.—A quarrel for the possession of Kent Island, in the Chesapeake, and the country east of the bay, created and for a long time kept up ill feeling between the Marylanders and the Virginians, some of whom had settled on the island before the charter of Maryland was granted. William Clayborne, the most bitter opponent of the Marylanders, claimed to own Kent Island, and resisted the Maryland authorities with an armed force. The title of Maryland, east of the Chesapeake Bay, was not fully established until 1646.

[The territory of Maryland was part of the grant to the Virginia company; but that company having been dissolved, the king thought it right to bestow the unoccupied land upon new favorites. The Virginia claims were based upon the rights of settlers under the original company.]

118. Churches and Schools.—Among the early settlers of Maryland, there were people of all the churches, but the majority were Catholics. There was no great activity in building churches. The proprietor received a large revenue from the sale and rent of lands, but he never helped to build churches or schools. Education in the early colony was very backward.

119. The Indians were friendly to the first colonists, teaching the men to hunt, and the women to make bread from maize. The Jesuit priests **(176)** instructed the Indians, and established the only Catholic mission in the English colonies. Their influence probably helped to keep the Indians friendly, for Maryland seems never to have had any serious Indian troubles.

120. The first Maryland Assembly met in 1637. The colony was laid off into counties like those of Virginia. There were no restrictions to the right to vote. A considerable number of Puritans settled at Providence. There was a stormy time during the English civil war, and the Puritan element had to be allowed to manage the colony during the Commonwealth **(41)**. But the mixture of religions prevented persecution or exclusion, and Catholics and Protestants continued to live side by side, no church molested by another.

[In 1660 the population of Maryland was about 12,000.]

SOUTHERN COLONIES. 63

CHAPTER X.
1660-1750.
SOUTHERN COLONIES.

For Explanation.—Barony; manor; bankrupt; immigration; commission; retaliate; Salzburgers; menace; evasion; siege; insurrection; itinerant.

To be Pronounced.—Chowan (chō-wän′); O′gle-thorpe; Berkeley (bĕrk′le); Shaftsbury (shafs′ber-re); Salzburgers (sạlts′bŭrg-ers); Darien (dā′re-en).

Map Work.—Copy diagram, and fill out with eight settlements in order of date:

Date.	Settlement.	Present State.
1670.	Old Charleston . . .	South Carolina.

What part of the Carolinas are mountainous? Were there any hindrances to early travel from Virginia southward? Why did the first settlers locate near the coast or on some river? In what way did Georgia check the extension of Spanish settlement? What reasons can you find why the same ways of living should prevail from Virginia southward?

NORTH CAROLINA.

121. Offshoot from Virginia.—Virginia, first born of England's colonies, was the parent of North Carolina. As soon as Virginia gained a firm footing, stragglers began traveling southward and penetrated the forests of the Chowan River. The first regular settlements were made along the Chowan River as early as 1653, under the authority of Virginia. Charles II., after his restoration to the English throne, wanted to reward his friends; and in 1663 he gave the land of North and South Carolina, westward to the "South Sea," to a company of his noble supporters. These proprietors spread invitations to settlers, and, with the help of Governor Berkeley (134), a government was set agoing like that of Virginia.

122. The Fundamental Constitutions.—The most active of the proprietors, the great Earl of Shaftesbury, in 1669, had his friend John Locke, a great English philosopher, draw up a plan for a government. This document, known as the "fundamental constitutions," was an attempt to revive the worn out forms of feudalism upon the fresh soil of America. There were to be baronies and manors, and all the divisions of a land-owning aristocracy. It was folly to expect such classes among people engaged in clearing forests for corn fields, and in fighting off Indians. But the wisdom of the philosopher did not understand the life of the pioneer. Religious freedom was guaranteed, and that was the one good thing in these constitutions.

123. The Government.—The proprietors sent a great many governors from England, who tried to establish a government on Locke's plan, but their attempts resulted in quarrels and confusion. The only real government was that of the assembly, composed of representatives elected by the land owners.

124. The Progress of North Carolina was very slow. Its political history is full of bad government and unjust laws. Its population was lawless and reckless, for it received many of the worst elements of Virginia. Virginians complained that it was the refuge of bankrupts and escaped criminals. It received additions from New England, and also Quakers, fresh elements of discord (97). A colony of Swiss founded Newbern in 1711.

125. Division.—The original territory being thought too

large for one government, was divided into two counties, called Albemarle and Clarendon, which finally became North and South Carolina. These had each an assembly and a separate government most of the time. In 1729 the proprietors, tired of sending governors to the Carolinas to quarrel with the people, sold their rights to the king, who sent out the governors thereafter. North and South Carolina, as royal provinces, date from 1729.

South Carolina.

126. The first settlement was made on the Ashley River, at Old Charlestown, in 1670. Ten years later the settlement was moved to a better location, at the junction of the Ashley and Cooper Rivers, and the name of the place afterwards came to be Charleston. It was the capital of the colony, and a flourishing town. Many French Protestants came to South Carolina. Their immigration was not confined to South Carolina, but she received the largest number, and they formed afterwards some of her leading families. Scotch, Irish, and Germans also were among the settlers of South Carolina.

127. The early life of South Carolina, like that of her northern sister, was turbulent and lawless. The people had the same quarrels with the governors, and both maintained the right to make their own laws. They were much annoyed by pirates, many of whom made their headquarters at Charleston, and thence attacked Spanish commerce in the West Indies. The Spaniards retaliated with inroads upon the English settlements. Finally a new neighbor on the south served as a protection to South Carolina.

Georgia.

128. The Purpose.—From the troubles with the Spaniards, attention was early directed to the land lying between the Savannah and the Spanish settlements in

Florida, but no settlements were made until after the Carolinas had become royal provinces. Some of the colonies, as Virginia and New York (141), were founded for commercial gain. Others, as Massachusetts and Pennsylvania (145), to secure asylums for peculiar religions. Georgia owes its foundation to charity.

129. [**James Oglethorpe** was a brave soldier, "sprung from an ancient family, which had sacrificed both life and fortune in the cause of the Stuarts" (**42**). He was also an honest, kind-hearted man, and devoted himself to a generous enterprise. While he was in Parliament his attention was called to the wretched condition of men imprisoned for debt, according to the law of that time. He was appointed a commissioner to investigate the condition of the jails, and he persevered, until, "from extreme misery he restored to light and freedom multitudes who, by long confinement for debt, were strangers and helpless in the country of their birth." More than this, he formed a plan of making a home in America for these unfortunates.]

130. The Plan.—A Board of Trustees was formed, with power to govern and defend the colony. The liberties of English citizens were guaranteed, and freedom of religion to all except Papists. The trustees had high hopes for their scheme. A company of thirty-five families went with Oglethorpe as governor, and began a settlement at Savannah in 1733. Augusta was laid out in 1735.

131. The management of Oglethorpe was energetic and wise. Treaties were made with the Indians, houses were built, and everything prospered under his care. Immigrants came from many places. Salzburgers, persecuted for their religion, settled at Ebenezer. A Scotch colony was located at Darien. The trustees attempted to exclude rum and slaves from the colony; but the colonists did not quietly submit. The law against rum was a source of continual trouble and corruption, and was repealed in 1742. There was a growing demand for slaves, and after Oglethorpe had returned to England, in 1743, there was open

---
128. For what religion was Massachusetts the asylum? Pennsylvania?

evasion of the law excluding them. At last, in 1749, the trustees gave way, and admitted slavery.

132. [**The Spaniards.**—The hostility of Spaniards in Florida was a long standing menace. War with Spain was formally declared by England in 1739. This war was still in progress when, in 1744, a war known as "The War for the Austrian Succession," involved the nations of Europe in a general conflict **(180)**. In 1740 Oglethorpe led a fruitless expedition against St. Augustine. But he successfully resisted a Spanish invasion two years later, saving Georgia and South Carolina to England by gallant fighting and shrewd generalship.]

133. A Royal Province.—The trustees became disappointed. Their grand hopes had not been realized. In 1752 they resigned their charter to the king. A government was established, similar to that of other royal provinces, as Virginia and the Carolinas.

The Southern Group.

134. The Restoration in Virginia.—The influence of the Restoration of Charles II. **(41)** checked the growth of the democratic government in Virginia. Large numbers of cavaliers, the supporters of Charles I. against the Commons in the Puritan Revolution in England **(42)**, had emigrated to Virginia, when the Commons triumphed. They strengthened the old feeling in Virginia against Puritans. Virginia rejoiced when Charles II. was crowned. Berkeley, the cavalier leader of the colony, was reëlected governor by the Virginians, and he was continued in the office by the king. The royalist, or cavalier party, now in the bloom of reviving prosperity, was disposed to go to extremes. The House of Burgesses gave the governor and his council the right to levy the taxes for three years. The Church of England was declared reëstablished, and severe laws were made against non-conformists. Worse than all this for Virginia, the government of Charles II. passed and proceeded to enforce the Navigation Acts **(91)**, which made tobacco worth less, and all imported goods cost more. No elections were allowed, and the royalist House of Burgesses was continued by adjournment from time to time. Would Virginians endure such treatment?

THE CAVALIER.

135. [**The Virginians.**—Turn to the map of Virginia and count the rivers that divide the land between Blue Ridge and Chesapeake Bay. With abundant water, a rich soil, a warm climate, and the tobacco plant, Virginia offered easy wealth to all who should own land. There was no staying together in towns for the first settlers. Laws were passed for building towns, but laws cannot make towns when people will not live in them. In 1660, even Jamestown had only a state house, one church, eighteen houses, and a dozen families. Over the broad land of Virginia, well watered and wooded, the first settlers spread, taking up land to their liking, "not minding anything but to be masters of great tracts." These were the plantations. The planters built their homes on the river banks; ships came to their doors for the crops of tobacco which Europe, Asia, and Africa were ready to buy, and returning ships brought whatever the planters needed of manufactured articles, and also what they desired most, cheap labor. Men condemned to servitude for a number of years, vagrants picked up in the streets of London, were shipped to Virginia, and their labor sold to the planters; and the children of Africa were enslaved to cultivate tobacco in Virginia and the Carolinas.]

136. **Loyalty and Independence.**—The Virginians of 1670 were chiefly native to the land. From childhood they had lived amid the freedom of a new land, and the independence of pioneers. Wealth could make the planters aristocratic; as Englishmen and churchmen they were loyal to the Stuart kings (41), but as Virginians they would not submit to tyranny. Still they lacked the power and the means of organization. There were no schools and few educated men. They had neither a newspaper nor a print-

ing press. The rivers and woods impeded land communications. They did not take the trouble to build either roads or bridges, but traveled either by boats or on horseback, following the paths through the woods and swimming the rivers. The Virginians could not keep up a steady, persevering, well planned effort to throw off oppression. They had the spirit to act, but they needed a leader to direct their movements.

137. [**Insurrection.**—Trouble arose with the Maryland Indians in 1675, some of whom crossed the Potomac and attacked Virginia plantations. Governor Berkeley did nothing to protect the settlements, and even disbanded troops that had gathered against the savages. The people, left by their governor exposed to the Indian attacks, found a leader in Nathaniel Bacon, a young Englishman, "brave, rich, eloquent, well meaning, apparently ambitious, but certainly far from wise." Bacon led a band of volunteers against the Indians, but Berkeley proclaimed him and his followers rebels. Then followed a general uprising of the southern counties against the governor, who was finally compelled to commission Bacon as military commander. But even when Bacon was fighting the Indians, the old governor, never forgetting his hatred of an enemy, again proclaimed him a rebel and a traitor. Bacon and his followers laid siege to Jamestown, but the flight of Berkeley left them the masters of the capital. A council of war decided to burn the place, that its fortifications might not again give protection to the enemy. Thus was destroyed the only town of Virginia, sixty-nine years after its foundation. Only ruins now mark the foundation of Jamestown. Williamsburg became the capital. Soon after the burning of Jamestown, Bacon died of malarial fever, and his followers, left without a leader, scattered. Berkeley resumed his office, and gratified his revenge by hanging all the rebels he could catch. This insurrection is known as "Bacon's Rebellion." On the whole, it was disastrous to Virginia, for it checked the development of her popular government. Berkeley was removed, and governors followed who devoted themselves to money making.]

138. **Education.**—Through the influence of James Blair, an active, energetic Scotchman, a charter was gained for William and Mary College in 1699. Maryland established a free school at Annapolis in 1696. The rank of a college could not have been very high, for there was almost an entire lack of preparatory schools. Education was very back-

ward throughout the entire South. The poor had almost none at all, and private tutors were depended on for the children of the rich. In Maryland a law was passed in 1728, requiring free schools in every county; but they were kept under the influence of the church, and never prospered. There was no system of public schools in Virginia until after 1776. North Carolina had no schools until just before independence (274). In South Carolina there was no general education until afterwards, but the sons of the wealthy received good educations in Europe. In Georgia itinerant schoolmasters, who were loose characters and frequently intemperate, did most of the teaching.

[State Universities were established in the South after independence.]

139. **The Church.**—Except in Maryland, the majority of the settlers in the southern colonies were in sympathy with the Church of England, and in them this church was established by law and supported by taxes. The establishment was made in Maryland, also, in 1692, and the Catholics, who had founded the colony, were put under restriction. South of Virginia there was no very energetic suppression of non-conforming churches.

140. [**Rich and Poor.**—Agriculture, the life of the South, tended to the production of a few staples, as tobacco and cotton, and these, with slave labor, divided the freemen into classes of rich and poor. The rich lived in easy luxury, while the poor fell into rough habits. But in rich and poor alike there was a spirit of freedom even to lawlessness.]

CHAPTER XI.
1609-1750.
MIDDLE COLONIES.

For Explanation.—Rival; treason; nominal; era; signal; reprieved; imperious; devised; artisans; turbulent.

To be Pronounced.—Gus-tä′vus; Christina (kris-tee′na); Leisler (Lis′ler); Sloughter (slō′ter); Courant (koo-ränt′).

Outline of Paragraph 141.—Hudson, an English sailor serving Holland, discovers Hudson River; Dutch locate on Manhattan Island at mouth of river, calling settlement New Amsterdam; West India Company organized with monopoly of trade; founder of colony of fifty persons entitled to estate of sixteen miles on the Hudson; Indian claims paid for; settlers called patroons; only great rivals of English settlers.

[*Make a similar outline of other paragraphs.*]

NEW YORK.

141. Foundation by the Dutch.—Henry Hudson, an English sailor in the service of Holland, and in search of a northwest passage, discovered, in 1609, the river named for him. The Dutch, realizing the fine opportunity for Indian trade afforded by the Hudson and the harbor at its mouth, soon made a location on Manhattan Island. This trading post grew into a settlement which, in 1623, received the name of New Amsterdam. A great company, called the West India Company, was formed in Holland, having a monopoly of the trade; and any member founding a colony of fifty persons, received a right to an estate with a river frontage on the Hudson of sixteen miles. The Indian claims were paid for.

[These great land owners were known as patroons, and were the ancestors of the noted Dutch families of New York. The Dutch were the only formidable rivals to the English colonies on the Atlantic coast.]

142. Capture by the English.—King Charles II., claiming the land for England, and wishing to injure the growing

MIDDLE COLONIES.

power of Holland, gave all the Dutch territory to his brother James, Duke of York, afterwards James II. In 1664 an English fleet appeared before the town of New Amsterdam. No preparation for resistance had been made. The Dutch government had been entirely in the interest of the great company, with no regard for the people. The English commander promising liberty and representative government, easily gained possession. The Dutch governor and his soldiers sailed for Holland. New Amsterdam became New York. English laws were introduced, but the easy Dutch customs generally prevailed.

[In 1673 England and Holland being at war, the Dutch recaptured New York; but the following year possession was returned to the English.]

Map Questions.—Write the settlements in the order of their date, by the following Model:

Place.	Date.	Present State.	By What Nation. (See Text.)

What are the natural approaches to the interior of New York? of Pennsylvania? To what territory is Delaware naturally joined? From how many directions was New Jersey easily approachable? What reasons can you find for a commercial center at New York?

NEW JERSEY.

143. The Territory of New Jersey was first settled by the Dutch from New York, and passed with New York into the possession of the English in 1664. The Duke of York gave it to Lord Berkeley and Sir George Carteret. These proprietors established a government composed of a Governor, a Council appointed by themselves, and an Assembly chosen by the colonists.

A DUTCH HOUSE.

144. Towns were started rapidly, the first being Elizabethtown, by Puritans in 1664, Newark in 1666, by people from Connecticut, and Burlington in 1667, by Quakers. The Puritan element was strong, and left its impression on the early laws.

[With New York, New Jersey went over to the Dutch, in 1673, and again to the English the following year.]

PENNSYLVANIA.

145. The early history of Pennsylvania centers around the life of the man whose name was given to the province. William Penn had a large claim against the English govern-

WILLIAM PENN.

ment, inherited from his father, who had been a brave commander. His only chance for pay was to take land in America. A tract of 40,000 square miles was given to William Penn, in 1681, and christened by King Charles "Pennsylvania" (Penn's forest country). Penn was a Quaker, a man of ability and high aims. His scheme was to found a government in accordance with Quaker principles. "Perfect liberty of conscience was guaranteed to all. Capital punishment was to be inflicted only for murder and treason; and other penalties were to be imposed for reformation, and not for revenue. Trial by jury was assured not only to white men, but to Indians." The liberal principles of Penn's government, and his offer of land, at forty shillings for 100 acres, attracted Quakers in large numbers, and other settlers, from all over Europe.

146. [**Quakers** were a religious sect, calling themselves "Friends," founded by George Fox, in England, in the seventeenth century. They believed in the natural nobleness of humanity, and that conscience is the true guide of conduct. Fox taught that doctors should have no more quarrels, but study the laws of life; that lawyers should give up tricks, and not try to shield a guilty man; that preachers should find

the highest truth in the purity of conscience. The Quakers believed in an Inner Light, which was regarded as a true inspiration and revelation. This belief easily turned weak-minded persons into the fanatics who troubled the solemn Elders of Massachusetts Bay (**97**). One noticeable habit was simplicity of speech and dress. They refused to take an oath, or to serve as soldiers.]

147. Foundation of the Colony.—Penn himself went out with a company of 100, in 1682, made a famous treaty of peace with the Indians, and laid out the city of Philadelphia in 1683. Immigration was very rapid. In one year, 7,000 are said to have been received. At the end of the century, the population is estimated at over 20,000. Chester, the oldest town in Pennsylvania, had been founded by Swedes in 1643.

148. [**Philadelphia** means "brotherly love," the great idea of the Quakers. The city was laid out on the checker-board pattern, now so universal in the United States, and its streets were kept clean and orderly.]

149. [**Penn's Treaty.**—Penn met the Indians under a large elm tree, the location of which is now marked by a monument. "We meet," said Penn, "on the broad pathway of good faith, and good will; no advantage shall be taken on either side, but all shall be openness and love. We are the same as if one man's body were to be divided into two parts; we are all one flesh and blood." The chiefs were touched by his honest and kindly words. "We will live in love with William Penn and his children," they replied, "as long as the sun and moon shall shine." This treaty was never broken. It is even said that no drop of Quaker blood was ever shed by an Indian.]

150. Troubles arose in the colony, between the Quaker element and those not of that sect. Penn was in disfavor in England after the accession of William and Mary, in 1688, and charges of misgovernment caused the office of governor to be taken from him in 1693. Having acquitted himself of the charges, he gained his province again the following year. The proprietorship of the province remained in the family of Penn until American Independence. The legislative department continued as first planned by him, and was as democratic as any in New England. There was, however, continual discord between the governor appointed by the proprietor, and the assembly chosen by the people.

DELAWARE.

151. Three nations contended for the little territory of Delaware. The Dutch were the first to settle, establishing, in 1623, a trading post only. Their possession was nominal. The next were the Swedes. Gustavus Adolphus, the great ruler of Sweden, hoped to found colonies in America. His plans were carried on after his death, and, in 1638, a settlement was made near the site of Wilmington, and a fort built, called Fort Christina. The English attempted to come in from Virginia, but the Dutch and Swedes united against them. Having expelled the English, the Dutch and Swedes struggled with each other. The Swedes were overpowered, and in 1655 the Dutch ruled supreme from Delaware to New York. In 1664 the Delaware settlements gave way to English rule, and Delaware became an appendage to New York, until it passed into the hands of Penn, in 1682, and formed thereafter a part of his province. Under the government of Penn, Delaware prospered.

MIDDLE COLONIES TO 1750.

152. Government of the Restoration.—We have seen the effects on the older colonies of the rule of Charles II. and his friends (93, 134). The colonies in the middle group also felt the evils of the plan of government through men appointed by the king, and responsible to him alone. The English revolution of 1688 formed an era in the history of all the colonies then founded. The exclusion of the bigoted tyrant, James II., from England, and the accession of William and Mary, was a signal of fresh hope for the growing democracies of America. But they were doomed to disappointment, for the revolution in England was an aristocratic, and not a democratic movement.

153. [Popular Movement in New York.—In spite of the promises of the English commander at the time of the Dutch surrender, no colony suffered more under the Stuart plan of government than New York. The champion of the popular party was Jacob Leisler, a native of Ger-

many. On several occasions he had headed resistance against Andros
(98) and his associates. When news of the downfall of James II.
reached New York, Leisler, as the leader of the people's party, was made
lieutenant-governor by a "committee of safety," chosen from several
towns and the city. He addressed letters to the leaders of the neighboring colonies, in the name of William and Mary, and
was advised to act with caution. But he was hot-headed, and his treatment of opponents was severe. In outside matters he did better, and
was active in defending the frontier from the Indians and the French.
In 1691, Sloughter, a worthless drunkard, received a royal appointment
as governor, and the enemies of Leisler sought revenge. He had resisted English troops, and with others was arrested, tried, and found
guilty of treason. Sloughter reprieved them until the king's will should
be learned. But Leisler's foes were not satisfied, and persuaded Sloughter, while drunk, to sign the death warrants of Leisler and his son-in-law, who had been his chief aid. They were immediately hanged.
Leisler's death was legal; nevertheless, it was a political murder,
prompted by revenge. It created bitter parties in New York, whose
strife lasted for many years.]

154. Pirates.—New York harbor at this time (1692), was the shelter of a gang of pirates. Fletcher, the corrupt successor of Sloughter, was in league with them, sold them licenses, and is said to have shared their plunder. A plan was formed in England to suppress piracy by making recaptures. Bellomont, the next governor of New York, was one of the movers. Severe measures finally put a stop to piracy in American waters about 1723.

155. [Captain Kidd.—Bellomont commissioned the famous Captain
Kidd, a Scotch sailor, to capture pirates. Kidd sailed for Madagascar,
then the nest of pirates, and was gone a long time. Finally the word
reached England that he had turned pirate himself. When at last he
came back to America, he was arrested and sent to England, and there
hanged in 1701, for murder and piracy. On his return, he had buried
his spoils on Long Island. These were recovered by Governor Bellomont; nevertheless there grew a popular story that Kidd had buried
vast amounts of gold and jewels somewhere on the shore of New England or Long Island, and many a fortune seeker has dreamed of finding the treasure of Kidd, but has dug for it in vain.]

156. Walpole's Administration.—The system of managing the colonies through governors appointed by the English king, begun by Charles II. and continued by his successors, caused the same quarrels in all the colonies, and yielded the same story of imperious demands by the ambitious governors, and stubborn resistance by colonial assemblies. Under the easy administration of Walpole (101) the Middle Colonies, together with the others, prospered and were at peace.

157. Quakers and Military Service.—The Quaker element in Pennsylvania, in accordance with the principles of the sect, refused to do military service, no matter what the danger on the outside. This refusal was a cause of trouble until 1744, when Benjamin Franklin devised and set in order a system of volunteer service.

158. [Benjamin Franklin (1706-1790) was born in Boston, where his father, originally a dyer, was carrying on the business of candle and soap making. He was the youngest son of a very large family. As a boy he had some instruction at school, but at the age of ten was put to work, first with his father, then with an older brother, who had a printing office, and published a newspaper, the "New England Courant." Benjamin did not prosper with his brother, and at the age of seventeen, he struck out for New York, and then for Philadelphia. Here he arrived with only one dollar in his pocket, and no friends in the city. He found employment as a printer, and later on became the publisher of the "Pennsylvania Gazette," and one of the most influential citizens of Philadelphia. He was distinguished for practical common sense, as well as for superior intellect. As an able writer, a clear thinker, a wise statesman, and a noble patriot, Franklin deserves to be well known to all the boys and girls in the United States. (See portrait of Franklin, Chapter XVII.)]

159. People and Occupations.—The descendants of the Dutch settlers formed a large part of the people of New York, but in time they acquired the English language and adopted English customs. The people of New Jersey were mostly English. Pennsylvania received a large non-English immigration during the first half of the eighteenth century. Germans were the most numerous, Irish next; together they outnumbered the English settlers. They furnished many excellent citizens—farmers and artisans, but shiftless and turbulent elements as well. Agriculture was, of course, the great dependence, and the climate allowed a greater variety of crops than in the south, while the excellence of the soil gave a greater profit than in New England. Pennsylvania exported grain, and manufactured paper, glass, and cloth. New York and Philadelphia were centers of thriving and growing commerce.

160. Education.—The Dutch early established schools in New York, partly supported by the government. These declined under the English mastery, except in the city. There Columbia College, first called King's College, was founded in 1754, but being in the interest of the Church of England, it was not a general favorite. New Jersey had schools in the towns of New England origin (144). The Presbyterians established the College of New Jersey in 1746, the fourth in age in the United States. Located first at Elizabethtown, it was moved to Princeton in 1757, and is frequently called Princeton College. In Pennsylvania and Delaware, schools in the rural districts were poor, sometimes kept by ex-convicts. In the towns they were better, and best in Philadelphia, where a public school was opened in 1711. The University of Pennsylvania was planned by Franklin, in 1743, opened as a school six years later, became a college in 1755, and a genuine university in 1779. It was a popular institution.

161. The Church.—The conflict of races and of languages in New York made no conflict in religion, for the Dutch were Protestants, and the early English settlers were Non-Conformists (40). But the government, from 1692 onward, most unwisely sought to impose the worship of the English Church, and to compel its support. Dislike of the English Church was a prominent cause of decline in loyalty toward England. In New Jersey the Church of England existed only in name. Puritan and Quaker influences were strong. In accordance with Quaker principles, genuine religious freedom was enjoyed in Pennsylvania, and the policy of that colony may be said to have become that of the United States.

ABSTRACT OF FIRST ENGLISH SETTLEMENTS.

Copy and complete the following Review of the Early Settlement of the Thirteen English Colonies:

Name.	First Location.	When.	By Whom.	Chief Purpose.	Became English.	
					How.	When.
Virginia.	Jamestown.	1607.	Englishmen.	Adventure and gold.		At the beginning.
Massachusetts.						
New York.					By conquest.	1664.
New Hampshire.						
Connecticut.						
Maryland.						
Rhode Island.						
Delaware.						
North Carolina.						
New Jersey.						
South Carolina.						
Pennsylvania.						
Georgia.						

CHAPTER XII.
THE THIRTEEN COLONIES IN 1750.

For Explanation.—Prevailingly; felony; malice; tithing; penal; postal.

Outline of Paragraph 167.—Colonial governments divided into three classes; *charter*—people electing governor; *proprietary*—owner appointing governor; *royal*—king appointing governor. At first, charter government, three colonies; proprietary, eight; royal, one; changed to charter, two; proprietary, three; royal, seven. In all colonies, people elect legislature, with power of taxation.

[*Outline other paragraphs in a similar way.*]

---

162. **The colonial governments** are frequently divided into three classes: charter governments, in which the colonists elected their governor; proprietary governments, in which the owner of the land appointed the governor; and royal governments, in which Great Britain appointed the governor. Massachusetts Bay colony was an example of a charter government, Maryland of a proprietary government, and Virginia, after the charter of the company was revoked (**106**), of a royal government. The thirteen colonies belonged to these classes, as follows:

AS FOUNDED:

Charter.	Proprietary.	Royal.
Rhode Island	Maryland	Virginia (after 1621).
Connecticut	Pennsylvania	
Massachusetts Bay	Delaware	
	New Hampshire	
	New York	
	New Jersey	
	The Carolinas	
	Georgia	

After the early experiments of the proprietary companies, and the annihilation of the Massachusetts charter, they became and were,

IN 1750:

Charter.	Proprietary.	Royal.
Rhode Island	Maryland	. . . Massachusetts.
Connecticut	Pennsylvania . . .	. . . . Virginia.
	Delaware	. . New Hampshire.
		. . . . New York.
		. . . . New Jersey.
		. . North Carolina.
		. . South Carolina.
		. . . . . Georgia.

More important than these distinctions in the choice of governors, is the fact seen in the history of every colony, that the people managed all their local affairs. They were represented in a legislature of their own choosing, and which had the sole power of taxation, and in general sought only the good of the people.

163. [**The people** of the thirteen colonies were prevailingly of English stock. In New England there was pride of race and origin. "God sifted a whole nation," said an old governor, "that he might send choice grain to this wilderness." Among the southern planters there was pride of family and descent from Cavalier aristocracy. Southern plantations passed by inheritance from father to son, and in the same way the estates of the Dutch settlers of New York were preserved. In New England there were few large estates. The English descendants changed somewhat in appearance from their forefathers, becoming less ruddy in face, and less stout in form.]

164. The slave population was quite numerous in all the colonies, and especially so on the plantations from Maryland south. Slaves were held in bondage by laws, the severity of which indicates "the widespread fear among the masters of a slave insurrection." "The slaves had no rights which any white man was bound to respect. If a master killed a resisting slave, it was no felony, for no man could be presumed to have any malice in destroying his own property. Slaves were debarred from giving evidence, except at the trial of one of their own race for capital

163. Describe the difference between pride of race and pride of family.

offense." However, they were generally "mildly treated, well clothed and fed. Many of them had gardens and poultry, and, as they were carefully kept in a state of densest ignorance, it is not going too far to say they were tolerably contented and happy."

165. Occupations.—Agriculture was the leading occupation in the whole land. Hay, grain, and cattle were shipped from New England to New York and Philadelphia. Indian corn had been a blessing to the early settlers, for it could be easily raised where wheat would have failed. Corn bread remained a staple of food. New England whale and cod fishermen carried on an extensive and profitable business. There was considerable trade along the coast and with the West Indies, which supplied the colonies with molasses and sugar. In the middle colonies, especially Pennsylvania, manufactures, as leather, paper, glass, and linen cloth, began early and grew steadily. The southern planters raised corn and wheat for their own use; tobacco, rice, and indigo for export. Along the western frontier every man was a hunter. Women all knew how to use the spinning wheel and the hand loom, and homespun cloth was worn by the majority. Every man knew the use of tools, and could be his own mechanic.

166. Professions.—Aside from the clergymen there was little calling for professional men in the early colonial times. This changed as the colonies grew, and law became the leading profession, attracting men of foremost ability. The colonies were not excessively quarrelsome, but their strict defense of personal rights gave plenty of work to courts and lawyers. There were no trained physicians in the land till about 1750, Philadelphia first establishing a medical school. Druggists and quacks enjoyed whatever medical practice existed among a hardy and healthy people.

Puritans Going to Church.
Engraved from Boughton's celebrated painting.

SUNDAY MORNING IN VIRGINIA.

167. Clergymen were the leading class in early New England. Their influence controlled the laws and habits of the people. Their power gradually weakened as the affairs of government came to be separated from the church. They were stern, severe men, hard workers, and finely educated, versed in all the ancient, and, occasionally, in the modern languages. Outside of New England there was no such body of educated clergymen. Those who officiated in the English Church where it was established were generally jolly, good natured men, easy-going in their own habits, and careless of the state of their parishes.

168. [**The observance of the Sabbath** illustrates the difference in religious spirit between the North and the South. The Puritan "Sabbath" began at six o'clock Saturday evening, and lasted until sunset on Sunday. All work of every description was suspended, while amusements and sports, rare enough on week days, were absolutely prohibited. There was no traveling, no movement in the streets, nothing but religious exercises at home and in church. In some places, if any one was absent from church for more than one Sunday, the tithing man sought the offender out, and he was obliged to offer sufficient defense, or be fined, set in the stocks or in a wooden cage, or whipped. Rules were less strictly enforced in later days, but the spirit remained. The church services were tediously long. A sermon often lasted two hours, with prayers in proportion. On account of the scarcity of books, the hymns were given out one line at a time, by a "leader," and then sung by the congregation. Only about five tunes were common to which hymns were sung. The churches were plain wooden buildings. The congregations sat on benches or in high-backed pews. The tithing man carried a staff with a brass knob on one end and a feather on the other, with which he rapped the heads of men or tickled the noses of women if they chanced to be overcome with slumber. Virginia began with Sabbath laws as strict as those of New England, but they soon passed away. Sunday became a day for visiting and social enjoyment. The average clergyman "hunted the fox and raced horses, turned marriages, christenings, and funerals alike into occasions for mirth and revelry. Stricter habits characterized the newer sects, as Presbyterians, Baptists, and Wesleyans."]

169. Houses in early New England were all of wood. The log cabin gave place to the "lean-to," a frame house with a steep roof sloping only one way. After this came houses with hip-roofs and also with gables. They were solidly built with heavy hewn timbers. Inside were great fireplaces with massive stone chimneys. The winter evenings spent before the blazing hearth were a cheerful feature

NEW ENGLAND COLONIAL FIRESIDE.

in early New England life. Furniture was home-made, heavy, and substantial. In South Carolina the better houses were of brick, with broad verandas. In Virginia some were built of cut stone. Southern homes tended to luxurious living, with costly furniture, silver plate, and servants to do all the work. The South allowed a great deal more of open air life and enjoyment than the North.

170. Dress.—Officials and wealthy persons indulged in expensive and showy dress. Men made even a greater display than women. Broadcloth and velvet, lace ruffles at wrists and neck, silk stockings, diamond shoe buckles, powdered hair, and a sword by the side, made up the costume of the colonial gentlemen of leisure. Women sometimes displayed silks and brocades, high head-dresses and ostrich feathers. The majority of both men and women, however, were clothed in homespun.

171. Amusements.—In New England, after the decline of Puritan severity, there were some simple forms of relaxation. Sleigh rides, picnics, tea parties, quiltings, corn husk-

A HUSKING BEE

ings, and spinning-bees made a round of fun the year through. Thanksgiving Day, partly a social and partly a religious holiday, marked the great holiday season in New England, while Christmas celebration prevailed in the South. Places of public amusement came only with the growth of large cities. Theaters were resisted as evil, wherever Puritan influence extended.

172. Military System, Penal Laws, Etc.—The colonies had neither army nor navy as regular institutions. New England, however, had from the start a regular militia system, by which every citizen was trained to arms. Pennsylvania and other colonies established the system later. Indian wars kept all the colonists familiar with fighting. In the seventeenth century, all men, even farmers, carried small weapons. Training days, in New England, when all the men gathered in their towns for military drill and inspection, were among the great events of the year. After the drill, there was shooting at a mark, games and feasting, with plenty of cakes and cider. Criminal classes existed in the colonies, rather from importation than home production. According to the ideas of the world at the time, punishments were everywhere severe. At least seven crimes were generally punishable by death. Fines and imprisonment were the lightest penalties. Insolvent debtors were liable to imprisonment. The nineteenth century has brought about a different system of punishments, designed for the correction of criminals, not for revenge upon them.

173. Streets, Roads, Postal Communication, etc.—Some attention was paid to street paving in the larger cities, as Philadelphia and Boston, and to lighting with oil lamps along the sidewalks. Franklin carried out a great many improvements in Philadelphia, and, among other things, improved the postal system introduced into the colonies by the British government. Postal communications extended only to larger places, and was extremely slow when compared with railroad time. The mail was carried in post chaises, and later on in stage coaches, which were introduced a short time before Independence. Wheeled vehicles were not at all common. The colonial governors had the first coaches, drawn by six horses. Rich men followed with four-horse carriages, heavy and clumsy. Little was done at road building, in colonial times, outside of New England,

and travelers straggled through the forests on horseback or afoot, getting across rivers as best they could, and in the outside country spending the night at farmhouses. In the South, traveling was especially difficult. A visitor was a great relief to the monotony of life, and any one was sure of a welcome in a Southern home, and of hospitable entertainment as long as he wished to stay. The first newspaper of the colonies was the "Boston News Letter," first published in 1704; there were seven small sheets in the colonies, appearing once a week, and spreading through the country by slow stages. Two days between New York and Philadelphia was remarkably quick time in 1762.

COLONIAL HISTORY TO 1750.

Copy and complete the following Review:

Colonies.	Character of the Country.	Chief Occupations.	Principal Cities and Towns.	Leading Events.
New England Colonies. Chapters (VI., VII., VIII.)	Hilly, rocky. Many small streams and valleys.	Farming. Fishing {Whale. Cod.} Shipping. Manufactures.	(See map following p. 96.)	Confederacy, 1643. King Philip's War, 1675-7. Navigation Acts, 1651-61. Trouble over Charters. Quaker Persecution. Salem Witchcraft.
Southern Colonies. Chapters IX., X.				
Middle Colonies. Chapter XI.				

CHAPTER XIII.
1600-1750.
CANADA AND LOUISIANA.

For Explanation.—Pompous; stages; monastic orders; on parchment; stupendous; accession; savannahs; ally; Spanish succession; Austrian succession; squadron; Gibraltar; metropolis; Sultan of Versailles.

To be Pronounced Before Reading the Chapter.—Eu-ro-pē'ans; Loyola (loi-ō-'la); Joliet (zho-le-ā'); Marquette (mar-ket'); Ar-kan'săs; Il-li-nois'; Navarre (na-vär'); Versailles (ver-sälz'); New Or'le-ans.

Outline of Paragraph 174.—From 1600 to 1750 English had settled narrow border between Alleghanies and Atlantic; west of the Alleghanies unknown to them; St. Lawrence and Mississippi Valleys in possession of France.

[*Make a similar outline of other paragraphs.*]

1. FRENCH EXPLORATION OF THE INTERIOR—1600-1750.

174. English civilization, planted along the coast, in a century and a half had subdued the narrow strip of the continent drained by the rivers that run into the Atlantic. The vast and fertile region west of the Alleghanies, although claimed in the pompous charters of the English, was to them an unknown land. The St. Lawrence and the Mississippi, the natural approaches to the interior of the continent, fell to the possession of France, the great rival of England.

175. Explorers of Canada.—With a steady and far seeing purpose the French kept their hold on the St. Lawrence, and during the seventeenth century extended their explorations inland from Quebec (**45**). Samuel de Champlain, enterprising and fearless, a master of navigation, a careful observer, and the leading spirit in exploration for the first third of the century, made Canada known to his countrymen in well written accounts, illustrated by his own hand. For many years he was lieutenant-governor of New France, as the French possessions were called; but he is to be remembered as the discoverer of Lakes Champlain, Huron, and Ontario. In the steps of the explorers followed the fur traders, a class of men whose manner of life was formed by their business. Hardy and fearless, they adopted many of the habits of the savages, but pushed their trade with the energy of Europeans. They traveled the rivers in birch bark canoes, hunted the deer and the bison, trapped the beaver, and bought furs of the Indian hunters. The fur trade was the life of Canada. Even early in the century, from 15,000 to 20,000 beaver skins were annually bought from the Indians and shipped to France.

176. The Jesuits.—As companions of the explorers and the fur traders, went the Jesuit missionaries, members of a great religious order, sent to subdue the children of the wilderness to the spiritual rule of the Church of Rome. Also hardy men and fearless, selected for especial fitness, trained in severest schools to obey unquestioning an authority of more than military strictness, the Jesuits "aimed at the conversion of a continent." The French government followed up the advance of explorers, traders, and priests with a line of forts along the great lakes.

[Various stages in the history of the Church of Rome have been attended by the formation of societies for its advancement. Dominicans, called Black Friars, and Franciscans or Gray Friars, are monastic orders founded in the thirteenth century. The order of Jesuits, or the Society of Jesus, was founded by St. Ignatius Loyola, a converted Spanish soldier, in the early part of the sixteenth century, for the purpose of fighting the growing power of Protestantism.]

177. Exploration in the West was continued in the latter half of the century by Cavalier de La Salle, the famous discoverer of the Ohio, and by Louis Joliet, native of Quebec, a man educated by the Jesuits and trained among the

---
175. *What does the phrase " illustrated by his own hand" mean?*

fur traders. Joliet was sent to find the Mississippi, and Father Marquette, a Jesuit, was appointed to accompany him. Their starting place was a trading post on Lake Huron. Their outfit was two birch canoes, a supply of smoked meat and Indian corn, and five Indians as paddlers. Their course was along Lake Michigan to Green Bay, and up Fox River. From the head of Fox River they dragged their canoes across the prairie to Wisconsin River, and again embarked. In June, 1673, they steered their canoes into the rapid current of the Mississippi. They descended the great river to the mouth of the Arkansas, and then fearing to go farther, they returned by way of the Illinois River, and thence overland to Lake Michigan.

[These overland crossings from water to water are called portages.]

178. Louisiana.—In 1682 La Salle descended the Mississippi to its mouth, gave the name "Louisiana" to the whole valley, and took formal possession in the name of "the most high, mighty, invincible, and victorious Prince, Louis the Great, by the grace of God, king of France and of Navarre, Fourteenth of that name."

["The realm of France received, on parchment, a stupendous accession. The fertile plains of Texas; the vast basin of the Mississippi from its frozen northern springs to the sultry borders of the Gulf; from the woody regions of the Alleghanies to the bare peaks of the Rocky Mountains,—a region of savannahs and forests, sun-cracked deserts, and grassy prairies, watered by a thousand rivers, ranged by a thousand warlike tribes, passed beneath the sceptre of the Sultan of Versailles; and all by virtue of a feeble human voice, inaudible at half a mile."—*Parkman.*

2. WAR BETWEEN THE FRENCH AND ENGLISH COLONIES—1689-1748.

179. France and England.—In direct contrast to the growth of the English government (42), the sovereignty of France became more and more the possession of the king alone. Louis XIV., king of France from 1643 to 1715, ruled as an absolute monarch. There was no law above

---

178. What is meant by the "feeble human voice" referred to in the last line?

the king's will. When the English people deposed a tyrannical king (James II., 1688), Louis gave him refuge and support. There were many other reasons for hatred between the two nations, and long, bloody, and expensive wars between France and England were the result. The French and English colonies in America were naturally rivals, and the wars in Europe made them foes.

180. [The wars between the colonies are frequently designated by the names of the English rulers. King William's War, 1689-1699; Queen Anne's War (War of Spanish Succession), 1702-1713; King George's (War of Austrian Succession), 1744-1748. The French colonies were far weaker in numbers than the English, but better protected by their position. The Frenchmen armed their Indian allies and sent them to destroy the frontier settlements of New York and New England. Captives that were spared the knife and the tomahawk were driven through the woods to Canada. New York and New England sought vengeance in expeditions by land and water against the strongholds of Canada. But land expeditions were always failures, because defeated by the difficulties of the march. The important strongholds of Canada were Port Royal (now Annapolis), Montreal, Quebec, and later, Louisburg. Port Royal was captured in 1690, by a fleet fitted out by Massachusetts; but it was recaptured the next year by a French ship. In 1710 it was again captured, and this time retained as an English possession, together with the province of Acadia. In 1745 troops from all the New England colonies, aided by artillery from New York, and provisions from Pennsylvania, and by an English squadron, captured the strong fortress at Louisburg, built in 1720. Louisburg, the Gibraltar of America, commanding the entrance to the Gulf of St. Lawrence, surrendered to New England mechanics, farmers, and fishermen. By the treaty that pacified Europe in 1748, Louisburg was given back to the French, but the boundaries of the colonies were left undetermined, the ground for future trouble.]

3. GROWTH OF NEW FRANCE TO 1750.

181. The Iroquois, sometimes called the Five Nations, occupying the fertile land of New York, and extending their war paths south to Carolina, east to Maine, and west to the Mississippi, were a permanent obstacle to French progress. The Algonquin tribes of Canada and New England were the deadly foes of the Iroquois, and the region of Lake Champlain was an annual battle ground. The Algonquins were weakening when Champlain and his early successors came to their assistance against the Iroquois, with whom the best efforts of French leaders and priests failed, afterward, to establish friendship. Common hatred of Frenchmen tended to unite the Iroquois with the English, and although they seldom took an active part as English allies in war, they were at all times a hindrance to the French, and therefore a defense for the English.

[A treaty was made in Albany, in 1684, by a convention composed of Iroquois warriors, and representatives of Virginia, Maryland, Massachusetts, and New York. The invitation had been sent by the Governor of New York, at the wish of the Iroquois, and the convention is notable as the first in which English colonies, north and south, met to consult for the common good. Said a Mohawk chief: "We now plant a tree, whose top will reach the sun, and its branches spread afar off, and we shall shelter ourselves under it, and live in peace, without molestation." The tree did grow to the heavens, but its leaves were as poison to the red men.]

182. **Growth of Louisiana.**—Through the first half of the eighteenth century, French occupation pushed on down the Mississippi. A fort built at Natchez, in 1716, was the beginning of the first permanent settlement in the valley south of the Ohio. New Orleans dates from 1718, founded by a trading company (called the Western, or the Mississippi Company), which had gained a grant of Louisiana the previous year. New Orleans became the metropolis of the valley. Mobile, commenced in 1702, was also an important location. In 1732 the ownership of Louisiana returned to the crown of France.

183. **The French population** of America never became very numerous. Quebec, the capital of New France, was a town of considerable size. Generally, however, the French did not settle the country and build towns as the English did. Yet, their hold on the country was a strong one, for their forts and trading posts lined the great rivers, in a semicircle from the Gulf of St. Lawrence to the Gulf of Mexico.

Except in Canada and around New Orleans, Frenchmen left no permanent mark on the country, but they weakened and pacified the Indian tribes, preparing the way for other masters.

REVIEWS.

Copy and complete the following reviews:

1. FRENCH EXPLORATION OF THE INTERIOR—1600–1700.

Chief Explorers.	Office or Purpose.	Regions Visited.	Dates.
1. Champlain.	Lieutenant-Governor of New France.	Canada, Lakes Champlain, Huron, and Ontario.	Early part of 17th century
2. Fur traders.			All the time.
3. Jesuits.			
4. La Salle.			
5. Joliet and Marquette.			

2. WAR BETWEEN THE FRENCH AND THE ENGLISH COLONIES—1689–1748.

General Cause.—European wars involving France and England.

General Method. { Raids on frontier English settlements. Expeditions by land and water against the strongholds of Canada.

Name of War.	Time.	Chief Events.	Result, if any.
1.			
2.			
3.			

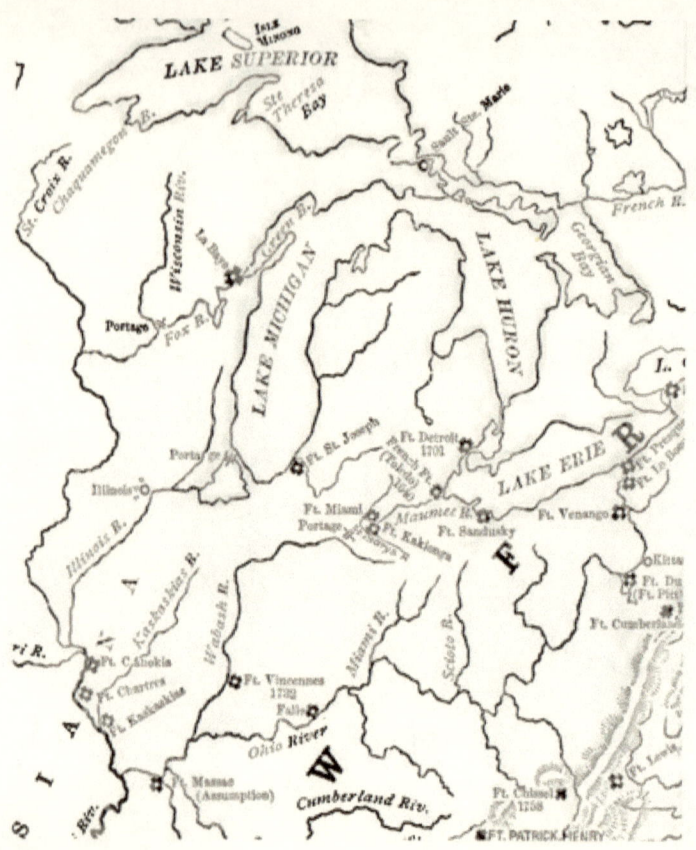

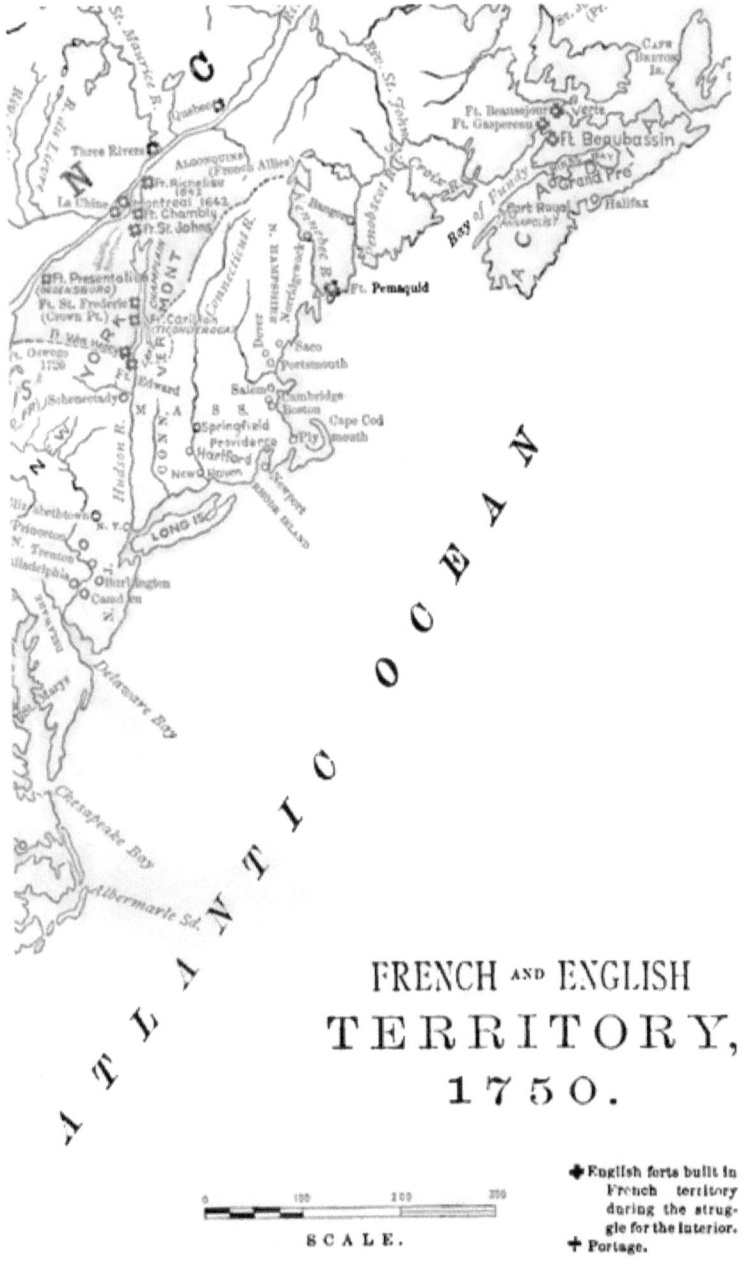

CANADA AND LOUISIANA.

3. GROWTH OF NEW FRANCE TO 1750.

[See map following p. 96.]

	Territory.	Chief Places.	Occupations.	Government.
Canada.	Basin of the St. Lawrence and Great Lakes.		1. Farming in Acadia and a little elsewhere.	Governor appointed by the king of France.
			2. Trapping and hunting. (175)	
			3. Trading with Indians. (175)	
Louisiana.	(178)		4. Fishing in Canada waters.	From 1718 to 1732 by the Mississippi Company. Subsequently, with Canada, by Governor appointed by the king of France.
			5. Military service.	

COMPETITION FOR NORTH AMERICA—1492 TO 1750.

Nation.	Territory Occupied.	Becoming Previous to 1750.
Spanish	Florida Mexico California	New Spain.
French	Louisiana Canada (Acadia)	New France. (English province).
Dutch Swedish	New Netherlands { New York New Jersey Delaware	
English	New England Pennsylvania Maryland Virginia Carolinas Georgia	The thirteen English colonies.

Review the settlement of North America by nations and by territory.

CHAPTER XIV.
1750-1763.
THE STRUGGLE FOR THE INTERIOR.

For Explanation.—Alert; parallel; frontier; reflections; pretensions; original; commissioner; flank; counter; envoy; emblems; spare; agile; swooped; compromise; ambush; emissary; foray; base; scale; sentries; onset; cruisers; privateers.

To be Pronounced Before Reading the Chapter.—Frŏn-te-năc'; de Bienville (deh be-ăn'vĕl); Gist; Le Boeuf (leh bŭf); Kanawha (ka-ngw'wä); Du Quesne (du käne'); Dinwid'die; Dieskau (dees'kow); Beausejour (bo-se-zhoor); Ma-drid'.

Outline of Paragraph 191.—Florida and Mexico and southward acknowledged Spain; exception; England and France contest for the north; *England*—thirteen growing states, with the best of people and laws; *France*—with scattered population, often corrupt, under military rule; English settlers ten times as many as French; *France*—controls the great St. Lawrence and Mississippi waterways; *England*—the Hudson and Susquehanna; *France*—difficult position to attack; *England*—exposed on the ocean, east, and on her frontier, west; *France*—definite plan and one head; *English Colonies*—undecided and divided.

[*Make a similar outline of other paragraphs.*]

184. Rival Powers in America.—Spain had led the way across the Atlantic; and the new world, from Florida and Mexico southward, excepting only Brazil, yielded to Spanish arms, and paid rich tribute to the monarch at Madrid. The contest for the control of the country to the northward lay between the English and the French races. England was represented by the thirteen growing States, reproducing and developing in America the best of England's institutions and laws; France, by a scattered population, under a military government, alert, but despotic, and often corrupt; for Canada swarmed with official thieves. The English in America outnumbered the French more than ten to one. But the contest did not rest in numbers alone. France had the control of the great waterways, the Mississippi and the

St. Lawrence; the English the minor ones of the Hudson and the Susquehanna. France had the defenses of position difficult of attack; the English settlements were exposed along two parallel lines—one the line of their coast, and the other of their frontier. Chief of all, France had a definite plan, namely: to stop the English growth at the line of the Alleghanies; and all her movements were carried out with the directness of military orders, issued from a single head. The English colonies did not all feel the danger alike, had no means of acting in concert, and their legislatures grumbled and quarreled over the expenses of defense.

185. [**This an American War.**—Previous conflicts between the French and English in America had been only reflections of hostilities begun in Europe (**180**). The one we are now to study began in the valley of the Ohio, and extending to the mother countries, was finally merged into the great European conflict known as the "Seven Years' War" (1756-1763). The vital question in America was whether the English language, popular government, and Protestant religion; or the French language, monarchical government, and the Church of Rome should prevail in the valley of the Mississippi.]

186. Conflicting Claims.—The territory of New France, according to French notions, included practically all land drained by the St. Lawrence and the Mississippi. England, besides her original pretensions (**56**), had set up the claim that the Iroquois tribes, through their treaties, had become English subjects, and that England, therefore, was entitled to rule all land ever conquered by the Iroquois braves.

[After the treaty of 1748 (**180**) commissioners met at Paris, and for three years discussed the rival claims of France and England without fixing on any boundary. Acadia, which had been an English province since 1713 (**180**), was the chief ground of dispute. England claimed all Nova Scotia and a part of New Brunswick, under the name of Acadia. France would limit it to the southern end of the peninsula, desiring the northern end for land communication between Quebec and Louisburg. As a match to Louisburg, England built a strong fort at Halifax, in 1749, and began a town which in three years had a population of 4,000.]

187. Outposts.—The activity of France in erecting military defenses on the frontier was met with counter movements by the English colonies. As early as 1726 New York put a fort at Oswego to face the French at Fort Frontenac. As a sort of flank movement the French built a fort at Crown Point, thus guarding Lake Champlain and blocking the natural route to Canada from the south. For years these outposts threatened each other, emblems of the deadly rivalry of their owners.

188. [**Traders** from Virginia and Pennsylvania had reached the headwaters of the Ohio, and then carrying their merchandise on pack horses or in canoes, they visited the Indian villages, even to the Mississippi. These enterprising peddlers alarmed the authorities of Canada. Celoron de Bienville was sent into the Ohio Valley in 1749, to warn the English traders, and at the mouths of rivers to bury leaden plates, on which was inscribed the title of France to all the land drained by the streams. In nearly every village Bienville found the intruding peddlers in high favor with the Indians. A Frenchman reported at this time, "The Indians like our brandy better than English rum, but they prefer English goods to ours, and can buy for two beaver skins, at Oswego, a better silver bracelet than we can sell at Niagara for ten."]

189. [**The Ohio Company.**—While Bienville was planting his leaden plates, the Ohio Company, comprising some of the leading men of Virginia and Maryland, was preparing to occupy the land penetrated by the traders. The Ohio Company had received through the government of Virginia a grant of 500,000 acres between the Kanawha and the Monongahela Rivers, on condition that a fort should be built, and one hundred families established on the land within seven years. The company in 1750 employed Christopher Gist, a frontiersman, to prospect their possessions, and he reported "a fine, rich, level land, well timbered with large walnut, ash, sugar trees, and cherry trees; well watered with a great number of little streams and rivulets; full of beautiful natural meadows, with wild rye, blue grass, and clover; and abounding in turkeys, deer, elk, and most sorts of game, especially buffalo."]

190. New French Forts.—In 1752 Marquis Duquesne was made governor of Canada. His movements were prompt and well directed. A new chain of forts was to connect Lake Ontario and the headwaters of the Ohio. In the spring of 1753 an expedition sent from Canada built a fort at Erie. Fort LeBoeuf was the next point, and the

summer ended with French garrisons at these forts, and a
few men stationed at Venango, a trading post. Here, in
the beginning of December, 1753, arrived Major George
Washington, Adjutant-General of the Virginia militia, only
twenty-one years old, but the chosen envoy of Governor
Dinwiddie of Virginia, bearing a letter warning the French
trespassers to depart at once from the territory of the King
of Great Britain.

191. [**George Washington** was born in Virginia, February 22d, 1732.
A grateful nation honors the day as a general holiday. Every boy or
girl who expects to be a citizen of the United States should study the
brave deeds and the wise and noble words which make us acquainted
with the character of this great American. His boyhood passed with
little schooling, but with plenty of out of door sport and exercise, which
gave him good health and vigorous strength. He was a tall man, rather
spare, quick and agile, and a bold and graceful rider. From sixteen to
nineteen he was a land surveyor, and in this work he became acquainted with Virginia and the habits of its Indian people. When he
was nineteen the expected trouble with the French and Indians led
Virginia to make military preparations. The colony was divided into
districts, in one of which Washington was commissioned as a major.
In 1753 he was the man best fitted for the tedious journey from Williamsburg to Lake Erie, a journey made doubly perilous by the cold of
winter and the treachery of Indians. (See portrait, p. 189.)

192. Preparation in Virginia.—The French had no
thought of giving up the Ohio. The commission (**186**) had
failed to fix a boundary, and war must decide the question
of ownership. The home government authorized Dinwiddie
to act, but left him to get his men and money from the
colony. The House of Burgesses was slow to lay taxes
asked for by a royal governor, whom they delighted to
resist. Dinwiddie appealed to them and to his neighbors
north and south, and received help from North Carolina.
Pennsylvania, from rivalry with Virginia, would do nothing,
but Dinwiddie's efforts got together a few hundred men not
trained as soldiers, but ready for forest fighting.

193. Fort at Pittsburg.—The plan was to build a fort
where Pittsburg now stands, the site having been recom-

mended by Washington, and the advance began in the spring of 1754. Forty men were hurried to the place and commenced work. Washington was following with a larger party. But the French governor, having no unruly assembly to deal with, could act more quickly. In April a French party of about 500 swooped down on the unfinished fort, demolished it, and began at once to build one in its place much larger and better, which they named Fort Duquesne.

194. [**The First Fight, 1754.**—Washington regarded the capture of the fort as the beginning of war. He sent for reinforcements, and worked forward to find a place for a new fort. When near a place called Great Meadows, word came, through an Indian ally known as Half King, that a French force was approaching. With forty men Washington went to the camp of Half King, and together they made a night attack on the French scouting party. "I heard the bullets whistle," wrote Washington to his brother, "and believe me, there is something charming in the sound." Washington lost one man. The French had ten killed, including the commander; the rest were made prisoners. This sudden attack of the youthful Washington was the beginning of the great war.]

195. [**Fort Necessity.**—While waiting for reinforcements, Washington erected some rude defenses, to which he gave the name Fort Necessity. Here a superior French force arrived July third, and firing was kept up through the whole of a rainy and dismal day. Although the English lost more than their assailants, terms of surrender were offered by the French commander and readily accepted by Washington, who was allowed to lead out his men with the honors of war. Virginia's efforts had failed, and in all the great valley no flag floated save the lilies of France.]

196. **The British Ministry** (42) desired to put the burden of the war upon the colonies. For a long time the view had been a common one in England that the French in Canada were a good check to the colonies, and kept them dependent upon England. The ministers advised the colonies to act together, and ordered the governors to summon a convention of delegates from all the colonies, to consult

---

195. What valley is referred to?

for the common defense. Thus came about a memorable assembly, which convened at Albany, in June, 1754.

197. The Albany Convention was composed of able men representing the New England Colonies and New York, Pennsylvania, and Maryland. The first business was to renew the treaties with the Iroquois, whose chiefs gathered tardily, sullen and distrustful because of the slowness of the English in resisting French encroachments. Next came the discussion of a plan of union for the colonies, and here was displayed the genius of Franklin (**158**), present as a delegate from Pennsylvania. He presented a plan of union which recognized the colonial governments as well as the authority of the king. It was discussed and adopted by the convention, but being a compromise, it found favor neither in England nor in America.

198. [**Franklin's plan** provided for a general colonial government, made up of a Grand Council, Colonial Assemblies, and a President-General appointed by the king. This general government had specified powers, chiefly with respect to Indian affairs, land, and military defenses. It could levy taxes for these general purposes. The President-General was the chief executive officer, and had a negative on all the acts of the Grand Council. All laws had to receive the approval of the king.]

199. Military Plans for 1755.—Although both England and France still politely assured each other that there was no war, both governments sent troops to America. General Braddock took two British regiments to Virginia, and assembled the colonial governors for consultation. Four lines of attack were agreed upon, designed to sweep the French from America:

1. Braddock, the commander-in-chief, was to capture Fort Duquesne (**193**).

2. Shirley, governor of Massachusetts, was to march by way of Oswego against Fort Niagara.

3. Johnson, a land owner on the Mohawk, and a leader among the Indians, was to capture Crown Point.

104   HISTORY OF THE UNITED STATES.

4. An army of New Englanders was to attack the Acadians.

200. [The Campaign of 1755.—Braddock's fine army of trained soldiers worked its way nearly to Fort Duquesne, but was there caught in

EVANGELINE, THE ACADIAN MAIDEN.

an ambush and sent in miserable retreat to Philadelphia. Nearly 1,000 men were lost. Braddock was killed, and all his papers captured, revealing the English plans to the enemy. Shirley got as far as Oswego, but dared go no farther, lest he should be cut off by French from Frontenac. Johnson's army contained several men from New England, who knew better than he how to fight on the frontier. A French army, commanded by Baron Dieskau, coming down by way of Lake Champlain, was hurled back in defeat from the shores of Lake George, but Johnson did not follow up this advantage, and only strengthened the lines at Forts Edward and William Henry. The expedition against Acadia resulted in the capture of Fort Beausejour, the seizure of about 4,000 Acadians, and their transportation to the English colonies.]

201. The Acadians.—[The French inhabitants of Acadia in 1713 (**186**) were allowed to remove within a year, but all who chose were free to remain, keeping their own religion and laws. Most of them staid and prospered under English protection. In 1745 and afterwards, the Acadians ought to have been neutral, but French emissaries among them, especially their priests, kept them stirred up against the English authorities. They repeatedly refused to swear any allegiance to England. But all their quarrels and defiance did not justify the breaking up of their homes, and the separation of families in their forced removal to places strange to them and their customs. Although the Acadians were far from being the quiet, peace loving, and thrifty people described by the poet, still the treatment that they received is a lasting blot upon the history of English government in Nova Scotia. (Read Longfellow's poem " Evangeline " for the story of their banishment.)]

202. Declaration of War and Fighting in 1756.—England and France, in 1756, made formal declaration of the war already two years old in the colonies, and at this time the European conflict began (**185**). For two years the French remained generally victorious. Marquis de Montcalm was their military commander, a man whose ability made up for the fewness of his soldiers, and the hindering jealousy of the governor of Canada. In 1756 Montcalm captured Oswego, destroying the English hold on Lake Ontario, and strengthened the defenses at Ticonderoga. On the English side Colonel Webb, Major-General Abercrombie, and the Earl of Loudon were appointed commanders. Not one of these was an efficient officer, and all of them offended the provincial troops by making all officers who held commissions in the regular British army rank above

---

200. For a fuller account of this battle, read Lesson 109, Second Reader, California Series.

202. Who are meant by " provincial troops?"

every officer who held a commission in the colonial militia. A major in the regular army ranked above a provincial major-general. The only effective fighting on the English side in 1756 was done by bold rangers like Robert Rogers of New Hampshire, and Israel Putnam, a Connecticut captain, who checked the Indian forays on the frontier.

203. [**Events of 1757.**—The French began the year with an unsuccessful attempt to surprise Fort William Henry. The Earl of Loudon failed miserably in an assault upon Louisburg, and having taken the best men from the frontier he left the way open to Montcalm, who now compelled Fort William Henry to surrender. By the terms of the surrender, the English garrison was to march to Fort Edward unmolested, but in spite of Montcalm's efforts to control his Indian allies, many an English soldier was murdered and many others stripped and maltreated.]

204. Success in the war changed sides in 1758, for then William Pitt, the great English statesman, was made Prime Minister of England (42), and he defended the colonies with a vigorous hand. The incompetent officers were gradually removed and better men put in their places. Provincial officers ranked the same as regulars. In this year Abercrombie led a disastrous expedition against Ticonderoga, but this was the last of the English failures. Colonel John Bradstreet destroyed Fort Frontenac and regained Oswego. Thus cut off from supplies, Fort Duquesne was blown up to prevent capture by a strong force led more skillfully than Braddock's by Brigadier John Forbes. An English fort was built on the ruins of Duquesne and named Fort Pitt; whence the name of the present city. The capture of Louisburg in July, 1758, Sir Jeffrey Amherst commanding the land forces, opened the St. Lawrence for a final assault on Quebec.

205. Events of 1759.—Niagara and the posts along Lake Erie fell during this year, and Ticonderoga and Crown Point were abandoned at the approach of an army led by Amherst, the abler successor of Abercrombie, for Montcalm

THE STRUGGLE FOR THE INTERIOR. 107

CAPTURE OF QUEBEC.

was compelled to withdraw his men from the frontier to defend the capital. Amherst was to have gone on to Quebec, but he was too slow in his movements, and the honor of capturing the great stronghold of Canada belongs solely to General James Wolfe, a young commander, only in his thirty-third year, but the choice of Pitt for the most important work of the war. On September 19th, 1759, the English flag was unfurled over Quebec and the war in America was practically ended, for the strength of New France had been exhausted in the defense of her capital. New England was filled with rejoicing at the downfall of her enemy.

206. [**Capture of Quebec.**—The site of Quebec has the finest natural defenses on the continent. A steep promontory between two rivers makes a walled fortress on top, almost impossible to capture. Montcalm had extended his fortifications along the St. Lawrence from the River Charles to the Montmorenci. The whole number defending the intrenchments and the fortress, including Indians, was about 16,000 men. Wolfe had about 9,000 free for operations on land. The guns on board his ships could not be elevated sufficiently to reach the fortress, and Wolfe carried a part of his men to Point Levy. Bombardment from that point resulted only in driving the non-combatants from the lower part of the town at the base of the promontory. Montcalm's policy was to tire out his adversary, and Wolfe tried in vain to provoke a general conflict at the lower camp and to land troops on the St. Lawrence bank above the city. In this way time passed from June to September. One plan remained: to scale the heights back of the fortress, called the Heights of Abraham, and fight the French upon the top. While a part of the army pretended an attack on Montcalm's camp, Wolfe ran his boats up the river above the city and made another pretense to attack the French defenses there. Then a moonless night was chosen for the grand assault. Volunteers passed the sentries on the shore by giving the name of a French regiment, and made a landing in a small cove where a steep ravine gave a chance to climb to the heights above. The negligent French guard on top was overpowered, and morning revealed the bulk of Wolfe's army drawn up in fighting order on the Plains of Abraham. There was still the fortress wall ahead, but Montcalm decided on a sudden onset, and with a more numerous army came out to meet his foe. The two lines exchanged volleys at close range, and Wolfe gave the command to charge. As he was leading the charge two shots hit him, and a third lodged in his breast. Montcalm, borne backward by the flight of his troops, was also mortally wounded. Both generals lived to learn the result of the fight. Wolfe's words were, "God be praised, I die in peace." Montcalm said, "I am happy that I shall not live to see the surrender of Quebec."]

205. *What place was the capital?*

207. Conquest of Canada.—No attempt of the French forces was able to recover the surrendered fortress, and the arrival of additional English troops both by land and water brought about the surrender of Montreal and the remaining French forts in the west in 1760. Canada was conquered, and the English colonists hoped to sit under their own vines and fig trees, with none to make them afraid.

208. War in the West Indies.—The war went on in other places. British forces relieved from service in Canada were turned against the French islands in the West Indies. Colonial soldiers went with the regulars and helped the British navy sweep French merchantmen from the sea. The king of Spain became the ally of France in 1761, and in the next year English and colonial cruisers paid him for it by destroying Spanish colonial commerce, and by capturing Havana, the capital of Cuba and the key to the Gulf of Mexico. These operations were very profitable to the colonies. The privateers were rewarded by plunder, the merchant vessels got the trade of the West Indies, and the whole country the business of supplying provisions to fleets and armies. Pitt, whose vigor and boldness had brought the victories, was the idol of America.

209. [**Pontiac**, chief of the Ottawas, took up the war in which Montcalm had failed, and formed a formidable conspiracy among the tribes from the Ottawas to the lower Mississippi. The Iroquois alone kept out of it. Pontiac rehearsed the wrongs his race had received at the hands of the English. He showed his fellows that English occupation was death to them, and he said that the French king was coming with an army to protect his children of the forest. This plan was to keep up a show of friendship, while organizing his forces, and, at an appointed time, to surprise and capture all the western forts and drive the English back to the settlements. In accordance with this plan, attacks were made in May and June, 1763; eight out of twelve forts were captured, and three years of Indian fighting, with great loss and expense to the colonies, were required to crush the power of Pontiac.]

210. The Peace of Paris, in 1763, formally closed the European war and established territorial boundaries in

America. Spain gave up Florida **(48)** in return for Havana, and excepting New Orleans, all North America east of the Mississippi was recognized as a British possession. New Orleans and Louisiana, restricted now to the west half of the Mississippi Valley, were ceded to Spain. English statesmen had questioned whether Canada should be retained or not, but pride in the empire that was growing up in America, prevailed, and Canada was retained as British territory. A moderate amount of wisdom and regard for American interests would now have preserved to England the fairest colonies she ever had.

[Florida was returned to Spain by Great Britain in 1783.]

ABSTRACT OF THE STRUGGLE FOR THE INTERIOR.

Copy and complete the following review:

The War between the French and the English Colonies, 1754-1763.

1. Question at issue **(192)**.
2. Movements that led to fighting.
   1. Activity in building military defenses.
   2.
   3.
3. Military movements and results.
   - 1754.
     1.
     2.
   - 1755.
     1. Braddock attempts to capture Fort Duquesne. Fails.
     2.
     3.
     4.
   - 1756.
   - 1757.
     1.
     2.
   - 1758.
     1.
     2.
     3.
     4.
   - 1759.
     1.
     2.
     3.
   - 1760. 1763.
     1.
     2.
     3.
4. Boundaries established 1763.

CHAPTER XV.
1763-1775.
THE BIRTH OF THE NATION.

For Explanation.—Measures; unanimous; tariffs; duties; revenue cutters; cabinet; finances; seer; revision; press; ministry; substantially; platform; common; impetus; dissolved; Tarquin; memorial; Cæsar; raged; embodied; official; ministerial; fatal compliance; indictment; prime minister; preamble; expedient; quarters; rescind; toast; tumults; redress; men-of-war; raids; scruple; signature; executed; extortion; freeholders; outlaws; capital; subversion; culmination; representative; subsist; grievous; redressed; league; conciliation; policy; stealthily; detachment; flash in the pan; drenched; alternative; virtually; Chevy Chase.

Outline of Paragraph 211.—Conquest of Canada gave America to the English race; colonists share in the glory; military spirit brought out; 20,000 colonial troops in service; 400 American privateers; trained fighters in every settlement; many trained to command.

[*Make a similar outline of other paragraphs.*]

---

211. **The Results of the War.**—The conquest of Canada decided that the English race was to rule in America. The colonists gloried in the victory, in which they were vitally interested, and for which they had toiled and fought. The war had done much for them, besides subduing their rival. It had brought out their military spirit in its full strength. In the closing years, more than 20,000 colonial troops—10,000 from New England alone—had been in service, and more than 400 privateers were fitted out in the harbors of the colonies. At the end of the war, there were men in every village who knew what fighting was, and many a man like Putnam, Stark, and Washington had been trained for the command of armies.

212. **A New Name.**—Before the war the colonists were proud to call themselves Englishmen, and there was no greater honor among them than to have been born in the mother land. To go to England was to go home. But the

war showed them that their life was different from that of Englishmen, and perhaps suggested that it was an equal honor to be an American. Americans, therefore, they will hereafter be called.

213. [England's Debt.—One result of the war was more important than military training. It was the taxation of the colonies to pay the English national debt. This debt, £70,000,000 at the beginning of the war, was doubled at its close. This was the price that England paid for the vast extension of her territory in America and India. Only by the greatest vigilance and economy could England hope to guard her great empire, and make good her indebtedness. What so natural as a demand upon America to bear a part of the burden incurred largely in her defense. Taxes in England bore heavily on the land owners, and they formed just at this time the ruling class in Parliament. At the same time, these land owners had no direct interest in America, no knowledge of its people, and no sympathy with their ideas. The English Parliament proceeded, therefore, to tax Americans.]

214. **The feeling of Americans** toward the home government was never more loyal than at the close of the French war. Royal governors asserted that the colonies were aiming at independence, but Americans, with one voice, denied the charge. They looked forward to a great development, but under the British flag. The colonies loved England far more than they loved one another. Some in America feared to lose the authority of England, lest the colonies should split up into a number of petty States forever quarreling. There were Virginians, Pennsylvanians, and Massachusetts men, but as yet there was no sentiment of union to exalt the name American above provincial titles. There was a common territory, with natural boundaries, the common interests of commerce, the same language, religious sentiments, and free local government, but the stronger bond of resistance to oppression that bore on all alike, was needed to unite thirteen provinces into one nation. American patriotism was born of resistance to English oppression, and the blood of patriots made the union lasting.

---

214. What is meant by "provincial titles?"

215. [George III. and his Influence.—The measures, which in a dozen years changed Americans from loyal English subjects into the defenders of a new nationality, "fighting for their just and equal position among the powers of the earth," must not be regarded as the unanimous will of the people of England. George III., king from 1760 to 1820, assumed the crown as a young man obstinately minded to rule in his own fashion. He did not, like the Stuarts, seek to override Parliament (42), but he made a corrupt Parliament the servant of his will. The English monarch united with the aristocracy ruling in Parliament to suppress public opinion in England and self-government in America. Even a king cannot stop the growth of nations, and beneath the tyranny of George III. arose government by the people in both England and America.]

216. Trade Regulation.—The monopoly of American trade secured by the Navigation Acts (91) made English manufacturers, merchants, and ship owners rich. These trade laws laid tariffs upon goods imported into America, but the British government received very little revenue, for the tariffs were universally evaded. The colonies paid duties at the custom houses when they could not avoid them, but no one regarded these duties as taxes. The colonies were willing to contribute to English wealth as the price of their protection. But the right to tax themselves through their own representatives had been maintained by Englishmen in America against governors, proprietors, and kings (162). Born of a free race, their inherited love of freedom, strengthened in a hundred ways by life in a new land, the Americans of 1765 were not the men to submit to tyranny. When the English Parliament, in which America had no representatives, proposed to tax Americans, the country rang with the cry, "Taxation without representation is tyranny." Loyalty to king, love of motherland, and mutual jealousies, were consumed when once the fiery love of freedom was kindled.

217. Enforcement of the Trade Laws.—The war for the interior had directed the attention of English statesmen to the colonies, of which previously they had been very ignorant. The English Ministry said that smuggling must be stopped, and the trade laws be enforced. A sharp-eyed official, George Grenville, discovered that it was costing England annually over £7,000 to collect a revenue of £1,000 to £2,000. The custom house officers waked up when investigation began. To aid them in detecting smugglers, "writs of assistance" were employed in Massachusetts, which, by authority of the Superior Court, permitted officers to search private houses for smuggled goods. Swift revenue cutters were provided, manned by rough seamen, whose special business it was to suppress the illegal trade.

218. [**James Otis.**—The use of the "writs of assistance" was denounced by the press and contested in the courts. The contest in the court-room brought into public notice James Otis—"a lawyer of Boston, with a tongue of flame and the inspiration of a seer." "To my dying day," he exclaimed, "I will oppose, with all the power and faculties God has given me, all such instruments of slavery on the one hand and villainy on the other." Otis was born at Barnstable, Massachusetts, 1725, and died, struck by lightning, in 1782. The prophet of the American Revolution, his full energy was devoted to the defense of American liberty until his mind became shrouded in insanity.]

219. The Stamp Act.—George Grenville came to the head of the English Cabinet in 1763. His long experience had made him familiar with the finances of America, but neither nature nor experience had given him a statesman's wisdom. He resolved "to enforce strictly the trade laws, to establish permanently in America a portion of the British army, and to raise by parliamentary taxation of America at least a part of the money which was necessary for its support." In 1764, along with a revision of the trade laws, Grenville announced in the House of Commons that "for further defraying the expense of protecting the colonies it may be proper to charge certain stamp duties in the said colonies." Time was allowed the colonies to suggest some other way of raising money if they saw fit, but no attention was paid to protests against the stamps. In February of 1765 Grenville introduced his measure requiring all bills, bonds, leases, insurance policies, newspapers, and legal documents of all kinds to be written or printed on stamped paper, to be sold by public officers at fixed prices. Along with this was an act restricting trial by jury. The bill became a law with very little opposition in Parliament. It was to take effect November 1st, 1765.

[Pitt (**204**) was out of power and absent from Parliament on account of sickness. One opponent of the bill, however, spoke of Americans as "sons of liberty," trained by hardship and danger to maintain their rights. His words received no attention in England, but the "sons of liberty" heard them in America.]

220. Its Reception in America.—The proposed stamp law had been quickly announced in the colonies, for America now had a vigorous press. Newspapers were published in Boston, New York, Philadelphia, Annapolis, Williamsburg, and Charleston, and from these news centers were spread the ideas of resistance and revolution. The colonial assemblies during 1764 protested against the stamps. The whole country took up the discussion from the newspapers, and all minds were occupied with questions of government.

221. Americans Divided.—Discussion of the stamp taxes divided Americans into two parties. Those who opposed the English taxes were called Whigs, Patriots, or Sons of Liberty, and those who supported the English ministry were Loyalists, Tories, or Friends of Government. At the beginning the Patriots were in the minority in some colonies, but their numbers grew rapidly until they included, substantially, the whole people. Their platform was drawn up in the Declaration of Independence, and their political ideas are to be found in the Constitution of the United States. (See Appendix.) The chief men of the Loyalists were office holders appointed by the king, and persons of wealth and high social position.

222. Correspondence Between the Colonies.—Massachusetts formed a committee of correspondence, and sent a circular letter to the assemblies in the other colonies, proposing harmonious action. This letter received cordial responses throughout the land, and finally, when the Act "that will be remembered as long as the globe lasts" was passed, in March, 1765 (219), it found a public sentiment in America ready to resist it. The Patriots were convinced that submission to such a law would be a badge of slavery.

223. **Massachusetts and Virginia.**—James Otis, in the Massachusetts Legislature, suggested a meeting of committees from all the colonies, to consider the common danger. Virginia set the plan moving with a powerful impetus. The House of Burgesses, already near the end of their session, had delayed action. A vacancy was filled by the election of Patrick Henry. On a blank leaf torn from a law book he wrote a series of resolves, to the effect that the people of Virginia, as British subjects, had the right to govern themselves, through their own assemblies, in the matter of taxes, and that they were not bound to obey any other law imposing a tax. Before all the resolutions were adopted the governor dissolved the assembly; but the newspapers reported the bold words of the "forest-born Demosthenes," and they were echoed in every community.

224. [**Patrick Henry**, a native of Virginia, was born in 1736, and died in 1799. He had failed as a merchant, but succeeded as a lawyer, and now his "gushing, fiery eloquence" startled the House of Burgesses, with "a warning flash of history" in the words: "Tarquin and Cæsar had each a Brutus; Charles the First, his Cromwell; and George the Third"—— "Treason," interposed the Speaker, and others repeated the word; but the orator, with steady voice, closed his sentence,—" may profit by their example."]

225. **Sons of Liberty.**—Associations calling themselves "Sons of Liberty" (221), paraded the streets, shouting "Liberty, Property, and No Stamps!" These words became the motto of newspapers, and the favorite toast at American dinners. As might be expected, these demon-

---

223. Who is meant by the "forest-born Demosthenes?"

strations broke over the bounds of right, and were attended with the plundering and destruction of buildings, and with personal wrong to the supporters of Parliament. All the better people deplored these outbreaks, and learned the valuable lesson of caution, lest it might be said that America was ruled by mobs. Stamp officers were forced to resign their appointments, and promise never to accept them again. Sometimes they were even made to stand on a platform and shout "Liberty, Property, and No Stamps!"

226. The Stamp Act Congress met on October seventh, in the City Hall of New York. In this city the conflicts of opinion were most bitter, for here were the headquarters of British strength. Yet nowhere were the Sons of Liberty more determined. Nine colonies were represented by twenty-eight delegates, many of whom were lawyers, a profession that now included some of the ablest and most progressive Americans. This Congress was an assembly "graced by large ability, genius, learning, and common sense. It was calm in its deliberations, seemingly unmoved by the whirl of political waters." It adopted and forwarded a declaration of rights and grievances, and "an address to His Majesty, a memorial to the House of Lords, and a petition to the House of Commons." These documents plainly stated the rights of Americans in taxation and jury trial.

227. [**Prominent Members.**—"James Otis stood in this body as the foremost speaker. The brothers Robert and Philip Livingston ably represented New York. John Dickinson, of Pennsylvania, was soon to be known through the colonies by 'The Farmers' Letters' (addressed to 'The American People,' and printed in the newspapers). Thomas McKean and Cæsar Rodney were pillars of the cause in Delaware. Edward Tilghman was an honored name in Maryland. South Carolina, in addition to the intrepid Gadsden, had in Thomas Lynch and John Rutledge, two patriots who appear prominently in the subsequent career of that colony." In the course of the discussion, Gadsden said: "There ought to be no New England man, no New Yorker, known on the Continent; but all of us Americans." The presiding officer, Timothy Ruggles, of Massachusetts, was a Tory.]

228. The Stamp Act a Failure.—The resistance went further than processions and petitions. Americans entered into agreement to import nothing from England, and began to manufacture for themselves. "Frugality and Industry," was the cry. The richest citizens dressed in homespun, rather than wear imported cloth. On November first (219), business was stopped, bells were tolled, and flags hung at half-mast. Copies of the Stamp Act were peddled in the streets, labeled "The folly of England, and the ruin of America." The stamp legislation had failed.

229. Repeal.—In England merchants were threatened with ruin by the loss of American trade and petitioned for a repeal. Grenville had lost his position (217). Pitt declared "This kingdom has no right to lay a tax upon the colonies. I rejoice that America has resisted." Fierce debates raged in Parliament on the question of repeal, for Parliament had deliberately proclaimed its right to tax the colonies, and was reluctant to take back its words. The repeal was carried in March, 1766, but at the same time a Declaratory Act was passed, opposed only by Pitt and a few others, stating the right of Parliament "to bind the colonies and people of America in all things whatsoever." An outburst of joy in England and America greeted the news of repeal. Americans cared very little about the declaratory act so long as nothing was done to enforce it. "They blessed their sovereign, revered the wisdom and the goodness of the British Parliament, and felt themselves happy."

230. [A National Spirit.—The resistance to the stamp act had created a national spirit, soon to be embodied in a national government. Otis said that "one single act of Parliament had set people thinking in six months more than they had done in their whole lives before." A British official prophesied that the repeal would be followed by "measures for rebellion." But the Patriots said, "We utterly deny that such an intention ever entered into our hearts." Otis declared that "British

219, 229. *How long was the stamp act in force?*

America would never prove undutiful till driven to it as the last fatal resort against ministerial oppression, which will make the wisest mad and the weakest strong." The Sons of Liberty (225) disbanded, and the "colonies cheerfully and affectionately acknowledged their dependence on the crown of Great Britain." But their affection was misplaced.]

231. The King's Policy.—George III. regarded the repeal as "a fatal compliance." In 1766 Charles Townshend, a brilliant but reckless politician, assumed the lead in the House of Commons (42), and in June announced as his opinion that the government of America should be made "independent of the people." He was soon the leading spirit in the ministry, and urged putting taxes on America with an army to see them collected. This was the spirit of the succeeding English legislation that led to the American Revolution—the legislation of an English Parliament which did not represent the will of the English people, but was controlled and managed by George III. We can not take up all the acts of the stubborn king and his obedient Parliament from 1767 to 1775, nor examine all the arguments and appeals of American patriots. In these years the national spirit sprang into vigorous life. Americans never fell back a single step from the stand they had taken in defense of their right to govern themselves, which right the king was equally persistent in trying to overthrow. Read the Declaration of Independence for the indictment against the last king to whom Americans acknowledged allegiance. In the words of an English historian: "The shame of the darkest hour of English history lies wholly at his door."

232. The Townshend Act.—By act of Parliament, in 1767, a duty was laid on paper, glass, painters' colors, and tea, all of which were regular exports from England to America. This duty might easily have been collected in England, and Americans would never have complained; but the English government desired to make the collection in America, so that Americans might know that they were being *taxed*. Townshend died before his revenue acts took effect, and their execution fell to Lord North, a more determined enemy of American liberty and a more obedient favorite of the king. He became Prime Minister in 1770, and in this office he served the king for the next twelve years.

233. [**The preamble** of the Townshend Act stated that it was "expedient" to raise a revenue for defraying the expense "of the administration of justice and support of civil government," and for the general defense of the provinces. That preamble was supposed to state the right of Parliament to tax Americans, and whatever might happen to the duties or to the revenue, this preamble had to stand to keep up the dignity of the English government. "It is the weight of that preamble," said the noble-minded Burke, defending the rights of Americans on the floor of the House of Commons, "and not the weight of the duty, that the Americans are unable and unwilling to bear." (Read the oration of Edmund Burke on American Taxation.)]

234. Organization in America for fresh resistance followed the news of the Townshend Act. The assembly of New York had been forbidden to meet until a demand for quarters for the king's troops was complied with, and this was a warning of the treatment that other colonies would receive. Massachusetts acted first, her legislature sending another respectful and plain statement of American rights in a letter to the English ministry, and another circular to her sister colonies. Governor Bernard of Massachusetts ordered the legislature to rescind the circular letter. The legislature refused to rescind, was dissolved by the governor, but its members, reëlected by the people, met again and the government went on in defiance of the governor. Next the king tried his hand and ordered the Massachusetts legislature to rescind, and the legislature by a vote of ninety-two to seventeen again refused. This vote was published in the newspapers, and "The Illustrious Ninety-two" became another favorite toast all over the country. The king, never learning anything, ordered the other colonial assemblies to take no notice of the circular letter, but they all resolved to stand by Massachusetts.

THE BIRTH OF THE NATION. 121

235. [The New Agitation.—Taught by the riots of 1765 (**225**), the Patriots set themselves for united, organized resistance. James Otis denounced mobs, and declared that no circumstances could justify private tumults and disorders. John Dickinson, of Pennsylvania, wrote: "Our cause is a cause of the highest dignity; it is nothing less than to maintain the liberty with which Heaven itself has made us free. I hope it will not be disgraced in any colony. We have constitutional methods of seeking redress, and they are the best methods." The agitation in Massachusetts brought some new men to the front. Among these were Samuel Adams, "a poor man, a universally good character, and of rising influence as a popular leader," and John Hancock, a generous and steady patriot, whose personal services and great wealth were freely given to the cause.]

236. British Troops in Boston.—Massachusetts was regarded in England as the center of rebellion, and troops were ordered to Boston, "to suppress riots." In September, 1768, vessels arrived in the harbor with 700 men, who were landed under cover of the guns of men-of-war, an insult to a peaceable people. Before the end of the year, there were 4,000 regulars in and about Boston. The king withdrew troops needed at the western forts, for it was the plan of his advisers to expose the frontier, so that the terrors of Indian raids might help to humble the colonies. Americans thought of arms, but only for defense.

[In April, 1769, Washington wrote to a friend: "At a time when our lordly masters in Great Britain will be satisfied with nothing less than the deprivation of American freedom, no man should scruple or hesitate to use arms in the defense of so valuable a blessing," but only "as the last resource."]

237. ["Boston Massacre, 1770."—Americans hated the British soldiers, now stationed both at New York and Boston, for their presence was a constant reminder of threatened slavery. Ill feeling and insolent talk soon grew into street fights with fists, stones, and clubs. In Boston, March 5th, 1770, a few soldiers, without command, fired upon an insulting crowd, killed three, and wounded several. The killed had a public funeral, the soldiers that fired were tried and convicted of manslaughter, and the governor was compelled to remove the troops outside the city.]

238. Repeal of Duties.—In April, 1770, Lord North, urged on by a petition from London merchants, who were suffering from American non-importation, carried the repeal of the Townshend duties, on all articles except tea. He knew that the duties produced nothing but trouble and expense, and he was glad to get rid of them; but it would not do to abolish all the taxes, for the king insisted that "there must always be one to keep up the right." Americans saw that this repeal settled nothing. They were fighting for a principle, and not against the amount of the tax.

239. **Government by Royal Orders.**—George III., in 1770, began a method of ruling the colonies by royal orders. Not waiting for the formality of an act of Parliament, he sent instructions, over his own signature, to be executed by the colonial governors through military force, if necessary. By these orders, colonial assemblies were dissolved, unusual places were set for their meeting, and their organization was interfered with. Americans for the most part were opposed to the slave trade, but the king ordered them to cease their efforts to stop it. Prompted by such authority, it is not strange that colonial officers were guilty of outrages upon a peaceful people. There was extortion in fees, unjust seizure of property, and unwarranted imprisonment of citizens. But all the time a sentiment of union grew stronger, and organizations for defense were perfected.

240. [**Violent Acts.**—The free spirit of Americans had ample ground for collision with British authority. In North Carolina the tyranny of Governor Tryon and the extortions of his officers were unbearable. An organization of "honest freeholders," under the name of "regulators," sought redress, but got nothing save more ill treatment. In 1771 Tryon, with a military force, marched into the country of the regulators, and declaring them outlaws he destroyed houses and crops. A battle was fought, resulting in the killing of thirty men and the flight of the farmers, few of whom were armed. Despising Tryon's proclamation of peace to all who would swear to obey the laws and pay the taxes, the fugitives crossed the mountains, and in 1772, formed a government by written association, the foundation of the state of Tennessee, and an example to all Americans to govern themselves independent of the British king. The anger of the people of Rhode Island at the commander of the royal schooner *Gaspee*, engaged in compelling submission to the

revenue laws, led them to capture and burn the *Gaspee* one night in June, 1772, when it had accidentally run aground. A recent English law had made the destruction of a royal vessel a capital offense, and allowed transportation of accused persons to England for trial; yet in the very teeth of this law the *Gaspee* was burned, and even a reward of £500 failed to induce any man in Rhode Island to betray a countryman.]

241. The Tea Tax, 1773.—Americans up to this time had been in the habit of expressing loyalty to the king, and of blaming only his ministers and corrupt majorities in Parliament for their troubles. They did not know that the king's will controlled both ministry and Parliament (215). The king was anxious "to try the question with America," and the tea tax was selected for the experiment. Since 1770 there had been no chance to collect the tax, for American merchants ordered no tea. Americans had used none except what they could smuggle from Holland. Tea came to England from India and paid a duty on entering English warehouses. In 1773 the shrewd scheme was adopted in Parliament of forcing tea on Americans by offering to refund the duty collected at the English custom house on condition that the tea be reshipped to America. Thus the tea, after the duty was paid in the American custom house, could be sold even cheaper than it could be bought from the Dutch. But Americans cared nothing for the cheapness. They were being taxed by a power that had no right to tax them. Indignation burst out fiercer than that against the Stamp Act. "All America was in a flame." All the colonies were affected alike, and united resistance silenced local quarrels.

242. The Tea Disposed Of.—To Philadelphia and New York came shiploads of tea, but the captains were compelled to sail back to England, their cargoes untouched. At Charleston tea was landed, but left to rot in damp cellars. At Boston the people would not let the tea be landed, and the governor would not let the ships sail back. At last, there was a grand meeting on December 16th, 1773, at the Old South Meeting House, and in the evening a party of fifty young men, disguised as Indians, took possession of the tea ships lying at the wharf, hoisted the chests from the hold, and poured the contents into the bay. There was perfect order and rapid work. No one was allowed to carry off any tea, and to this day no one knows the names of the men who took part in what has since been famous as "The Boston Tea Party."

243. Punishment.—The Tea Act had produced indignation throughout America, uniting the colonies in resistance. The destruction of the tea at Boston produced counter-indignation in England. The people called it a subversion of the constitution; Lord North, the culmination of years of riot; Parliament, actual rebellion, flowing from the desire for independence. To punish rebels was the purpose of the next legislation. In March, 1774, was passed the Boston Port Bill, prohibiting all trade at Boston, and transferring business to Salem. The same session of Parliament passed four other acts, all in the same spirit. The Massachusetts Regulating Acts aimed to overthrow the representative government of Massachusetts by transferring power from the legislature to the governor. The other three severally provided for the protection of magistrates in executing English laws; for quartering British troops in America; and for making the country north of the Ohio between the Alleghanies and the Mississippi a part of Canada, thus aiming to cut off the growth of the colonies westward.

244. Continental Congress, First Session, 1774.—The punishment of Massachusetts awakened sympathy in the whole country. Washington, in a Virginia convention (August, 1774), said: "I will raise 1,000 men, subsist them at my own expense, and march myself at their head for the relief of Boston." "We shall have to resist by force," was the feeling of the country, when delegates, elected by one impulse throughout the land, assembled at Philadelphia, September fifth. The name "colonial" being abandoned, this assembly was named a Continental Congress. Georgia sympathized with the movement, but alone was unrepresented.

[Among the fifty-five members there were many men of positive character and wide influence. A number had served in the Stamp Act Congress (226), but the majority now saw one another for the first time. In them all parts of the country met and became acquainted. John Adams, a man of great ability, and Samuel Adams, a man of great influence, were there from Massachusetts. John Jay, of New York, was a man of high character and learning. Christopher Gadsden, of South Carolina, represented the genuine American. There were wealthy merchants like Philip Livingston, of New York, competent farmers like John Dickinson, of Pennsylvania, accomplished and influential lawyers like the Rutledge brothers, of South Carolina. The Virginia delegation was especially strong. It presented "in Richard Henry Lee, statesmanship in union with high culture; in Patrick Henry, genius and eloquence; in Washington, justice and patriotism." For "solid information and sound judgment" Washington was said to stand foremost among them all. Franklin had not yet returned from England, where for several years he had acted as agent for the colonies and spokesman for American interests, winning universal respect and the honored title of Dr. Franklin.]

245. Its Acts.—Congress approved the doings of Massachusetts, and pledged the support of the continent. It adopted a Declaration of Rights, claiming the protection of the English Constitution, and specifying eleven acts of Parliament which must be repealed in order to restore harmony between England and America. To these grievous acts Americans would never submit, but "for the present" Congress "had only resolved to pursue the following peaceable measures:"

1. An Association for non-importation and non-consumption of English goods and non-exportation to England.
2. Addresses to the people of Great Britain, to the colonies, and to the people of Canada.
3. A loyal address to His Majesty.

All these documents were carefully prepared by able committees, and on October twenty-sixth Congress adjourned, having issued a call for another meeting on the tenth of the following May, unless in the meantime the grievances should be redressed.

246. [**The association** for abolishing commerce with England was the most important work of the Congress. It was in the form of a voluntary pledge, which was signed by fifty-two members of Congress, and afterwards by the Patriots throughout the land. The association thus united the citizens of the colonies, not as through a league of independent states, but as individuals forming a nation. Rules were laid down for the government of those who took the pledge, and any who broke it were condemned as "the enemies of American liberty." The address to the people of Great Britain called them "Friends and Fellow Subjects," and said: "Permit us to be as free as yourselves, and we shall ever esteem a union with you to be our greatest glory and greatest happiness." The address to the colonies warned them to be ready for mournful events, and said, in closing: "Above all things we earnestly entreat you, with devotion of spirit, penitence of heart, and amendment of life, to humble yourselves, and implore the power of Almighty God." Daniel Webster (**473**) advised young men who wished to breathe the spirit of our revolutionary ancestors, to study these immortal papers.]

247. Preparations for defense went on throughout the colonies after the adjournment of the Congress. All eyes were fixed on Massachusetts, where it was evident the struggle would begin as soon as England should attempt to use *force*. From every community there came to Massachusetts letters of encouragement, and to Boston, donations for the relief of those who suffered from the closing of the port. October 27th, 1774, the Massachusetts legislature selected a "Committee of Safety," to whom was given the care of "warlike stores." The militia was organized, one fourth to be ready for service at any moment. These men signed pledges to be ready to fight at a minute's warning, and are now remembered as "The Minute Men." Officers were appointed to command the militia, and the committee of safety was authorized to call out the force whenever General Gage, whom the king had appointed military governor of Massachusetts, should attempt to enforce the Regulating Acts (**243**). In Virginia Washington headed a movement for organizing militia.

THE BIRTH OF THE NATION.

248. [**The king** could not understand Americans. He thought that a few blows would bring the rebels to submission. In Parliament there were great debates on American affairs. Burke delivered an immortal speech in favor of conciliation (March 22d, 1775), proclaiming that the fierce spirit of liberty in America could not be conquered, but his eloquence fell unheeded upon a nation whose pride of mastery had been wounded. The policy of the king and ministry went on unchecked. They tried to break the union by offering conciliation to separate colonies. But as long as the English plan to overthrow the government of Massachusetts remained unchanged, the American determination to stand together was unshaken. Friends of the king were proclaiming in England that "the Americans were a nation of noisy cowards," but the answer across the ocean was, "America must and will be free."]

Map Questions.—What water was crossed by the British in leaving Boston for Concord? Why were British troops safer in Boston than outside? How could supplies be furnished them in Boston?

249. Lexington, April 19th, 1775.— A secret attack was planned by General Gage to destroy military stores which the Committee of Safety (247) had placed at Concord, twenty miles from Boston. On the evening of April eighteenth, a detachment stealthily left Boston, but was barely under way when the church bells in the villages began to rouse the minute men to arms. Paul Revere had ridden from Boston to give the alarm ahead of the advancing soldiers. Word was sent back to Gage for more men, and the detachment marched on. A little before sunrise the advance company, commanded by Major Pitcairn, reached Lexington Common, where about

---
249. See "*The Midnight Ride of Paul Revere*," *California Third Reader*, p. 322.

seventy minute men had gathered under the leadership of Captain John Parker. As he rode up, Pitcairn yelled, "Disperse, rebels, disperse," and his men fired a volley, killing seven Americans. The minute men returned a few scattering shots, killing one English soldier. The war had begun.

[Both parties were reluctant to fire first and thereby be the beginners of a war. Both commanders had given the word not to fire until fired upon. But some of the British soldiers saw a "flash in the pan" and fired, followed by the whole company. Probably one of the seven Americans that were killed had without command raised his musket, the gun missing fire, but giving the "flash in the pan," a sufficient signal for the English soldiers.]

250. Concord.—The march was continued to Concord, where a part of the stores was found and destroyed. There was another encounter at Concord bridge. The English had commenced to tear up the planks, when a company of militia-men rushed upon them across the bridge. The English soldiers fired first, the Americans returned the volley, and more men were killed. It was ten o'clock A. M., and militia-men were hurrying toward Concord from all directions. The English soldiers set out to march back to Boston.

251. The march to Boston soon grew into a run, for American blood had been shed and American blood was up. From behind stone walls and fences the farmers poured a deadly musket fire upon the soldiers in the road. After firing once, they would reload, run rapidly across lots to a new position, and fire again. To the English soldiers they seemed "to drop from the sky," they were so thick. Near Lexington the exhausted soldiers were met by 1,000 men, commanded by Lord Percy, sent from Boston to help them. As Percy marched out that morning, the band playing Yankee Doodle, a Roxbury boy had shouted, "You go out to Yankee Doodle, but you will dance by and by to Chevy Chase." Percy had brought a few small cannon, which served to some extent to keep off the assailants, but the attack did not entirely cease until the tired English soldiers gained the protection of the gunboats in Boston harbor. Never again did General Gage send an armed man into the country.

[The British loss in killed, wounded, and missing was 273. The minute men, of whom not more than 400 were in the fight at any one time, had eighty-eight killed or wounded.]

252. Lexington and Concord raised the courage and the military spirit of Americans. "Unhappy it is," wrote Washington, "that a brother's sword has been sheathed in a brother's breast, and that the once happy and peaceful plains of America are to be either drenched with blood or inhabited by slaves. Sad alternative! But can a virtuous man hesitate in his choice?" A committee in Mecklenburg county, North Carolina, asserted that the English Parliament, by declaring the colonies in rebellion, had given up its authority, and a set of rules was provided to govern the selection of new officers with the authority of the people. A war for independence had virtually commenced, although as yet there was no actual declaration either of war or of independence.

CHAPTER XVI.
1775-1783.
WAR FOR INDEPENDENCE.

For Explanation.—Republican; outlawed; expedition; skirmish; besiege; brigadier; martial law; eminence; zig-zag; windrows; parapet; dispelled; conciliatory; promoted; condign; enlistment; ravages.

1. FIRST HOSTILITIES.

253. Continental Congress, Second Session.—Congress reassembled at Philadelphia (May 10th, 1775), according to adjournment (245). It met in a two-story building that had been erected for the Pennsylvania government, and which is still remembered as the State House. Its lower room, in which Congress assembled, is called Independence Hall. All the colonies were represented.

[Nearly all the members of the former session were present. George Clinton, one of New York's great men, and Franklin, recently returned from England with a world-wide fame, were among the few new members.]

254. Power of Congress.—With the authority of the American people, Congress began the general government of the country. "It was the head of a great movement, based on general consent; and as such was recognized and obeyed." The idea of a monarch was lost, and the government of the country became wholly republican, the will of the majority of the people being the source of law.

255. "Green Mountain Boys" and Ticonderoga.—Settlers in Vermont had no regular government, but were united in a sort of military league under the name of "Green Mountain Boys." Rough and ready men, they were just the ones to strike a blow when the alarm came from Lexington. An expedition planned in Connecticut, but composed chiefly of Green Mountain Boys, and commanded by their leader, Ethan Allen, surprised and captured Fort Ticonderoga and a British garrison of about fifty men (May 10th, 1775).

State House—1876.

Fort Crown Point was captured two days later. Beside the forts, these bold moves put the Americans in possession of 220 cannon, and a quantity of much needed ammunition.

[By Allen's account the surprise at Ticonderoga occurred as follows: As the attackers rushed upon the fort, a sentry snapped his gun and fled. But before the sleeping garrison could make any defense they were prisoners. Allen compelled a watchman to show him to the quarters of the commanding officer, who sprang out of bed at the summons to surrender. "By whose authority?" asked the astonished officer. "In the name of the great Jehovah and the Continental Congress," was Allen's reply. And the Englishman thought best to submit.]

[Vermont had been claimed both by New York and New Hampshire. As most of the settlers held titles from New Hampshire, the land was often called the "New Hampshire Grants."]

256. **A Continental Army.**—The militia that gathered after the Lexington skirmish encamped around Boston to besiege General Gage. So far as they could the people of Boston withdrew, and left the city to the British troops. Congress having adopted the assembled militia as a Continental Army, on June fifteenth, by a unanimous vote made George Washington commander-in-chief, with rank as General. Four major-generals and eight brigadiers were also appointed. Washington left Philadelphia on June twenty-first, for Boston, and on the way learned that the great battle of Bunker Hill had already been fought.

[The major-generals were Artemas Ward, Massachusetts (soon retired), Charles Lee, Englishman, Philip Schuyler, New York, and Israel Putnam, Connecticut. Horatio Gates, an English officer living in Virginia, was made adjutant-general, with rank as Brigadier. The eight brigadier-generals were Seth Pomeroy, Massachusetts (soon retired), Richard Montgomery, New York, David Wooster, Connecticut, William Heath, Massachusetts, Joseph Spencer, Connecticut, John Thomas, Massachusetts, John Sullivan, New Hampshire, and Nathanael Greene, Rhode Island.]

257. **The militia men**, whom the news of Lexington summoned from farm and workshop, obeyed various local chieftains, but had as yet no regular organization. Promi-

WAR FOR INDEPENDENCE.

nent leaders were Israel Putnam of Connecticut, John Stark of New Hampshire, William Prescott and Artemas Ward

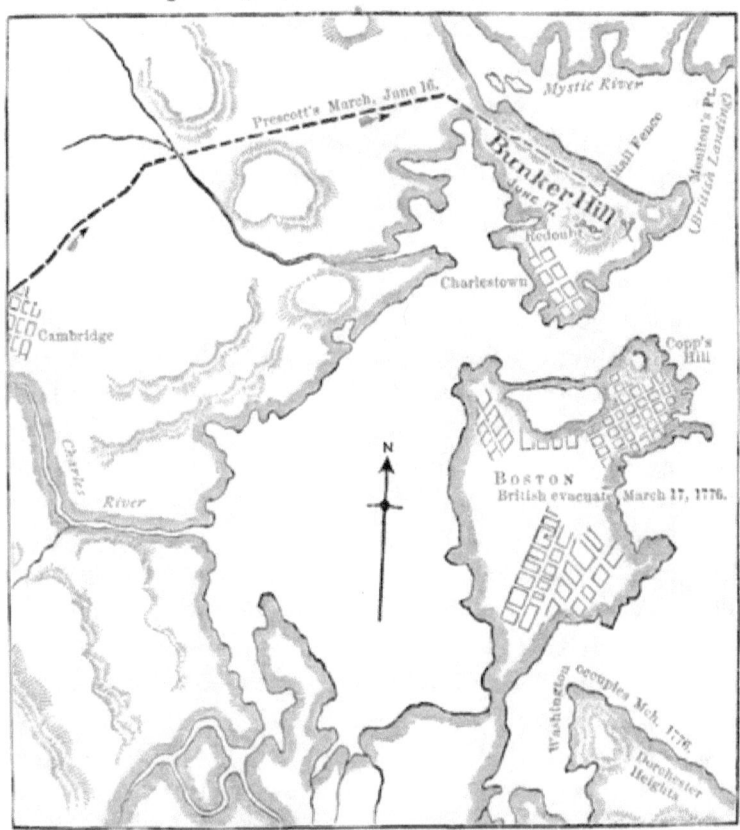

MOVEMENTS AROUND BOSTON.

Map Questions.—On what natural division of land was Bunker Hill? What waters nearly surround it? On what part of the peninsula did the British land? In what direction from the peninsula was Boston? What town on this peninsula? From what point and from what direction did Prescott advance to Bunker Hill? On what day? On what day was the battle fought? How would an opposing fort on Bunker Hill affect the safety of British troops in Boston? Supposing all the American troops to have been sent with Prescott to Bunker Hill, how could their position have been endangered? What other suburb commanded the city? When did Washington occupy Dorchester Heights? How does Boston lie with reference to Dorchester Heights and Bunker Hill? When did the British evacuate Boston?

of Massachusetts, Ward being recognized as highest in rank. Cambridge was general headquarters.

258. Fortification of Bunker Hill.—It became known to the militia commanders that General Gage, who was proceeding to enforce martial law, intended to fortify the low hills about Boston, and they anticipated him. On the evening of June 16th, 1775, three regiments (about 1,000 men), commanded by Colonel William Prescott, and a party of Connecticut men under Captain Knowlton, left Cambridge for the hills back of Charlestown. After some doubt as to choice of ground, earthworks were commenced about midnight upon a low eminence, known then as Breed's Pasture, but memorable since as Bunker Hill. The position was less than a mile from the British battery on Copp's Hill, and almost within hearing distance of British war ships in the bay. Morning revealed the night's work to the British watchmen. One of the ships opened fire upon the intrenchers, doing no damage, however, and the work was continued till eleven o'clock. Before that time General Gage had ordered the cannonading stopped, and an assault to be made to drive the Americans from the hill.

259. [**The Arrangement of the Troops.**—At noon General Howe, commanding the attack, landed at Moulton's Point, with 2,000 men. The boats made a second trip for more men, while the first regiments calmly ate their lunches. When the plan of attack was seen at the American fort, the best possible arrangements were made for defense. Knowlton's men were placed on the left, where a low stone wall, topped with two rails, gave some protection. In front of this stone fence, in farmer fashion, they quickly built a zigzag stake and rider fence, and filled the space between the two with hay, which was lying in windrows on the ground. Here came two New Hampshire regiments, commanded by Colonel Stark and Colonel James Reed, the only reënforcements that came that day to men tired with a night's hard work, without water to drink or anything to eat, except the little they had brought in their knapsacks. On the American side, about 1,400 men took part in the battle; on the British side, 3,800.]

260. [**The Battle.**—The first assault was made about three o'clock in the afternoon. The British advanced in two divisions—one led by

General Pigot, to drive the Americans from the hill; the other, led by General Howe, along the Mystic River, to drive them from behind the fence, and cut off the retreat from the hill. From the roofs of Boston an anxious people viewed the conflict. Powder was scarce at the American works, and none must be wasted on shots at long range. "Wait till you see the whites of their eyes!" "Not a shot sooner!" "Aim at the waistbands!" "Aim at the handsome coats!" "Pick off the commanders!" "Wait for the word; every man steady!" were the words that passed from Prescott along the impatient line at the fort. Steadily up the low hill came the regular ranks of the British army, under a burning sun. There were a few harmless shots from Pigot's men, but in the fort was silence that threatened death. At last came the word, "Fire!" A sheet of flame burst from the whole line, and the ground was strewn with dying men. The British line was broken, and retreated in disorder. At the rail fence the same saving of powder was enforced by Putnam, Stark, and other officers. Howe's men shot first, and shot too high; then the same deadly fire poured over the parapet of hay, from hill to river. Howe's loss was even greater than Pigot's, and followed likewise by a retreat. Charlestown was now set on fire, by order of General Gage, hoping that the smoke of the burning town would conceal the movements of his troops. The British lines again advanced, the faltering soldiers spurred on by their officers, Howe himself marching at the head. A second time they retreated, with even greater loss, before the same deadly musket fire from fort and fence. Americans thought that they had won, but a third time Howe formed his men; this time in column, and led them against the fort alone. Another volley made the British falter, but they gained the parapet. Prescott's men had exhausted their powder, and he ordered a retreat, which was protected by Stark's men, who retired from the fence. The British were in possession of the hill in an hour and a half after the first assault; but it had cost them in killed and wounded 1,054 men, of whom 157 were officers. The American loss was 150 killed, 270 wounded, and thirty prisoners. Just at the moment of retreat from the redoubt, Dr. Joseph Warren was killed. A young man, one of the noblest of Massachusetts patriots, a member of the committee of safety; he was serving at the redoubt as a private soldier. His ability, integrity, and purity of character made his early death a loss to his countrymen. See portrait, p. 172.]

261. Results of the Battle.—Englishmen had boasted that the "Yankees" would not stand a steady fight; the courage and endurance shown on Bunker Hill dispelled all such illusions. The heavy loss crippled the king's army for the time, and irritated the king and Parliament. A

---

260. *Read the poem, "Grandmother's Story of the Battle of Bunker Hill," by Oliver Wendell Holmes.*

conciliatory petition that had been sent by Congress received for answer a proclamation from the king, that rebellion existed in the colonies in North America. General Gage was superseded by General Howe.

262. **Washington's Army and the Siege of Boston.**—On his arrival at Cambridge, the headquarters of the American forces, Washington took formal command, reminding his troops that they were now "the troops of the United Provinces of North America," and hoping that "all distinction of colonies would be laid aside." He found about 16,000 men without regular enlistment or military discipline. Ammunition hardly existed. Powder was gathered from all the colonies, bought from France, and captured from England; but still its scarcity was a great drawback for a long time. Mines in Connecticut furnished lead. No man ever worked harder or more patiently than Washington. The army was gradually trained, and its lines were drawn more tightly around the inactive British army besieged in Boston.

263. [**Uniform and Flag.**—Blue and buff were the colors adopted for the uniform of the Continental army. Officers wore blue coats with yellow trimmings, and yellow or buff vests. The soldiers seldom had uniforms. Hunting shirts, dyed brown, were the nearest approach to it. British soldiers had scarlet coats, and this gave them such names as "redcoats," "lobster backs," etc. The Americans were called "rebels." At first the Americans had no regular flag. Regiments adopted colors and designs that pleased them. A flag showing a rattlesnake in the act of striking, and bearing the inscription, "Don't tread on me," was a favorite of the privateers (269). The rattlesnake had thirteen rattles, the number of the colonies. On January 1st, 1776, Washington unfurled before the army around Boston the flag adopted by Congress—thirteen stripes, alternately red and white, with the united British crosses in the corner, red and white in a blue field. Thirteen stars in a circle took the place of the crosses in 1777. A new star has been added for each new state; otherwise no change has been made in the flag which our forefathers adopted.]

264. **Capture of Boston.**—In March, 1776, Washington occupied Dorchester Heights in the night-time, a repetition of the movement at Bunker Hill, and, helped by a stormy

day, completed strong fortifications before General Howe could attack. Unable to hold the city any longer, the British army embarked on the fleet, March seventeenth, and sailed to Halifax.

[From this time on no great effort was made to conquer New England, which was, for the most part, spared the ravages of warfare. New England contributed by far the larger part of the national army, but the scene of war was shifted to the middle and southern colonies.]

2. INVASION OF CANADA—1775–6.

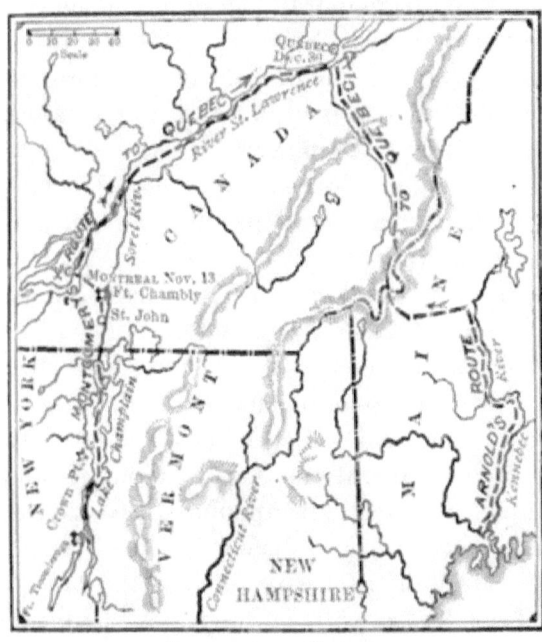

INVASION OF CANADA.

Map Questions.—What two generals marched for the invasion of Canada? At what season of the year? At what point did Arnold begin his march? In what general direction did he go? At what point did Montgomery start? In what general direction? Which had the easier natural route to Canada, Montgomery or Arnold? Why? At what point on Montgomery's route did a battle take place? Where did the two invading armies meet? When was the assault on Quebec made? With what result? (Defeat of the Americans.)

265. Invasion Planned.—Congress, having learned that the governor of Canada intended to recapture Crown Point, General Schuyler (**256**) was sent to the outpost with orders to advance into Canada if he found it practicable. On account of poor health, Schuyler soon yielded his place to General Richard Montgomery, an Irishman who had served in the British army in the war with

France, and had married and settled in New York. Montgomery, a brave and spirited officer, led a small army into Canada.

266. [Allies were expected from the Canadians, but they gave neither British nor Americans any vigorous support. Through the influence of prominent Tories, the Indians of New York and Canada were arrayed on the British side.]

267. **Montreal and Quebec, 1775.**—The feeble British garrisons posted in Canada gave way before Montgomery's troops. Montreal was captured (November 13th), and the course turned toward Quebec. Meanwhile another force of 1,100 men, led by Benedict Arnold, a brave but reckless man, had been struggling up from New England through the forests of Maine, to aid Montgomery before Quebec. Arnold arrived first, more than half his men having perished from cold and starvation. Repeating Wolfe's plan, he placed his force upon the Plains of Abraham, under cover of night, but the British commander staid within his walls in safety. Montgomery having arrived, Quebec was besieged, amid all the discouragements of a northern winter. An assault was made (December 30th), nearly successful, but in the end disastrous, for Montgomery was killed. Arnold and several others appointed in succession to the command, kept the force before Quebec through the spring of 1776. More British troops arriving, the Americans fell back to Ticonderoga, with nothing gained by the campaign in Canada.

3. STATE GOVERNMENTS.

For Explanation.—Anarchy.

268. **From Colonies to States.**—Most of the royal governors and other officials sought safe places when the fighting commenced. With the news of Lexington, British rule

---

267. *In what respect did the conduct of the English commander differ from that of Montcalm?* (206). *What made the capture of Quebec difficult?* (206). *Was any other way of reaching Quebec possible for Americans? Why?* (268).

in the colonies was practically over. After the king's proclamation (**261**), the majority of Americans had little thought of allegiance. But with the death of allegiance to the king, died also the legality of all legislatures and courts. Had not the people throughout colonial times been trained to self-government, anarchy would have added its perils to those of war. But the people were ready to be sovereigns. Through the old forms the local government went on; the colonies became states, some with their old constitutions, some with new ones, formed by themselves through conventions. Governors elected by the people took the place of the king's appointees.

[All these State Constitutions provided for Republican government. Three departments, Legislative, Executive, and Judicial, were kept generally distinct. Most of the legislatures were composed of two houses. Certain qualifications—as ownership of land, property to a certain amount, or profession of religious belief—were common requisites for office holding and for voting.]

4. Along the Coast.

269. American Privateers.—The Americans had no navy, while England's was the best in the world. In 1775 Congress authorized Washington to employ armed vessels, and steps were taken for the building of fourteen small war vessels as the beginning of a navy, which, however, were never completed. In 1776 private vessels were commissioned to sail under the American flag, and carry on war against English ships. These privateers could not do much against English war fleets, but they seriously injured English commerce, and by the capture of provisions and military supplies gave help to the American army.

270. [American seaports were the prey of British fleets. The town of Falmouth (now Portland), Maine, was wantonly burned in 1775, by permission of General Gage. Other towns suffered the same fate during the war.]

271. The Attack on Charleston, June 28th, 1776.—It was suggested to George III. by the ex-governors of Vir-

Map Questions.—What waters wash three sides of Charleston? On what natural division is the city located? Describe Charleston Harbor. Why should a British fleet choose Charleston for a point of attack in the South? Was Fort Moultrie well located? Why? Could land forces easily be brought against it? What difficulties would land forces meet in marching upon Charleston from the neighboring coast?

ginia and North Carolina that the southern colonies might easily be brought into subjection by an armed force. Tories were numerous in the South, but the Patriots held the upper hand, and when a British fleet, with land forces, commanded by Sir Henry Clinton, appeared off Charleston Harbor (May 31st, 1776), defenses had been constructed for the city. Chief among these was a fort of palmetto logs upon Sullivan's Island, a low, sandy island at the harbor's entrance. The fort was built so as to inclose a small swamp in its center. After a long delay, the attack was made (June 28th), but the best efforts of the British gunners made no impression upon the fort, balls sinking into the soft palmetto logs without splitting them, and shells sinking harmlessly into the swamp. Having themselves suffered considerable loss, the British forces, after one day's work, sailed for New York, and Americans rejoiced over a victory at Charleston.

[Colonel William Moultrie was the brave commander of the fort, and in his honor it was named Fort Moultrie.]

5. INDEPENDENCE.

For Explanation.—Identified; reference to a record; harassed; executive.

272. Growth of the Sentiment.—On New Year's Day,

1776, when Washington first unfurled the flag of the United Colonies, there was in New England a public opinion in favor of independence; but in the Middle and Southern Colonies there was only the preference of the foremost men. After the receipt of the king's proclamation (**261**), the newspapers everywhere boldly advocated separation. In the center and south the majority of the people clung to the hope of reconciliation. Pennsylvania especially opposed independence, for the popular influence of the old proprietary government was in favor of connection with England. Still the sentiment for independence grew rapidly after the beginning of 1776. The bitterness of war, and fierce words from the king, continually showed the American people that they had no hope but in themselves.

[A single pamphlet stirred the hearts of hesitating Americans, and carried them for independence. This was a pamphlet entitled "Common Sense," written by Thomas Paine, and first published in Philadelphia, January 9th, 1776. In a plain and spirited style, it made clear to the colonists that everything right and reasonable pleaded for independence. Edition after edition was exhausted, and the work was reprinted in the principal American cities, and in England and France.]

273. [**The popular leaders** who are found first identified with independence are Samuel Adams, John Adams, Joseph Hawley, James Sullivan, Elbridge Gerry, and James Warren, from Massachusetts; Matthew Thornton, of New Hampshire; Nathanael Greene and Samuel Ward, of Rhode Island; Benjamin Rush and Benjamin Franklin, of Pennsylvania; Thomas McKean, of Delaware; Samuel Chase, of Maryland; Richard Henry Lee, George Wythe, Patrick Henry, Thomas Jefferson, and George Washington, of Virginia; Cornelius Harnett, of North Carolina; and Christopher Gadsden, of South Carolina. Thomas Paine was an Englishman, of Quaker family, who came to America in 1774, and, through the help of Franklin, found employment as editor of the "Pennsylvania Magazine."]

274. Fourth of July.—On July 2d, 1776, Congress adopted the resolution, "*That these United Colonies are and of right ought to be free and independent states; that they are absolved from all allegiance to the British Crown, and that all political connection between them and Great Britain is and ought to be totally dissolved.*" "Now," wrote John Adams, who had been the great orator in Congress in favor of independence, "the greatest question has been decided which was ever debated in America, and a greater perhaps never was or will be decided among men." July third and fourth were spent in carefully examining the expressions of the Declaration, previously prepared by a committee, and on the evening of the fourth the Declaration of Independence, in the words that we now read, was formally adopted. Americans will never cease to celebrate the Fourth of July.

LIBERTY BELL.

It is a curious fact that this bell, though cast twenty-three years before, had inscribed on it the Bible quotation: "*Proclaim liberty throughout the land unto all the inhabitants thereof.*"

275. [The committee appointed to draft the Declaration was chosen in Congress by ballot, and its members were Thomas Jefferson of Virginia (**412**), and John Adams of Massachusetts (**401**), Benjamin Franklin of Pennsylvania, Roger Sherman of Connecticut, and Robert Livingston of New York. Jefferson had entered Congress in June, 1775, with a reputation already established for ability in writing state papers. He received the highest number of votes in the choice of the committee, and the writing of the Declaration was left to him. Only a few verbal changes were made by Adams and Franklin. Jefferson was so familiar with the affairs of his time that he wrote the whole paper without reference to a single record. " He so discharged the duty assigned him that all Americans may well rejoice that the work of drawing the title deed of their liberties devolved on him."]

WAR FOR INDEPENDENCE.   143

276. How the News Was Received.—As soon as the Declaration was printed, copies were sent to all the state governments, and through them the Declaration was formally announced. The army listened to it with uncovered heads, and everywhere the people ceased from business and

TABLE AND CHAIRS IN INDEPENDENCE HALL.

gathered in imposing audiences to hear its words. There were military salutes, flags flying, and general rejoicing. The State House bell at Philadelphia, which led the rejoicing peal, is still preserved as "Liberty Bell." The symbols of royalty were destroyed, and in New York a leaden statue of George III. was pulled down and used for bullets to be shot at the king's soldiers. In England the news of the Declaration produced general indignation.

277. United States Government.—The great political idea of the Declaration of Independence is that the people of a country have a natural right to say how they shall be governed. Congress continued to act as the national government, but its powers were not defined. A committee was appointed in June, 1776, to form a plan of confederation or government of the states in the Union. But the work of preparing a national constitution could not go on rapidly in a country harassed by war. The plan of government presented in the Articles of Confederation was not adopted in Congress till November 15th, 1777. To give this plan of government the force of law, required acceptance by all the states, and four years passed before this was gained. There were naturally many perplexing questions connected with so great a subject. Meanwhile the states went on arranging their own constitutions, and thus the attention of political leaders was kept at home. Congress continued to represent the national government.

278. [**The Acts of Congress** were those of general authority. Before the Declaration it invited Canada to join the Union, provided for the organization of an army, ordered Tories to be disarmed, opened the ports to foreign trade, and held correspondence with foreign powers. Arthur Lee, of Virginia, corresponded with Congress from London, and Silas Deane, of Connecticut, was the agent of Congress in France. Immediately after the Declaration of Independence, Franklin, now seventy years old, was sent as the national representative to the Court of France. He was already known there as a man of science, and in his plain clothes and simple manners he was the object of universal notice and admiration. His work in France was of supreme value. As the difficulties of war increased, the strength of Congress grew weaker. Its numbers fell from fifty to seventeen, and even to nine. It was necessarily slow in action, for it had no regular executive. But it wisely trusted Washington, and his name and influence kept up the army.]

6. WASHINGTON'S CAMPAIGNS—1776–1780.

For Explanation.—Maneuver; base; regulars; stand; threatened; indecisive; Hessians; cavalry; foraging; futile; accessible; meditated.

To be Pronounced Before Reading the Section.—De Kälb; Thăd′e-us Koscinsko (Kos-se-ŭs′ko); Căs′i-mĭr; Steuben (stü′ben); d'Estaing (ĕs′tăng).

279. **Washington's army,** enlisted under the authority

of Congress, was composed principally of farmers and mechanics, very largely from New England. As no one expected a long continued war, the first enlistments were for short terms, and throughout the war there was constant going and coming. As a result, Washington often had to depend upon unskilled recruits for meeting armies trained in Europe under strictest discipline. Yet the deeds and sufferings of the American army form a record of heroism never to be forgotten.

WASHINGTON'S CAMPAIGNS.

Map Questions. — Locate Washington's winter quarters, 1775-6? 1776-7? 1777-8? 1778-9? Which way, then, did the seat of war travel from winter to winter? To capture Philadelphia, the British sailed up Chesapeake Bay and marched across the country from Elktown; tell from the map why they could not take the city by going up the Delaware Bay and River. Name the battles. After reading the story of Washington's campaigns, write these battles in the order of their dates.

10-II

[The total number of American soldiers employed during the war is put at 291,971. This includes 56,163 militia, or men serving under state authority. Often Washington had less than 5,000 under command, so much did men come and go. At the beginning Americans had no artillery, no military engineers, no system of tactics, and few experienced officers. There were a few mounted troops, of whom Morgan's Virginia riflemen were famous. They were said to be able to put a rifle ball through a seven-inch target at 200 yards, even when advancing rapidly.]

280. Battle of Long Island, August 27th, 1776.—After being driven from Boston, New York was the next place for the British to attack. Washington transferred his army from Boston, and began defenses before the arrival of General Howe with the British army. A battle was fought on Long Island, where the Americans were commanded by Generals Putnam and Sullivan. A hard fight left the Americans in heavy defeat, with Sullivan and nearly 1,000 men prisoners.

281. Loss of New York.—All the troops were removed from Long Island in a single night, a skillful maneuver, conducted by Washington himself, who was for hours without sleep, and most of the time in the saddle. New York was held, until to stay longer would have put the whole army in peril. Some advised that the city should be burned. Not being destroyed, it afforded the British shelter, and a base of operations, both on land and water, for the rest of the war. The disasters around New York discouraged Americans. Half of Washington's army deserted him. "The militia went off," he says, "in some instances almost by whole regiments; in many instances by half ones, and by companies at a time." The same spirit infested the regulars.

282. [Execution of Nathan Hale.—One incident in the operations around New York is to be remembered as an example of the cruelty of war. Washington, while in New York, desired some information of the British arrangements on Long Island, and Nathan Hale, a young Connecticut Captain, just graduated from Yale College, talented and beloved, volunteered to go in disguise within the British lines. He had completed his observations, and was on the point of returning to the city, when he was seized and taken before General Howe. Here he frankly avowed his name, position, and purpose, and, without a trial, was next day hanged as a spy. Not his death, for that was to be expected, but his cruel treatment beforehand, aroused the anger of Americans. Even a Bible was denied him, and a letter written to his mother was destroyed. His last words, remembered and reported by an English officer, were: "I regret that I have but one life to lose for my country."]

283. **Retreating and Skirmishing.**—Howe's plan was to cut off Washington from New England, and force him to fight a decisive battle. Washington's hope was to gain time—resisting, delaying, but not risking a general battle, which would have been destruction. There was a brilliant skirmish at Harlem, a well defended stand at White Plains; but the Americans had to fall back northwards. The English captured Fort Washington (November 16th), with 2,600 prisoners. Fort Lee was abandoned. Howe now crossed into New Jersey, and Washington turned to the southward for the defense of Philadelphia.

284. **Washington's memorable retreat** across New Jersey is distinguished in military records, not for fighting, but for skill in escaping it. By breaking down bridges he made less than seventy miles in a level country cost his pursuers nineteen days; and by crossing the Delaware and destroying boats for seventy miles, he made them decide to postpone attempts to follow him further until the river should freeze over.

285. [**General Charles Lee,** who now ranked next to Washington (256), had been left in command of troops at North Castle. He was a man of English birth, boasting a large military experience, on account of which the offer of his services was accepted by Congress. He seems, however, to have had neither military ability nor affection for the American cause. Being commanded to bring his force to the support of Washington, he not only disobeyed, but acted so carelessly that he was himself taken prisoner. General Sullivan (**256**), who had been

---

282. *Why was Hale's death expected?*

exchanged, was put in Lee's place, and promptly brought the force to Washington's assistance. While a prisoner at New York, Lee offered a plan of conquest to General Howe. The Americans afterwards received Lee in exchange, not knowing his treason, which was brought to light by the investigation of recent years.]

286. The situation in December, 1776, was discouraging to Americans. The British had captured Newport, Rhode Island, and held New York and nearly all New Jersey. Philadelphia was threatened, and Congress withdrew to Baltimore. Patriotic spirit in Pennsylvania was feeble. The Quakers, always opposed to war, in a meeting at Philadelphia, refused "in person or by other assistance" to join in carrying on the war. In New Jersey people became afraid, and in numbers sought the protection of British arms. Washington, although many in the country were ready to join with Lee in calling him indecisive, never despaired, and now showed his alertness, decision, activity, and skill. Howe's army, spread over New Jersey to keep down the Patriots, was enjoying comfortable winter quarters and Christmas festivities.

287. Recovery of New Jersey.—On Christmas night, in boats, the trip made perilous by blocks of drifting ice, Washington recrossed the Delaware with 2,400 men, surprised a force of 1,500 Hessians and a party of English cavalry, at Trenton, captured nearly 1,000 prisoners with their arms and stores, and returned safe into Pennsylvania, with the loss of only four men, of whom two were frozen to death. On December thirtieth, Washington took possession of Trenton, and by skillful movements and a battle at Princeton (January 13th, 1777), in which the British loss was four times the American, he obliged the British army, commanded by Lord Cornwallis, to give up the whole of New Jersey except Brunswick and Amboy. Washington placed his army in winter quarters at Morristown, a well chosen position. Through the spring Howe, the British Commander-in-Chief, exhausted all his skill in trying to provoke a general engagement, and to reopen a land route to Philadelphia. Unsuccessful in these endeavors, he finally withdrew all his troops to New York.

WASHINGTON CROSSING THE DELAWARE.

288. Condition of the American Army.—All this time Washington had less than 5,000 men fit for duty. Smallpox raged in the camps, and the dread of it made men slow to enter the service. Many foreigners, especially Frenchmen, came to America at various times to join the American army. The commissioners in Paris (**278**) were free with promises of high positions, which only the strong protests of Washington and other officers kept Congress from fulfilling with equal lavishness. Some of these new-comers were mere adventurers, seeking position and pay, but some were genuine patriots, willing to work anywhere for the American cause.

289. [**The most prominent foreign patriots** who aided the American army were Marquis de Lafayette, a young French officer, who became an intimate friend of Washington, and rendered brave service for America; John de Kalb, an Alsatian; Thaddeus Kosciusko, a young

Polish noble and a skilled military engineer; Casimir Pulaski, also a Pole; and Frederick W. A. Steuben, a Prussian, who had served in the Seven Years' War under Frederick the Great, king of Prussia.]

290. The British plan for 1777 was to cut off New England by means of an army made up of British regulars, Tories, and Indians, and commanded by General Burgoyne, which was to move from Canada by way of Lake Champlain and to connect with the force at New York. (For Burgoyne's fate, see **306**.) At the same time Howe planned to attack Philadelphia from the sea. Washington, with vastly inferior forces, undertook to defend the city, trying by a show of energy to raise courage in a people indisposed toward war.

291. Movements Around Philadelphia.—Since the entrance to Delaware Bay was guarded by forts Mifflin and Mercer, Howe's forces entered the Chesapeake, and were landed at Elktown. Washington was there to dispute the advance through an open country, inhabited chiefly by Royalists and Quakers. His plans were well laid, but the battle which took place, known as the battle of Chad's Ford, or the battle of the Brandywine (September 11th, 1777), through blundering information, ended in a serious defeat. Nevertheless Washington maneuvered, and preserved his army. It took Howe fifteen days to advance the thirty miles to Philadelphia. Howe occupied the city on September twenty-sixth, and all England exulted over the capture of the American "capital." In reality, the capture only gave comfortable winter quarters to the British army. Congress moved to Lancaster, and afterwards to York.

292. Germantown and the Opening of the Delaware.—Washington struck a skillful, but unsuccessful blow at a British outpost at Germantown (October 4th). Then after a six weeks' struggle, the British opened the Delaware, but Howe reported that the country could not be conquered without additional armies, and offered his resignation. His army spent the winter in Philadelphia, fiddling, dancing, gambling, and getting up amateur theatricals.

293. Valley Forge.—Washington's army went into winter quarters at Valley Forge, a place of which it is said that our forefathers could not speak without a shudder. The days of that winter were for Americans the darkest of the war. When the army reached the location (December 19th), there was no protection save a forest, which could furnish logs for huts, branches for thatch, and fuel for camp fires. Nearly 3,000 men lacked either shoes or other clothing. Numbers were sick with fevers and diseases resulting from exposure and lack of food. Washington had no supplies. The English had hard money to pay for meat and flour, and lived in plenty; but the Americans had only the paper money of Congress (**343**), which was so cheap that a general's pay would not keep him in clothes. Foraging parties alone kept the army from dying of starvation. Desertions, of course, were frequent.

294. [Plot Against Washington.—Men judge of merit by success. Many men who, in comfortable homes, at safe distances from the enemy, judged of Washington's campaign, thought that somebody else could have done better. Washington knew that there were intrigues against him; but, with heroic patience, he stayed at his post and his work. A council of war, appointed in Congress from among Washington's enemies, sent a remonstrance against putting the so called army into winter quarters, and wanted an immediate attack on Philadelphia. The leading spirit of this council was an Irishman, named Conway, whom Congress had appointed Inspector-general of the army. Anonymous letters to members of Congress suggested that a Gates, a Lee, or a Conway could take those barefooted, half-starved men, and "in a few weeks render them irresistible." However, the confidence of the soldiers in their chief was never shaken, and the eyes of Congress were soon opened to the truth. Conway was dropped. Steuben, the experienced Prussian officer, was appointed to the place, and began to organize and discipline the army. But the feebleness of Congress made relief slow to come, and the terrible sufferings of the army at Valley Forge lasted through the winter.]

295. French Alliance.—In May, 1778, news came to America that startled the British army in its gaiety and cheered the Americans in their distress. On February sixth a treaty had been formally made by the king of France and the American representatives in that country, John Adams having taken the place of Silas Deane (278), in which the independence of the United States was set down as the object of the treaty, each party agreeing to fight until that independence was acknowledged by the world. France was to furnish a fleet of sixteen war vessels and an army of 4,000 men.

296. Philadelphia Abandoned.—The news of the French alliance roused the English people against France. A few Englishmen saw that the war to subdue America was hopeless, but as yet there was no general wish to give it up. General Howe's resignation was accepted and Sir Henry Clinton was made commander-in-chief. The British government made some futile attempts to reconcile the colonies; at the same time, however, Clinton was ordered to abandon Philadelphia, to hold New York, to lay waste Virginia by means of war ships, to attack Boston, Providence, and all accessible ports, destroying wharves and shipping, and to spur on the Indians from Detroit to Florida to ravage the frontier. Clinton left Philadelphia, crossing the Delaware (June 17th, 1778), with more than 17,000 men, closely watched by Washington, his Valley Forge heroes now somewhat strengthened. The departure of the British army filled Philadelphia Tories with dismay, and crowds of them fled, following the army and taking all their property that they could carry with them.

297. Monmouth, June 28th, 1778.—Washington followed Clinton across New Jersey along a parallel line, ready to strike a blow at right angles. When near Monmouth Court-House (now Freehold) Washington arranged a plan of attack. Movements of the British army brought on an engagement (June 28th), which is known as the battle of Monmouth. A day's hard fighting ended with the

WAR FOR INDEPENDENCE.   153

general result in favor of the Americans. Leaving his dead unburied, Clinton withdrew his army in the night, and made a hasty march to New York.

WASHINGTON REBUKING LEE.
(From the celebrated painting by Leutze, in Library of the State University at Berkeley.)

298. [**General Charles Lee** commanded the vanguard of the American army, which began the battle. He was careless and inactive, disregarding Washington's orders. His troops, "the flower of the American infantry," were soon in retreat—"through their obedience to the commands of a leader who meditated their disgrace." Washington, with the rear of the army, arrived in time to stop the retreat and save his troops. He demanded of Lee an explanation of his conduct, and later, finding that Lee was doing nothing to retrieve the day, ordered him to the rear. Washington rearranged the troops and conducted the battle till nightfall. The loss in the battle was about equal on both sides. The day was intensely hot, and many died from the effects of the heat.

After the battle Lee sent disrespectful letters to Washington, was tried by a court-martial, and suspended for a year. He never returned to the army, and never was regretted. (The picture represents the first meeting of Washington and Lee. Lafayette and Alexander Hamilton appear just behind Washington.)]

299. Siege of Newport, August, 1778.—The French fleet of fifteen vessels, commanded by Count d' Estaing, reached America in July, 1778, too late to intercept the English vessels which had escaped from Philadelphia to New York. Washington had only a feeble army with which to coöperate, but a joint movement was planned to attack Newport, and to drive the British forces from Rhode Island (286). The allies met with unfortunate delays. The British fleet was reinforced. A naval contest was beginning, when a terrible storm scattered and damaged both fleets and drenched the land forces. The French fleet, after making repairs at Boston, sailed off for the defense of French possessions in the West Indies. The American troops, which had gathered before Newport, were withdrawn, after fighting one indecisive engagement at Quaker Hill (August 29th).

300. For the next two years Washington fought no great battles, but his tireless efforts kept the army recruited, his brilliant genius planned important movements, and his experienced judgment directed them. The winter of 1778-79 was spent by the American army in winter quarters that formed a great semicircle around New York, reaching from the Connecticut shore of Long Island to the Delaware River. In the middle point of the semicircle West Point was fortified to defend the Hudson and to keep the line of communication from east to west. This line around New York was held for the rest of the war.

[Shut up in New York, Clinton was able only to send out ravaging and foraging parties into New Jersey and Connecticut, and, by water, to Virginia. The burning of buildings and towns was freely allowed, and not a few of the inhabitants were put to the sword. At times, however, Clinton himself was made to feel the want of food and fuel.

301. [**Stony Point, July 16th, 1779,** was the field of one of the most brilliant achievements of the war. An attack on the British garrison

WAR FOR INDEPENDENCE.

posted there was planned by Washington and executed by General Anthony Wayne, an officer who had distinguished himself at Monmouth, and by his daring gained the nickname of "Mad Anthony." At the head of 1,000 chosen men he captured the strong fortress by a night assault, and made prisoners of the garrison without firing a single shot, and with only a small loss. Wayne did not try to hold Stony Point, which was reoccupied by the British, but afterwards abandoned.]

302. [Paulus Hook.—In August Major Henry Lee, of Virginia, known as "Light Horse Harry," made a daring night attack on the British at Paulus Hook (Jersey City), and took 150 prisoners.]

7. BURGOYNE'S DEFEAT AND THE FRENCH ALLIANCE.

For Explanation.—Panic; intrepid; ordnance; vain; mercenary; impotent.

To be Pronounced.—Ma-hŏn′; Wȳ-o′ming; Bon-hŏm′me; Se-rä′pis; Scarborough (skär′bŭr-eh).

303. General Burgoyne's Advance.—Having followed the campaigns of Washington from 1776 to 1780, we return to Burgoyne's invasion of Canada in 1777 (**290**). This seemed at first to promise a British success and an end to the war, but patriot strength in the North was underestimated. General Schuyler, commander of the American forces in the North, was familiar with the ground (**265**). Abandoning Ticonderoga, he put every possible obstacle in the way of the invaders, obstructing roads and destroying provisions. Burgoyne reached Ticonderoga in July. From that point his advance was difficult and slow. On the first of August, however, he had reached the banks of the Hudson.

304. In the Mohawk Valley.—The Indian tribes were to help the invaders, but this resort to Indian warfare roused the indignation of the people of New York, and brought out their full strength. Near Fort Stanwix (Rome), the brave "freeholders" of the Mohawk Valley, led by Nicolas Herkimer (August 4th), fought a body of mingled Indian and English invaders, commanded by General St. Leger, and the approach of an American force, under Benedict Arnold (**267**), completed the victory, sending St. Leger's party off to Canada in defeat and panic.

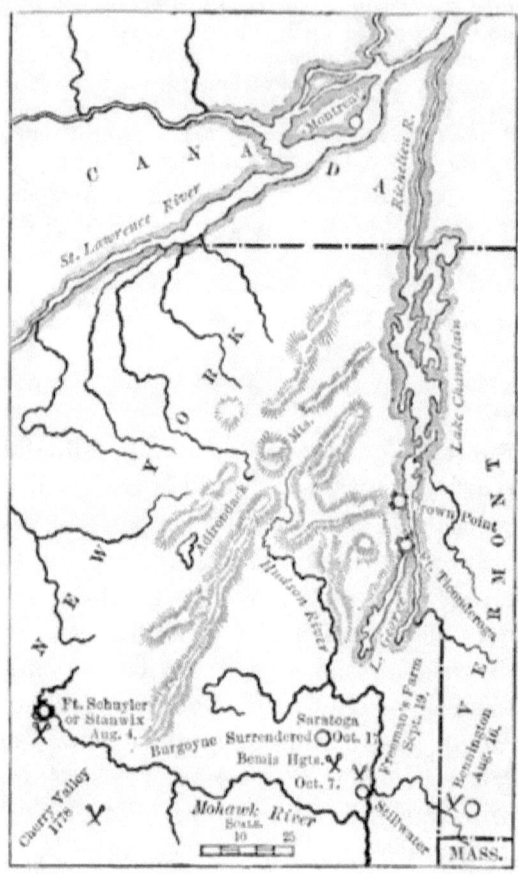

BURGOYNE'S INVASION FROM CANADA—1777.

Map Questions.—Make a list of the four battles that took place during this invasion, in the order in which they were fought, according to the following Model:

Date.	Places.	Result. (See text.)

Why should British troops, seeking to cut off New England from the South, invade from Canada, rather than march northward from New York? What difficulties lay before Burgoyne?

305. Bennington.—A detachment detailed by Burgoyne to capture supplies in Vermont, was defeated at Bennington August sixteenth, by farmers from Vermont, New Hampshire, and Western Massachusetts, under the standard of General Stark (257). This was "one of the most brilliant and eventful victories of the war." It raised the courage of Americans for the destruction of Burgoyne's army.

306. Main Battles.—Burgoyne, without help from New York city, and with no supplies for a retreat northward, had to fight on ground selected and fortified by Kosciusko (289). On August first, Congress had elected General Gates to succeed Schuyler, and given him full power to call for militia. Washington added to the northern army 500 picked riflemen, commanded by the intrepid Morgan (279). Two battles were fought—one at Freeman's Farm, near Stillwater (September 19th); the other at Bemis Heights (October 7th). The American army outnumbered the English, and Burgoyne was crippled past recovery. Howe's army was busy around Philadelphia, and a relief movement from New York, feebly resisted by an American army under Putnam, was too late to help Burgoyne. At Saratoga (October 17th), Burgoyne surrendered his whole army. Americans were overjoyed at their great victory, and Gates won high favor with Congress and the people, although really he had done but very little.

[The total loss of the British in this campaign was nearly 10,000 men. The Americans gained thirty-five pieces of the best ordnance, and over 4,000 muskets.]

307. [Opinions of Englishmen.—After Burgoyne's surrender, the Earl of Chatham (Pitt) **(204)**, in the English House of Lords, repeated what Burke had proclaimed to the House of Commons in 1785: "My Lords," he said, "you cannot conquer America. In three years' campaign we have done nothing and suffered much. You may swell every expense, accumulate every assistance you can buy or borrow, traffic and barter with every little pitiful German prince, your efforts are forever vain and impotent, doubly so from this mercenary aid on which you rely, for it irritates to an incurable resentment. If I were an American, as I am an Englishman, while a foreign troop was landed in my country, I never would lay down my arms—*never*, NEVER, NEVER." In the House of Commons Burke continued to speak for the Americans, supported now by Charles James Fox, the youngest defender of the American cause, and one of the most brilliant of English statesmen. Even now Fox demanded the recognition of American independence **(274)**.]

308. Burgoyne's Defeat Brings French Aid.—From the first, France had lent secret aid in arms and money, and this was all that the English government had counted on.

But many influences brought the king of France to do more. The representatives of America and American principles were agreeable to the French people. France felt the defeat of the last war, and longed for revenge on England. Frederic the Great, King of Prussia, although unable to take part himself, freely advised the king of France, saying: "The independence of the colonies will be worth to France all that the war will cost." When the news came of Burgoyne's defeat, and of Washington's successful escape from Howe, in 1777, the king of France paused only to consult with Spain, and then concluded the treaty (295). In England the news of the alliance had a tremendous effect. No one seemed fit to govern except the aged Earl of Chatham, whom ill-health had for years kept from the government. All the laws offensive to Americans were repealed, and commissioners were sent to America (296) offering peace, but without independence. Nothing less than full independence would now satisfy Americans, and the war went on—England on one side; America, aided by France, Spain, and finally Holland, on the other.

309. [Chatham had denounced the war from the first, but he was inflexibly against American independence. Bundled up in flannels, pale and wasted away, he hobbled to his place in the House of Lords, supported on either side by his son, William Pitt, and his son-in-law, Lord Mahon. "My Lords," he said, "I rejoice that the grave has not closed upon me, that I am still alive to lift up my voice against the dismemberment of the ancient and most noble monarchy." Again attempting to speak in answer to arguments, the great statesman fell in the agony of death.]

310. **The war was divided into two periods** by the treaty with France. IN THE FIRST PERIOD (1775–1778), the Americans fought alone; generally defeated in the pitched battles, but showing to the world that although their armies might be scattered, their cities captured and plundered, their country impoverished, they could not be subdued. In England during this period there was no enthusiasm for the war. No men of great ability came forward to lead the

armies or the fleets. The freemen of the land did not recruit the ranks, and King George had to resort to the hireling soldiers whom English money could obtain from the petty German states. Thousands of Hessians fought in America under the British flag, and many a deed of cruelty and robbery is remembered against them. Serving for hire, they considered that America was a fit field for plunder, and British officers did not try to restrain them. IN THE SECOND PERIOD (1778-1781), the spirit of the English people was aroused, for now there was a war with France in India, on the sea, and wherever English and French interests conflicted, as well as in America. The English navy was at once recruited, and it successfully resisted the navies of France, Spain, and toward the close of the war, of Holland also. But no more great armies were sent to America, and no one but King George persisted in the hope to force America into submission. At the same time the war in America took more savage methods. The destruction of wharves and shipping was ordered, and plundering of private citizens was freely permitted (**321, 329**). On the other hand, it must be said of the Americans, that as their hopes brightened through foreign help, their own national spirit grew cool, and the tireless efforts of Washington could hardly keep his army recruited. Only when a district was invaded did the people come forward for vigorous defense. When the war was far away business and money making kept them at home.

8. ON THE FRONTIER.

For Explanation.—Upland; neutrals.

311. Cherokees.—The instinct of the Indian allied him with England, for the war seemed to him an opportunity to win back his lost hunting grounds. Moreover, the emissaries of the English government supplied him with arms

---

310. What especially distinguished the first from the second period of the war?

and urged him to fight. In 1776, at the time of the attack on Charleston (271), 2,500 Cherokees, accompanied by the king's men, fell upon the people of East Tennessee (240) and spread onward to the western settlements of the Carolinas and Georgia. They were beaten back by a general rally of upland Patriots from Virginia to Georgia, pursued beyond the Alleghanies, and "forced to beg for mercy."

312. **Wyoming Valley** in Northern Pennsylvania was the scene of a terrible massacre in 1778. An offshoot from Connecticut, the thrifty people of this valley had sent their best men to the national army in 1776, and for their own defense had built a line of ten forts. To the north were tribes of the Iroquois. Their chiefs, bribed by English money, desiring revenge for their loss in the Mohawk Valley (304), were stung to hatred of the Americans on account of the alliance with their old enemies, the French. A band of Seneca warriors (one of the Iroquois tribes) entered Wyoming with Tory leaders and under the British flag (July, 1778). The few brave men left to defend their homes were caught in an ambush; 225 scalps were taken in less than half an hour; every fort and house was burned, and a wailing procession of the survivors, mostly women and children, fled over the hills into the eastern settlements.

313. [**Cherry Valley.**—A few months later, about thirty people, most of them women and children, were murdered in Cherry Valley, New York. (See map, page 156.)]

314. **Vengeance** was taken on the Senecas the following year (1779). Washington sent General Sullivan with 3,000 men into their country, and their villages and crops were burned as far as the Genesee River. The Iroquois, finding that the king of England did not protect them, were glad to be neutral.

315. [**The secret purpose of Spain** during the war was to confine the American states within narrow bounds on the south and west. But

---

311. *In what direction from East Tennessee did the Indians move?*

the power of Spain in the New World, as well as in the Old, was fast decaying, and backwoodsmen of Virginia, opening the way for free institutions, baffled the efforts of the Spanish monarchy, and in 1776 organized the county of Kentucky, under the state of Virginia. The frontiersmen held their ground against both Spanish and English, and in 1780 established Fort Jefferson, on the Mississippi, four miles below the mouth of the Ohio.]

9. NAVAL AFFAIRS.

316. American privateers did honorable service, although no match for English fleets. The best work was the capture of English supply ships. France assisted in fitting out these privateers, and Holland gave them shelter when they cruised around the British islands.

The number of British vessels captured during the war was about 700.]

317. [**John Paul Jones**, a native of Scotland, is one of the most noted of the commanders of American vessels. In 1778 he sailed about Great Britain in the *Ranger*, and even ventured land attacks at places on the coast. In 1779, in the same waters, he captured many prizes with a fleet of five old merchant vessels, fitted out in France by Franklin. In September, Jones fell in with the British merchant fleet from the Baltic, under convoy of two frigates of the royal navy, the *Serapis* of forty guns, and the *Countess of Scarborough* of twenty-two guns. Jones's own ship, which he had named the *Bonhomme Richard* (or good man Richard, in honor of Franklin, who had once published "Poor Richard's Almanac"), fought with the *Serapis* one of the most desperate of sea fights. The *Serapis* was the stronger, but Jones bore down to close range, and succeeded in fastening the anchor of the *Serapis* to his own vessel. After two hours of bloody fighting, in which both vessels were repeatedly on fire, the *Serapis* nearly a dozen times, the British flag was struck. The next day Jones transferred his crew to the *Serapis*, for the *Richard* was already sinking. Jones's companions had captured the *Countess of Scarborough*, and Jones found shelter for his prizes in a Dutch harbor.]

318. French fleets, after the treaty (**295**), kept the English navy busy, especially in the West Indies, where both countries had possessions to defend. To some extent English war vessels were withdrawn from the American coast, but Clinton, at New York, always had vessels in which he could send troops or communicate with other ports.

10. Arnold's Treason.

319. [Clinton's Bribery.—From the time of assuming command Sir Henry Clinton (**296**) had reported to the British government that he could not successfully carry on the war without new armies, and new armies were not to be had. Hopeless of success in open war, Clinton resorted to bribery, and was encouraged in his efforts by the advice from his government, that "next to the destruction of Washington's army, the gaining over of officers of influence and reputation among the troops would be the speediest means of subduing the rebellion." He worked the corruption of one notable man. Benedict Arnold, placed in charge of Philadelphia after the removal of the British army, lived extravagantly, and extravagance brought him to dishonesty and treason. In the winter of 1778-1779 Clinton took him into pay, Arnold furnishing information of American affairs. In February, 1779, he let Clinton know that he desired to change to the British side. Arnold's open preference for Tories had disgusted the Patriots of Pennsylvania. Charges of misconduct were brought before Congress. Arnold was tried by a court-martial, on charges that touched his honor, and according to his sentence was reprimanded by Washington, though with the greatest forbearance.]

320. Plot to Betray West Point.—In 1780 there was need of a new commander at West Point, an important American fortress recently built under the direction of Kosciusko (**289**). Acting in concert with Clinton, Arnold sought and obtained the post, urging wounds as an excuse for keeping from the field. The plan to betray West Point required a messenger to complete the bargain. Major John Andre, a young and ambitious English officer, who had been in correspondence with Arnold, undertook to meet him, and boldly entered the American lines. The arrangements were made, but as Andre could not get back on the English ship on which he had come up the Hudson, he set out in disguise, provided with a pass from Arnold, to ride on horseback to New York. When nearly within the British lines he was arrested by three Americans. He was searched, and papers revealing the treason were found in his boots. Through the stupidity of an American officer, word of Andre's capture was sent to Arnold, who escaped to a British ship. Andre was tried by a court-martial of American officers, sentenced, and hanged as a spy. The plot had failed at the last moment, but the British government kept its promise, giving Arnold a commission as brigadier-general, £6,315 as compensation for pretended losses, and pensions for his family.

11. War in the South—1778-1781.

For Explanation.—Pillaged; profligate; wreaked; paroles; cowed; disposed; malignant; obnoxious; corral.

To be Pronounced.—Che'raw; de Grässe; Ca-taw'ba; Rochambeau (ro-shong-bo).

321. Capture of Savannah and Attempt on Charleston.—For 1778 the English government planned an extensive campaign in the South. "Large numbers of the inhabitants," it was said, "would doubtless flock to the standard of the king," and the English rule would easily be restored as far north as Virginia. Little was done until after the summer heats, but Savannah was easily captured, December 29th, 1778. The plundering of the country by the British army brought out the strength of South Carolina for the defense of Charleston, the next point of attack. General Benjamin Lincoln was placed in command of the American army in the South, and on his approach the British retired into Georgia, having pillaged far and wide, and having destroyed what it was impossible to carry away.

322. [An attempt to recover Savannah (September, 1779), by the French fleet commanded by Count d' Estaing, aided by Americans under Lincoln, proved unsuccessful. The American loss was heavy; that of the French still greater. The French fleet sailed off to France, and the remains of the American army fell back to Charleston.]

323. Fall of Charleston, 1780.—Sir Henry Clinton, commander at New York, who had failed to capture Charleston in 1776 (271), decided to try again, and withdrawing his troops from Rhode Island sailed from New York on Christmas day, 1779. His fleet was scattered by a storm and damaged by privateers; still his force was strong enough to capture the city (February 12th, 1780); as well as Gen-

164   HISTORY OF THE UNITED STATES.

eral Lincoln and his army of 2,000 men who had unwisely remained inside. Again the British army found rich plunder, and spared nothing; carrying off the rich plate of the planters and seizing their negroes to send them to the West Indies to be sold. To complete the outrage, Clinton attempted to force Americans into the support of the king's government.

WAR IN THE SOUTH.

Map Questions.—Of the three sections of country embraced in this map—lowland, upland, and mountain—in which did most of the battles occur? What reasons for this can you suggest? Who commanded

WAR FOR INDEPENDENCE. 165

the Americans at Camden? Who superseded him? Taking command at what place? Which way did the Americans travel when attacking? When retreating? What is the last march shown of Cornwallis? Where do Greene's campaigns end? What battle did Morgan fight? Write the military events in the order of their dates, by the following Model:

Date.	Event.	Result of Battle. (See Text.)
1. December 28th, 1780.	Savannah captured by the British.	
2.		
3.	Gates takes command at Hillsborough.	
4	Battle of Camden fought. . .	British victory.
5.		
6.		
7.		
8.		
9.		
10.		

324. [**Lord Cornwallis**, a rival of Clinton, an able officer and also most determined to root out "rebellion," was placed in command in the South (1780). South Carolina was practically subdued, and Cornwallis proposed to be the conqueror of North Carolina and Virginia. He had only a small army, and vigorous steps were taken to induce the weak or compel the profligate to enter the service of the king. Communication was kept up by a chain of forts at Georgetown, Charleston, Beaufort, and Savannah, along the sea; and inland at Augusta, Ninety-Six, and Camden.]

325. **Partisan Warfare.**—The Patriots were quick to retaliate the outrages of the British invaders and their Tory helpers, and thus civil strife raged in the South, the most savage and destructive of the war. Bands of Patriot exiles gathered around brave leaders like Thomas Sumter and Francis Marion, and wreaked unceasing vengeance on the

plunderers of the land. They would strike suddenly, fight with desperate courage, and be off again to safe hiding places in the mountains. The personal dash, courage, and narrow escapes of these heroes form the most exciting chapter in the history of the war.

326. Gates, the American Commander in North Carolina.—Washington sent all troops that could be spared, for the help of the South against the invasion of Cornwallis. Virginia nobly spared her own defenders for the protection of North Carolina. Washington desired that General Nathanael Greene should be placed in command of the southern army, but contrary to his recommendation, Congress appointed General Gates (306). Joining his army at Hillsborough, Gates chose to march in a direct line on Camden, occupied by a part of the British army commanded by Lord Rawdon. The advance of Gates raised the courage of Carolinians, and they gathered to join him, some, even, who had been forced into British service, escaping to swell the number. Cornwallis hastened up from Charleston for the defense of Camden, and skillfully disposed his men for the battle (August 16th, 1780).

327. Gates Defeated at Camden.—Gates ordered his men into a fight, in which he took pains not to expose himself, and from which he disappeared at the first flight of his untrained militia. The battle, however, was nobly borne by experienced troops from Maryland and Delaware, led by the brave Baron de Kalb (289), who was mortally wounded. The British had the victory, although "their great loss," wrote Marion (325), "was equal to defeat."

[From Camden Gates rode alone to Hillsborough, making 200 miles in three days and a half, and leaving his army behind him. In October Congress put Greene in his place, whom Washington introduced to his friends in the South as "a man of abilities, bravery, and coolness."]

328. Cornwallis and the People.—The battle at Camden made Cornwallis the chief figure in the British army in

America, and his government hoped for success through him. According to his plan of conquest, Cornwallis began a reign of terror in the Carolinas. The destruction of property and of life was terrible. Paroles were not respected; no faith was kept with prisoners, no mercy shown the defenseless, and none were safe save those in the active service of the king. Cold-blooded assassinations were committed, even by men who held commissions in the king's army. But the more cruel and barbarous the methods of the king's servants in the South, the stronger grew the Patriot cause among the people.

329. [**British treatment of prisoners** was extremely cruel throughout the war. Prisoners were generally confined in worn-out ships, where scant room, food, and clothing made them the victims of disease. There were several prison ships at New York; one of which, the *Jersey*, became notorious. Twenty-five hundred prisoners from Charleston were confined on one ship in Charleston harbor. In thirteen months one third of the number died from malignant fevers. Other captives were forced to serve on British ships.]

330. [**King's Mountain, 1780.**—After the battle of Camden, Cornwallis sent 1,100 men to arouse and arm Tories, and to disperse Patriots in western North Carolina. This party was surrounded at King's Mountain (October 8th, 1780), by Patriot riflemen gathered from North Carolina and the western frontier. The British party was completely defeated, 800 being made prisoners. Many of them were Tories, the most obnoxious of whom were hanged, after the example set by Cornwallis. The Patriots had gathered at King's Mountain in the spirit in which they had gathered at Concord. The victory cowed the Tories, gave fresh zeal to the Patriots, and turned the course of the war in the South, as the victory at Bennington had done at the North in Burgoyne's invasion (305).

331. **The Army after Camden.**—General Greene assumed command of the remains of Gates's army at Charlotte (December 4th, 1780). He found 970 regulars and 1,013 militia; but such was their condition, that Greene wrote to his wife, "I have been in search of the army I am to command, but without much success, having found only a few half-starved soldiers, remarkable for nothing but pov-

erty and distress." He made himself familiar with the country, and got together all possible recruits.

332. Morgan at the Cowpens, 1781.—Advancing his camp to Cheraw, Greene sent Morgan, at that time the ablest commander of light troops in the world, with 600 men to rouse the country west of the Catawba. To meet the danger of a Whig uprising, Cornwallis sent his favorite officer, Tarleton, to destroy Morgan's corps. Tarleton soon overtook the Americans; but Morgan, by his wise choice of ground and skillful management, utterly defeated the British force (January 17th, 1781), at the Cowpens, a place so named on account of a corral built there for marking cattle. Tarleton, with only a few companions, escaped to carry the news of disaster to Cornwallis.

333. Guilford Court House, 1781.—Cornwallis at once set out to catch Morgan before he could unite with Greene; but Morgan and Greene were too quick for him. The two divisions were united, yet not strong enough for battle; they fell back to the northward; the Catawba, the Yadkin, and finally the Dan being crossed, with Cornwallis in close pursuit, but delayed at each river by a rise of the stream, just after the Americans had forded. Finally at the Dan, Cornwallis gave up the chase, and turned back to Hillsborough. Greene, having been reinforced by militia, returned from Virginia, and with an army superior in number, fought Cornwallis at Guilford Court House (March 15th, 1781). The inexperienced American militia fled as at Camden (327), leaving the battle to be fought by the regular troops. Cornwallis won the field; but so great was his loss that he could not follow up his victory, and he retired toward the sea. Greene followed, and recovered all of North Carolina, except Wilmington, where Cornwallis lodged the remnants of his force (April 7th).

334. Cornwallis to the North, Greene to the South.—At

Wilmington, Cornwallis received more troops by sea from Charleston, and not willing to acknowledge the failure of his plans, set out at the end of April with 1,435 men for the Chesapeake. Greene had determined to carry the war into South Carolina. His force numbered only 1,800, and the risks were great. Yet, coöperating with the Carolina leaders, Sumter, Marion (325), and Pickens, he broke the British line of communications, fought a fierce battle at Hobkirk Hill (April 25th, 1781), unsuccessfully besieged Ninety-Six, and after resting his men among the hills on the Santee, fought the last formal battle in the South, at Eutaw Springs (September 8th). Both the battles are classed as British victories; but the effect was to make the British give up all their posts, except Charleston and Savannah.

[Greene said: "We fight, get beaten, and fight again." He had been in command less than two months, and the three southern states had been recovered, except the three places on the coast, and of these Wilmington was soon abandoned. In gratitude for Greene's services, South Carolina voted him an estate. Georgia added 5,000 guineas, and North Carolina 24,000 acres of land in Tennessee.]

12. THE LAST CAMPAIGN, 1781.

For Explanation.—Devastation; vigilant; sally.

335. The War in Virginia.—In James Otis (218) and Patrick Henry (224), Massachusetts and Virginia had each an apostle of freedom. Their statesmen worked together in the committees of Congress. From one state came the leader of the American armies; from the other, the largest number of recruits. In Massachusetts was shed the first blood of the war; the soil of Virginia was to be stained with the last. In January Clinton had sent Benedict Arnold (320) to hold a position on the Chesapeake, and to harass Virginia. Thomas Jefferson, now governor of Virginia, called on the militia, but so many had gone for the protection of North Carolina that no sufficient force could be gathered at home. Richmond was burned. To protect Virginia and to catch Arnold, whom Americans longed to hang, Washington sent a force under Lafayette by land, and asked the French fleet to cut off escape by water. The fleet moved too slowly, and the plan failed, for Lafayette was not strong enough to operate alone. On the arrival of Cornwallis in Virginia, Arnold was ordered back to New York.

336. [**Arnold.**—After joining the British, Arnold had increased his infamy by writing insolent letters to Washington, inviting all Americans to desert their colors, and by urging the British to break up the American army through bribery. He displayed a character so sordid that British officers shrank from serving with him. After the close of the war he spent the rest of his life in England, without the respect of his fellow men, and with no country to call his own.]

337. **Cornwallis** began the devastation of Virginia, but was ordered by Clinton, now seriously threatened in New York by Washington, to seek and fortify some strong position near the sea, that he might be ready to sail to Clinton's assistance. Cornwallis selected and fortified Yorktown.

338. **Siege of Yorktown, 1781.**—Washington arranged with De Grasse, commander of a French fleet from the West Indies, to blockade the Chesapeake. Washington's army was moved southward quickly, crossing the Hudson on August thirtieth and reaching Yorktown late in September. Already De Grasse had arrived and had blocked up the James River, shutting off Cornwallis' escape. More French ships brought troops and cannon from Newport. On September seventeenth Cornwallis had written to Clinton: "This place is in no state for defense; if you cannot relieve me at once, you must be prepared to hear the worst." But Clinton had been deceived by Washington's maneuvers, expecting him to make New York the point of attack, until it was too late to interfere. The allied armies drove the British within the Yorktown fortifications, chiefly rude earthworks (September 28th). Cannonading began (October 9th), and in two days the British were scarcely able to

return the fire. On the fourteenth two redoubts were taken by assault—one by the Americans, the other by the French. A spirited sally on the morning of the sixteenth failed. On the seventeenth Cornwallis called for a cessation of hostilities, and two days afterwards surrendered.

THE SIEGE OF YORKTOWN.

Map Questions.—On what natural division of land is Yorktown located? By what river? What prevented Cornwallis from escaping across York River? What from escaping in his ships? What prevented his crossing the peninsula to James River? Can you see any way in which he could escape except by overpowering his enemies? Beginning on the west, north of York River, name, in their order, the forces by which he was surrounded.

172   HISTORY OF THE UNITED STATES.

339. The surrender of Yorktown, October 19th, 1781, practically ended the war. In America there was rejoicing at the news. Congress voted special honors to Washington

1. Lafayette.   2. Cornwallis.   3. Greene.   4. Warren.

WAR FOR INDEPENDENCE. 173

and the French commanders, and thanked all officers and troops. In England Lord North received the news "as he would have taken a bullet in his breast," exclaiming, "It is all over." Greene's army in the South was strengthened. Washington returned to his old position around New York.

[The British continued to hold New York, Charleston, and Savannah, but there were no more battles. There was, however, considerable fighting on the frontier against Indians incited by Tories.]

13. THE CLOSE OF THE WAR.

For Explanation.—Negotiations; confiscating; depreciation; magnanimous; redeem; furloughs; Cincinnati.

340. Treaty of Paris, 1783.—The final treaty of peace was delayed until September, 1783, by tedious negotiations, largely between the European nations. Then a treaty was signed at Paris, by which Great Britain acknowledged the independence of the United States. The treaty admitted the title of the United States to all land between the Mississippi and the Atlantic, from Canada and the Great Lakes to Florida. Great Britain retained Canada, and transferred Florida to Spain, who owned the Louisiana territory also (210). Thus the neighbors of the United States were Great Britain on the north, with only a roughly marked boundary line on the northeast, and Spain on the south and west, with the southern boundary fixed at the thirtieth parallel.

341. [The Tories had fought for England, and had given assistance and shelter to the enemies of America. Most of the states had passed laws confiscating their property. When the contest ended, there was little for them to enjoy in the United States. Numbers left the country, moving to Canada, to the West Indies, and to England. When the passions of the war had passed away, some returned to live again in the land of their birth.]

342. "Continental Money."—The demand for money to conduct the war, had been, for the Americans, a demand harder to meet than that for men. Congress adopted the ready expedient of issuing a paper continental currency, in the form of "bills of credit," or promises to pay coin. These promises could not be fulfilled until the war was over, and some regular plan arranged for a revenue. At the beginning of the war, people readily accepted these "bills of credit" as money, and at one time Congress had to hire twenty-eight men to put signatures on them, in order to get them out fast enough. With the third year of the war depreciation began; the "continental money" became every year more plentiful, and every year was worth less and less. The British flooded the country with counterfeit bills. Crops were poor in 1779-1780, making food scarce. Before the end of the war paper money was almost worthless; cash loans from Europe alone afforded relief.

343. [**Paper Money.**—Colonies had issued paper money before independence, and their experience ought to have taught Congress that unless some limit was put to the amount of paper currency, and some plan arranged for future payment, there would be trouble. But then, as now, men were influenced by the impression that a government stamp had power in itself to give value to a slip of paper; that if a shoemaker would sell a pair of shoes for five silver dollars, and Congress ordered him to sell the same shoes for five paper dollars, he would have to do it. Congress made laws to regulate prices, but as the length of the war grew greater, and the day of redeeming the paper promises seemed further off, people became reluctant to receive them in trade. Moreover, the war interfered with the raising of crops, and the making of things for sale, and when the "paper money" became cheaper, everything else became scarcer, and therefore dearer. It is outside the power of any government to control prices, and during the war they rose enormously. Although over $357,000,000 of paper money was issued, the expense of the war, in coin, was about $135,000,000. The cheapness of the paper money is shown in the expression, "Not worth a continental," meaning not worth a dollar of continental money.]

344. **The pay of the American army** had consisted chiefly of promises, which for years there was no government strong enough to fulfill. Had not Washington's men shared the spirit of their commander, the army would have gone to pieces utterly, long before peace permitted disbanding. Twice there was tumult, once in 1781, again in 1783, when men proposed to go in arms and force pay from Congress, which had little to give. These tumults are some-

times called revolts or mutinies. Suppressed as they were without force, they hardly deserve such names. Washington by his own desire served without pay, except to receive back what he had taken from his own pocket for necessary expenses, of which he presented an exact account at the end of the war.

345. The Disbanding of the Army.—Soldiers were allowed to go home on furloughs all through 1783. Then a final proclamation fixed November third as the time for "absolute discharge" of the whole army. At New York, Washington bade an affectionate farewell to his officers who had served with him so long and so nobly, and then surrendering his commission to Congress, retired to his home at Mount Vernon, on the Potomac River. The soldiers became scattered and lost in the country for which they had fought.

[Under the name of "Cincinnati," officers of the army formed a "society of friends" to aid one another, and to cherish union between the states.]

346. [**The spirit of the war** lived in Washington, "calm in the midst of conspiracy; serene against the open foe before him and the darker enemies at his back. Washington inspiring order and spirit in troops hungry and in rags; stung by ingratitude, but betraying no anger, and ever ready to forgive; in defeat invincible, magnanimous in conquest, and never so sublime as on that day when he laid down his victorious sword and sought his noble retirement—here indeed is a character to admire and revere; a life without a stain, a fame without a flaw."—*Thackeray.*]

HISTORY OF THE UNITED STATES.

PRINCIPAL MILITARY EVENTS OF
Copy and complete the following Review of principal

Place.	Event.	Date.	Com- American (or French).
1. Lexington and Concord.	Skirmish.	Apr. 19.	
2. Ticonderoga.	Surprise.	'75.	
3. Bunker Hill.	Battle.		
4. Boston.	Siege.		
5. Canada.	Invasion.		
6. Charleston.	Attack.		
7. East Tennessee.	Indian raid.		
8. Long Island.	Battle.		
9. { Harlem. White Plains. } { Ft. Washington. Ft. Lee.	Skirmishes. Assault. Retreat.	'76.	
10. Trenton.			
11. Princeton.			
12. Mohawk Valley.			
13. Bennington.			
14. Brandywine Creek.			
15. Freeman's Farm. (Stillwater.)		'77.	
16. Germantown. (Ft. Mifflin.) (Ft. Mercer.)			
17. Bemis Heights.			
18. Monmouth C. H.			
19. Wyoming Valley. (Cherry Valley.)		'78.	
20. Newport.			
21. Savannah.			
22. Western New York.			
23. North Sea.			
24. Stony Point. (Paulus Hook.)		'79.	
25. Savannah.			
26. Charleston.			
27. Carolinas.		'80.	
28. Camden.			
29. King's Mountain.			
30. Cowpens.			
31. Guilford C. H.			
32. Hobkirk Hill.		'81.	
33. Ninety-Six.			
34. Eutaw Springs.			
35. Yorktown.			

THE WAR FOR INDEPENDENCE.
Military Events of the War for Independence.

manders. British.	Victory for.	Greater loss for.	Results.
Pitcairn and Percy.	Americans.	British.	America aroused and the war commenced.

The Path Toward American Independence.

ENGLAND. Parent and Sovereign. — PEACE AND UNION — **AMERICA.** Colonies and Subjects.

ENGLISH LEGISLATION.

1. Enforcement of trade laws. Writs of Assistance. .... 1763-4.
2. Stamp taxes proposed and ordered. .... 1764-6.
3. Stamp Act repealed. .... March, 1766.
4. Policy of taxes and troops carried out by the king's ministers. .... 1768-70.
5. Duties repealed, except on tea. .... April, 1770.
6. Official outrages. Government by royal orders. .... 1770-3.
7. Tea forced on Americans. .... 1773.
   Punishment of rebels. Boston Port Bill. Massachusetts Regulating Acts, etc. .... 1774-5. Fight at Lexington (April 19, 1775), begins the War for Independence.

AMERICAN RESISTANCE.

1. Opposition by newspapers and in colonial courts.
2. Patriotic party formed. Colonial correspondence. Colonial Congress (1765). (Declaration and petitions.) Non-importation. Americans loyal.
3. Organization for resistance.
4. Fights with British soldiers. Boston massacre (1770). Americans firmly defiant.
5. Violent acts. N. C. Regulators (1771). Burning of Gaspee (1772).
6. Tea sent back or destroyed.
7. Continental Congress, 1st Session. (Rights and grievances.) Association for non-importation. Preparations for military defense.

CHAPTER XVII.
1783-1789.
The Formation of a National Government.

For Explanation.—Title; cede; vague; Nestor; ratify.

Outline of Paragraph 347.—Articles of Confederation not a national constitution; conveyed no sovereignty; represented states, not the people; each state one vote; assent of nine states sometimes required; no provision about foreign trade; taxes levied on states, Congress no power to enforce collection; states to obey, no power to enforce obedience; no executive, no courts. Nevertheless of great benefit, providing for the present time and teaching the people how to do better.

(*Outline other paragraphs in the same way.*)

347. **The Articles of Confederation** were not suitable for the constitution of a national government. Under them there could be no true government, for they conveyed to Congress no true sovereignty. The Congress of the Confederation represented thirteen states, and not the people of America. In this Congress votes were taken by states, the members from one state casting one vote. For certain acts, as making war and coining money, the assent of nine states was necessary. There was no provision for regulating trade with foreign nations. National expenses were to be paid by an assessment levied upon the states in proportion to their taxable property. Every state was expected to obey the laws of Congress—but there was no power in Congress to enforce obedience. Congress had no means to collect the taxes it assessed.

[The government of the Confederation had no regular executive department for the enforcement of law, and no courts for the adjustment of disputes. "The Confederation, notwithstanding its defects, was of extended benefit. It met the pressing wants of the Union, and thus strengthened it. It conferred a great educational service through the experience of its defects; and it carried the nation along until a more efficient system was provided for."]

348. **Causes of Dissension.**—The enthusiasm of war had kindled a national feeling that kept the states united as

long as the war lasted. At its close, quarrels and dissensions could not be prevented, and could be remedied only by a competent national government. The army was unpaid, and the states, burdened by debts of their own, were slow to take upon themselves any part of the common load, and naturally quarrelsome about their shares. At the close of the war, settlers, many of them ex-soldiers, set out from the older locations to find new homes on the lands beyond the Alleghanies. But to whom did these western lands belong, or who had a right to give a title to them? The vague terms of colonial charters, instead of establishing definite bounds for the American states, only furnished grounds for jealousy and dispute. The claims of several states overlapped one another, and serious quarrels were sure to arise, when one state began to sell land claimed by another.

349. [**Western Claims.**—New Hampshire, Rhode Island, New Jersey, Pennsylvania, Delaware, and Maryland were definitely bounded by their charters. New York was not limited on the west. Massachusetts, Connecticut, Virginia, North Carolina, South Carolina, and Georgia, claiming at first to extend to the Pacific, limited themselves at the Mississippi River after Louisiana was ceded to Spain in 1763. These rival claims to western land were gradually settled by states giving up their title in favor of the United States. New York was the first to act, giving up her claim in 1780. Virginia followed in 1784, Massachusetts in 1785, Connecticut in 1786, South Carolina in 1787, North Carolina in 1790, and Georgia in 1802. Connecticut retained for a time a large tract of land in the northeastern part of Ohio, which thus came to be known as the Western Reserve.]

350. [**The Northwest Territory,** including all the ceded land north of the Ohio, was organized in 1787. A government was established for the territory, a governor and judges to be appointed by Congress, and a legislature to be elected by the people of the territory, after they had reached a required number. The law establishing the Northwest Territory is known as the Ordinance of 1787. It forever prohibited slavery within the territory, and provided for the encouragement of public schools, popular government, and the future formation of states.]

351. [**Regulation of Commerce.**—Englishmen did not believe that the American states could maintain their union, and proceeded to enforce restrictions on American trade. British garrisons were retained in American frontier forts, for the purpose of controlling the fur trade.

American goods were excluded from the British islands in the West Indies, unless carried in British ships. "They mean," wrote John Adams, representing Americans at the British court, "that Americans should have no ships, nor sailors, to annoy their trade." An effort was made in Congress, in 1785, to secure a general and uniform trade law throughout the Union, which should favor American ships and levy duties upon imported goods. The effort failed, because a few states, having no ships, feared that they might be giving a monopoly to those that had ships. In the absence of any general trade laws, states began to act for themselves. New York established a custom-house, turning over the duties collected into her own treasury, and thus acting as a thoroughly independent state. Some of the states began to levy duties upon the imports from other states.]

352. Discussion of a New Government.—The leading men of the country clearly perceived the need of an efficient general government. In 1783 Washington wrote to Lafayette: "To form a new constitution that will give consistency, stability, and dignity to the Union and sufficient powers to the great council of the nation, for general purposes, is a duty incumbent upon every man who wishes well to his country." Before surrendering his commission (345), Washington addressed a circular letter to the governor of every state, by him to be placed before every legislature. "It is indispensable," he wrote, "to the happiness of the individual states, that there should be somewhere a supreme power to regulate and govern the general concerns of the confederated republic. . . . Whatever measures have a tendency to dissolve the Union, or to violate or lessen the sovereign authority, ought to be considered as hostile to the liberty and independence of America." Among all the great men who studied and discussed plans for a general government, James Madison of Virginia (**429**), and Alexander Hamilton of New York are distinguished as men who clearly understood the needs of the time and labored actively for reform.

353. [**Alexander Hamilton** was born on one of the West Indies in 1757. At the age of fifteen he was sent to New York to be educated and he entered Columbia College (**160**). Two years later, in a brilliant and stirring speech, he "electrified a public meeting" at New York, called to denounce the Boston Port Bill (**243**). He displayed remarkable intellectual powers, and became at once one of the ablest writers in the American cause. At twenty he was a trusted officer on Washington's staff, "and to the proud day at Yorktown was as chivalrous, generous, and gallant a soldier as ever drew his sword for his country." He was an acknowledged admirer of the British form of government, and the plan which he favored for the United States contained life-tenure for all the high offices, legislative and executive, tending toward monarchy rather than democracy. He died at Weehawken, New Jersey, in 1804, shot in a duel into which he had been drawn by Aaron Burr, then Vice-President of the United States.]

354. A convention to reform the Articles of Confederation had been several times suggested from 1780 to 1786. The legislature of Virginia, in 1786, invited the other states to elect delegates to consider reforms. Delegates were elected in most of the states, but those from five states only came together at Annapolis in September, 1786. As the representation was so unsatisfactory, no business was undertaken. All the states, however, were urged to send delegates to meet at Philadelphia in May, 1787, and Congress sanctioned the movement.

355. [" **Shays' Rebellion.**"—Throughout the land people were burdened with debts contracted during the war. Forced collections through the courts and the imprisonment of debtors caused great distress, and debtors were disposed to resist the law officers. In Massachusetts there was bitter opposition to forced collections, and for a time the courts were powerless. In the western part of the state, during the winter of 1786-7, this opposition grew into an armed insurrection, known as "Shays' Rebellion," from the name of the principal leader, Daniel Shays. The insurrection was easily subdued by a military force called out by the governor of Massachusetts. It was, however, an uprising of people against a government established by themselves. By the enemies of the country it was taken as a sign of anarchy; to Americans it was a valuable lesson, teaching the need of a national government.]

356. The Constitutional Convention assembled May fourteenth, but a majority of the states not being represented, adjournments were taken until the twenty-fifth. On that day the delegates present organized by electing George Washington President. Sixty-five delegates had been elected, representing all the states except Rhode Island, which took no part in the convention. Ten delegates did not take their places, and many dropped out during the long session. The states showed the greatest wisdom in sending their ablest men to this convention. They were men distinguished by their services during the war period, both in Congress and in the state governments. The delegates from Virginia, headed by Madison, brought with them the rough draft of a National Constitution. The sessions of the convention were secret.

[Franklin was the Nestor of the convention. Now at the age of eighty-one, he had been prominent in public affairs since the Albany convention (197). Three members had been in the Stamp Act Congress; seven in the Congress of 1774; eight had signed the Declaration of Independence. Eighteen were members of Congress at the time, and only twelve had never served in Congress. "Nine were graduates of Princeton (160), four of Yale, three of Harvard (100), two of Columbia, one of Pennsylvania." Several were from William and Mary's, and several more had been educated at English or Scotch colleges. Many had made careful study of forms of government, and were familiar with the best writings on the subject. They were "the goodliest fellowship of lawgivers whereof this world holds record."

357. Difficulties before the Convention.—The early sessions of the convention were far from being quiet and harmonious. It was soon decided to throw aside the Articles of Confederation entirely and to prepare a new Constitution. Then all the errors, prejudices, and jealousies of the various states were brought to the surface. The smaller states feared being overwhelmed by the larger ones. The question of allowing representation for slaves provoked stormy dissension. At one time Washington wrote that he almost despaired of a favorable issue to the proceedings. Franklin showed the necessity of compromise, and compromise became one of the foundation stones of the American government.

[During the time of stormy debate, Franklin, in an impressive speech, moved that the convention be opened each morning with prayer. "The longer I live," he said, "the more convincing proofs I see that God governs in the affairs of men." His motion was not voted on, but a better spirit thenceforth prevailed. At another time, speaking of the diversity of opinions, he said that when a carpenter is making a broad table and

1. Hamilton.   2. Madison.   3. Morris.   4. Franklin.

the edges of his boards do not fit, he planes a little from each and makes a good joint. So in the convention, opposite sides must each give up a little in order to gain a just settlement.]

358. Difficulties Removed.—It was early decided to establish a national Congress of two houses (Senate and House of Representatives). The question of representation was settled by allowing one representative to each state for every 40,000 (changed later in the session to 30,000) inhabitants, three fifths of all slaves being added to the number of white persons in making the apportionment. The claims of small states were recognized by giving to each an equal vote in the Senate.

[The question, whether the chief executive should be one or more, and, after one was decided upon, how he should be elected and how long he should serve, provoked prolonged debate. The adjustment of power between the general government and the states was the most difficult problem before the convention. Hamilton would have made the states clearly dependent upon the general government, by having Congress appoint state governors, etc. Madison, although desiring to maintain the states, wished Congress to have a negative on state laws. These views did not prevail. The majority thought to leave the states sovereign in their own sphere and at the same time to erect the general government above them, supreme in all matters of national concern. Around this question of the relation of the states to the general government centers the political history of the United States from 1787 to 1865.]

359. The Constitution Completed.—The convention did not conclude its labors until the middle of September. The result of their work was the Constitution which Americans still honor and obey. It was to be submitted through Congress and the state legislatures, to the vote of the people in each state. When the people in nine states had voted in favor of it Congress was to appoint the time and place for holding elections for the new offices. The Constitution was signed on September 17th, 1787, all members then in attendance appending their names, except three, Edmund Randolph and George Mason of Virginia, and Elbridge Gerry of Massachusetts. Each of these had taken an active part in the convention, but felt dissatisfied with the result.

Hamilton took a broader view: "No man's ideas," he said, "are more remote from the plan than my own are known to be; but is it possible to deliberate between anarchy and convulsion on one side, and the chance of good to be expected from the plan on the other?" The Constitution was a nobler work than the majority in the beginning had dared hope to make. Yet at this day we may say that no one of those men fully realized the grandeur of the work they had accomplished.

360. Before the People.—The newspapers quickly made the country acquainted with the work of the convention, and discussion of the document at once began. Farmers, mechanics, and merchants in general welcomed it; but it was opposed by many men of ability and influence, who thought that the proposed government would injure the already existing state governments, which they knew and loved. Thus arose a division of the people. Those who favored ratification of the Constitution took the name of Federalists; those who preferred to reject it were known as Anti-Federalists. Many leading statesmen in all the states were among the Federalists. A few, however, like Patrick Henry, of Virginia, and George Clinton, of New York, were violent Anti-Federalists. Washington and Franklin and John Hancock cast all their great influence in favor of the Constitution. Hamilton and Madison worked in state convention, and argued in the newspapers, publishing a series of eighty-five essays in a New York newspaper, in which the whole Constitution was explained and defended.

[These eighty-five essays, collected and published as a book, are now known as "The Federalist," one of the great works in American political literature. Six essays were written by John Jay (**369**).]

361. Adopted.—Delaware, Pennsylvania, and New Jersey were the first states to ratify the Constitution. New Hampshire has the honor of casting the decisive vote, she being the ninth state to ratify. Her approval was given in

FORMATION OF A NATIONAL GOVERNMENT. 187

June, 1788. New York and Virginia followed soon after New Hampshire. Rhode Island and North Carolina withheld their approval until after the Constitution went into force. On July 2d, 1788, the President of the Congress of the Confederation declared that the Constitution of the United States had been adopted. Preparations to put the new government into operation began at once.

[Elections for members of the first Congress and for President and Vice-President were held according to directions of Congress. When the votes of presidential electors were counted, it was found that George Washington was chosen first President of the United States by a unanimous vote. John Adams, having received the second votes of thirty-four out of sixty-nine electors, was duly elected Vice-President.]

QUESTIONS.

When did local or "town" government begin in America? (**66, 67**). State government? (**268**). Government by the states in union? (**274**).

What then was the order of growth, from local governments upward; or the opposite, from a central government downward?

STUDY OF THE CONSTITUTION.

Who established the Constitution (see Preamble)? Voting in what manner? (**359**).

Where did legislative powers not granted to Congress (Art. I., Sec. I.) remain?

* How are representatives chosen, and for how long? (Art. I., Sec. II.; 1.)

How are vacancies filled? (Art. I., Sec. II.; 4.)

Who presides over the House of Representatives? (Art. I., Sec. II.; 5.)

† How are senators elected, and for how long? (Art. I., Sec. III.; 1.)

How are vacancies filled? (Art. I., Sec. III.; 2.)

Who presides over the Senate? (Art. I., Sec. III.; 4.)

How often and when does Congress assemble? (Art. I., Sec. IV.; 2.)

Where must revenue bills originate? (Art. I., Sec. VII.; 1.)

How much legislative power does the President have? (Art. I., Sec. VII.; 2.)

Study carefully Article I., Section VIII., for the powers of Congress.

Study carefully Article I., Section IX., for prohibitions upon Congress.

---

* *How many Representatives has California? Who is the Representative from your district?*

† *Who are the Senators from California?*

What time was guaranteed to the foreign slave trade? (Art. I., Sec. IX.; 1.)

Do you find the word "slave" anywhere mentioned?

Study carefully Article I., Section X., for prohibitions upon states.

What must the United States do for every state? (Art. IV., Sec. IV.; 1.)

Who is our chief executive officer? What is his term? (Art. II., Sec. I.; 1.)

* What was the manner first provided for electing a President and Vice-President? (Art. II., Sec. I.; 3.)

Who has power to declare war? (Art. I., Sec. VIII.; 11.)

Who is commander-in-chief of the army and navy? (Art. II., Sec. II.; 1.)

Who has power to make treaties? (Art. II., Sec. II.; 2.)

What is the method of appointing officers? (Art. II., Sec. II.; 2.)

What is said about power of removal or cause for removal? (Art. II., Sec. IV.)

How are United States judgeships filled? (Art. II., Sec. II.; 2.) For what term? (Art. III., Sec. I.)

What cases come under the judicial power of the United States? (Art. III., Sec. II.; 1.)

What constitutes treason against the United States? (Art. III., Sec. III.; 1.)

How may a person fleeing from justice in one state be recovered from another state? (Art. IV., Sec. II.; 2.)

What is the supreme law of our land? (Art. VI.; 2.)

How may the Constitution be amended? (Art. V.)

What were the great defects of the Articles of Confederation? (**347.**) Show that the Constitution corrected these defects.

Consider what the word *nation* means and then give as many reasons as you can find for saying that the people of the United States were a nation in 1787.

What is the difference between a league of states and a national government?

Give reasons showing that the Constitution was suitable for a national government.

---

* *How many electoral votes has California?*

CHAPTER XVIII.

1789-1797.

THE UNITED STATES GOVERNMENT ESTABLISHED.

For Explanation.—Quorum; coxswain; sound; ordeal; scrutiny; levied; defalcation; per diem; mileage; national securities; assumption; chamberlains; punctilious; tinged; abdicated; patrician; cant; envoy; refugee; partisan; calumny; coinage; turnpikes; epidemics.

George Washington, *Virginia*, President.
John Adams, *Massachusetts*, Vice-President. } 1789-97.

1789-93.	1793-7.	
Thomas Jefferson—State.	Thomas Jefferson, Edmund Randolph, Timothy Pickering,	State.
Alexander Hamilton—Treasury.	Alexander Hamilton, Oliver Wolcott,	Treasury.
Henry Knox—War.	Henry Knox, Timothy Pickering, James McHenry,	War.
Edmund Randolph—Attorney-General.	Edmund Randolph, William Bradford, Charles Lee,	Attorney-General.

1. WORK OF THE FIRST CONGRESS.

362. Inauguration of Washington.—The fourth of March, 1789, had been appointed for the first Congress under the Constitution, to assemble at New York, the temporary capital of the United States. No quorum, however, of either Senate or House of Representatives was present until April first. George Washington, President elect, arrived on April twenty-third. A decorated barge, with twelve rowers and a thirteenth man for coxswain, brought him from the Jersey shore. Vessels in the harbor, flying the flags of all nations, saluted with thirteen guns. Governor Clinton of New York, attended by civil and military worthies, escorted the honored hero over a carpeted path from the water-steps to a carriage of state, and citizens arm-in-arm fell in behind the military procession, while the madly ringing bells strove to express the nation's joy. One week later, on the balcony of Federal Hall, both houses of Congress being assembled within, Washington solemnly repeated the words of the oath of office, and with closed eyes whispered the words, "so help me, God!" kissing the Bible as he concluded. Then rang out the joyous cry of the people: "Long live George Washington, President of the United States!" and the artillery thundered the first of presidential salutes. After the inaugural address, modest, calm, and hopeful, appealing to the Almighty for help and guidance, there were religious services in a neighboring chapel. The ceremonies of the day ended with brilliant fireworks.

363. Congress had weighty work before it. Laws that should put a great government into operation were to be made. The first Congress was composed of sound, experienced men, with enough of the opponents of the government among them to make every measure pass the ordeal of close scrutiny and sharp debate.

[In those days the people could not keep posted on congressional discussions, for reports of debates were not published. The Senate, endeavoring to assume an imposing station, sat with closed doors, that no intruder might break in upon its dignified counsels. Vice-President Adams, in the chair, would sternly rebuke a whisper, if any member were speaking on the floor. The House of Representatives was less punctilious, and visitors were allowed in the gallery. Madison, whom Patrick Henry and the Anti-Federalists of the Virginia Legislature had defeated for the Senate, had been elected a Representative by the people of his district. He was on intimate terms with the President, and was soon recognized as a leader in the House.]

364. Revenue.—The national treasury was empty. To provide a revenue for government expenses was the first care. Soon after the House of Representatives organized, Madison moved a resolution that certain duties ought to be levied upon imports, and the first of American tariff debates followed. Madison's plan was adopted in substance. Moderate duties were levied upon articles of general importation, the purpose being to raise a revenue, but in the choice of articles that should pay the duties, there was also a clear purpose to foster home productions and manufactures. Custom Houses and the regular machinery for the collection of duties, were provided. Duties were payable only in gold or silver coin.

365. [Revenue Tariff.—Tariffs are sometimes classified as Revenue tariffs and Protective tariffs. If the object of a government in establishing a tariff is simply to raise a revenue, the duties would be laid upon articles of general use which are not produced within the country. The tax is then widely distributed, and does not in any way affect the manufactures of the country. For instance, the United States, desiring simply a tariff for revenue, might lay a duty upon tea and coffee, which are used by almost every one, and are not produced in the United States.]

366. [Protective Tariff.—The idea of a Protective tariff is quite different. If a government desires a Protective tariff, it will place duties upon articles which are produced within the country, but which can be imported for a less price. For instance, iron is produced both in the United States and in Great Britain, and for some reason—as better methods in the reduction of iron ore, lower wages paid to workmen—British iron can be sold in the United States cheaper than domestic iron. Without a tariff, therefore, the manufacture of iron cannot be carried on in the United States. If, however, our government charges a duty on imported iron, our manufacturers can get higher prices, and are protected against foreign competition. The government, meantime, gets a revenue from the tariff, provided the importation of iron continues under the tariff.]

367. The Executive Departments.—Congress established three departments—a department of Foreign Affairs, of War, and of the Treasury—the man in charge of each to be called a Secretary, and to be appointed by the President. All together were to act as his advisers. Later was created the office of Attorney-General, or legal adviser of the President.

[Washington set an example of appointing prominent men to these positions. "I want men," he used to say, "already of marked eminence before the country, not only as the more serviceable, but because the public will more readily trust them." In consulting with his advisers, Washington generally put questions, and demanded opinions in writing, but after a few years adopted the practice of calling them together for oral consultation. In this way the chiefs of departments came to be called the Cabinet.]

[The Department of Foreign Affairs soon received the name of the Department of State. In 1798 the affairs of the War Department were divided, and the Navy Department was created. Post Offices were managed by the Treasury Department until 1829, when the Postmaster-Gen-

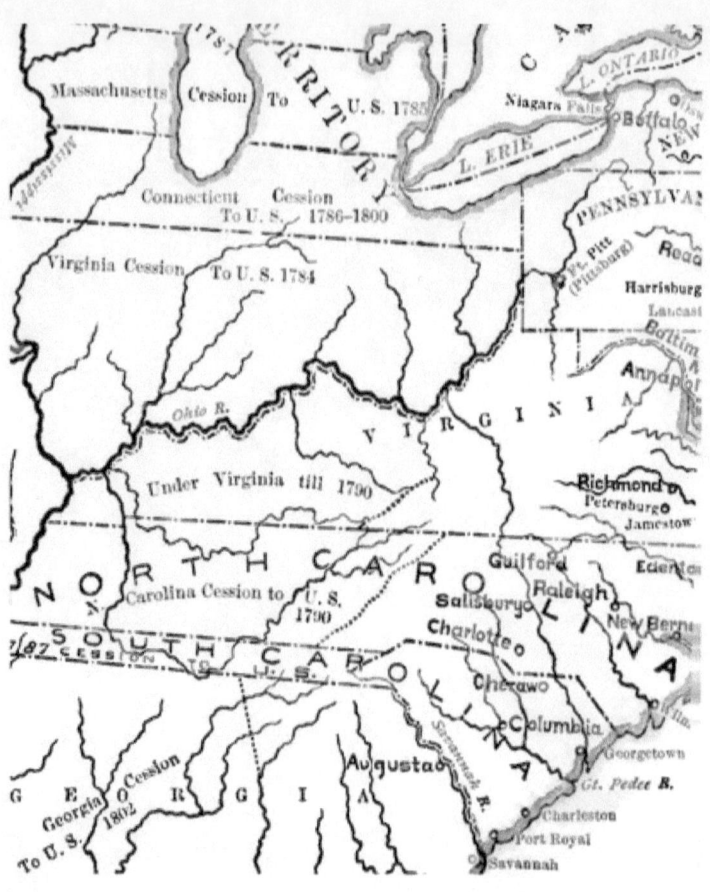

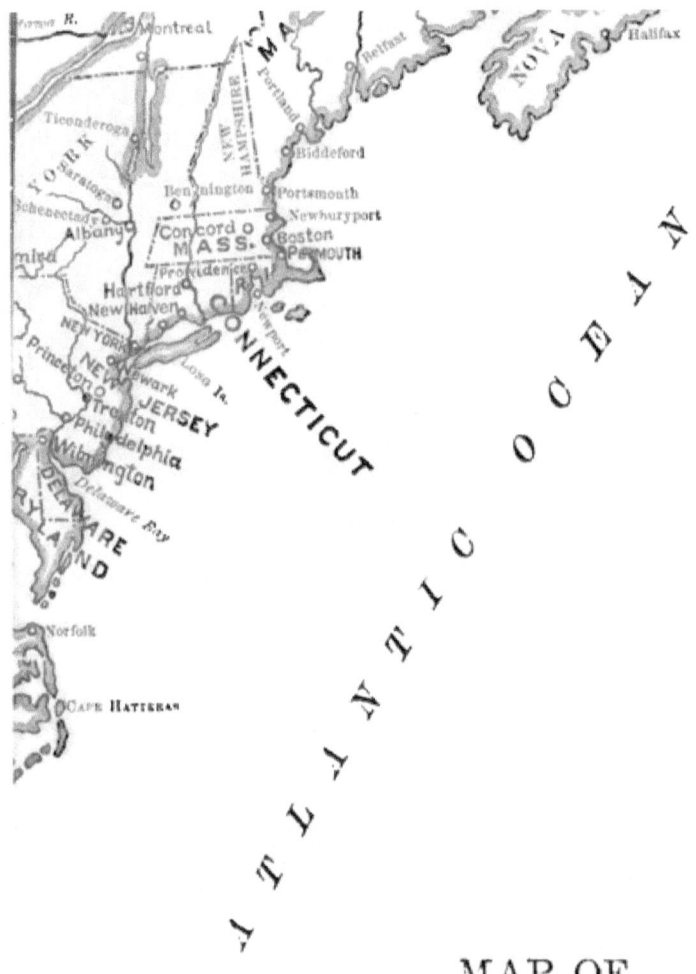

MAP OF
TERRITORY OF 1783.

SCALE.

eral was added to the Cabinet. The Department of the Interior, which manages public lands, patents, pensions, the census, etc., was organized in 1849.]

[The Treasury Department was organized with a complicated system of inspection. An Auditor examines public accounts, a Controller reviews them, a Treasurer under heavy bonds is the actual guardian and disburser of the funds, and a Register keeps a record of receipts and payments. The special duty of the Secretary of the Treasury is to prepare plans for national finance. He supervises the whole department, but can appoint only his own assistants. The United States Treasury has never been dishonored by any serious defalcation.]

368. United States Courts.—Other important legislation was passed at the first session of Congress, which later years have not changed, but only extended. The United States Supreme Court was organized with a Chief Justice and five (now eight) Associate Justices appointed for life. For subordinate courts the country was divided into districts, in each of which was organized a District Court. These judicial districts were grouped into circuits, in which provision was made for Circuit Courts. Congress gave the courts the necessary officers of clerks, marshals, and attorneys, but built no jails.

369. [John Jay was appointed Chief Justice. Born in New York in 1745, of Huguenot descent, a graduate of Columbia College and a lawyer, he was a stanch patriot and one of our ablest statesmen. He was a prominent member of the Continental Congress, Minister to Spain in 1779, whence he joined Adams and Franklin at Paris **(295)**. In 1795 he resigned the office of Chief Justice to become Governor of New York.]

370. Territories.—Provision was made for the organization of territorial governments, under the authority of the United States, in all the land which had been ceded to the United States **(349)**. Provision was also made for territories to enter the Union as states on equal terms as soon as sufficient population should be gained. Several states on ratifying the Constitution had demanded amendments. These made a large number when brought together. Congress cut them down to ten, which were adopted and added

---

370. Read Articles I–X., Amendments to the Constitution of the United States.

to the Constitution. They were regarded as additional safeguards to the rights of the people.

371. [The salaries fixed for the various officers were low as compared with present figures. Washington had desired that only his official expenses should be paid, but Congress liberally gave him $25,000 a year. The yearly salary of the Vice-President was $5,000, of the Chief Justice $4,000, while the pay of members of Congress was fixed at $6 per diem with mileage according to distances. The sum of $216,000 was sufficient for the first year's expenses, including the army and the pension list. Since the second administration of President Grant the President has received $50,000. The present salary of the Vice-President is $8,000, of the Chief Justice $10,500, of members of Congress $5,000 with mileage.]

372. The national debt was not touched at the first session of Congress, but it formed an important part of the work the second year, 1790. Secretary Hamilton had been carefully maturing his plans and his financial report was the political sensation of the early government. It startled Congress and the country by the amount of indebtedness it revealed (nearly $12,000,000 of foreign debt, over $42,000,000 due at home, and $25,000,000 of state debt incurred in the common cause of war), and by the bold determination to pay every dollar of the huge amount.

[Hardly any one had expected that the government would keep its promises in full, and the mere publication of Hamilton's report made the price of national securities rise from fifteen cents to fifty cents on the dollar. New York capitalists rushed their agents through the country to buy up all the bills they could find, before the news of this proposed payment could reach their holders. This made Congressmen oppose payment in full, for it was argued that only speculators would be benefited, and not the patriots who had given their services and their means to the country.

373. The assumption of the state debts was fiercely opposed, as tending to centralize power in the United States government. A compromise settled the matter. The state of Virginia was opposed to assumption, but was desirous of getting the national capital. It had been generally agreed to build a new city for the capital, and the competition

---

373. In this compromise, what parties made concessions, and what concessions did each make?

for the site lay between the Delaware, Susquehanna, and Potomac Rivers. By the compromise, state debts to the amount of $21,500,000 were assumed by the United States, and our capital city was located on the Potomac.

374. [**The National Capital.**—The government went from New York to Philadelphia in 1791. The site of the national capital was selected by the first President in the last year of his administration, and the country unanimously named it WASHINGTON. Work was commenced on government buildings, which were occupied in 1800, when President Adams congratulated Congress on "a residence not to be changed."]

2. THE PRESIDENT AND THE COUNTRY.

375. Presidential Etiquette and Entertainments.—In New York and Philadelphia, Washington set to future presidents an example of elegant receptions, and rich banquets to limited and select companies. John Adams would have had numerous chamberlains and masters of ceremonies. While discarding these attendants of royalty, Washington was, however, "punctilious in the smallest matters of etiquette." Himself a true gentleman, and "as genuine a man as ever came from his Maker's hand," carefulness in etiquette was to him a matter of honor and gentlemanly breeding. With wealth of his own, he had no wish to make money out of his office, and was accustomed to spend his whole salary in the discharge of his official duties. His wife, in her youth a Virginia belle, adorned her position as a leader of society, and her fame is made lasting in the title of "Lady Washington," accorded to her by common consent. Washington spent the intervals between the sessions of Congress in tours through the states, partly as a rest from office, but mainly to acquaint himself with the condition of his fellow citizens.

376. The prosperity of the country began with the establishment of the national government. The fierce debates that had rent the people over the adoption of the Constitution were stilled. Heaven gave fruitful seasons. American grain was in demand in Canada and in Europe. Commerce and manufactures were growing, and everything promised better times to come. The President's message to Congress at the beginning of the second session (January 4th, 1790), spoke of the growing importance of the United States as a nation. Convinced of their helpless condition outside of the Union, the two stubborn sisters at last joined hands, North Carolina ratifying the Constitution in November, 1789; but little Rhode Island holding out till the following year.

[The United States had cut off political connection with England, but remained English in nearly everything else—in language, law, religion, traditions, and habits of thought. The wealthy wore powdered wigs and frilled shirt bosoms, following English fashions of the eighteenth century. Jefferson, who from the study of French writers, and a long residence in France (**412**), had become strongly tinged with French ideas, recommended to Congress the adoption of the French decimal system in money, weights, and measures. This wise advice was followed only in the decimal system for United States money. Even in this it took people a long time to change their prices and accounts from pounds, shillings, and pence, previously used, to dollars and cents, recently invented. The use of the French metric standards was made legal in the United States in 1866. They are now almost exclusively used by scientists of every nation.]

377. [**Death of Franklin.**—After returning from France, Franklin served as Governor of Pennsylvania, where his wise guidance rescued the state from civil dissensions. His death occurred April 17th, 1790, at the age of eighty-four. His last public work was to head a petition to Congress from a society of Pennsylvania for the abolition of slavery. "Equal liberty," the petition said, "was originally the portion and is still the birthright of all men." Of all the illustrious men of American Independence, he alone stands out as a leader in advance of his age; in him was a glorious prophecy of what American character might become. America regretted her loss, and France mourned for him as for a favorite son.]

378. **Vermont and Kentucky** were admitted to the Union in 1790. The Constitution of Vermont prohibited slavery; that of Kentucky tolerated it. In this way Congress began a "miserable policy of halving the national territory between freedom and slavery."

379. [**Slavery**, chiefly of African races, had been introduced into the English colonies of America at an early date (**135**). Descended from the customs of Roman conquerors and approved by the precepts

of Jewish law, the right of ownership in human beings was recognized in the laws of Christian nations until the fuller light of the Christianity of the nineteenth century condemned it. In the American colonies the growth or the decay of slavery was determined not by the ideas of the people, but by the conditions of their life. Only the industry of free laborers could bring a return from the meager soil of New England farms; only skilled workmen could manage the shops in the North and the center; but in the river bottoms of the South, with the toil that could be wrung from the lazy and ignorant slave, tobacco, rice, and indigo gave the planter an easy income. The African could not endure New England winters, but in the heat of the South he lived in health. Only negro slavery increased. White men, condemned to servitude, found, in the new country, means to escape, and the Indian's wild spirit fretted itself to death when put in fetters. During the latter part of the colonial period there was a growing spirit in condemnation of the slave trade, but the English government would not allow its suppression. In his first draft of the Declaration of Independence (275), Jefferson denounced the slave trade as "piratical warfare against human nature itself," but his words offended some and were stricken out; again, in Congress, in 1784, he sought to prohibit slavery in all the western lands then being ceded to the United States (349), but failed by a single vote. Massachusetts was the only one of the original states to enter the Union with a constitution prohibiting slavery. The United States prohibited the importation of slaves after January 1st, 1808. There was talk of general emancipation during the early years of our government, but slaves had become so numerous in the southern states, and their presence had so worked itself into southern society, that the problem of emancipation was perplexing.]

3. THE INDIANS.

380. United States Indian Policy.—Americans failed always to make permanent friendships with the Indian tribes, for the life of one race meant the death of the other. Settlers constantly pressing westward fought back the Indians as they did the wild beasts, and the government had to protect the settlers when they were in danger.

[The power of the Iroquois was crushed in 1778 (**314**), but north of the Ohio there were other tribes, who, crossing the river, made the lowland of Kentucky "dark and bloody ground." In 1790 the Indians of the Northwest numbered from 20,000 to 30,000. The Wabash was the chief tribe. In the Southwest were the Chickasaws, Choctaws, Cherokees, and Creeks, numbering about 70,000.]

381. War was made on the northwest Indians to defend the settlers who had entered Ohio. In 1790 General Harmar was defeated near the site of Fort Wayne. In 1791

General St. Clair led United States troops against the Indians, and he, too, was led into ambush and badly defeated near the head of the Wabash. In 1794 General Anthony Wayne (301) was more successful, destroying the force of the Indians in a battle near the site of Toledo and bringing them to a treaty by which they surrendered the territory of the present state of Ohio. Treaties were concluded with the southwestern tribes by peaceful means.

4. EXCISE AND THE WHISKY INSURRECTION.

382. Tax on Liquors.—The payment of the national debt required additional United States taxes, and an excise was placed on distilled liquors. This tax belongs to the class of taxes called indirect, because not borne entirely by the persons who pay it, and being supposed to discourage the use of liquors by raising their price, it recommends itself to great numbers of people. To the first Congress the excise seemed a tax the least liable to be opposed.

383. The Tax Resisted.—In the mountain counties of North Carolina, Virginia, and Pennsylvania the people were in the habit of turning their surplus grain crops into whisky, which they could haul to market much more easily than the grain. These people, many of them of foreign birth, fought off the tax collectors, and in Pennsylvania even balked the state militia brought out against them. Fearing the effect of a lawless example, President Washington called out an army of 15,000 men from the militia of the neighboring states and sent it into western Pennsylvania. Order was restored on the appearance of the army. The disturbance is known as the Whisky Insurrection.

5. UNITED STATES BANK.

384. The national debt was paid off in the following manner: All the old bills were collected, the holders receiv-

---

382. *Explain how it is that the tax described in this paragraph is not borne by the people who pay it to the government.*

ing in exchange new paper, or bonds of the United States, bearing interest at fixed rates and payable after a period of years. For the regular payment of the interest and the gradual reduction of the principal, certain revenues, or funds, were set aside. A debt provided for in this way is said to be funded.

385. A United States Bank was an important feature of Hamilton's financial scheme. A bill for incorporation brought out strong opposition from Congressmen who believed that such an institution would enable the United States government to swallow up the state governments. They pronounced the bank "unconstitutional," arguing that the constitution nowhere gave the United States power to establish a bank. In reply, Hamilton brought forward his doctrine of "implied powers," arguing that as the bank would be a useful means of collecting taxes and of borrowing money, it was authorized by the clause of the constitution empowering Congress "to make all laws which shall be necessary for carrying into execution" the powers that were expressly granted. (See Constitution, I: VIII: 18.) The bill became a law in 1791, and a bank was chartered for twenty years. The view which pronounced the bank unconstitutional is frequently called "a strict construction" of the constitution; Hamilton's view is called "a loose construction."

[Hamilton took for his model the Bank of England, an institution that has been in operation for a long time, and has been a source of strength to the English government. A large part of its capital stock is composed of bonds representing the English national debt. Bank of England notes circulate as money, and every one holding them is interested in keeping up the government, for with the downfall of the government the bank notes would become worthless. A similar bank, called the Bank of North America, planned and managed by the financier of the Revolution, Robert Morris, had done good service for Americans toward the close of the war.]

385. Explain the difference between "implied" and "expressed" powers. Give an illustration of each.

6. FOREIGN AFFAIRS AND POLITICAL PARTIES.

386. The old-time monarchy of France came to an end in 1789, in what is called the French Revolution. The old order of things in society, government, and religion was swept away; a republic was set up, but did not long continue. A new monarch, in the person of Napoleon Bonaparte, supported by the army, gradually supplanted the republic.

387. [**Napoleon Bonaparte** was born in Corsica, in 1769. His genius was for war, and in the affairs of the Revolution he found opportunity for service. The monarchies of Europe conspired to suppress democracy in France. Bonaparte, having extended the military sway of France over Italy; having humbled Austria, and overrun Syria and Egypt, was, in 1802, proclaimed consul for life, and two years later he gained his true title, being crowned by the Pope as Napoleon I., Emperor of the French. For ten years Napoleon continued to dazzle the world by his military achievements, fighting the combined armies of northern Europe. Defeat came in 1814, Napoleon abdicated his power, and retired to rule the island of Elba; but not to rest from ambition. In February, 1815, invited by a conspiracy of his old supporters, Napoleon escaped to France, resumed his former position, gathered another grand army, but met final defeat in the great battle of Waterloo (June 18th, 1815). The rest of his life he lived a prisoner of Great Britain, on the little island of St. Helena. He died in 1821.]

388. The growth of political parties in the United States was greatly influenced by affairs in Europe. The division between Federalists and Anti-Federalists passed away at the successful inauguration of the government. Then began a new division. Washington tried always to be of no party— to be for the nation as a whole, and the country so trusted him that few men could ever be found to say that they were against him. But the opinions of Washington inclined toward those of Hamilton, and Hamilton was the natural party leader of the Federalists. The opponents of the Hamilton Federalists began in 1792 to call themselves Republicans. Hamilton admired the British form of government as the best in the world, and his enemies accused

---

387. Where is Elba? St. Helena?

him of aiming at a monarchy in America. This was probably not true, but Hamilton and his fellows did desire a sort of patrician or ruling class, composed of "the men of sense and property, a little above the multitude." Jefferson was the chief opponent of the political ideas of Hamilton, and became the leader of the Republicans.

389. The new party of Republicans, headed by Jefferson, had as yet little strength among the people, and in 1792 Washington was unanimously reëlected; and Adams, who was a pronounced Federalist of aristocratic notions, again received the Vice-Presidency by a handsome majority over George Clinton of New York, the candidate of the Republicans. From this time on, however, the strength of the Republicans grew steadily. They received the remnants of the old Anti-Federalists, the men who still feared that the Union would crush the states. They received, also, the support of a considerable number of Americans who sympathized strongly with the democratic ideas of the French revolution.

[Thus this growing party, the name changing from Republicans to Democratic-Republicans, and finally dropping the last part altogether, represented, in Jefferson's time, on one side the old-time opposition to American union, and on the other the hope of the future for the political equality of men. The Federalists, having established union and nationality above state distinctions, remained the defenders of the social order of the past.]

390. [Genet's Mission.—The ideas of the French revolutionists were dangerous to the ruling classes of England, and there was open war between the two countries most of the time till 1815. The French republic claimed aid from the United States in return for the help which the French monarchy had given in the war for independence. In 1793 the French Government sent Genet as minister to the United States. Many in the country were disposed to help the French against England. Although President Washington had proclaimed the neutrality of the United States in the war between France and England, Genet, immediately on his arrival in America, began to organize "Democratic societies" in sympathy with French revolutionists, and to commission privateers to prey on English commerce. His insolent operations were soon checked by firm measures on the part of Washington, and after a year Genet was recalled at the President's request. Enthusiasm for France, kindled by Genet's visit, lived, after his departure, in "Democratic societies" organized by him in the leading cities. The spirit of these societies to disregard law brought upon them the censure of President Washington, and as societies they soon disappeared.]

391. Jay's Treaty.—England had reluctantly acknowledged the independence of the United States, and continued willfully to injure the young republic. She had delayed to surrender Detroit and other forts in the Northwest, and her war ships seized American vessels trading with France. Chief Justice Jay went to England as a special envoy, and, in 1795, brought home a treaty providing for the surrender of the forts, for payment of damages to American merchants, but allowing damages to England for certain debts unpaid on account of the Revolution, and leaving the northern boundary poorly defined, with privileges on the ocean in favor of England. The treaty was ratified, although very unpopular. It postponed serious difficulties with England for twelve years.

7. IMMIGRATION AND WESTERN DEVELOPMENT.

392. The young republic of the United States attracted attention in all parts of Europe. The general war in Europe made a demand for American produce, and offered rich profits to American commerce. The flag of the United States became well known in foreign harbors. In the United States there was a constantly growing demand for labor, and an unmeasured extent of new land in the West. These advantages, combined with a government founded on freedom and equal rights, attracted multitudes from Europe for whom, in their native land, there was no hope of advance and hardly the chance of a comfortable life. The United States welcomed them as workers, and allowed them to become citizens after a brief residence.

393. Western Development.—During Washington's second administration an immigration began, so vast that "it seemed to our citizens as if all Europe were flowing in upon them." There were refugees from France, laborers from

England, Ireland, and Germany. This influx of population entered by the great harbors of Boston, New York, and Philadelphia, and thence joined in a movement to the westward, which began to build new states in the northwest, Ohio being the first.

394. [**Census.**—The first United States census, taken in 1790, showed a total population of 3,929,214. Of this number negro slaves made between one fifth and one sixth.]

8. Washington Retires.

395. Washington longed for release from public duties, and declined to be a candidate for a third term. In 1796 he published his Farewell Address to the American People, in the preparation of which he had labored long and carefully. "In words of solemn benediction, and free from all cant or partisanship," the foremost of Americans expressed the truths taught him by a life-long experience in founding American nationality. He warned the people against entangling alliances with foreign nations; against the danger of geographical parties, and the spirit of faction and disregard of authority, and urged them to make religion, morality, and general education the pillars of the government. On relief from office, Washington spent his few remaining years in quiet life on his Mount Vernon plantation.

396. The presidential election in 1796 brought out a partisan contest in full strength. Proceeding from the quarrels of leaders like Hamilton and Jefferson, there had grown up, especially in Philadelphia, a partisan press, whose attacks upon men of opposing views have never since been exceeded in bitterness and calumny by American newspapers. The leaders themselves in those days joined in controversies, which sometimes grew into duels, a fashion of settling quarrels introduced into America from France. Vice-President John Adams was recognized as the Federalist candidate for the first place, while Jefferson represented

---

395. What is meant by "geographical parties?"

the Republicans. Of the 138 electoral votes, Adams received 71, Jefferson stood next with 68. This gave the country a President of one party, and for Vice-President, the leader of the Opposition.

397. The United States at the end of Washington's administration had prosperity but not wealth. There was an immense debt, and very little money to support either an army or a navy. Fortunate it was for the young nation that its early government had the firmness of Washington, whom the people loved and trusted, the force and energy of Hamilton, who created financial stability, and the wisdom and experience of Congressmen like Madison, who had a regard for the whole people. The United States mint, located at Philadelphia, began to give the country a uniform coinage, facilitating home trade. The government issued patents protecting inventors and helping manufactures. Good turnpikes were built between the principal cities, making travel easier and quicker. New England began canals, which made freighting cheaper. Colleges increased in number, and began to rise to higher scholarship. Noah Webster published "The American Spelling Book" and other simple text-books, laying the foundation for American common school education. The health of the people was generally good, but at times epidemics, like yellow fever at Philadelphia in 1793, showed how little the physicians of that time knew about diseases, and challenged them to improve their methods of treatment.

398. The South grew more rapidly in wealth, for a great staple had been added to her products. Cotton had been raised in the southern colonies, but it was not a profitable crop until Eli Whitney, in 1793, invented the cotton gin, a machine for cleaning out seed from the cotton. By hand a slave could clean only one or two pounds of cotton a day, but with the machine he could clean a thousand. This in-

THE UNITED STATES GOVERNMENT ESTABLISHED. 205

vention had a great and far-reaching effect upon the southern people. By vastly increasing the profits of slave labor it greatly strengthened the power of the slavery system. Manufactures, for which slave labor is unsuited, did not flourish, and the South came to live almost entirely by exporting raw products.

399. [**Eli Whitney** was born in Massachusetts and graduated from Yale College. He went to Savannah to study law, and while there his attention was directed to cotton cleaning. He received but very little from the invention of the cotton gin, but afterwards he became rich by manufacturing improved firearms for the government. (See portrait, p. 268.)]

SUMMARY OF WASHINGTON'S ADMINISTRATION.

Make a summary of this chapter by filling in notes after the following topics:

First Congress.
1. National Revenue.
2. Tariff. { 1. Revenue. 2. Protective.
3. Executive Departments.
4. Treasury.
5. Courts.
6. Territories.
7. Amendments.
8. Funding the debt.

The Country.
1. Prosperity.
2. New ideas.
3. New states.

The Indians.
1. Tribes and numbers.
2. Wars.

Excise.
1. Reasons for the tax.
2. Resistance.

United States Bank.
1. Arguments. { 1. For. 2. Against.
2. Model and purpose.

Foreign Affairs and Home Politics.
1. Parties.
2. Leaders.
3. French influence.
4. Treaty with England.

Immigration and Growth.
1. Reasons for immigration.
2. Movement of population.

Washington's farewell advice.
Progress under the administration.

CHAPTER XIX.

1797-1801.

GOVERNMENT BY THE FEDERALISTS.

For Explanation. — Burly; stickler; stanch; naturalization law; aliens; sedition; concerted.

John Adams, *Massachusetts, President.*
Thomas Jefferson, *Virginia, Vice-President.*

Timothy Pickering, } State.
John Marshall,
Oliver Wolcott, } Treasury.
Samuel Dexter,
Benjamin Stoddert, Navy.

James McHenry, } War.
Samuel Dexter,
Roger Griswold,
Charles Lee, } Attorney-General.
Theophilus Parsons,

1. THE NEW ADMINISTRATION.

JOHN ADAMS.

400. The President and the Vice-President of the new administration stand out in American history in strong contrast. Adams, the Federalist, was stout and burly, a stickler for forms and ceremonies and English notions in dress and etiquette, an admirer of English aristocratic government, yet a true defender of freedom and representation of the people. Jefferson, tall and lank, careless of dress and social distinctions, a devotee to the new French ideas of equality and the "rights of man," saluted as the "friend of the people," yet lacked the warm nature of a popular leader.

What new department appears in the Cabinet of this Administration?

401. [**John Adams** was born in Massachusetts, in 1735. He graduated from Harvard College, became a lawyer, and one of the most prominent patriots and early statesmen. After serving in France (**295**) until the treaty of 1783, he went to England, the first representative of the United States at the court of Great Britain. He returned to America to serve as Vice-President with Washington (**361**). As President he desired to follow in Washington's path, and retained the old Cabinet. In doing this he made the mistake of trying to fit himself to another man's armor. These men were faithful to Washington, but when he was gone they looked to Hamilton for guidance, and not to Adams. Toward the end of his term Adams reorganized his Cabinet, but too late to make a harmonious administration.]

2. "Adams and Liberty."

402. Troubles with France made Adams's term an unquiet time. The French government, at war with the rest of Europe, but secure through the military achievements of Napoleon, wanted to make the United States pay tribute for peace. One minister was driven out of the country, and the capture of American ships by French war ships was unchecked. A special embassy sent by Adams met with trickery and double dealing, the only plain assurance being that bribes to the men controlling the French government would stop the offenses. The embassadors came home disgusted, and the angry President stated to Congress: "I will never send another minister to France without assurance that he will be received, respected, and honored as the representative of a great, free, powerful, and independent nation."

403. The bold stand of the President brought out the enthusiasm of the country. Sympathy for the French revolutionists had long since subsided, and now a baseless dread of being forced to serve a foreign power set the country wild. "Millions for defense, but not one cent for tribute," became the cry. "Towns and private societies, grand jurors, militia companies, merchants, the Cincinnati" (**345**), sent addresses to the President, approving his conduct. The badges of revolutionary patriots came out again, and a man found wearing the French tricolor was in danger of rough handling.

[Two new songs expressing the national sentiment were sung at every gathering. One, "Hail Columbia," written by Joseph Hopkinson, has become a lasting possession; the other, "Adams and Liberty," by Robert Treat Paine, Jr., although of equal poetic merit, passed away with the events that gave it life.]

404. [The **Federalist Congress** made actual preparation for war, establishing the Navy Department, building war frigates, and reorganizing the army with Washington at the head and Hamilton second. President Adams, honest and stanch, for once proudly felt himself a popular hero. Federalist newspapers grew rich, while the Republican papers nearly starved. Carried away by this burst of popularity, the Federalist leaders formed a scheme of permanently establishing their rule by silencing their opponents and putting free speech under checks. In this moment of their pride they ran counter to the spirit of American freedom and their downfall was sudden and forever.]

3. Downfall of the Federalists.

405. The Federalist Measures, 1798.—(1) A new *naturalization law* lengthened the time of residence necessary for citizenship from five to fourteen years, and required all white aliens to be registered so that they might be watched. (2) The *alien law* gave authority to the President for two years to compel any alien whom he thought dangerous to the peace of the United States to leave the country. (3) The *sedition law*, also temporary, made it a high misdemeanor, punishable by heavy fine and imprisonment, for any persons unlawfully to combine to oppose any law of the United States or to publish anything maliciously tending to bring the officers of the government into disrepute. The purpose of the naturalization law was to counteract the influence of foreigners, chiefly French, who generally sided with the Republicans.

[President Adams made no use of the authority given him by the alien law, but several persons were prosecuted under the sedition law, among them a Congressman from Vermont, who was fined and imprisoned for four months for publishing a letter accusing the administration of thirsting for power, turning worthy men out of office, etc.]

406. The Republicans opposed the alien and sedition laws with spirit in Congress and with defiance outside. The Federalists had designed them as war measures to protect the country from the emissaries of France, but the people regarded the sedition law as an attack on freedom of speech and of the press, and the Republican party grew stronger. The legislatures of Virginia and Kentucky, near the end of the year 1798, protested against the alien and sedition laws, boldly declaring them unconstitutional and therefore "of no force." These protests are the celebrated "Resolutions of '98." They expressed a dangerous doctrine of defiance to laws of the United States, a doctrine which came not from the people, but from a few party leaders. Many legislatures speedily condemned the spirit of the resolutions.

407. [**Resolutions of '98.**—Jefferson concerted these resolutions with Madison, and himself wrote the first draft of the Kentucky protest, Madison writing that of Virginia. Jefferson's first draft, which was modified before adoption, declared that whenever the General Government should abuse its authority under the Constitution, "a nullification of the act is the rightful remedy;" any state thus having the right to countermand a United States law, provided the state could set up the claim that the law was unconstitutional. Jefferson was never afterwards willing to father this doctrine of "nullification," and Madison, who thoroughly understood the Constitution, always disapproved it.]

408. The death of Washington occurred December 14th, 1799. Europe mourned his loss, and America felt that the shaft of death had pierced the heart of the nation, when the grave closed over its chieftain, "first in war, first in peace, and first in the hearts of his fellow-citizens." His noble character is summed up in these words, "the best of all great men, and the greatest of all good men."

409. The presidential election, in 1800, was a war of party leaders. Adams was again a candidate, and again did not receive the full Federalist support. The Republican electors all voted for Jefferson and Burr, who received seventy-three votes each, against sixty-five for Adams. According to the Constitution at that time, it was left for the House of Representatives to decide whether Jefferson or Burr should have the first place. Hence arose plots and schemes, many Federalists thinking that they would rather have Burr than Jefferson. The House spent several days in balloting, without a choice; but on the thirty-sixth count gave the presidency to Jefferson, clearly the people's choice from the beginning.

410. [**Adams** had saved the country from a war with France, and handed over to his successor a nation in prosperity, with a navy organized to protect American commerce in distant seas. But so much did Adams feel his defeat that he left Washington, now the seat of government, early in the morning of March 4th, 1801, that he might not be present at the inauguration of his rival. He spent the remainder of his life on his farm at Quincy, Massachusetts.]

QUESTIONS.

Read carefully Art. II., Sec. I., 3, of the Constitution, and Art. XII. of the Amendments. Then answer these questions:

What was meant in Adams's time by "the double chance" for the Presidency? What change is made by the amendment? What reasons were there for the change? How is the vote taken in the House? How many state votes were required to elect Jefferson?

SUMMARY.

Summarize this chapter under the following topics:

Government by the Federalists. { 1. Cause of popularity.
2. Acts passed. { 1. 2. 3.
3. Effect of legislation.

CHAPTER XX.
1801-1809.
New Ideas and a New Party.

For Explanation. — Traversing; installment; Moslem; Barbary States; corsairs; blockade.

To be Pronounced. — Bĕr′lin; Mil′an; Trĭp′o-li (le); Trĭp-ŏl′i-tans; re-div′i-va; Ful′ton.

Thomas Jefferson, *Virginia, President.*
Aaron Burr, *New York,* } *Vice-President.*
George Clinton, *New York,*

CABINET.

James Madison—State.
Albert Gallatin—Treasury.
Henry Dearborn—War.

Benjamin Stoddert, }
Robert Smith, } Navy.
J. Crowninshield, }

Levi Lincoln, } Attorney-General.
Robert Smith, }

Thomas Jefferson.

411. Inauguration.—The first two Presidents went to inauguration in carriages, attended by formal escorts, through the streets of populous cities. Through the bushes and trees then covering the site of Washington, Jefferson is said to have ridden, hitching his own horse in front of the unfinished capitol. His inaugural address "remains a model of its kind."

["Full of hope and confidence, he pictured a rising nation spread over a wide and fruitful land, traversing all the seas with the rich productions of their industry, engaged in commerce with nations who feel power and forget right, advancing rapidly to destinies beyond the reach of mortal eye." "I believe this," he said, "to be the strongest government on earth. I believe it is the only one where every man, at the call of the laws, would fly to the standard of the land, and would meet invasions of the public order as his own personal concern." He desired to secure equal justice to all men; peace, commerce, and honest friendship with all nations, the support of state governments, and the preservation of the general government, freedom of speech, of the press, and of religion; the encouragement of agriculture and commerce and general education. "Peace, and not pride," was the foundation of his system.]

412. [**Thomas Jefferson** was born in Virginia, in 1743. He had two years' study at William and Mary College (**138**). He became an eminent lawyer, and rendered public service in the Virginia House of Burgesses before going to Congress (**275**). He was Minister to France from the close of the war for independence until he returned to fill the office of Secretary of State in Washington's Cabinet. He was always an earnest student in science and literature.]

413. [**Changes in the Country.**—The change from Adams to Jefferson marks the change from eighteenth- to nineteenth-century ways. The Republicans made fun of the powdered wigs and stiff, ceremonious manners of the Federalists. On the other hand, the Federalists took counsel with one another, dreading the rule of mobs. Like many a fallen hero, they thought the country would perish with them. They sneered when dairymen expressed their admiration of the President by sending "the greatest cheese in America to the greatest man in America;" but when Jefferson cordially accepted and divided the cheese among his intimate friends, then the dignity of Federalism was horrified. The country, however, stood on the verge, not of ruin, but of wonderful progress. Public education began to improve. Newspapers gave up personal quarrels, and aimed for the higher office of news gatherers and public instructors.]

414. Inventions.—Attempts were made to construct mowing machines, for which there was great need in the level lands of the West. Successful machines, however, did not come into use until after 1835. Pennsylvania anthracite coal was discovered in 1791, but needing a powerful draft, it would not burn in the small open stoves in general use, and people considered it worthless. After a time, however, it was put to good service in large furnaces and steam engines. The *first successful steamboat*, the *Clermont*, was constructed in 1807, by Robert Fulton, of Pennsylvania.

415. [Fulton's Steamboat.—Several men in the United States, before Fulton, had tried to move boats with paddles revolved by steam power, but there was very little interest in the project until the development of the West brought the great rivers into the service of trade. Fulton went to France, and built a boat in 1804; but his heavy engine broke through the bottom and sank into the mud of the Seine. He returned to America and tried again, and this time his steamer, the *Clermont*, a side-wheeler, made a trip on the Hudson River, from New York to Albany, a distance of 150 miles, in thirty-two hours.]

416. Use of Steamboats.—Within a few years there were steamboats on all the western rivers, making travel easy, quick, and pleasant, and freighting, up stream or down, quick and cheap. New Orleans began to grow as the outlet of Mississippi trade. The country around Pittsburg furnished the iron for steamboat machinery, and coal for fuel. Lumber was plentiful all along the Ohio. The first steamboat on the Ohio was built in 1811; the first ocean steamer crossed the Atlantic from Savannah, Georgia, to England, in 1819.

[The steam engine is the invention of James Watt, a Scotchman, born in 1736. His engines came into use for stationary work about 1775.]

417. The purchase of Louisiana was Jefferson's great achievement. Louisiana had been ceded by Spain to France. Napoleon (387), at the head of France, and aiming to rule the world, had grand designs of a new French empire in America. But wars in Europe taxed the attention of Napoleon and the resources of France. Jefferson, believing in the growth of the country and seeing the danger of having an ambitious neighbor like France, opened propositions for purchase. James Monroe (455) was sent as special envoy to France, the President assuring him that "on the event of this mission depends the future destiny of the Republic." Napoleon being in need of money, and fearing that England would wrest the country from him, Louisiana was bought, in 1803, for $15,000,000. The barrier to American progress was now removed; the great river of rivers became the outlet of western commerce.

[Only a part of the purchase money was paid down. Eleven and one fourth millions were to be paid in annual installments after fifteen years, with interest at six per cent.]

418. Lewis and Clarke Expedition, 1804.—The territory purchased was an unknown land even to Americans. Jefferson, always interested in perfecting science, selected two army officers, Meriwether Lewis and William Clarke, and sent them to ascend the Missouri River to its headwaters. Their explorations were extended to the Pacific, giving to the public the first definite information about the Northwest, and to our government a fair claim to ownership of the Oregon country. (See Territorial Map of 1876.)

[The explorers set out in 1804 with a party well selected and equipped. They worked up the Missouri in small boats for 2,600 miles, then on wild horses, which they had caught, they crossed through the mountains to the streams flowing into the Columbia, which they followed to the sea. On the way they met many an Indian tribe that had never seen a white man. Two rivers preserve upon our maps the names of these explorers. The Columbia River had been discovered in 1792 by Robert Gray of Salem, Massachusetts, who sailed in the *Columbia Rediviva*.]

419. The navy, organized by Adams for war with France (**404**), now did good service against another foe. The Moslem princes of the Barbary States, from being robbers on land, had taken to the ocean and waged piratical warfare against Christian nations. Such was the fear of these corsairs that the nations of Europe paid heavy tribute to be let alone. Washington had made a treaty with Algiers, and the ransom of prisoners had cost the country a million dollars. Another million had been paid for a so called respect for our country's flag. But bribes only tempted the pirates to further outrages. In 1800 the Dey of Algiers had compelled an American man-of-war to carry his dispatches to Constantinople, and thus the first American man-of-war to enter the Bosporus was seen under a pirate flag. In 1801 the tribute was stopped. American men-of-war visited the Mediterranean to fight, not to serve, Algiers, and a few brisk encounters brought the Barbary powers to honorable terms in 1805.

420. [**The war** was chiefly with Tripoli. One especially brave achievement is remembered. A United States frigate, the Philadelphia, had run aground in the harbor of Tripoli and been captured by the Tripolitans. Lieutenant Stephen Decatur, a few days afterwards, with twenty picked men, entered the harbor and burned the prize.]

421. The Napoleonic wars, which filled all Europe with alarm from the beginning of the century until the great battle of Waterloo (1815), cast their shadows over America and made the last years of Jefferson's administration dark with coming trouble. England's strong navy began to blockade the harbors of France in 1806. Napoleon answered with his *Berlin Decree*, which ordered the vessels of all nations to keep out of British ports. By the *Orders in Council* of 1807, England ordered American ships to keep out of every European port except those of Great Britain and Sweden, then her friend. Napoleon retorted with his *Milan Decree*, ordering any American vessel which was caught entering a British harbor to be seized and sold.

[The Berlin and Milan Decrees were named for the places whence Napoleon issued them.]

422. American commerce came near to ruin between these two ferocious powers. America hardly knew which one to fight, and the President did not approve fighting either. England had the best navy in the world, and did the most damage to our commerce. Moreover, England was in need of sailors, and claimed the right to search American vessels, and to take off men, on the ground that they were English subjects or runaways from the English navy.

[In 1807 the *Leopard*, a British war frigate, fired upon the United States war frigate *Chesapeake*, off the Chesapeake Bay, killing three men and wounding eighteen. Four men, claimed to be British deserters, were taken from the *Chesapeake*. This outrage was sufficient grounds for war. "This country has never been in such a state of excitement since Lexington," wrote Jefferson. However, he decided not on war but on an embargo.]

CHAPTER XXI.
1809-1817.
YOUNG AMERICA AND THE WAR OF 1812.

For Explanation.—Hotspur; sail; flag ship; catastrophe; pennant; laconic; tactics; dismantled; hulk; mediator.

James Madison, *Virginia, President.*
George Clinton, *New York,* } *Vice-President.*
Elbridge Gerry, *Massachusetts,*

CABINET.

Robert Smith, James Monroe, } State.	William Eustis, John Armstrong, James Monroe, Wm. H. Crawford, George Graham, } War.		
Albert Gallatin, Geo. W. Campbell, Alexander J. Dallas, Wm. H. Crawford, } Treasury.			
Paul Hamilton, William Jones, } Navy.	Cæsar A. Rodney, William Pinckney, Richard Rush, } Attorney-General.		

428. Madison was the last of the presidents who had taken active part in founding the government. The three presidents before him were men of strong characters and masterful wills. After him come presidents who are able to stand first, not so much by their own wills as by consulting the views of others. As the country grows, party organizations strengthen, and the presidents become not so much the makers as the representatives of party doctrines. Madison belongs with the first three presidents in his early services, but to the latter class in his methods of administration.

429. [**James Madison** was born in Virginia in 1751. After graduating at Princeton, he became a lawyer. He entered public service as a member of the Virginia legislature, served for four years in the Continental Congress (1780-84), and was again in the legislature. He was one of the foremost men in the Constitutional Convention (1787), and in the first Congress (1789). After serving in Congress for eight years, he was Jefferson's Secretary of State. He was not a natural orator, and one year he lost an election to the Virginia legislature from weakness as a speaker, and from refusing to treat voters. Yet he was always a clear reasoner, and long practice made him an effective public speaker. With the Republicans elected their candidate, James Madison, the friend, and, to a considerable extent, the disciple of Jefferson.

[The Federalist nominees in 1804 and 1808 were Charles C. Pinckney of South Carolina, and Rufus King of New York. In 1804 they received fourteen, and in 1808 forty-seven electoral votes out of 176.]

427. [Jefferson, who had regained the friendship of John Adams, like him, retired to the quiet of his home, Monticello, Virginia; no longer active, but still interested in the country, the character of which his ideas had done much to form. " Liberal education, liberal religion, a free press, America for Americans, faith in the simple arts of peace, in science and material progress, in popular rule, in honesty in government economies; no kings, no caste, room for the oppressed of all climes; hostility to monopolies, the divorce of government from banks and pet corporations; foreign friendship and intercourse with foreign alliance; faith in the indefinite expansion of this union on this continent,—all this, though others inculcated some of these maxims too, is Jeffersonism, and Jeffersonism is modern America."—*Schouler*.]

REVIEW.

Two parallel threads run through the history of Jefferson's terms. On one lies the growth and improvement of the country. On the other, a situation in foreign affairs that brought trouble to Americans. Under these lines, make a list of events, with a note explaining each.

Growth and Improvement.
1. Change.
2. Inventions.
3. Use of steamboats.
4. New territory.
5. Exploration.

Foreign Affairs.
1. Barbary States.
2. European Wars. { 1. Commercial Orders. 2. Results to America.
3. Embargo. . . { 1. Plan. 2. Results.

CHAPTER XXI.
1809-1817.
Young America and the War of 1812.

For Explanation.—Hotspur; sail; flag ship; catastrophe; pennant; laconic; tactics; dismantled; hulk; mediator.

James Madison, *Virginia, President.*
George Clinton, *New York,* } *Vice-President.*
Elbridge Gerry, *Massachusetts,* }

CABINET.

Robert Smith, } State.
James Monroe, }
Albert Gallatin,
Geo. W. Campbell, } Treasury.
Alexander J. Dallas,
Wm. H. Crawford, }
Paul Hamilton, } Navy.
William Jones, }

William Eustis,
John Armstrong,
James Monroe, } War.
Wm. H. Crawford,
George Graham,
Cæsar A. Rodney, }
William Pinckney, } Attorney-General.
Richard Rush,

428. Madison was the last of the presidents who had taken active part in founding the government. The three presidents before him were men of strong characters and masterful wills. After him come presidents who are able to stand first, not so much by their own wills as by consulting the views of others. As the country grows, party organizations strengthen, and the presidents become not so much the makers as the representatives of party doctrines. Madison belongs with the first three presidents in his early services, but to the latter class in his methods of administration.

429. [**James Madison** was born in Virginia in 1751. After graduating at Princeton, he became a lawyer. He entered public service as a member of the Virginia legislature, served for four years in the Continental Congress (1780-84), and was again in the legislature. He was one of the foremost men in the Constitutional Convention (1787), and in the first Congress (1789). After serving in Congress for eight years, he was Jefferson's Secretary of State. He was not a natural orator, and one year he lost an election to the Virginia legislature from weakness as a speaker, and from refusing to treat voters. Yet he was always a clear reasoner, and long practice made him an effective public speaker. With great mental powers there was "united a pure and spotless virtue which no calumny has ever attempted to sully." (See portrait, p. 184.)]

430. [**Indian Outbreak.**—In dealing with the Indians it was the plan of President Jefferson to purchase their land by fair bargains, and carefully to respect the treaties. For several years there had been no Indian troubles, but in 1811 there was a fresh outbreak among the Wabash Indians in the Northwest. The Indians felt the loss of the fur market caused by the war in Europe, and contact with the frontier traders had given them acquaintance with firearms and frontier whisky. Tecumseh, a chief, eloquent, brave, and crafty, aided by his brother, a pretended prophet, stirred up an insurrection which was bravely and skillfully met by William Henry Harrison, Governor of Indiana Territory (513). With a force made up of settlers and volunteers from Kentucky, Harrison fought a hot battle at the Indian village of Tippecanoe, near the present site of Lafayette, Indiana, defeating and scattering the Indians. This victory stopped the Indian troubles and gave fame to Harrison. The country believed that the Indians had been set on by English agents, and this belief increased the hatred for England.]

431. The War-cloud Darkens.—Madison was for a firm attitude toward both England and France, with preparation for armed defense, but he could not enforce his policy in Congress. Dissension ruled among the Republican leaders, including the Cabinet. The non-intercourse law (426) was given up in 1810. Then Napoleon, deceitfully representing that he had repealed his offensive decrees, non-intercourse was revived against England alone, who instantly became more aggressive than ever. Our country was swept rapidly on to a war with England. British cruisers watched American shores, trying to capture ships bound for France, and occasionally overhauling American ships and pressing American seamen into British service. Interference with American commerce and the impressment of American seamen led to the war of 1812 (**436**).

432. ["**Little Belt**" **and** "**President.**"—In one of these affairs the British sloop-of-war *Little Belt* was riddled with balls by the American frigate *President.* Each vessel claimed that the other fired first.]

433. The Rising Generation.—The Republicans were still the ruling party, but its leaders were new and younger men. The country wanted active measures in place of the worn out peace policy of Jefferson, and the neutrality which no European nation respected. "War men" were the favorites in Congressional elections, and this was the chance for young aspirants. The presence of this new element in American affairs, the power of men who had grown since the Revolution, and the fact that the original thirteen states no longer controlled the Union, are shown by the election of Henry Clay as Speaker of the House of Representatives, in 1811.

434. [**Henry Clay** was a Virginian by birth, the son of a Baptist clergyman, whose death left a widow and seven small children with very meager support. A poor boy with no one to depend upon but himself, he managed to get a little schooling, and afterwards a knowledge of law sufficient for admission to the Virginia bar. He began practice at Lexington, Kentucky, rose to fame as a criminal lawyer, and then entered political life in the Kentucky legislature. He was twice elected to fill vacancies in the United States Senate before his election as a Representative in 1811. On the very day of his appearance in the House he was elected Speaker. When this "tall, slender son of Kentucky, with long brown hair, blue eyes, large mouth, peaked nose, and shaven face," took into his hand the Speaker's gavel, he began a public career of forty years, ending only with death. His power was in his eloquence, bold, strong, and flashing with fire, which warmed even the cold-hearted and made the timid bold. (See portrait, p. 243.)]

435. [**John C. Calhoun**, of South Carolina, was another of the young Hotspurs of the House, as they were called from their zeal for war. Calhoun entered the House of Representatives with Clay, was for a time his friend and political companion, and for about the same period equally conspicuous in public affairs. He was, however, a man of far different character. Born in South Carolina, in 1782, grave and handsome in appearance, of Irish lineage, a graduate of Yale College, a successful lawyer, careful, studious, and tireless, Calhoun also entered Congress through the legislature of his state. He had eloquence clear, plain, concise, and logical, but seldom impassioned like Clay's. The public career of the two men forms a large part of the history of the United States government until 1850. (See portrait, p. 243.)]

436. **War against Great Britain** was declared by Congress June 18th, 1812. Considerable preparation had been made by the United States. The influence of the western states, where there was little confidence in the United States

navy, caused the greater preparation to be made for operations on land, chiefly with a view toward invading Canada. The United States had no trained army, not even experienced officers. Armies were raised and put in charge of men who were appointed for political reasons, and knew nothing of war; and consequently the Americans were beaten in nearly every land fight, until the forces were reorganized and drilled under competent officers. The British navy, numbering nearly 1,000 sail, some of them the most powerful vessels known, sneered at the little United States frigates, a dozen in number. Yet our seamen won many a brilliant fight, surprising their own countrymen as well as the people of England.

437. [**The United States Military Academy** was established at West Point in 1802, with a small number of cadets, who were trained chiefly in artillery and military engineering. In 1812 the work was extended, and has since included full instruction in all matters of military science, with a liberal education in mathematics, French, and general sciences. Each congressional district is entitled to have one cadet at West Point, appointed by the Congressman. The District of Columbia and the territories have one each, appointed by the Secretary of War, and the President appoints ten more at large. The United States allows each cadet his rations and $500 a year, against which are charged all his expenses for clothes, books, etc. Cadets are admitted between the ages of seventeen and twenty-one, upon examinations showing perfect soundness of body and proficiency in the English language, arithmetic, geography, and United States history. On graduation they receive commissions in the United States military service.]

438. **Opposition to the war** was very strong in New England, where the Federalists had still a great deal of strength. Always favoring England rather than France, they now condemned the war as useless. This opposition grew worse as the war went on; but it brought no return of power to the Federalists. Madison came out for reëlection in 1812, as a war candidate, and was successful.

[Madison received 128 electoral votes out of 218. The Federalists voted for De Witt Clinton of New York, nominated by a part of the Republicans as a better war manager than Madison.]

THE SONS OF THE FOUNDERS DEFEND THE FLAG. 223

WAR OF 1812.

439. On to Canada had been the cry of the war party, and the fighting began on the Canada frontier in 1812. Congress had planned an army of 25,000, but for a long time there were very few disciplined troops. General Henry Dearborn was commander-in-chief.

MILITARY MOVEMENTS ON THE NORTHERN FRONTIER.

Map Questions.—Estimate by the scale the length of the northern frontier from Fort Meigs to Plattsburg. Are there any natural barriers to land troops along the line? Where were the natural entrances to Canada? Did these become battle-grounds? (See **442**.) Why was a lake navy extremely valuable to either side? From what states were troops likely to be sent to Detroit? To Sackett's Harbor? To Plattsburg? Make, from the map, a list of battles, in the order of occurrence, by the following Model:

Date.	Name and Locality.	American Commander. (See Text.)	Results. (See Text.)

440. Movements in 1812.—General William Hull, Governor of Michigan, had 2,000 men at Detroit. He set out to capture the British fort at Malden, but became frightened and returned. Then the British commander, General Brock, besieged Detroit, and Hull quickly surrendered with about half his force, the other half being absent on detached expeditions. Next, a body of regular troops and New York militia, under General Van Rensselaer, assembled on the Niagara and invaded Canada. On Queenstown Heights they fought the British troops under Brock, and gained a temporary advantage, Brock being killed. Later the Americans, now commanded by Lieutenant-Colonel Winfield Scott, but not reinforced, were driven from their ground and compelled to surrender. The American loss was about 1,000 men.

441. Movements in 1813.—Our forces were arranged in three divisions—the Army of the West (Michigan), General William H. Harrison; the Army of the Center (Western New York), General Henry Dearborn; the Army of the East (around Lake Champlain), General Wade Hampton. In January a part of Harrison's army, under General Winchester, was surprised at Frenchtown (now Monroe), on the River Raisin, by Indians and British troops under Colonel Henry Proctor. The Americans surrendered, and were massacred by the Indians. Harrison built Fort Meigs, which Proctor attacked, but failed to capture. Later, Proctor and Tecumseh, the Indian chief, made an attack on Fort Stephenson and were repulsed. General Dearborn transported troops from Sackett's Harbor and captured York (now Toronto), an unimportant place and abandoned in a few days. Dearborn next landed his troops near the mouth of the Niagara, captured Fort George, and in time gained the Niagara frontier, but lost most of it shortly after. In Dearborn's absence a British attack on Sackett's Harbor was beaten off by General Jacob Brown, with troops hastily gathered in New York. Dearborn was superseded.

442. On the lakes in 1813 we made up for our failures on land. At Presque Isle (now Erie) an American squadron was built, supplied with guns, and placed under command of Captain Oliver H. Perry of Rhode Island. In August,

Perry sailed out to meet the British fleet, and gained a brilliant victory September 10th, 1813. Ships were built on Lakes Ontario and Champlain, and these lake fleets were of constant service throughout the war.

443. [Perry's Victory.—"In officers and men the fleets were about equally matched; there were six British vessels to the American nine, but the former carried more guns, and were greatly superior for action from a distance. With thirty long guns to Perry's fifteen, Barclay (British commander) had the decided advantage at first, and our flagship, the *Lawrence*, exposed to the heaviest of the British cannonade, became terribly battered, her decks wet with carnage, her guns dismounted. Undismayed by this catastrophe, Perry dropped into a little boat, with his broad pennant and banner, and crossed to his next largest vessel, the *Niagara*, the target for fifteen minutes of a furious fire while being rowed over. Climbing the *Niagara's* deck, and hoisting once more the emblems of commander, our brave captain now pierced the enemy's line with his new flagship, and, gaining at last the advantage of a close engagement, which nearly three hours had eluded him, he won the fight in eight minutes. . . . . 'We have met the enemy, and they are ours,' was Perry's laconic dispatch to Harrison, written in pencil on the back of an old letter, with his navy cap for a rest; 'two ships, two brigs, one schooner, and one sloop.'"—*Schouler.*]

444. Battle of the Thames.—Perry's victory opened the way for Harrison's army to enter Canada. It won a fierce battle on the River Thames (October 5th), in which the Indians held out to the end, their chief, Tecumseh, being among the slain. The British commander, Proctor, escaped in a carriage. Harrison captured Malden.

445. Land movements in 1814 were more skillfully conducted. Failures had taught the need of discipline. The government displaced incompetent officers, and reorganized the army, the work going on slowly under the direction of General Jacob Brown and Colonel Winfield Scott, who had to translate a book from French, in order to get any satisfactory system of tactics. In July, Brown crossed the Niagara with his new army, defeating the British force at Chippewa Creek (July 5th). Their numbers being increased, they fought our army, from sunset to midnight, at Lundy's Lane (July 25th). Both armies suffered, but ours had the advantage. Both Brown and Scott were wounded, and the advantage was not followed up. During the summer, fresh troops were sent to Canada to invade our country by Burgoyne's route (303). Their advance was checked by our fleet on Lake Champlain, which fought and defeated the British fleet in the harbor of Plattsburg (September 11th, 1814). The invasion was then given up.

[Commodore Thomas Macdonough commanded our fleet. The enemy was under Commodore Downie. Macdonough had four war vessels and ten gunboats—in all eighty-six guns and 882 men, of whom he lost about 200. Downie had four war vessels and twelve gunboats, carrying ninety-two guns and 937 men. His loss was about 300. Macdonough announced his victory in the dispatch: "The Almighty has been pleased to grant us a signal victory on Lake Champlain, in the capture of one frigate, one brig, and two sloops-of-war of the enemy."]

446. British Ravages on the Coast.—British fleets had blockaded our shore during 1813 and 1814. At first they spared New England, as a friend to them; but soon they extended their depredations from Maine to Georgia, burning defenseless towns and seizing private property. The larger cities were defended by torpedoes, and New York by a floating battery, the invention of Robert Fulton, and the beginning of steam gunboats. In 1814 the British took possession of Maine as far as the Penobscot River, causing great alarm throughout New England.

447. Capture of Washington.—In August, 1814, a British fleet arrived in the Chesapeake, with an army of 5,000 men, under General Ross. Our capital was without defense, and fell an easy prey to the invaders. The government officers escaped, but the capitol and other public buildings were burned. Baltimore was the next point of attack. It made a brave and successful resistance. The British land force was repulsed, Lord Ross being among the slain. The fleet bombarded Fort McHenry all night, without reducing it. Fleet and troops were now withdrawn—the fleet to continue plundering along the coast, the army to join an expedition against New Orleans.

THE SONS OF THE FOUNDERS DEFEND THE FLAG. 227

[Our total loss in the capture of Washington was about $2,000,000. Our most valuable government papers had been removed, but the British vandals spared not even the library of Congress. The attack on Fort McHenry was the occasion of the familiar song, "The Star Spangled Banner," written by Francis S. Key, who had fallen into the hands of the British, and was detained on a vessel in the harbor. He composed the song while anxiously pacing the deck of the vessel during the early morning hours, watching to see if our flag still floated over Fort McHenry.]

Map Questions.—Has Washington any natural defenses? Was it protected by neighboring forts? Was there any reason why Baltimore could be defended more successfully than Washington?

448. War in the south was waged between the Indians, fighting in the interest of the British, and militia from the southern states under the command of Andrew Jackson of Tennessee. Jackson was entirely successful in subduing the Creeks, the most hostile tribe, and he was put in charge of military affairs in the south, with a commission as major-general. By energetic management he was ready to defend New Orleans against a British army of 12,000, which arrived in December, 1814, under Sir Edward Packenham. There were several night attacks and skirmishes, with no advantage on either side. On January 8th, 1815, the whole British army moved forward to attack Jackson's inferior force, protected, however, by hasty intrenchments. That

Map Questions.—Did the region around New Orleans offer any barriers to the approach of land troops from the southward? Why would the possession of New Orleans have been valuable to the British?
(Read Lessons 84, 95, and 106, California Second Reader.)

assault was terribly fatal to the British army. Packenham was killed, and what was left of his army retired to the ships and sailed to the West Indies.

[The secret purpose of the attack on New Orleans was to capture and hold it after the conclusion of peace, as a means of wresting from us the territory of the Louisiana purchase. Jackson's closing victory was the most creditable of the land exploits and made him the hero of the war. In the battle the British loss was over 2,500. Jackson had eight men killed and thirteen wounded.]

449. On the Ocean.—Our navy began its brave and successful work immediately after the declaration of war, and continued it until after the treaty of peace. The *Essex*, Captain Porter, made the first capture (August 13th, 1812), taking the *Alert* after a fight of only eight minutes. The first duel between ships equally matched was fought off the Gulf of St. Lawrence (August 19th), by our frigate *Constitution*, forty-four guns, Captain Isaac Hull, and the British frigate *Guerriere*, thirty-eight guns, Captain Dacres. There was no advantage in either ship, and bravery and skill decided the fight. After a skirmish at long range, the ships grappled, tried to board, and again cut loose. At the end of the fight the British frigate was a dismantled hulk, while the *Constitution* was in good trim, with only fourteen men lost. Never before had an English frigate hauled down her colors in equal fight. We had invaded Great Britain's empire of the sea. It was the beginning of a series of naval contests which made America rejoice and England grow alarmed, which, more than anything else, gained honorable terms for us at the end of the war, and which brought the powers of Europe to respect the rights of commerce on the high seas.

[Our ship-builders had been studying their business, and they turned out new ships that were improved sailers. Our gunners had put sights on their guns, while the Englishmen still handled their guns without sights. Moreover our captains and seamen were fighting for the honor of their country, and to win respect where they had been subjected to insults.]

450. Peace had come to Europe in 1814 through the overthrow of Napoleon (387), allowing Great Britain to send her armies against us. Negotiations for peace with Great Britain were under way during almost the whole war. In 1813 the Emperor of Russia offered to act as umpire to decide the question of our war, and our representatives went at once to St. Petersburg. Great Britain was not so prompt to accept Russia as a mediator. Finally, the English ambassadors met ours at Ghent, a city of Belgium, and, after an argumentative skirmish of several months, a treaty was agreed upon (December 24th, 1814), very satisfactory to both parties. This treaty of Ghent left all the original questions of the war unmentioned; nevertheless, they were practically settled, for the American flag has never since been treated with disrespect on the high seas. Our boundaries remained the same as before the war.

[Knowledge of the treaty would have prevented the battle of New Orleans, and also the four naval combats of 1815; but news traveled slowly in those days. A British sloop-of-war, under a flag of truce, brought the treaty to New York, February 11th, 1815. From that point messengers on horseback hurried the good news through the land.]

TABLE OF COMBATS ON THE OCEAN—WAR OF 1812.

American.			British.		
Ship.	Commander.		Ship.	Date.	
Essex	Porter	Captures	Alert	Aug. 13	
Constitution	Hull	Captures	Guerriere	Aug. 19	
Wasp	Jacob Jones	Captures	Frolic	Oct. 18	1812
Wasp	Jacob Jones	Is captured by	Poictiers	Oct. 18	
United States	Decatur	Captures	Macedonian	Oct. 25	
Constitution	Bainbridge	Captures	Java	Dec. 29	
Hornet	Lawrence	Captures	Peacock	Feb. 24	
Essex	Porter	Captures	Sever'l prizes on the Pacific		
Chesapeake	Lawrence	Is captured by	Shannon	June 1	1813
Argus	Allen	Is captured by	Pelican	Aug. 14	
Enterprise	Burrows	Captures	Boxer	Sept. 5	
Essex	Porter	Is captured by	{ Phœbe { Cherub	Mch. 28	
Peacock	Warrington	Captures	Epervier	Apr. 28	1814
Wasp	Blakeley	Captures	Reindeer	June 28	
Wasp	Blakeley	Captures	Avon	Sept. 1	
President	Decatur	Is captured by	A fleet	Jan. 15	
Constitution	Stewart	Captures	{ Cyane { Levant	Feb. 20	1815
Hornet	Biddle	Captures	Penguin	Mch. 23	
Peacock	Warrington	Captures	Nautilus	June 30	

Merchantmen captured by Americans, about 1,800.
Merchantmen captured by British, about 500.

THE SONS OF THE FOUNDERS DEFEND THE FLAG. 231

451. The Hartford Convention.—The New England dissatisfaction with the war **(438)** culminated in a convention of twenty-six Federalist politicians, at Hartford, Connecticut (December 18th, 1814). They represented the New England states, but hardly the New England public sentiment. Their sessions were secret, but the general belief credited them with a plan to rebel against the United States in case of further continuance of the war. This belief was the finishing stroke to the Federalist party. Nothing ever came from the work of the convention, for the war had ended successfully. The news of peace and of Jackson's victory traveled through the land, filling it with rejoicing. The convention published a report calling for several constitutional amendments, chiefly to restrict the power of Congress in declaring war and in laying embargoes on commerce. This convention represented the doctrine of state sovereignty as opposed to the sovereignty of the United States, but the unpopularity of its schemes shows how strong the love for the national government was becoming.]

452. Difficulties and Lessons of the War.—Our country began the war with the spirited plan of conquering Canada **(439)**, but in a short time was hard pushed to defend our northern line. It was difficult and expensive work to maintain armies along an almost uninhabited frontier, and impossible to support them in an enemy's country. New England, the most populous and wealthy section, had held aloof, and the sudden peace in Europe set free the British armies. The true strength of the country was shown when it became necessary to repel invasion. The war showed the need of trained soldiers and sailors. The army was never again reduced to Jefferson's standard; the navy was kept up. The spirit of rebellion died with the war. The trust of the country was lodged more deeply in the national government, as our security against oppression from abroad and jealous strife at home.

453. The end of Madison's administration found the country rapidly regaining prosperity. Imports increased with the revival of commerce, and the tariff yielded a revenue to pay the national debt (about $127,000,000 in 1815, $80,000,000 due to the war). Our navy had again brought the Barbary States to terms, and made them pay for ships they had captured during our war with Great Britain. James Monroe had done efficient duty in Madison's cabinet, and the Republicans chose him as Madison's successor. He was elected with very little opposition. Daniel D. Tompkins, who had been the "war governor" of New York, was elected Vice-President.

[The Federalists voted for Rufus King, of New York, for President. Monroe had 183 electoral votes; King only thirty-four.]

REVIEW.

Copy and complete the following review:

War of 1812—Conducted by what party and what leaders in Congress?

- Causes.
  - 1.
  - 2.
- Chief events.
  - 1. Unsuccessful invasion of Canada.
  - 2.
  - 3.
  - 4.
  - 5.
- Treaty of Ghent.
  - 1.
  - 2.
- Results.
  - 1. Need of an army and navy realized.
  - 2.
  - 3.
  - 4.

Make a table of the military events of the war like that on page 176.

CHAPTER XXII.
1817-1825.
North and South Set a Dividing Line.

For Explanation.—Diversified; paramount; tide water; caucus; dubbed; paralytic.

James Monroe, *Virginia, President.*
Daniel D. Tompkins, *New York, Vice-President.*

CABINET.

John Quincy Adams—State.	B. W. Crowninshield, }
Wm. H. Crawford—Treasury.	Smith Thompson, } Navy.
	Samuel L. Southard, }
George Graham, } War.	Richard Rush, } Attorney-General.
John C. Calhoun, }	William Wirt, }

---

454. **The era of good feeling** is the name often given to the time of President Monroe's first term. The Federalist party was dead, and no new division into parties had yet been made. For twelve years all candidates and almost all voters claimed to be Republicans. Political conflicts were calmed, and the nation, now free from foreign interference, strode forward toward wealth and power.

455. [James Monroe was born in Virginia in 1758. His studies at William and Mary College (138) were interrupted by the outbreak of the Revolution, and he joined the continental army together with most of the professors and students. He served with credit as a captain, and after the war studied law under Jefferson. He was elected to the Virginia legislature, and afterwards to the Continental Congress. He opposed the Constitution, but was chosen United States Senator in the first Congress. He was envoy to France (1794-7); Governor of Virginia (1799); envoy to France, Spain, and England (1803); again in Virginia legislature (1810); Governor in 1811, and Madison's Secretary of War (1811-17). He followed Jefferson in politics. At his second election as President he received every electoral vote but one. He died at New York in 1831.]

456. **Florida** was the ground of a new Indian war, and of a new purchase. Runaway slaves from Georgia had always found shelter among the Seminole Indians of Florida. During the war of 1812 the Seminoles had received

arms from English officers. Georgians were annoyed by the hostility of the Seminoles, and especially by the shelter given to runaway slaves. Florida was Spanish territory, but Spain was too weak to maintain authority. During 1817 there were frequent fights on the frontier. General Andrew Jackson, in command of the United States troops in the south, brought the long standing troubles to a close in a daring and reckless manner. Being ordered to take charge in Georgia, he immediately entered Florida, laid waste the Seminole country, seized Pensacola, a Spanish post, and hanged two British subjects on the charge of inciting the Seminoles to commit depredations. In five months he had conquered Florida. Jackson's violent acts gave the government trouble with both England and Spain, but increased his popularity, especially in the South. Pensacola was given back to Spain, but further negotiations resulted in the purchase of Florida for $5,000,000.

[Although the purchase was made in 1819 the treaty was not fully confirmed until 1821. It settled a dispute about the line between Louisiana and Texas, yielding to Spain all land west of the Sabine River.]

457. Negro slavery had at times entered into many public questions, but did not by itself challenge the attention of the country till about 1820. Washington's advice against geographical parties (**395**) was set aside when southern slave labor and northern free labor spread westward into new territory along parallel lines. Time only increased the difference in social and business habits between the two sections, and this difference tended to separate them in politics.

458. [**Conflicting Interests.**—The early leaders, like Jefferson, who had struggled to abolish slavery (**379**), or at least to pen it up within its ancient bounds, failed. The South was gradually given up to the few industries for which slave labor was practicable. On the other hand, commerce and manufactures were developed at the North, side by side with a diversified agriculture. Hence arose a conflict of interests between North and South, revealing itself in national affairs, especially in the discussion of tariff questions.]

459. New States and Slavery.—Owing to the more rapid increase of population at the North (**393**), the South feared that the slave states would, in time, be overwhelmingly outnumbered in Congress. It therefore became southern policy to oppose the admission of free states, and to increase as rapidly as possible the number of states admitted with slavery. New England, on the other hand, opposed the admission of new states in the southwest, for with the decay of Federalism it seemed to New England that her power was passing from her. The matter of the extension of the slave system came up as a paramount question in 1818, when the people of Missouri applied for admission to the Union, with a constitution permitting slavery. Congress had agreed that it had no power to interfere with slavery, either in state or territory where it had existed at the beginning of the government. Now there was a new question: "Shall slavery be legalized in territory where there were no slaves when the United States gained possession?"

[After Vermont and Kentucky (**378**) new states were admitted as follows: Tennessee, 1796, Ohio, 1802, and Louisiana, 1812—two with slavery and one without. Then Indiana, 1816, was followed by Mississippi, 1817; and Illinois, 1818, by Alabama, 1819—a free state paired off with a slave state each time.]

460. Missouri Compromise.—For three years the question of the admission of Missouri was debated in Congress. A majority of the House opposed her admission as a slave state; a majority in the Senate favored it. The contest was practically ended in 1820, by a measure known in history as the Missouri Compromise, arranged chiefly by Henry Clay, Speaker of the House. This measure provided for admitting Maine as a free state, and Missouri as a slave state; but it prohibited slavery forever in all the rest of the Louisiana purchase north of the parallel 36° 30′, the southern boundary of Missouri.

[The compromise bill was passed by a large **majority in both houses.**]

461. [**The Negro Republic, Liberia,** on the west coast of Africa, was founded in 1822, and honors President Monroe in the name of its capital, Monrovia. The republic was the work of the American Colonization Society, organized in 1817, for the return of freed negroes to their native land. Several prominent men were connected with the society, but our government never took part in its work.]

462. Internal Improvements.—Secretary of War Calhoun recommended to Congress a system of roads and canals, not only to facilitate commerce and the transportation of United States mails, but also as the best means of defense in time of war. This plan of employing national funds for internal improvements had been generally disapproved by Jefferson and his followers. Congress, however, undertook the construction of a national road with easy grades and strong bridges, for the use of the westward emigrants. This road, known as the Cumberland road, beginning at Cumberland, Maryland, was extended into Ohio, and finally into Indiana.

463. The Erie Canal extends from Buffalo to Albany, joining Lake Erie with tide water on the Hudson. This great work had been proposed to the national government before the war of 1812, but the government declined, and the canal was finally constructed by the state of New York, chiefly through the influence of DeWitt Clinton, governor of the state during most of Monroe's administration. Clinton's "Big Ditch" was strongly opposed as a useless expenditure of public money. Its first cost was $7,600,000, nearly half of which the canal has sometimes paid in a year's earnings. It is now operated by the state of New York without any charge to the persons using it. It has connections with the central lakes in New York, and with the Alleghany, St. Lawrence, and Susquehanna Rivers. The success of the Erie Canal led other states to follow the example of New York.

464. The Monroe Doctrine.—Spain held to the plan of

taxing American colonies to the last dollar she could wring from them, until the decline of her power, and her weakness after the Napoleonic wars (387), enabled them to win independence. The entire Spanish possessions on the American Continents thus passed from her control. After establishing their independence, the colonies began to form republics. At this point several of the great monarchies of Europe were disposed to interfere, and to help Spain reconquer her lost possessions. England, however, protested, and declared for the independence of Spanish-American republics. These events were referred to in the message of President Monroe to Congress, December, 1823, and his words on that occasion contained what has become known as the Monroe Doctrine. Briefly stated, it is as follows: 1. No more European colonies on the Western continents. 2. No more extension of European monarchical systems this side of the Atlantic. 3. No European interference with Spanish-American republics.

[These principles are in accordance with Washington's advice to keep free from European politics, and with Jefferson's idea of America for Americans. They are broad principles of American patriotism, plainly stated by a patriotic President. Monroe's firm stand was in accordance with the advice of Adams, his Secretary of State, whose long residence in Europe made him well qualified to advise. It might be called also the doctrine of Washington, Jefferson, Adams, or any genuine American.]

465. Lafayette, who had survived the perils of the French Revolution (386), was invited in 1824 to visit our land, for whose independence he had fought in the days of his youth. Now an old man of sixty-eight, accompanied by his son, George Washington Lafayette, he spent a year in a tour through the country, so wonderfully changed since the war for Independence. Then every state touched salt water, and now there were states beyond the Mississippi. Everywhere he was received with rejoicing, and treated as the nation's guest. He was present at the laying of the corner-stone of Bunker Hill monument, June 17th, 1825, the oration being delivered by Daniel Webster (473). At the end of his visit, he was carried back to France in a new United States frigate, the *Brandywine*, so called in honor of Lafayette's share in the battle of that name (291). The United States also made him a present of $200,000, and a township of public lands.

[Bunker Hill monument was completed in 1842, and dedicated the following year, Webster again being the orator of the day. The monument cost something over $150,000.]

466. The presidential election, in 1824, was a personal struggle between numerous candidates, all of them claiming to be Republicans. Up to this time there were no great party conventions, such as we have now, to nominate candidates, and nominations were usually made by a caucus of Congressmen. William H. Crawford, of Georgia, who had entered Congress with Clay (434) and Calhoun (435), was the caucus

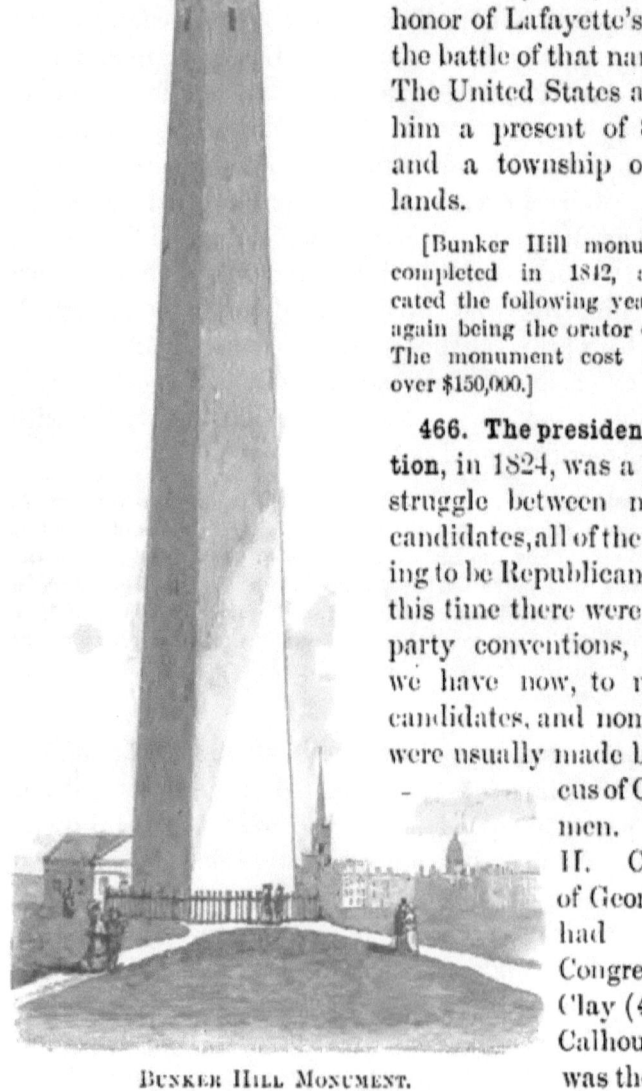

BUNKER HILL MONUMENT.

nominee for President. John Quincy Adams (**468**) was a candidate, and having served as Secretary of State stood in the line of promotion, which several elections had established. Andrew Jackson (**479**) was a candidate, as a war hero, and Henry Clay, as a parliamentary hero. Calhoun also desired the presidency, but was contented with the second place. The election made Calhoun Vice-President, but for the first place no candidate had a majority of electoral votes, and the choice, therefore, rested with the House of Representatives. The House elected John Quincy Adams. From the number of candidates, this election was dubbed "the scrub race for the presidency."

[The electoral vote stood: Jackson ninety-nine, Adams eighty-four, Crawford forty-one, and Clay thirty-seven. By the Constitution (see XII. Amendment), Clay could not be a candidate before the House of Representatives, and Crawford having become a paralytic, the contest lay between Adams and Jackson. The influence of Clay was sufficient to decide, and he preferred Adams to Jackson. The vote in the House stood for Adams thirteen, Jackson seven, Crawford four.]

QUESTIONS.

Give all the causes you can find that made the "era of good feeling."
What were the circumstances of the acquisition of Florida?
Bound the United States, January 1, 1804. (See map following p. 256.)
Bound the United States, January 1, 1820. (See map following p. 256.)
What was the contest over the admission of Missouri?
Explain how the Senate and House of Representatives came to be opposed.
What was conceded on either side?
If extended to the Pacific, where would the line of the Missouri compromise cut California?
What reasons can you give why the United States should control post offices and the carrying of mails?
What canals do you know of in California? Who constructed them?
What difficulties hinder private parties from digging canals?
Who builds and takes care of roads in California? Make a list of all the republics on the American continents.
Find out what you can about a Panama canal. Who do you think should have the control of such a canal? Of the first six Presidents, who had been Secretaries of State? Who Vice-Presidents?

468. How had preceding elections established "a line of promotion?"

CHAPTER XXIII.

1825-1829.

A Protective Tariff and New Political Parties.

John Quincy Adams, *Massachusetts, President.*
John C. Calhoun, *South Carolina, Vice-President.*

CABINET.

Henry Clay—State.
Richard Rush—Treasury.
Samuel L. Southard—Navy.

James Barbour, } War.
Peter B. Porter, }
William Wirt—Attorney-General.

John Quincy Adams.

467. The administration of J. Q. Adams does not mark any return to the Federalism of his father (**401**). Like his father, however, the President was a self-willed, independent man, who had no skill to act as a leader, and who would not follow the leadership of any one else. During his term new political questions came before the people, and new party lines were drawn. The country in general continued on its prosperous course.

468. [**John Quincy Adams,** the son of John Adams, was born in Massachusetts in 1767. Having graduated at the age of twenty, with high standing at Harvard College, he established himself as a lawyer in Boston. At the age of twenty-seven he was appointed Minister to The Netherlands, by President Washington. Returning to Boston in 1801, he was elected by the Federalists to the Massachusetts legislature, and thence to the United States Senate; but so little did he act with the Federalists that he was regarded as a traitor to the party. President Madison appointed him minister to Russia (1809), the first officer of the

United States to live at St. Petersburg. Afterwards he was Minister to England (1815-17), and Monroe's Secretary of State (1817-25). Defeated for a second presidential term, he was elected and reëlected to the House of Representatives, performing there, till his death, in 1848, the most honored services of his life. When a majority in Congress tried to shut out petitions for the abolition of slavery and to cut off all discussion of slavery questions (**509**), Adams stood up fearlessly fighting for the right of petition and freedom of speech, with all the power of a masterly intellect and a biting sarcasm in debate which made him respected even by his foes.]

469. Fourth of July, 1826, was celebrated with more than usual spirit. To us it is still memorable as the end of the earthly life of two great men, Thomas Jefferson, the author, and John Adams, the foremost defender of the Declaration of Independence (**275**). They had passed down the declining years of life in genuine friendship, and in the feebleness of age their one last wish was to see the sun rise on the fiftieth birthday of the country that they loved. To that day their lives were spared. "To their country they yet live, and live forever."

470. A Congress at Panama of representatives of all the republics (**464**) of North America and South America was planned, in 1826, to consider the independence, peace, and security of the continents. President Adams approved the movement and appointed commissioners to represent our country, but Congress delayed providing for expenses, and the meeting was over before our commissioners reached Panama.

[The delay was caused by the reluctance of United States slave owners to be associated with the Spanish-American republics which had extinguished the slave system.]

471. The tariff had remained substantially as arranged by the first Congress (**364**) until 1816. Then the debt incurred in the war of 1812 led to a revision of the duties. The experience of the country had tended to bring a protective tariff into favor (**366**), and the law of 1816 established low protective rates. Four years later there was a

16-II

call for higher rates, the argument being that peaceful years in Europe had lessened the demand for American grain, and that it was desirable to induce capitalists to undertake further manufactures at home, thus creating a market at home for the products of agriculture. A bill providing for high protective rates was defeated in Congress in 1820, but a similar bill was passed in 1824. In 1828 a new tariff was established with still higher protective rates.

472. [**Growth of Sectional Opposition.**—In 1816 the opposition to a protective tariff was not sectional. Calhoun, representing the opinion of South Carolina, favored it, while strong opposition came from New England. In 1824 Clay, representing Kentucky, was the foremost defender of protective ideas, general support coming from the Middle States, while Webster (**473**), representing to a considerable extent the opinions of New England, stood strongly for unrestricted trade. In 1828 New England had joined with the Middle States, and Webster became henceforth the companion of Clay in the defense of the protective system. Webster explained the change by saying that New England had accepted the verdict of the nation in 1824 in favor of protection, and had given up commerce and shipping in favor of manufacturing. At the same time general opposition to protective tariffs had grown up in most of the Southern States—strongest in South Carolina. Agriculture had become the one great industry of the South, the people living by the sale of raw products, and importing goods extensively from Europe.]

473. [**Daniel Webster** was born at Salisbury, New Hampshire, in 1782. Being a weak and tender child, he was spared the farm work of a New England boy, and had all his time to roam the woods, to read, and go to school. At Dartmouth College he read everything "he could lay hands on, and remembered everything he read." He could learn anything he tried to learn, and with wonderful quickness. At college he began his life as an orator. He loved to speak, and his audience loved to listen. His family was poor, every member toiling and sacrificing to give him an education. He, too, shared the burden, working hard for himself and the others, and his education and power of oratory brought him wealth and prominence. After becoming known in New Hampshire as a lawyer and legislator, he moved to Massachusetts, and was sent to Congress, where he won political leadership, national fame, and the love of New England. He was Representative from Massachusetts (1823-7), Senator (1827-41), Secretary of State (1841-3), again Senator (1845-50), and again Secretary of State till his death, in

---

Read extracts from the public speeches of Webster, Lessons 114, 124, 128, 144, 159, 172, Third Reader, California State Series.

1852. No man ever lived with greater power to control his fellow men by eloquence. An imposing presence, a powerful intellect, and vigor of imagination, combined to make him the greatest of American orators, and as great as any the world has known.]

1. Webster.   2. Calhoun.   3. Clay.

474. "The American System."—The clearest arguments of the time in support of protective tariffs are to be found in the speeches of Henry Clay. He admitted that a system of free trade, or of tariffs laid simply for revenue, was suited to a country like England—small, exhausted in soil, and a monarchy in government. On the other hand, he claimed that for America, a new and vast country of undeveloped resources, and democratic in government, the true system for general prosperity was a system of high protective tariffs, all revenue derived from duties in excess of government expenses to be expended by the national government in improving rivers, harbors, roads, etc. Hence a system of protective tariffs and internal improvements **(462)** came to be called "The American System."

475. New Parties.—The principles of the American System incorporated in the tariff laws of 1824 and 1828, found favor in New England and the Middle States, while most of the Southern States began a strong opposition. Western States were divided. Among leaders, Adams, Clay, and Webster defended the American System; Calhoun and Jackson fought against it. Hence arose a division between men who had called themselves Republicans. The followers of Adams, Clay, and Webster took the name of "National Republicans," the word "National" standing for the early Federalist idea of a powerful national government. The followers of Jackson and Calhoun now accepted the name of Democrats. Thus the old Democratic-Republican party **(389)** separated into two branches, dividing its name between them, and each claiming at the time to inherit its principles.

476. [State Sovereignty.—The difference between these two parties in regard to their views of the national government may be expressed by saying that the National Republicans favored a "loose construction" and the Democrats a "strict construction" of the constitution **(385)**. Calhoun and his immediate followers cherished the doctrine of "state rights," or state sovereignty, which had received expression in the Resolutions of '98 (406). Derived from the ideas of the early Republicans, who desired to be on guard lest the general government should absorb the powers of the states, the doctrine of "state rights" now meant that the United States constitution was simply a compact between independent, sovereign states, and that the general government belonged to the people, only through their states. In case of conflict between a state and the general government, men who cherished this doctrine would support their state and not the general government.]

477. The Presidential contest was decided as between two men, and not between two parties. Jackson was before the people as a candidate from the day of Adams's election, and the question had been simply who would gain the most support in four years. Jackson was elected President, and Calhoun was reëlected to the second place.

[The National Republican candidates, J. Q. Adams and Richard Rush, received eighty-three electoral votes against 178 for Jackson.]

REVIEWS.

Protective Tariff, 1828.
- 1. Reasons for. . . .
  - 1.
  - 2.
- 2. Supported by. . . .
  - 1. What section.
  - 2. What statesmen.
- 3. Opposed by. . . .
  - 1. What section.
  - 2. What statesmen.

Parties, 1828. . . . .
- Democratic. . . . .
  - 1. Origin.
  - 2. Principles.
  - 3. Leaders.
- National Republican.
  - 1. Origin.
  - 2. Principles.
  - 3. Leaders.

QUESTIONS.

Make a list of American republics at the present date. During what period should you say that our government was managed by men concerned in its foundation? In other words, what dates should you give for the "period of the founders?" Write a short essay comparing the United States July 4, 1826, and the United States July 4, 1776. What reasons can you give why the United States government should manage the improvement of rivers and harbors? Who owns San Francisco Bay? Write a sketch of the history of political parties in the United States from 1787 to 1828.

CHAPTER XXIV.
1829-1837.
JACKSON AND THE PEOPLE.

Andrew Jackson, *Tennessee, President.*
John C. Calhoun, *South Carolina,* } *Vice-President.*
Martin Van Buren, *New York,*

CABINET.

Martin Van Buren,	} State.	John H. Eaton, } War.	
Edward Livingston,		Lewis Cass,	
Louis McLane,		John Branch, } Navy.	
John Forsyth,		Levi Woodbury,	
Samuel D. Ingham,	} Treasury.	Mahlon Dickerson,	
Louis McLane,		John M. Berrien, } Attorney-General.	
William J. Duane,		Roger B. Taney,	
Roger B. Taney,		Benjamin F. Butler,	
Levi Woodbury,			

William T. Barry, } Postmaster-General.
Amos Kendall,

1. POLITICAL AFFAIRS.

478. The presidency of Andrew Jackson marks a change in the political methods of our country. In this time began the systematic organization of political parties, by means of state and local committees; the choice of candidates through great national conventions, and the publication of party principles in *platforms*, which nominees are pledged to support. The years of Jackson's presidency were distinguished by a series of stirring political contests, but they are especially memorable for great improvements made by our people in business life, and for advances made in scholarship and literature.

479. [**Andrew Jackson** was born in 1767, of Scotch-Irish parents. His birthplace, probably, was in North Carolina, although near the southern boundary of the state. Almost without education, he nevertheless became a lawyer in the frontier state of Tennessee, and through the native force of his character he won a prominent position. He was

---

What difference can you point out between President Jackson and his predecessors, in regard to experience in affairs of the national government? What had Jackson done to commend himself to the people?

JACKSON AND THE PEOPLE.

ANDREW JACKSON.

in Congress for brief periods as Representative (1796), and Senator (1797). From 1798 to 1804 he was a judge in the Supreme Court of Tennessee. Then he became a planter, but up to the age of forty-five he had established no great reputation, except as a man of violent temper, and an experienced duelist. The war of 1812 gave him a national fame. After his second term he retired to his plantation, the "Hermitage," near Nashville, Tennessee, but he held a controlling hand in politics until his death in 1845. His nickname, "Old Hickory," gives some idea of his character. He regarded an opponent as a personal enemy, and could see neither a fault in a friend, nor a virtue in a foe. He lived to see the defeat of all his rivals.]

480. Removals from office filled by presidential appointment were very rare under the early Presidents. A man who did his work well was seldom discharged, even when a President was elected from an opposite political party. The growth of the country had greatly increased the number of offices, creating many positions that paid good salaries, and under President Jackson a new system was introduced. Many men, who were not supporters of Jackson, were removed, and their places were filled by Democrats. This system of filling the offices of the country with the political supporters of the President was called "rotation in office." It is also known as the "spoils system," a name taken from the saying, "To the victors belong the spoils," put forward as a political maxim. The spoils system, followed very generally by political parties since Jackson's time, has been the cause of much evil and corruption.

[Removals by the first six Presidents amounted to seventy-four, most of them for unfitness. In his first year Jackson removed 491 postmasters and 239 other officers.]

481. Three Great Contests.—The United States Bank, protective tariffs, and state sovereignty were the subjects of fierce political warfare during these years. The President had come into office pledged to economy and the prompt payment of the national debt (**453**). Everything that he believed to be an abuse in the government he was ready to attack as he would a personal foe. He was opposed to the bank, believed in reducing tariffs to avoid a surplus in revenue, and swore "by the Eternal!" that he would maintain the authority of the United States. The bank was killed, the tariff was compromised, and the attempt to put ideas of state sovereignty into practice was defeated. These results were reached during Jackson's second term, and the issues leading to them made up chiefly the presidential campaign of 1832, which began early and was fought bitterly.

482. [**History of the Bank.**—Congress refused to renew the charter of Hamilton's bank (**385**), and it closed up its affairs in good order in 1811. In 1816 financial embarrassments from the war debts (**453**) brought about a new bank, modeled after the first, and likewise chartered for twenty years. The second bank was not always well managed, and gave offense to some by interfering in politics. Under the management of Clay, a bill was passed in Congress just before the presidential election of 1832, renewing the bank charter. The President promptly vetoed the bill, thus giving the people a chance to decide at the polls between "the bank" and "Jackson." After his reëlection President Jackson caused the government funds to be removed and to be deposited in local banks. In 1836 the bank tried to continue its life by taking out a charter in Pennsylvania, under the absurd name of the "Bank of the United States of Pennsylvania," but it perished in the general ruin of banks in the years following 1837 (**503**).]

483. The chief presidential nominees in 1832 were Clay, representing the National Republicans, and Jackson, representing the Democrats (**475**). Clay favored the American

---
482. In 1832 how many years had the charter to run?

JACKSON AND THE PEOPLE. 249

System (474) and the bank, to both of which Jackson was opposed. Jackson won a sweeping victory. Martin Van Buren (500), of New York, was elected Vice-President.

[Jackson received 219 electoral votes, Clay forty-nine. South Carolina cast her eleven votes for John Floyd, who represented opposition to the national tariff laws. Vermont gave her seven votes to William Wirt, the nominee of an Anti-Masonic party, which had a short-lived existence in a few northern states. It represented opposition to secret organizations, especially to the order of Freemasons.]

484. South Carolina against the United States.—Several southern states joined with South Carolina in protesting against the protective tariff of 1828 (471), but she alone proceeded to resist the law. Near the end of 1832 the state government called a convention, which declared the United States tariff law null and void, forbade all citizens of South Carolina to pay duties, and threatened secession from the Union and armed resistance should the general government maintain its custom house at Charleston. Resistance was to begin on February first. President Jackson promptly ordered two war vessels to Charleston, with sufficient troops to see the legal duties collected. At the same time a calm and dignified address, written by Secretary of State Livingston, was issued to the people of South Carolina. It presented the sound argument that to nullify a United States law was to destroy the Union, and appealed to the patriotism for which South Carolina had early been distinguished. The state paused, and meanwhile Congress undertook a revision of the tariff.

485. [Calhoun's Ideas.—South Carolina was acting upon the assumption that the protective tariff laws were unconstitutional (497). (The question of constitutionality could never be brought before the United States courts, for the reason that the words of the later tariff laws omitted the reference to protecting home industries, which the preamble to the first law (364) had contained, and there was no contest over the right of Congress to levy taxes.) In this attempt to nullify a national law, South Carolina followed the advice and leadership of Calhoun, who had given up his hope of the presidency and devoted himself to the affairs of his state. He believed that slavery was "a positive good," and that there was a permanent conflict of interests between the "staple states" of the South and the rest of the Union, because from their "soil, climate, habits, and peculiar labor," the southern states would always be devoted to their "ancient and favorite pursuit" of agriculture. From this conflict of interests he thought that there was constant danger of unjust laws. He wished not to destroy, but to preserve the Union, and fixed upon "nullification" as a means of avoiding conflict, and as a safeguard against secession, or withdrawal from the Union. Clear-headed and logical as he was, he did not see the absolute contradiction between nullification and government through law, between state supremacy and a united nation.]

486. **The Compromise Tariff, 1833.**—A bill to reduce tariff rates about one half within two years was before Congress during January, 1833, with no strong prospect of passage, but with support enough to make some friends of protection fear an approaching overthrow. In February, a new bill, planned and arranged by Clay, now in the Senate, was substituted. It was called a compromise bill, and provided for the gradual reduction of all duties over twenty per cent *ad valorem*, one tenth of such duties being deducted yearly until 1842, when it was calculated that all duties would have the uniform rate of twenty per cent. This bill became a law, and South Carolina repealed her nullification ordinance.

[Clay claimed that his bill preserved the principle of protective tariffs and averted civil war, for Congress about the same time had passed an "enforcement bill," authorizing the President to employ land and naval forces in the collection of revenue. President Jackson gained the credit of having defended the Union.]

487. **Whigs.**—While President, Jackson acted as the chief of the Democratic party, and his influence was felt everywhere. His administration has been characterized as "the reign of Andrew Jackson." His political opponents called him a tyrant, and adopted the name of Whigs, a name recalling the patriots, who, in revolutionary days, had withstood the tyranny of George III. (**221**). The Whig party was essentially the National Republican party under

486. Who were the parties to the tariff compromise? What concessions were made by each?

a new name, representing support of the American System, a United States Bank, and nationalism, as opposed to "state rights" (476).

488. [Webster-Hayne Debate.—The speeches of Webster, in the United States Senate, often set forth the national idea of the Whig party. One speech is especially memorable, delivered in a "great debate," during the winter of 1829-30. The original question, regarding the sale of public land in the west, was lost sight of in a general discussion of the nature of the Union, and the powers of our national government. Upon this theme came the grand contest between Webster and Robert Y. Hayne, of South Carolina, who was afterwards governor of that state during the nullification trouble (484). Hayne had desired that new states in the west might have the proceeds from the sale of land within their limits, believing independence and sovereignty of the state to be the life of the republic, and no evil so much to be feared as consolidation in the general government; and, in a formal speech, he set forth the doctrine of state sovereignty (476). In reply, Webster discussed the origin of the government, whether it was in fact created by state governments or by the people. He found for answer not that "it was the creature of thirteen wills, and now the servant of twenty-four," but that "it was the people's constitution, the people's government; made for the people, made by the people, and answerable to the people." Both speeches were widely read, and made a deep impression upon the country.]

489. The Presidential election of 1836 resulted in favor of the Democrats, with Martin Van Buren for President. The Whigs were not well organized, and their votes were divided between several men, William Henry Harrison (513) of Ohio, receiving the largest number.

[The total electoral vote was divided between five men: Van Buren, 170; Harrison, seventy-three; Hugh L. White, twenty-six (votes of Tennessee and Georgia); Daniel Webster, fourteen (vote of Massachusetts); and Willie P. Mangum eleven (vote of South Carolina).]

QUESTIONS.

How were candidates for the last election nominated for the offices of your county?

How were the last presidential candidates nominated?

If a presidential election is held this year, read the party platforms when they appear in the newspapers.

Who is your postmaster? How was he appointed?

2. Development.

490. The people of the United States during Jackson's time enjoyed universal prosperity. Immigration from Europe fluctuated from year to year, increasing from about 8,000 in 1820 to 80,000 in 1840. These new-comers did not generally press on to the new lands of the west, as the early immigrants had done (393), but settling in the great cities they began to form a wage-earning class, especially in the manufacturing centers. Becoming citizens and voters, their influence began to count in United States politics as "the foreign vote." They brought with them habits and prejudices from old world society, but no new institutions.

491. Social reforms were commenced in movements to do away with drunkenness, with cruelty of punishment in prisons, and with negro slavery. The movement against drunkenness was carried on by temperance societies, which began about 1830 to spread through the country. They required of members a pledge, not of total abstinence from the use of intoxicating drinks, but only of moderation. The movement for prison reform accomplished the abolition of imprisonment for debt, and of the harsh penalties that had been common in the laws of all countries. The penitentiary system was substituted, founded upon the belief that no human beings are utterly bad, and that prisons should offer opportunities for improvement through work and instruction. The movement against slavery was known as "abolitionism," and its promoters as "Abolitionists."

492. The Abolitionists, about 1831, began to speak and print their belief that negro slavery was sinful and injurious to the country. In 1833 they founded a national anti-slavery society, with branches throughout the northern states. The method of the Abolitionists was to print and circulate arguments against slavery, to petition Congress for its abolition in the District of Columbia, and to urge owners to emancipate their slaves, slave states to abolish the system, and free states and slave states alike to aid in the education of negroes.

493. The inventions of these years laid a foundation for new industries. John Ericsson (see portrait, p. 268), in 1836, invented the screw propeller, which was an advantage to ocean steamers and made them suitable for war ships. Steamers began to make regular trips across the Atlantic. A reaping machine was patented, and Colt's revolvers were a new thing in firearms. Friction matches came into use (about 1836), and displaced the patience-taxing flint and steel that our fathers used for kindling fires.

494. Railroads more than anything else changed American life to what it is now. Beginnings were made in the administration of Adams. In 1827 short lines of rails for horse cars were laid at Quincy, Massachusetts, and Albany, New York. Englishmen were working at locomotive engines from 1825 to 1829, and an English locomotive was brought to America and made its first trip in 1828, near Mauch Chunk, Pennsylvania. The same year a steam railroad was chartered to run westward from Charleston, South Carolina. During Jackson's time railroads multiplied throughout the Atlantic states.

[Americans made great improvements in the locomotive, and the locomotive made improvements in Americans, developing promptness and punctuality. The old stage-coach was slow and not punctual. The early river steamboats did not make regular trips and would wait two days to get a load, and stop anywhere along the bank for passengers to get on or off.]

495. General education became the subject of careful study on the part of earnest men. The founders of our government saw clearly that a republic can be founded only upon the intelligence of its citizens. Early in the century, religious test for office holders, and property qualifications for voters, began to disappear, and the democratic idea of manhood suffrage was sweeping into favor. Our fathers saw that if a state permits every man to vote, it must, for its own sake, see that every man has the education that will make him an intelligent voter. Common school education, for which Massachusetts colony (291) had laid the early foundation, extended to the western states, separated, however, from church control. Small private colleges multiplied in the new states, and the states themselves frequently established Universities upon broad principles of public education.

496. [National Schools.— A grand national University

LONGFELLOW.

BRYANT.

was a favorite plan with Washington. The United States has, however, never undertaken the work of public education, and states have arranged their school systems for themselves (733). In 1845 the United States established the Naval Academy, at Annapolis, for training naval officers, just as army officers were trained at West Point (437). By gifts of land (731) the United States has assisted state schools and colleges.]

497. **American Literature.**—After the great outburst of political essays at the time of the Revolution,

and the establishment of our government (360), little writing appeared to form an American Literature, until about 1830. Many reasons for this may be found in the life and education of our people. There was, however, some good writing all the time. Newspapers improved in form and style, and the introduction of steam printing presses brought about the modern dailies—papers of large size, wide circulation, and low price. Criti-

WHITTIER.

cal magazines, like the "North American Review," afforded miscellaneous reading, and stimulated an improved style in writing. From 1820 to 1840, many of the most distinguished writers of the nineteenth century began the great works which have built up the business of book publishing in America, given reading to the American public, and standing to the American branch of English literature.

LOWELL.

[Early in the century came the writers of the "Knickerbocker School," who centered at New York. The greatest of them is Washington Irving, who introduced an easy and graceful prose style into American writing. The novels of James Fenimore Cooper, begun in

1. Bancroft.   2. Prescott.   3. Motley.   4. Irving.

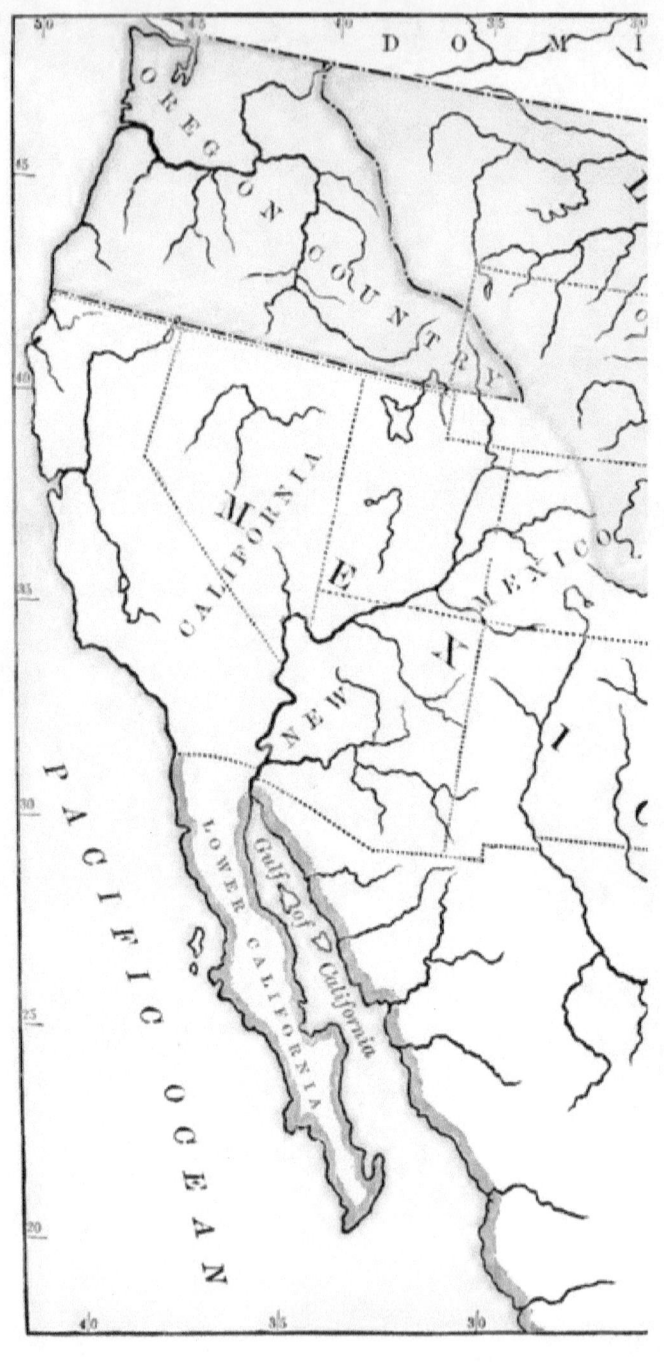

MAP OF
UNITED STATES IN 1830.

1821, were the first works in American fiction to be extensively read. Nathaniel Hawthorne, our greatest novelist, began publishing in 1837. The great poets, William Cullen Bryant, Henry Wadsworth Longfellow, John Greenleaf Whittier, Oliver Wendell Holmes, and James Russell Lowell were contemporaries of Hawthorne. Edgar Allen Poe was first known as a magazine writer, and later as a poet. George Bancroft published the first volume of his "History of the United States" in 1834. William H. Prescott, about this time, published his "Ferdinand and Isabella," and Motley, the historian of the Netherlands, was rising into prominence. American statesmen produced a few speeches that live in literature. Law and politics were professions attracting men of the highest ability.]

HAWTHORNE.

498. The country continued to enjoy peace with foreign nations, and President Jackson's vigorous management protected American commerce. The advance of settlements brought on the usual Indian conflicts. In Georgia the Cherokees, perhaps the most intelligent and progressive of the Indian tribes, gave annoyance in Adams's time by refusing to move west of the Mississippi. Under Jackson their transportation was accomplished. Indians in Illinois, Wisconsin, and Iowa, led by the chief Black Hawk, made war upon the settlers, and were subdued only after hard fighting. This is known as the Black Hawk war, from the name of the Indian chief. In Florida the Seminoles, under the lead of Osceola, gave even more serious trouble. In the end they were forced to move beyond the Mississippi. Our map shows the advance of population and the beginning of cities in the new states. Railroad building led to careful surveys, and surveys drew attention to mineral wealth hitherto unthought of. Still the Rocky Mountains and all beyond them were unexplored regions, save in the direction of Oregon. School geographies gave no information at all about the Sierra Nevada Mountains, and continued for many years to describe most of the land west of Kansas as the "Great American Desert."

REVIEW.

POLITICAL AFFAIRS.

"Spoils system."

Contests:
- Bank.
  - 1. Causes.
  - 2. Incidents.
  - 3. Results.
- Tariff.
  - 1. Causes.
  - 2. Incidents.
  - 3. Results.
- "State rights."
  - 1. Causes.
  - 2. Incidents.
  - 3. Results.

Whig party.

DEVELOPMENT.

People.
- 1. Immigration.
- 2. Indian troubles.

Reforms.
- 1.
- 2.
- 3.

Inventions.
- 1.
- 2.
- 3.

Education and Literature.
- 1.
- 2.
- 3.

Questions on Map of 1830.—Bound the United States in 1830. Name, in order, the states admitted since the original thirteen. Name the rivers that formed state boundaries. What rivers afforded avenues for inland commerce in 1830? Bound Louisiana as ceded in 1803. In 1830 how many states had been formed from it? Bound the Northwest Territory of 1830. How much had it been reduced since 1789? By what process? What was the general shape of the United States in 1830? In what direction was there the best opportunity for expansion? Where was the geographical center of the United States in 1789? The center of population? The geographical center in 1830? The center of population? How many states were there in 1830? Which had the largest population? Which the least?

CHAPTER XXV.
1837-1841.
Speculation and Panic.

Martin Van Buren, *New York, President.*
R. M. Johnson, *Kentucky, Vice-President.*

CABINET.

John Forsyth—State.	Amos Kendall, } Postmaster-General.
Levi Woodbury—Treasury.	John M. Niles, }
Joel R. Poinsett—War.	Benjamin F. Butler, } Attorney-General.
Mahlon Dickerson, } Navy.	Felix Grundy, }
James K. Paulding, }	Henry D. Gilpin, }

499. "Hard Times."—The prosperous years of Jackson's terms were followed by a period of business stagnation, bringing loss and even suffering. Besides business troubles, there were angry disturbances brought about by the bold utterances of Abolitionists **(492)**, and the beginning of annoyance in the west from the practices of Mormons **(510)**. The record of President Van Buren's term is one of troubles, business disaster being the chief.

500. [Martin Van Buren was born in New York, in 1782. With only a superficial education, he became a lawyer, and filled various offices in the state of New York. He was United States Senator (1821-8), and Governor of New York for three months (1828), resigning to become President Jackson's Secretary of State (1829-31). President Jackson appointed him Minister to England, but the Senate refused to confirm the appointment, whereupon he was elected Vice-President (1833-7), becoming, thereby, the presiding officer of the Senate. Defeated for reëlection to the presidency in 1840, and again in 1848 **(541)**, he passed the rest of his life in retirement. He died in 1862.]

501. Speculation.—The prosperous years of Jackson's first term were followed by speculation, chiefly in land. Eastern cities like New York were growing rapidly, and real estate rising everywhere in value, induced people to invest all their spare capital. The United States sold lands in the western states for $1 25 an acre, to any one wishing to buy. The Erie Canal **(463)** and improved steamboats made western lands more accessible, and therefore more valuable. City lots and western lands were bought and sold again, largely on credit. For a few years (1834-6) speculation on credit reigned supreme. Men deserted farming to become bankers and real estate brokers. But while cities were full of life and grew with marvelous rapidity, in 1836 it became necessary to import supplies of flour and wheat.

502. Banks.—Trading on credit was greatly increased through the agency of banks, which sprang up all over the country in great numbers. Bank notes, which were really only promises to pay coin, circulated as money. There were no laws controlling the formation of banks, or for inspecting their condition. The opposition to the United States Bank, and the withdrawal of the government funds (482), gave an impetus to local banking business. In fact, there came to be a mania for banks. Men stood in line for hours, and even fought for an opportunity to buy bank stock.

[A great many banks, especially in the west, were nothing but swindles, being started without any real capital, and operating through deception. They are often called "wildcat" banks.]

503. A change in affairs was bound to come, for the country could not long afford to import food supplies. It began in 1836, when an order known as the Specie Circular was issued from the Treasury Department to the land offices to accept nothing but coin in payment for land. This order was intended to stop the "wildcat" banks from cheating the government with worthless notes. It created a demand for coin. Holders of bank notes began to demand cash of the banks, and the banks had very little cash in reserve. To get cash, real estate was offered at reduced prices. Then owners, heavily in debt, became frightened and wanted to sell, but could not find purchasers. Soon there was a rush on the banks to collect notes, and banks all over the country had to close their doors. Honest banks were swept down as well as the dishonest.

504. A Panic is the name given to such a state of affairs as this. The panic of 1837 began with Van Buren's term, and lasted for more than a year, until business based on regular work and honest wages slowly made a new beginning. During this year there was widespread distress, sometimes even a lack of food.

505. The United States Government, also, was troubled by want of money, for its funds were in the keeping of banks which could not return them. In 1835 the national debt had been entirely paid off, and the government, having more money than it needed for expenses, had distributed its surplus among the states. In 1837, an extra session of Congress, called to consider the financial difficulties, issued treasury notes (similar to greenbacks) (**655**) to meet the current expenses. The chief result of the panic, so far as the government was concerned, was a United States treasury system, independent of all banks.

506. [**Our Sub-Treasury System** went into operation in 1840. It provides for the safe keeping of government money in the national treasury at Washington, in sub-treasuries at prominent cities, or in charge of depository banks. It was abolished by the Whigs, in 1841 (**514**), who tried to reëstablish the Bank of United States. In 1846 the independent treasury system was renewed.]

507. State Debts.—In the general spirit of speculation, many states had become involved in heavy debts for canals, railroads, etc. They, also, were hard pushed for money. No one can sue a state for the collection of a debt (Art. XI., Amendments to the Constitution), and some states that were heavily embarrassed voted not to pay. This refusal of a state to pay its debts is called repudiation. Some of the repudiating states afterwards paid off their debts.

508. Abolitionists and Slavery Riots.—The people of the North had generally accepted the theory of their statesmen (**459**), that slavery in the South was no affair of theirs. It might be a terrible sin, but the slave owners alone were responsible. The anti-slavery publications (492) alarmed and enraged the South, while at the North the Abolitionists were denounced as incendiaries and the destroyers of the public peace. Southern governors would have punished them, if they could, while at their public meetings northern mobs rotten-egged and stoned them. Anti-slavery printing presses were destroyed and buildings were burned, yet the movement made headway. The numbers of the Abolitionists increased enough to secure protection against mobs, but they never gained any important political strength.

[William Lloyd Garrison, the first of anti-slavery agitators, began the printing of the "Liberator" newspaper, in Boston, January 1, 1831. Wendell Phillips, a Massachusetts orator, and James G. Birney, of Michigan, a former slave owner, were Abolitionist leaders. Another leader, Elijah P. Lovejoy, a clergyman and an editor, was killed by a mob at Alton, Illinois, in 1837. John G. Whittier, the poet, was connected with the movement.]

509. **Anti-Slavery Petitions.**—More than by the utterances of the Abolitionists, the North was aroused by the refusal of Congress to receive petitions touching slavery. This rule was adopted by Congress in 1836, and soon other rules were passed which cut off all debate on slavery questions. These "gag" rules angered people at the North, who, led by John Quincy Adams in the House of Representatives (468), opposed them with unalterable resolution. After a struggle of four years these rules were given up, and petitions were admitted.

[Postmasters were allowed to search United States mails and to cast out anti-slavery pamphlets or papers "tending to promote discontent, sedition, and servile war." Slave-holders lived in fear of a slave insurrection, and their fear led to bitter feeling against the Abolitionists.]

510. **The Mormons,** or Latter-Day Saints, are a religious sect, founded in New York state in 1830. They made trouble in Missouri and Illinois during this administration, and afterwards moved to Utah.

509. Read Article I., Amendments to the Constitution of the United States.

[The founder of the sect was Joseph Smith, who pretended to preach a new gospel. He published his "revelation" as the "Book of Mormon," which he induced a small number of fanatics to accept as a new Bible. The sect located first in Ohio, in 1831, and next at Independence, Missouri, where their religious law brought them into conflict with the civil authorities. In consequence of this they moved, in 1838, to Illinois, where the legislature gave them a charter for a city, Nauvoo. Here Smith set the example of polygamous marriages and polygamy became the practice of the leaders, though not adopted by the Mormon church as a part of their creed until later. This custom, and numerous depredations upon property, brought the Mormons into trouble with the authorities of Illinois. Joseph Smith was shot in a riot (1844). The Illinois legislature revoked the charter of Nauvoo in 1845. Brigham Young took Smith's place at the head of the church, and under Young's leadership most of the Mormons emigrated to the vicinity of Great Salt Lake, in Utah Territory (1847-8).]

511. The presidential contest of 1840 was an exciting one. A Whig convention (December, 1839), nominated William Henry Harrison (513) of Ohio for President, and, to give the ticket strength in the South, John Tyler (515) of Virginia for Vice-President. Van Buren was the Democratic nominee for reëlection. The Whigs made a vigorous contest, charging upon Democratic administrations responsibility for the financial distress of preceding years, and stirring the enthusiasm of the people by large processions and mass meetings. They gained a sweeping victory.

[Harrison was a frontier man and had lived in a log-cabin. Therefore log-cabins became the style. Whigs built them in every city, and kept hard cider on hand for visitors. There were log-cabin cuff-buttons and log-cabin cigars. Log-cabin songs were sung at the great meetings, with the chorus of "Tippecanoe and Tyler, too." Harrison was known as "Old Tippecanoe," in memory of his victory over the Indians (444). Harrison and Tyler had 234 electoral votes out of 294. The Abolitionists voted for James G. Birney (505), but gained no electoral vote.]

QUESTIONS.

What were the causes of the panic of 1837? Would a panic be possible if all business were done on cash? What are some advantages of a "credit" system? Show how railroads make land more valuable. Why were northern people so enraged at the Abolitionists? Claiming their practices to be a part of their religion, what argument were Mormons able to make against prohibitory laws? (See Article I., Amendments to Constitution.)

CHAPTER XXVI.
1841-1845.
"TIPPECANOE AND TYLER, TOO."

William Henry Harrison, *Ohio, President.*
John Tyler, *Virginia, Vice-President and President.*

CABINET.

Daniel Webster,	} State.	George E. Badger,	} Navy.
Hugh S. Legaré,		Abel P. Upshur,	
Abel P. Upshur,		David Henshaw,	
John C. Calhoun,		Thomas W. Gilmer,	
Thomas Ewing,	} Treasury.	John Y. Mason,	
Walter Forward,			
John C. Spencer,		Francis Granger,	} Postmaster-
George M. Bibb,		Charles A. Wickliffe,	General.
John Bell,	} War.		
John C. Spencer,		John J. Crittenden,	} Attorney-General.
James M. Porter,		Hugh S. Legaré,	
William Wilkins,		John Nelson,	

For Explanation.—Extradition; rancorous.

512. **The election of Harrison** was the popular approval of a warm-hearted, patriotic man, put up by a strong party, because he was known to the country by a military and not a political record. It brought to Washington a swarm of Whig politicians, hungry for the offices which Democrats had held for twelve years. Harrison, however, wanted able men in his cabinet, and Webster became his Secretary of State. The President issued a call for Congress to meet in extra session in May, but his death occurred a month after his inauguration.

513. [**William H. Harrison** was born in Virginia, in 1773. He served as captain in the United States army, and removed to the west, in 1793. He was Governor of Indiana Territory (1801-13), commanding the western army in the war of 1812. He served in Congress as Representative from Ohio (1816-19), and as Senator (1825-8), and was sent as Minister to Colombia (1828-9). He died after a few days illness, April 6th, 1841.]

What may be inferred about this administration from the number of cabinet officers in each department?

514. Tyler and the Whigs.—Whig Congressmen expected President Tyler to coöperate with them in reëstablishing a United States Bank, and in strengthening protective tariffs. But Tyler was more Democrat than Whig, and had acted with the Whigs in his own state simply from personal opposition to President Jackson. He used the veto power against the Whig measures, and the Whigs were not strong enough in Congress to overrule him. Bitter animosity was created between Whig leaders and the President. This ill-will broke up the cabinet, which Tyler had accepted from Harrison, and subsequent quarrels weakened the Whig organization.

515. [**John Tyler** was born in Virginia, in 1790. He was a graduate of William and Mary College, a lawyer, a member of the Virginia legislature (1811-16), Representative in Congress (1816-21). Having left Congress on account of ill-health, he was again in the legislature of his state (1823-4), Governor of Virginia (1825-6), and United States Senator (1827-36), resigning, rather than obey instructions from his state, in favor of President Jackson. A third time he served in the Virginia legislature, acting with the Whigs. He died at Richmond, Virginia, in 1862.]

516. Webster-Ashburton Treaty.—Contrary to the wish of many Whigs, Webster refused to desert the cabinet of President Tyler until after important public business had been arranged. The boundary between Maine and Canada was in dispute (**340**). Serious difficulties had arisen out of a rebellion in Canada (1837), in which Americans were disposed to give help against Great Britain. In 1842 Webster arranged with Lord Ashburton, the British representative, a treaty which fixed our northern boundary from the Atlantic to the Rocky Mountains, as it now is.

[This treaty also provided for the extradition of criminals, each country agreeing to arrest and send back criminals who had escaped from the other.]

517. Texas was a Mexican state, from the formation of the Mexican republic (**464**) until 1835. A vast territory, one third as large as the original thirteen states together, with only a small population. Texas offered a favorable field for settlers, and many Americans from the southern states had gone into Texas. There they helped organize a revolt against Mexico. Mexican troops were driven out, and in 1835 an independent government was set up. The admission of Texas to our Union now became a question of great public interest, upon which our people were divided. President Tyler favored the annexation of Texas, and in 1844 arranged a treaty for that purpose, which the Senate rejected. The annexation of Texas then became the great issue in the presidential contest of 1844.

[If admitted, Texas would come in as a slave state. The question of annexation involved, therefore, the extension of the slave system, the center of most of the great political contests until 1860.]

518. Oregon, the name applying indefinitely to the country drained by the Columbia River (sometimes called the Oregon), began to attract settlers in 1840. Both the United States and Great Britain claimed ownership. Webster, as Secretary of State, tried to fix the boundary at the forty-ninth parallel, but neither country was willing to accept it. Our extreme demand was for the line of 54° 40', nearly the southern end of Alaska. England's claim reached nearly to California. The maintenance of our claims to the Oregon region was also a leading issue in the campaign of 1844.

519. The nominees in 1844 for President and Vice-President were, by the Whigs, Henry Clay of Kentucky, and Theodore Frelinghuysen of New Jersey; by the Democrats, James K. Polk (527) of Tennessee, and George M. Dallas of Pennsylvania. Van Buren had been a candidate for the Democratic nomination, but failed to get the two-thirds vote required for a choice in the Democratic convention. Polk stood for "the reoccupation of Oregon and the reannexation of Texas," on the theory that we had discovered and owned Oregon as far as 54° 40', and had acquired Texas in the Louisiana purchase (417). Clay stood for the American System (474) and United States Bank. Polk and Dallas were elected.

520. [**Two letters** decided the contest. Clay wrote that he would be glad to see Texas annexed, "without dishonor, without war, with the common consent of the Union, and upon just and fair terms," and he lost the votes of men strongly opposed to the extension of slavery. Polk, although a believer in free trade, wrote that it was the duty of the government to extend, "by its revenue laws, and all other means within its power, fair and equal protection to all the great interests of the whole Union." He won several protectionist states, without losing the states opposed to protective tariffs.]

521. [**Clay's Defeat.**—The Abolitionists voted again for James G. Birney (511). They were credited with defeating Clay, by "throwing away" their votes on Birney. The electoral vote was: Clay, 105; Polk, 170. New York went for Polk by a very small majority. Her thirty-six electoral votes would have elected Clay. Jackson lived to see this final defeat of his great adversary. "For twenty years these two great, brave men headed the opposing political forces of the Union. Whoever might be candidates, they were the actual leaders. John Quincy Adams was more learned than either; Mr. Webster was stronger in logic and in speech; Calhoun more acute, refined, and philosophic; Van Buren better skilled in combining and directing political forces; but to no one of these was given the sublime attribute of leadership, the faculty of drawing men unto him. . . . Clay held the advantage of rare eloquence; but Jackson had a splendid military record, which spoke to the hearts of the people more effectively than words. . . . In each of them patriotism was a passion. There never was a time in their prolonged enmity and rancorous contests when a real danger to the country would not have united them as heartily as in 1812, when Clay in the House and Jackson on the field coöperated in defending the national honor against the aggressions of Great Britain."—*Blaine.*]

522. **Texas Annexed.**—Polk's victory was considered the people's verdict in favor of annexing Texas. President Tyler, desiring to finish what he had begun, by means of a joint resolution from both houses of Congress, received authority to proceed. This resolution was forwarded to Texas, and the terms of annexation accepted by her gov-

521. How many times had Clay been a regular candidate for President? In what years?

ernment. She was admitted to the Union at the next session of Congress (December, 1845).

1. Whitney. 2. Fulton. 3. Ericsson. 4. Morse.

[Calhoun, Tyler's last Secretary of State, said that the admission of

Texas was "to uphold the interests of slavery, extend its influence, and secure its permanent duration." A broader view, leaving slavery out of consideration, would say that the admission of Texas was wise; for, not strong enough to remain independent, she would probably have formed European alliances dangerous to our interests.]

523. The States in 1845.—Arkansas became a state in 1836, Michigan in 1837. Florida and Iowa were admitted to the Union, March 3d, 1845. Iowa had trouble about her constitution, and did not get under way as a state until 1846. Counting Iowa, however, there were twenty-eight states the day on which Polk was inaugurated. Of the original thirteen, the seven north of Maryland had prohibited slavery, while the other six maintained it. Of the fifteen younger states, seven were free states, while in the eight south of Iowa and the Ohio River, slavery was legal. Thus free and slave states were equally represented in the United States Senate. Texas gave the majority to the slave states for a time. She was, however, the last state admitted with a constitution legalizing slavery. Wisconsin, a free state, was admitted to the Union in 1848.]

524. Telegraph.—The years 1840-4 brought about things more wonderful than political leadership, and greater in results to us and all the world than the annexation of Texas.

Franklin Press.

In 1837, Samuel F. B. Morse, artist and inventor, a professor in the University of New York, asked for a patent on an invention for employing electricity in sending messages between distant places. In 1845 Congress appropriated money for testing the invention, and the next year the first successful telegraph line in the world was in operation between Washington and Baltimore. In a few years, telegraph wires connected all the larger cities in the Union.

[The Morse system was adopted in Europe, and has been improved both in Europe and America. Morse received the highest honors from European powers, and gratitude and praise at home. For a long time electricity had been known as a force, fit to be applied to certain uses. The discoveries since 1840 have shown how to make these practical applications. The introduction of the telegraph facilitated and extended the work of newspapers. Improved presses were needed to supply the growing circulation of the great dailies. In 1846 was patented a cylinder printing press, in which the type placed on one cylinder imprints the paper revolving upon another cylinder. Improved cylinder presses do the rapid newspaper printing of the present time.]

MODERN BOOK PRESS.
(Used in printing this book.)

525. The country, at peace with foreign nations during Tyler's term, had some disturbances at home. In Rhode Island, in 1842, there was an attempt by force to overthrow the state constitution, which had been handed down from the days of Roger Williams, and allowed only freeholders and their oldest sons to vote **(74)**. The uprising is known as the "Dorr Rebellion," from the name of the leader. No blood was shed, and a new constitution removed the grievances. There was trouble also in New York over the land system of the Dutch patroons (141), which still existed along the Hudson. Farmers paid rent to the landlords, and were allowed no opportunity to buy for themselves. About 1844, many farmers refused to pay any more rent, and, as "Anti-renters," resisted the law officers. In the end the great land estates were broken up and sold. Thus far the mineral wealth of our land had received very little attention. The high lands of Virginia, North Carolina, and Georgia had furnished a little gold. Steam engines were bringing Pennsylvania coal and iron into use. New Jersey mines of iron ore were still older. Lead was found in northern Illinois and eastern Iowa, in the mineral, galena. The settlement of Michigan revealed the wealth of native copper on the shores of Lake Superior, and copper became one of our important exports.

QUESTIONS.

What is the advantage of a military over a political record for a presidential candidate? What grounds did Whigs have for resentment against President Tyler? What defense may be made for him? From the Atlantic to the Rocky Mountains what natural boundaries separate us from the British possessions? Do persons accused of crime sometimes escape from the United States to Mexico or Canada? Do they find there security from arrest? Why? Texas retained the ownership of all her unoccupied land—what advantage has this been to her over other states? What were the grounds of our claim to Oregon? (See Territorial Map of 1876.) What did Jackson do for his country in the war of 1812? What was Clay's part? How did the territory of free states compare in extent with that of slave states in 1845? See if you can find out how the electric telegraph works. How is telegraphing across the Atlantic Ocean accomplished? Learn what you can about the construction of ocean cables. Has the telephone any advantage over the telegraph? Has the telegraph any advantage over the telephone? Make a list of all the applications of electricity that you know anything about. Make a list of the metals mined extensively in the United States, with the important localities. What metals are mined in California?

CHAPTER XXVII.

1845-1849.

TEXAS AND MEXICO.

James Knox Polk, *Tennessee, President.*
George M. Dallas, *Pennsylvania, Vice-President.*

CABINET.

James Buchanan—State. George Bancroft, } Navy.
Robert J. Walker—Treasury. John Y. Mason, }
William L. Marcy—War. Cave Johnson—Postmaster-General.

John Y. Mason, }
Nathan Clifford, } Attorney-General.
Isaac Toucey, }

For Explanation.—Ranking; armistice; provisional.

To be Pronounced Before Reading the Chapter.—Nu-e'çes; Ri'o Gran'de; Re-sa'ca de la Pal'ma; Ve'ra Cruz (kroos); Bue'(bō)na Vis'ta; Pueb'la (pweb'la); Con-tre'ras; Mo-li'no del Rey' (ra); Chä-pųl'ta-pec; Chi-hua'hua (che-wä'wä); Gua(gau)da-lupe' Hi-däl'go; Chäl'co.

526. West of Texas (517) the almost uninhabited lands of Mexico stretched away to the Pacific. In 1845 no one realized the extent and fertility of the great Northwest, but the Southwest was an inviting field in which to extend our ownership. President Polk continued the policy of pushing out our lines in that direction.

527. [James K. Polk was born in North Carolina, in 1795, of Irish lineage. His family moved to Tennessee in 1806. Having graduated from the University of North Carolina, Polk became a lawyer. He was in the Tennessee legislature (1823-5), a Representative in Congress (1825-39)—twice elected Speaker,—and Governor of Tennessee (1839-43). He was always an efficient supporter of Jackson. He died in 1849.]

Map Questions.—What territory did Spain lose by the independence of Mexico? What territory did Mexico lose by the independence of Texas? By the war with the United States? Bound Mexico as left by the war. Name the harbors of Mexico. The chief cities. How many routes to the City of Mexico presented themselves to American armies? Were they all used? Why was it easy for the United States to gain possession of Arizona and California? Has California any natural connection with Mexico? Without railroads, which is the easier land journey—from Monterey to New Orleans, or from Monterey to the City of Mexico? Is California associated with Mexico by possessing the same climate and natural products?

TEXAS AND MEXICO.

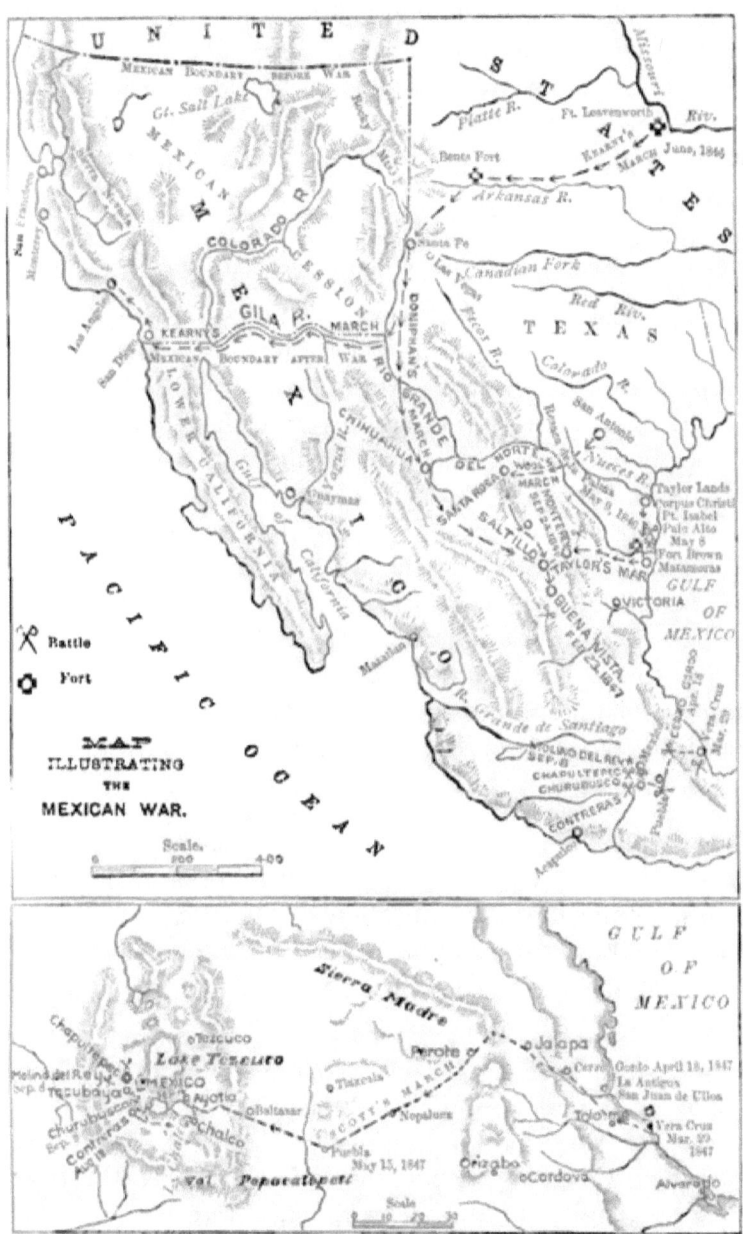

Map illustrating the Mexican War.

Map of Mexico.

528. The Oregon boundary (518) was settled by a treaty with Great Britain in 1846. The "Fifty-four forty or fight" doctrine (518) of the campaign was given up under the skillful management of James Buchanan, our Secretary of State, and the forty-ninth parallel was accepted by both nations as the line.

[Afterwards, a dividing line through the Pacific inlets, in our northwest corner, gave rise to further dispute, which was settled in 1871 (677).]

529. The boundary of Texas on the west was in dispute, also, when Texas was admitted. Mexico claimed the territory to the Nueces River, while Texas drew the line at the Rio Grande. Protection was given to the Texans by our troops under General Zachary Taylor, first as an "army of observation" before Texas was annexed, and afterwards as an "army of occupation" to guard the disputed territory between the Nueces and the Rio Grande. Taylor's army of about 3,000 men was gathered at Corpus Christi early in 1846. In March orders came from President Polk to advance to the Rio Grande. A position on the Rio Grande, nearly opposite Matamoras, was reached and fortified, and received the name of Fort Brown (now Brownsville).

The War with Mexico.

530. The Mexicans ordered Taylor back to the Nueces, on the threat of war. Taylor paid no attention to the order, and went on with his fortifications. The Mexicans crossed the Rio Grande and captured two companies of dragoons, killing a few men. Here began the war with Mexico.

531. The news of bloodshed aroused the nation. "Our country has been invaded," "American blood has been spilled on American soil," were the cries. President Polk, without waiting for word from the Mexican government, called on Congress for prompt action. May 13th, 1846, Congress passed a formal declaration of war, the preamble stating that war existed "by the act of the Republic of

Mexico." Ten days later Mexico declared war against the United States.

532. Battles of 1846.—Taylor was obliged to leave Fort Brown in charge of a small garrison, and to go with the body of his army to Point Isabel, to fetch supplies. During his absence Mexicans crossed from Matamoras in great numbers, and spread through the country between the fort and Taylor's army. On his way back to the fort, Taylor encountered and fought the Mexicans at Palo Alto (May 8th), and Resaca de la Palma (May 9th), driving them across the river. On receiving word of the declaration of war, Taylor transferred his army across the Rio Grande, and his "army of occupation" became an "army of invasion." He waited at Matamoras till August, and then, somewhat reinforced, advanced upon Monterey. The Mexicans, after defending Monterey for three days, were overpowered, and it was surrendered (September 24th). At Monterey Taylor was joined by General John E. Wool, who had marched from San Antonio, Texas, with 3,000 men.

533. Politics of the War.—The Democratic party commenced and conducted the war with Mexico. There was strong opposition, especially from Whigs, who believed the purpose of the war to be the acquisition of territory for the slave system. President Polk asked Congress to place a sum of money in his hands for the payment of Mexican claims, in the event of an early peace. A bill for this purpose was under way in Congress when David Wilmot, a young representative from Pennsylvania, introduced an amendment which divided not only Congress but the whole country in fierce debate.

534. The Wilmot Proviso, which was moved as an amendment to the bill appropriating money, declared it to be "an express and fundamental condition to the acquisition of any territory from Mexico, that neither slavery nor involuntary servitude shall exist therein." The whole question of the extension of slavery, which had been laid on the table in 1820 (**460**), was now before the country.

GENERAL SCOTT.

[The proviso never became a law, but to prevent the spread of the slave system over any more of the "free soil" of America became from year to year the inspiring purpose of a larger and larger number of men in the North. It was not Abolition; it was a command to halt. It was not attack, but defense. On the other hand, the South had grounds for fear in this new and surprising determination. The slave system was spurred on to seize a broader foundation for slavery, and to risk the Union in the attempt. The older leaders, who, loving the Union, had preserved it by compromise, were compelled to vote on the Wilmot Proviso, and they did so with sorrow. Webster voted for it, but with the words: "The future is full of difficulties and full of dangers. We appear to be rushing on perils headlong, and with our eyes all open."]

535. The campaign of 1847 was put in charge of General Winfield Scott (445), the ranking officer of the army. His plan was not to invade Mexico from the north (Taylor's route), but to land at Vera Cruz and march at once upon the Mexican capital. After some hesitation the War Department adopted Scott's plan, and dispatched him to Vera Cruz late in 1846, but with a smaller army than he had desired. Taylor's army was weakened in order to strengthen Scott before Vera Cruz. General Santa Anna, at the head of the Mexican army, thought to crush Taylor's smaller force, but was himself defeated in the hot battle of Buena Vista (February 23d). Scott captured Vera Cruz (March 29th), defeated the Mexicans at Cerro Gordo (April 18th), and entered the city of Puebla (May 15th). In this elevated region there was no fear of fevers, which had made a delay on the coast dangerous to the army, and Scott waited until the arrival of more troops in August.

536. Capture of Mexico.—The regular road to the capital lay between Lakes Chalco and Texcoco. As it was strongly fortified, the army found a new route around Lake Chalco and came upon the city from the southwest. Battles were fought at Contreras and Churubusco (August 19th), and the Mexicans were forced back upon their city. There was now an armistice, in which Mr. N. P. Trist, our commissioner accompanying Scott's army, vainly tried to induce General Santa Anna to accept peace and purchase money in return for New Mexico and California. Negotiations failing, fighting was resumed in the battles of Molino del Rey (September 8th), and Chapultepec (September 14th), strong positions from which the Mexicans were driven at heavy cost to us. The remaining defenses of the capital gave way, and Scott's troops entered the city

(September 14th), Santa Anna and the remains of his army having fled.

537. New Mexico and California.—Our authority was established in New Mexico by General S. W. Kearny, who, in 1847, marched from Fort Leavenworth with 1,800 men, and took possession of Santa Fe. Here he left Colonel Doniphan in command, and set out with a small party for California. Doniphan leaving a force to guard New Mexico, turned southward, and after two sharp battles near Chihuahua, he gained the city and the country around it. Doniphan then led his men into Texas. Before Kearny's arrival in California, the flag of the United States had been raised there by Captain John C. Fremont, who was in California with an exploring expedition at the outbreak of the war, and by Commodore Sloat, in command of our fleet on the Pacific. Thus, before Scott entered the city of Mexico, we were practically in possession of all the territory that we desired from Mexico.

538. Peace.—After the flight of Santa Anna, who was President as well as military commander, there was some difficulty in finding any one with whom to conclude peace. In February, 1848, a provisional Mexican government agreed to terms satisfactory to the United States—the cession of all territory from New Mexico to the Pacific, in return for $15,000,000, to be paid directly to Mexico, and $3,000,000 more to American creditors of Mexico. The treaty also guaranteed to us free navigation of the Gulf of California. This treaty is known as the treaty of Guadalupe Hidalgo, the name of the Mexican village where it was arranged. Our troops were now withdrawn from Mexico.

539. Our War with Mexico was conducted chiefly by the two able generals, Taylor and Scott, and it gave honor and fame to each. Our ranks were filled mainly by volunteers, who showed themselves excellent soldiers. Our armies met no reverses, though generally greatly outnumbered. The Mexican troops, in the words of U. S. Grant (**676**), were "poorly clothed, worse fed, and seldom paid." "With all this," he continues, "I have seen as brave stands made by some of these men as I have ever seen made by soldiers." The war with Mexico rounded out our territory into a broad belt from ocean to ocean. It also gave practical experience in tactics and engineering to the young officers trained at West Point, who afterwards became leaders on both sides in our civil war (**591**).]

540. In the Presidential contest of 1848 the exclusion of the slave system from the territory acquired from Mexico was the decisive question. Polk's negotiator (**536**) had refused Mexico an assurance that the ceded land should be kept free, and Polk was not renominated. His party nominated, for the presidency, Lewis Cass, a native of New Hampshire, and a citizen of Michigan. The Whigs nominated the hero of the war, General Zachary Taylor, a native of Virginia, and a citizen of Louisiana, an owner of slaves, yet a man who loved the Union, and would maintain it firmly. Taylor was elected, with Millard Fillmore, of New York, as Vice-President.

[The electoral vote stood 163 for Taylor, 127 for Cass. Some southern states voted for Taylor, and some northern states for Cass.]

541. [**Free Soil Party.**—Neither Whigs nor Democrats were willing to adopt the principle of the Wilmot Proviso (**534**), and both parties lost those men who desired some distinct assurance that the new soil should be forever free. These men joined in forming the "Free Soil" party; in favor of "Free Soil, Free Speech, Free Labor, and Free Men." Their nominee was ex-President Van Buren. The Free Soilers received the support of the former Abolitionists, and polled considerable votes.]

REVIEW.

ANALYSIS OF WAR WITH MEXICO.

War with Mexico, 1846-8.
- Cause.
- Politics.
  1. Democratic management.
  2. Wilmot Proviso divides the country.
  3. Free Soil Party organized.
- General Method.
  1. Invasion of Mexico.
     1. From Texas by . . .
     2. From the Gulf by . .
  2. Establishment of United States authority in New Mexico and California.
- Terms of Peace.
  1.
  2.
  3.
- Results.
  1.
  2.

CHAPTER XXVIII.

1849-1853.

EL DORADO, THE LAND OF GOLD.

Zachary Taylor, *Louisiana, President.*
Millard Fillmore, *New York, Vice-President and President.*

CABINET.

John M. Clayton, \
Daniel Webster,   } State.
Edward Everett,   /

Wm. M. Meredith, } Treasury.
Thomas Corwin,   /

George W. Crawford, } War.
Charles M. Conrad, /

William B. Preston, \
William A. Graham, } Navy.
John P. Kennedy,   /

Thomas Ewing,   } Interior.
Alex. H. H. Stuart,   /

Reverdy Johnson,   } Attorney-General.
John J. Crittenden, /

Jacob Collamer,   \
Nathan K. Hall,   } Postmaster-General.
Samuel D. Hubbard, /

542. The election of Taylor in no way settled the question of excluding slavery from the new territory, and before the United States had even adopted a plan for governing its new possessions, California had the population and the government of a state, and was demanding an equal voice in the management of the Union. All this wonderful progress was made between Taylor's election in 1848 and his death in 1850.

543. [**Zachary Taylor** was born in Virginia, in 1784. His father, a revolutionary officer, moved to a plantation near Louisville, Kentucky. In 1808 young Taylor entered the army, rising to captain in 1810, and for brave service in the war of 1812, was promoted to major by brevet, and later to full major. He served in the Black Hawk War (**498**), and afterwards in Florida, rising successively to lieutenant-colonel, colonel, and brigadier-general by brevet, with which rank he took command of the Army of the Southwest in 1840 (**529**). At this time he bought a plantation near Baton Rouge, Louisiana. He died at Washington, July 9, 1850.]

544. California attracted the attention of America and of the world by the discovery of gold in the foothills of the Sierras in the spring of 1848. In the gold region of California the yellow treasure could be found in the sand and gravel of every mountain stream. Through the remainder of 1848, stories of fabulous wealth crept eastward over the continent, so wonderful as hardly to be believed. The

GENERAL ZACHARY TAYLOR.

next year found thousands of people pushing westward, to dig gold in California. From the Atlantic shores they hurried to embark in sailing craft around Cape Horn; and from the "western" states they drove their emigrant wagons across plains, deserts, and mountains. Every danger by sea or land was braved for a chance to share the new found treasure. Every man's dream was to take his fortune from the "diggings" and return to enjoy his wealth in his early home. Few there were to find a fortune and return; the many stayed to build new homes and complete the foundation of a state.

[California never had a territorial government. United States military authority was represented by General Bennet Riley; but the people had come and had formed a political organization of their own before the civil arm of the government at Washington could be extended for their protection. At the call of General Riley, they elected delegates, who met at Monterey September 1st, 1849, and framed a constitution. This constitution was adopted by the people, officers under it elected, a state government inaugurated, and two men elected and dispatched to Washington to demand the admission of California as a state and to be Senators in Congress. All this was done before the end of 1849.]

545. Question of Admission.—The constitution of California prohibited slavery, and the question of admission called up all the enmities which had threatened to divide the Union over the admission of Missouri (**459**). Now, the question concerned the admission of a free state, instead of a slave state as in 1820. Thirty years, however, had only intensified the bitterness of the struggle. President Taylor recommended the admission of California with her constitution. His death, while the question was still pending, increased the difficulties of the situation, for the whole country, both North and South, trusted him. Vice-President Fillmore, who now became President, favored compromise measures, which were introduced, as in 1820 (**460**), under the leadership of Clay. Upon the basis of compromise, the question of admission was at last settled.

546. [**Millard Fillmore** was born in New York, in 1800. With only a limited education, and an apprenticeship as a fuller, he began the study of law. Being poor his study was done under great difficulties. He, however, succeeded in fitting himself, and began practice in 1823 in Erie county. He was a member of the New York legislature (1828-31), Representative in Congress (1833-5 and 1837-1843), an unsuccessful candidate for governor (1844), state comptroller (1847-9), and then Vice-President and President. He was the unsuccessful nominee of the American party (**569**) in 1856. He passed the rest of his life in retirement at Buffalo, New York, where he died in 1874.]

547. The Omnibus Bill is the name given to Clay's compromise, because it carried so many regulations. Its main provisions were: 1. The admission of California as a free state and with her present boundaries. 2. The organization of the rest of the Mexican cession into territories, Utah (including Nevada) and New Mexico (including Arizona), with nothing said as to slavery, and Texas getting $10,000,-000 to relinquish her claims on New Mexico. 3. The continuance of slavery in the District of Columbia (**492**). 4. The passage of a new Fugitive Slave Law.

548. The compromise of 1850 was effected by the passage of the essential features of Clay's bill as separate measures, the bill not passing as a whole. California was admitted as a state September 9th, 1850. The Fugitive Slave Law, passed about the same time, provided for the arrest and return of runaway slaves through the courts of the United States.

549. [**Fugitive Slave Law.**—Since the beginning of the anti-slavery movement (**492**), slave owners, especially along the border line, had lost heavily by the escape of slaves. There were people in the free states to shelter and aid them, and if they could reach Canada they were beyond pursuit. There came to be a secret system of stations for concealment through the free states to Canada, which was known as the "underground railroad." The provisions of this fugitive slave law were terribly exasperating to the people of the North. Any negro might be arrested, and, on the testimony of two persons, declared a runaway, his own statements counting for nothing. Any person concealing a slave, or assisting his escape, might be fined and imprisoned, and must pay $1,000 to the owner, if the slave got away. Daniel Webster, in reviewing the provisions of the Omnibus Bill, on March 7th, 1850, defended the fugitive slave law, and attacked the Abolitionists. This speech became historic, as Webster's "Seventh of March Speech." It was a bitter blow to many of his life-long friends in the North.]

550. Change of Leaders.—Again it was hoped that the agitation of slavery questions was laid to rest. The year 1850, however, marks a significant change of leaders in national affairs. Clay and Webster had fought neither for slavery nor against it, but always for the Union. Calhoun had fought for slavery, had prophesied disunion, but sought to guard against it (**485**). The generation of these men was gone. A younger generation was pressing on, marshaling itself gradually into two columns. At the head of one

1. Foote.   2. Stephens.   3. Toombs.

were Jefferson Davis and Henry S. Foote of Mississippi,

Howell Cobb, Robert Toombs, and Alexander H. Stephens of Georgia, and others, who would extend the slave system over the territories, or would, most of them, separate the slave states from the Union on the plea of state sovereignty. Leading the other were men like Charles Sumner of Massachusetts, William H. Seward of New York, and Salmon P. Chase of Ohio, who would admit no further advance of slavery upon free soil, and would, if need be, defend the Union by force of arms.

551. **The country** was prosperous in 1850. We were no longer a feeble people, living on the verge of a wilderness. We had conquered the wilderness, and become a great nation, reaching from sea to sea. To strengthen and more closely unite the country, men were beginning to think of a continental railway. In Europe there was peace, and the nations of the earth gathered to display and compare the products of their industry in the World's Fair at London, in 1851, the first of its kind. Hopeful men prophesied that war would be no more, and that nations, looking to the common interests of humanity, would agree to inhabit the earth in peace. Governments should be for the correction of evils, and not the instruments of pride and ambition.

<small>552. [The **Maine Law.**—In 1851 Maine passed what is known as the Maine Liquor Law. It prohibits the making or selling of alcoholic liquors within the state, except for medical purposes.]</small>

553. In the **Presidential** Campaign of 1852, both Whigs and Democrats tried to convince the country that the compromise of 1850 was a final settlement. The Democratic platform declaring that "the Democratic party will resist all attempts at renewing in Congress or out of it the agitation of the slavery question, under whatever shape or color the attempt may be made," was entirely pleasing to the South. The Whig convention declared that the party acquiesced in the compromise measures "as a settlement in principle and in substance of the dangerous and exciting

questions which they embrace." The Whig leaders were in a false position. They could neither gain the confidence

1. Sumner. 2. Seward. 3. Chase.

of the South, nor convince the North that an honest and

God-fearing man should accept the fugitive slave law as just, and obey it as a permanent regulation. Franklin Pierce, of New Hampshire, the Democratic nominee, was completely victorious over General Winfield Scott, a native of Virginia, the nominee of the Whigs.

[Pierce received 254 electoral votes to forty-two for Scott. The Whig party never organized for another election. Daniel Webster had been a candidate before the Whig convention for the presidency, but he had no support outside of Massachusetts. Clay, from his death bed, sent his last advice to his friends to oppose Webster. Webster himself died just before election day revealed the defeat and death of the Whig party, a party of which he and Clay more than any other men had been the founders and defenders.]

554. [**The Free Soilers** nominated John P. Hale of New Hampshire, but gained no electoral vote. In 1848 the Free Soil vote, considerably increased by dissensions among the Democrats, was 291,263. In 1852 it was only 156,149 out of a total vote of over three millions. This vote may be taken to represent the number of men in the free states at this time who were disposed to make the fight against slavery a national issue.]

QUESTIONS.

Review the terms of the Missouri Compromise, and see if you find therein anything preventing the admission of California as a free state. What was the cause of opposition to the admission of Missouri? What was the cause of opposition in the case of California? Counting thirty-three years as a generation, when did the first generation after the constitution (1787) end? The second generation? What were the ideas of leaders of the first generation, as Jefferson, repecting slavery? What were the ideas of leaders of the second generation, as Webster and Calhoun? Name early leaders of the third generation, and compare their ideas on the same subject. Who was sovereign of Great Britain in 1851? (43). Make a list of the great wars that have occurred in Europe and America since 1851. Account for the death of the Whig party. Find out how many states now have laws similar to the Maine Law.

CHAPTER XXIX.
1853-1857.
THE STRUGGLE FOR KANSAS, AND A NEW PARTY.

Franklin Pierce, *New Hampshire, President.*
Wm. P. King, *Alabama, Vice-President (died in office).*

CABINET.

William L. Marcy—State.   James C. Dobbin—Navy.
James Guthrie—Treasury.   Robert McClelland—Interior.
Jefferson Davis—War.   Caleb Cushing—Attorney-General.
          James Campbell—Postmaster-General.

To be Pronounced.—Bowdoin (bō′den); Koszta (kŏz′ta).

555. The administration of President Pierce began with the country quiet and prosperous. Before its close there was civil strife on the plains of Kansas, which divided the whole country in angry conflict.

556. [**Franklin Pierce** was born in New Hampshire in 1804. He graduated at Bowdoin College in 1824, a classmate of Nathaniel Hawthorne **(497)**, and became a lawyer. He was an ardent Jackson man. After serving in the New Hampshire legislature, he was elected to the House of Representatives in 1833, and to the United States Senate in 1837. In 1842 he resigned and returned to his profession. In the Mexican war he served as a colonel of volunteers and was promoted to brigadier-general. His nomination for the presidency was the result of a coalition. A two-thirds vote was required by rule of the convention. The prominent candidates were Lewis Cass, James Buchanan, Stephen A. Douglas, and William L. Marcy. After two days' balloting there was still no choice. On the third day Pierce's name was presented, and on the forty-ninth ballot he received a unanimous vote. During the civil war **(591)** he expressed sympathy with the Confederates. He died in 1868.]

557. The questions of slavery were reopened with greater fierceness than ever before, within one month after Pierce's first message to Congress. A bill was before the Senate to establish a territory of Nebraska. Stephen A. Douglas, a young and brilliant Democratic Senator from Illinois, and chairman of the committee on territories, reported certain amendments declaring that the compromise of 1850 **(548)**

had repealed the Missouri compromise (**460**). This declaration was defended "upon the great principle of self-government, that the people should be allowed to decide the questions of their domestic institutions for themselves." The proposed repeal was a surprise to the whole country, for the Missouri compromise had stood unchallenged for thirty-three years and no one had thought of its being touched in any way in 1850.

[Senator Dixon of Kentucky, Clay's successor, proposed to make a straightforward case of the Nebraska bill by an amendment, that "the Missouri compromise be repealed, and that the citizens of the several states be at liberty to take and hold their slaves within any of the territories." This amendment represented the common desire of pro-slavery leaders. The question, however, was not fought out on this plain ground. The southern leaders were content that Douglas should accomplish the admission of slavery into the territory north of 36° 30′, putting it on any ground that suited him.]

558. The Kansas-Nebraska Act is the name given to the act of Congress, which was finally voted upon and passed in May, 1854. It established territorial governments for Kansas and Nebraska, and declared that all laws of the United States should be in force in those territories, except the section of the Missouri compromise act prohibiting slavery north of 36° 30′. This section was declared to have been superseded by the compromise of 1850, and therefore was "inoperative and void." For each territory the act provided for a governor, secretary, and judges to be appointed by the President and Senate, and a territorial legislature to be elected by actual residents.

[In 1848 an attempt to extend the line of 36° 30′, through the Mexican cession to the Pacific, had failed. At that time, Douglas argued, the Missouri compromise was virtually abandoned. Then, in 1850, California was admitted with the free constitution formed by her people. This he claimed as a recognition that the United States had no power over slavery in the territories, and an acceptance of the principle of "popular sovereignty," as he termed it, or the right of people in a territory "to regulate their domestic institutions in their own way."]

559. The repeal of the Missouri compromise was to the

country a dividing sword. Douglas claimed at the time that it legislated slavery neither into the territories nor out of them, but left the whole matter to the territorial legislature. Quickly, however, the South set up the claim that the constitution recognized slavery; that, therefore, slave owners were entitled to full protection of their property in the territories, and no power could prohibit slavery until a state government should be formed. By the repeal, the plains of Kansas, unoccupied save by Indian owners, were held out as a prize to free labor or slavery, to be won by the swiftest in the race. Many southern Whigs joined with Democrats in voting for the repeal. All who opposed the repeal and the attempted extension of the slave system were quickly gathered into a new party.

560. [**Thomas H. Benton,** one of the ablest of the early Democrats, a constant supporter and admirer of Jackson, had entered the United States Senate on the admission of Missouri. For thirty years he was a Senator from Missouri, and for thirty years he had eloquently maintained the principles of the Democratic party. But his party passed from him, and he was at last defeated for the Senate (1850). Elected, however, to the House, in opposition to all the younger members of his party, he denounced the Kansas-Nebraska bill. He declared that the Missouri compromise had been forced upon the North by the South, and now it was to be repealed, "without a memorial, without a petition, and without a request from any human being."]

561. The Republican Party.—Few Congressmen from the North who had voted for the Kansas-Nebraska act were reëlected. They were voted against by every man opposed to the extension of the slave system, whether he had called himself Democrat, Whig, or Free-Soiler. Thus began a new and vigorous party, confined to the free states and distinctly maintaining the right and the duty of Congress to keep slavery out of the territories. Under the name of "Anti-Nebraska Men," the new party, in the fall of 1854, elected a majority of the House of Representatives. The name Republican was adopted immediately after this election.

562. The struggle for Kansas was a trial of strength between North and South. Emigrant aid societies were incorporated in free states to assist settlers in reaching Kansas. Secret political societies were formed in Missouri for the purpose of extending slavery into Kansas. The South had the advantage of nearness, Missouri being a slave state. The North had the advantage of a far greater number of persons free to move as emigrants and greater wealth to assist them. The efforts of the slave states, however, had the countenance of those who remained leaders in the Democratic party. Slave-owners having crossed into Kansas, held meetings and declared that slavery existed in Kansas and that free-state settlers should be ejected if they gave any annoyance.

563. [**Civil Strife in Kansas.**—Andrew H. Reeder, the first governor appointed, arrived in Kansas in October, 1854. In November he called an election for a territorial delegate to Congress, and another in March, 1855, for a territorial legislature. On both occasions armed bands crossed over from Missouri, took possession of the polls, stuffed the boxes with illegal votes, and after voting returned to Missouri. At the second election there was fraudulent voting on the part of the free-state settlers also. Governor Reeder tried in vain to have justice done. He was soon removed, and several successors continued the useless attempt to keep peace between the free-state settlers and the slave-state visitors. By the middle of 1856 there were two territorial constitutions, and two legislatures were competing to make laws for Kansas. The pro-slavery legislature was organized first. It fixed its capital at Lecompton, adopted Missouri laws in a body, and made an oath to support the Fugitive Slave Law a test for voters at all elections. The second legislature organized at Topeka under an anti-slavery constitution, but it was broken up by the arrest and imprisonment of its officers. There was now a civil war in Kansas, and the authority of the United States was only feebly exerted to keep the peace. Conflicts between small bands of armed men were frequent, with loss of life and destruction of property.]

564. Ruffianism, that ruled in Kansas, entered even the halls of Congress. Charles Sumner of Massachusetts was one of the boldest of the few Republican Senators. In a speech upon Kansas affairs, delivered in the Senate in May,

1856, Sumner criticised a Senator from South Carolina in bitter yet not unparliamentary terms. That Senator was not present, but his nephew, Preston S. Brooks, a Representative of the same state, having read Sumner's speech, resolved on punishment. Two days after the speech, Brooks, finding Sumner at his seat, writing, the Senate having adjourned, assaulted him, beating him over the head with a cane. Sumner was stunned by the blows, and was so seriously injured that several years passed before he recovered. This assault was regarded in the North as a bitter insult; in the South it was not condemned, and even received applause.

[The Republicans had a majority in the House, but could not get a two-thirds vote to expel Brooks. They, however, passed a vote of censure, upon which Brooks resigned. Within three weeks he returned, having been immediately reëlected. He challenged Senator Wilson, Sumner's colleague, for words denouncing his assault. Wilson declined a duel. Anson Burlingame, a Massachusetts Representative, accepted a challenge from Brooks, and named a place in Canada for the fight. Brooks then excused himself, on the ground that a trip through the states would risk his life. Other assaults, growing out of the same disputes, occurred outside of Congress.]

565. Cuba and Filibustering.—Cuba, as well as Kansas, invited conquest for slavery. In 1854 James Buchanan, our Minister to England, joined our Ministers to France and Spain, at Ostend, in Belgium, and the three issued a manifesto, called the *Ostend Circular*. It declared that we should be justified in seizing Cuba, should its possession by Spain be decided dangerous to our peace. There were filibustering expeditions against Cuba and other Spanish possessions, their object being to annex Cuba as a slave state. Attacks were made on Central America. These expeditions accomplished nothing beyond bringing dishonor upon our country. The leaders were frequently shot by Spanish authorities.

[William A. Walker, the most noted of the filibusters, was shot in Central America, in 1860.]

566. **The country** progressed and made great improvements, in spite of strife over slavery. In 1853 was held a second great World's Fair, in the Crystal Palace, in New York City, a large building of iron and glass, built for the purpose. In the same year New York established a Clearing House, which keeps accounts and does business between banks, just as banks do between persons. The rights of an American citizen were maintained before the world in the case of Martin Koszta, an escaped Austrian rebel, who had taken out his naturalization papers in the United States. He had afterwards gone to Asia Minor, where the Austrians arrested him; but one of our war vessels forced them to give him up as an American citizen. A beginning was made for commerce with Asia, when Commodore M. C. Perry, in 1854, forced his way into a Japanese harbor. He induced the Emperor of Japan to give up the policy of keeping his country shut out from the rest of the world, and gained his consent to commercial treaty with the United States. Railroad building went on rapidly, assisted by improvements in bridges.

[The rapid growth of the farming industry had led to important inventions in agricultural implements. In striking contrast to pounding the grain from the straw with flails and afterward winnowing it through an old-fashioned fanning mill, a thrashing machine was exhibited at the World's Fair in 1853 that not only thrashed the grain, but winnowed, sacked, measured, and recorded the quantity, all in one operation. In the year 1855, at the World's Fair in Paris, an American reaping machine was awarded the first prize for the rapidity and quality of its work. Up to this date, also, no less than 372 patents had been issued for improvements in plows.]

567. [**Gadsden Purchase.**—The treaty of Guadalupe Hidalgo (**538**) did not properly define the southern boundary of Arizona, and a dispute arose with the Mexican government over a strip of land lying south of the Gila River. This dispute was settled in 1853, by the purchase of the Mexican title, at a cost of $10,000,000. This is known as the Gadsden Purchase, James Gadsden, of South Carolina, having been our Minister to negotiate terms with Mexico.]

568. **The Presidential Election of** 1856 showed the vigor

of the Republican party. The Democrats desired a man who had not been concerned in the Kansas-Nebraska act, and found him in James Buchanan, who had been absent

OLD AND NEW IN HARVESTING.

in England during the strife over that measure. He was nominated for President. The Republicans nominated John C. Fremont of California, who had a favorable record

THE STRUGGLE FOR KANSAS, AND A NEW PARTY.

as an explorer and military officer, and a private character which won friends. Of the thirty-one states Fremont carried eleven, Buchanan nineteen. Buchanan was elected. Fremont received 114 votes, all from free states; Buchanan, 174.

569. [American Party.—Some southern Whigs joined the Democrats. Others joined a newly formed American party, which offered standing ground for all not prepared to take sides either for or against slavery. It proposed to require twenty-one years for naturalization, and to prohibit citizens of foreign birth from holding office. It maintained a secret organization, with initiations, passwords, etc., and from the secrecy of their proceedings the members were dubbed Know-Nothings. Their candidate for the presidency was ex-President Fillmore, also the nominee of remaining Whigs. He gained the eight votes of Maryland.]

REVIEW.

Repeal of the Missouri Compromise .....
- Proposed for what purpose.
- Accomplished. { By what means. Under what leaders.
- Result to political parties.
- Result for the nation.
- Result in Kansas.

QUESTIONS.

Why might even persons who thought the Missouri compromise wrong in itself, oppose its repeal? State the elements that made up the Republican party of 1856. What feelings between sections were shown at the time of the assault on Sumner? What spirit was shown in the expedition against Cuba? What kinds of bridges have you seen? What great bridges have you read about? State the benefits of World's Fairs. What smaller expositions have you visited? Bound Kansas. What slave state had to be crossed by northern settlers passing directly to Kansas?

CHAPTER XXX.
1857-1861.
FROM THE DRED SCOTT DECISION TO SECESSION.

James Buchanan, *Pennsylvania, President.*
John C. Breckinridge, *Kentucky, Vice-President.*

CABINET.

Lewis Cass, } State.
Jeremiah S. Black, }

Howell Cobb, }
Philip F. Thomas, } Treasury.
John A. Dix, }

John B. Floyd, } War.
Joseph Holt, }

Isaac Toucey—Navy.
Jacob Thompson—Interior.

Jeremiah S. Black, } Attorney-General.
Edwin M. Stanton, }

Aaron V. Brown, }
Joseph Holt, } Postmaster-General.
Horatio King, }

570. The administration of President Buchanan began under auspices very different from those of his predecessor. In 1853 the great majority of the people tried to believe that the question of slavery extension had been laid aside. In 1857 the majority could see that the time of neutrality was over. Buchanan's election had settled nothing, while the ballots cast for Fremont surprised Democrats everywhere and alarmed the South.

571. [James Buchanan was born in Pennsylvania, in 1791. After graduating from college, he became a lawyer. He served in the war of 1812, and was a Representative in Congress (1821-31), Minister to Russia (1832-4), United States Senator (1834-45), Secretary of State (1845-9), and Minister to Great Britain (1853-6). After his presidency he retired to his home near Lancaster, Pennsylvania, where he died in 1868.]

572. The Democratic Platform of 1856 had declared that the principles of our Constitution made "ours the land of liberty, and the asylum of the oppressed of every nation," but it had avoided any decided stand with regard to the domestic institution of slavery. Democratic leaders were inclined to leave to the courts the question whether or not slavery should be protected in the territories up to the time of forming a state government.

573. The Dred Scott Case.—The United States Supreme Court undertook to settle once for all the question of slavery extension, which was beginning to threaten the Union. A Missouri slave known as Dred Scott had been taken by his master into what is now Minnesota, at the time a part of Wisconsin territory, and also a part of the Louisiana purchase, north of 36° 30'. After a return to Missouri Dred Scott brought suit for freedom, on the ground that his master had voluntarily taken him where slavery was positively prohibited. The suit came at last before the Supreme Court of the United States, by which it was decided that the Constitution of the United States regarded negroes merely as property, that they could not become citizens, and had no rights in a United States court, and that the Missouri compromise and any United States laws prohibiting slavery were unconstitutional. The decision was given through Chief Justice Roger B. Taney, March 6th, 1857.

574. [**The decision was regarded** in the South as a victory, peaceably awarding all that was desired for the extension of slavery. In the North it was regarded as a perversion of justice and a disgrace to our country's history. Not less than the decision itself, its language, and the historical proofs cited for it, were exasperating to northern people. Chief Justice Taney, examining public opinion at the beginning of our government, claimed to find that negroes were then, in the prevailing opinion of the civilized world, regarded as an inferior race, with "no rights which a white man was bound to respect."]

575. The Lecompton Constitution.—The Dred Scott decision encouraged the pro-slavery leaders to continue the struggle to gain Kansas as a slave state. A convention called by the Lecompton legislature (**563**), drafted at that place in November, 1857, a pro-slavery constitution. An election was held, not upon the whole constitution, but only on the slavery sections. Free state settlers refused to vote. Thousands of fraudulent votes were returned by non-citizens, and admission to the Union was demanded for Kansas as a slave state. President Buchanan gave his approval to the acts which had nominally made Kansas a slave state. The "Lecompton Bill" was introduced in Congress, to admit Kansas with the Lecompton constitution. It was passed in the Senate, but could not be carried in the House of Representatives. The whole constitution was then submitted to the people, and it was defeated by an immense majority (January 4th, 1859).

[Senator Douglas resisted the Lecompton constitution as a wholesale outrage upon citizens of Kansas. He firmly maintained his doctrine of "popular sovereignty"—that the people of Kansas had the right to decide the question of slavery, but denied that the Lecompton constitution represented the will of Kansas citizens.]

576. [**Lincoln-Douglas Debate.**—In 1858 Senator Douglas was the Democratic candidate for reëlection before the Illinois legislature. Illinois Republicans nominated against him Abraham Lincoln, known to his neighbors as "Honest Abe," and in politics as an opponent of slavery, shrewd and ready in a stump speech, careful in his words, always absolutely truthful, and a master of humorous anecdote. Upon Lincoln's challenge, the current political questions were discussed by Douglas and himself in a series of joint meetings. This memorable debate on subjects of intense interest, such as the Lecompton constitution and the Dred Scott decision, fixed the attention of the whole country on Lincoln and Douglas. Lincoln gained the popular support of Illinois, but Douglas held enough of the legislators to be reëlected. Lincoln became a representative Republican, and his counsel and assistance as a political speaker were sought outside of his own state.]

577. New States.—Kansas formed a new constitution through a convention at Wyandotte (July, 1859). The Wyandotte constitution prohibited slavery, and was lawfully adopted. Kansas, however, did not gain admission to the Union until January, 1861. Minnesota became a state in 1858, and Oregon in 1859.

578. [**John Brown,** a native of Connecticut, a man of great bodily strength and unflinching courage, yet little wisdom, had fought against the pro-slavery bands in Kansas (**563**). He was a religious fanatic, and in the Kansas fights had formed the idea that he was divinely appointed to free the negroes from bondage. From some of the Abolitionists he obtained money. He then got together a number of reckless youth whom he trained for military service. His plan was to get free negroes to join him, advance rapidly into the mountains of Virginia, arm slaves, maintain his ground in mountain strongholds, and gradually get the 4,000,000 slaves of the southern states excited to armed and murderous conflict against their masters.]

579. John Brown's Raid.—On the night of October 19th, 1859, with a few confederates, Brown attacked and captured the United States arsenal at Harper's Ferry. He was quickly surrounded by Maryland and Virginia militia and ten of his men were killed. Brown and seven others, badly wounded, were captured. Brown was tried in a Virginia court, convicted of treason, conspiracy, and murder, and hanged. The sole effect of his crazy attempt was to inflame the South with anger.

580. Presidential Nominations, 1860.—The Democratic convention met at Charleston, South Carolina, in April, 1860, to nominate a presidential candidate. Jefferson Davis (550) in the Senate had already endeavored to have passed a series of resolutions to serve as the new Democratic platform. They declared that slaves were property, that neither Congress nor a territory had any right to interfere with this "property," and that it was the duty of Congress to protect it in case a territory failed to do so. These proposed additions to the platform of the Democratic party came before the Charleston convention. Northern Democrats, who recognized the leadership of Douglas, resisted their adoption. After a long struggle, the delegates from the cotton states—Alabama, Mississippi, Louisiana, South Carolina, Florida, Texas, and Arkansas—withdrew from the convention. Reconciliation was impossible. Two separate conventions were held at a later date. The northern Democrats nominated for the presidency Stephen A. Douglas of Illinois. The southern Democrats nominated John C. Breckinridge of Kentucky, then Vice-President. An enthusiastic Republican convention at Chicago nominated Abraham Lincoln of Illinois. The remnants of the Whig and the American parties (569), under the name of the Constitutional Union party, nominated John Bell of Tennessee.

581. Four Platforms.—Every candidate expressed his wish to maintain the Union. Every party was for government aid in building a railroad to the Pacific. The Republicans spoke for protective tariff and against any change in the naturalization laws. Both Democratic platforms called for the acquisition of Cuba (565), and denounced state interference with the Fugitive Slave Law (549). The grand distinction, however, was found in the attitude toward slavery. Republicans represented the belief that slavery was morally wrong and politically hurtful, not to be interfered with in the states, but by national authority forever to be excluded from the territories. Douglas Democrats proposed to leave the question to territorial settlers, and were willing to submit to the decisions of the Supreme Court. Breckinridge Democrats counted slavery morally right and slave labor an industrial advantage, and held that it was the duty of the national government to protect in the territories slave property as any other. The Constitutional Union men ignored slavery altogether, and were " for the constitution of the country, the union of the states, and the enforcement of the laws," words which were purposely indefinite.

582. The result was a Republican victory. Lincoln was elected, receiving the electoral votes of every free state except New Jersey. Missouri and New Jersey cast their votes for Douglas; Virginia, Kentucky, and Tennessee, for Bell; the others were for Breckinridge. The South regarded the election of a Republican President as a menace to the southern institution of slavery. To remain in the Union under him was represented as dishonor to southern leaders.

583. Secession.—South Carolina, through a special convention, passed an ordinance of secession, December 20th, 1860, and her governor declared South Carolina a separate, sovereign, free, and independent state, having a right to levy war, conclude peace, negotiate treaties, etc. By a general movement and through similar conventions, Georgia, Florida, Mississippi, Alabama, and Louisiana seceded in January, 1861. Texas followed in February.

584. The southern people had no opportunity to vote on secession. They elected conventions to consider public questions, and the conventions passed ordinances declaring the states out of the Union. It is believed by many that a majority of the southern people would have voted against secession. When once, however, a convention had declared a state seceded, its people, taught as they had been in the doctrine of state sovereignty (476), almost to a man felt bound "to follow their state."

585. The Confederacy.—The conventions of the seceding states elected delegates, who met at Montgomery, Alabama, in February, 1861, and formed a constitution for the "Confederate States of America." This same convention, in order to put its government into operation, declared itself a Congress, and elected as President of the Confederacy, Jefferson Davis of Mississippi, and Alexander H. Stephens of Georgia as Vice-President.(550). A flag was adopted, and preparations made for military defense.

[The Confederate constitution copied that of the United States, only substituting the word "Confederacy" for "Union," and making some changes to secure an undisputed sovereignty of states. The whole government was called provisional. Stephens, the Vice-President, had been a strong Union man, but followed his state when it seceded.]

586. The United States Government stood still. President Buchanan claimed to have no right under the constitution to force the seceded states to return, and was weak in protecting United States property. Secretary of War Floyd had ordered stores of war from northern arsenals to places where they were easily seized by Confederates. Southern Congressmen and other officials generally resigned, and joined their states. The Confederates seized, without resistance, all United States forts, arsenals, custom houses, mints, etc., within their territory. Fort Sumter, in Charleston harbor, and a few other posts on the coast, were alone defended.

587. [Excitement and Conspiracy.—The whole country was in a state of excitement and anxiety. All attention was directed to the new President. Lincoln passed from Springfield, Illinois, toward the national capital, the recipient of public honors until he reached Philadelphia. No honors were tendered him from Maryland, and evidence of a plot to assassinate him while passing through Baltimore, induced him to make the trip from Philadelphia to Washington by a night train, in advance of the time previously published. He arrived in safety at Washington (February 23d, 1861).]

REVIEW.

Find out all that you can about the following men, and then write an account of the part each one took in national affairs, from 1857 to 1861: James Buchanan, Roger B. Taney, Stephen A. Douglas, Abraham Lincoln, John Brown.

THE NATIONAL CAPITOL.

CHAPTER XXXI.
1861-1865.
THE WAR OF SECESSION.

Abraham Lincoln, *Illinois, President.*
Hannibal Hamlin, *Maine, Vice-President.*

CABINET.

William H. Seward—State.
Salmon P. Chase—Treasury.
Simon Cameron, } War.
Edwin P. Stanton, }
Gideon Wells—Navy.

Caleb B. Smith, } Interior.
John P. Usher, }
Edward Bates, } Attorney-General.
James Speed, }
Montgomery Blair, } P. M. General.
William Dennison, }

For Explanation.—Letters of marque; belligerent powers; guerilla.

588. The situation of the Republican administration was trying. Seven states had declared themselves out of the Union, and intended to stay out unless the administration would surrender to them on the subject of slavery. The states lying between the secession area and the free states were distinctly hostile to bringing back the seceded states by force. In the North there was a strong sentiment that it was better to let them go than to have a war; but a stronger sentiment declared that the unity of the nation must be preserved at any cost. The President's inaugural was thoroughly peaceful. He assured the people of the South that their property was not in danger, that fugitive slaves should be delivered up, and he questioned whether any constitutional right had ever been withheld from them. "In your hands, my dissatisfied fellow countrymen, and not in mine," he said, "is the momentous question of civil war. The government will not assail you. We are not enemies, but friends; we must not be enemies."

ABRAHAM LINCOLN.

589. [**Abraham Lincoln** was born in Kentucky, in 1809, of poor parents. The family moved to Indiana, and thence to Illinois. He had less than a year's school instruction in all his life, but he educated himself thoroughly by patient and careful study. From his boyhood up he was used to hard work. When he was sixteen, he served as ferryman on the Ohio. Three years later, he made a trip on a flatboat, with a cargo to New Orleans. He could already make stump speeches, and was famous for his muscular strength and talent in telling anecdotes. In Illinois he split rails, worked as a farm hand, and in a country store. Still, poverty clung to him. He went to the Black Hawk War as a Captain of volunteers (**498**). In 1832 he ran for the legislature, and was defeated. He studied law, and by hard work won a good practice. He was a Representative in Congress (1847–9).]

590. **Fort Sumter.**—Early in April President Lincoln ordered provisions sent from New York to Fort Sumter. When this word reached the South an order was tele-

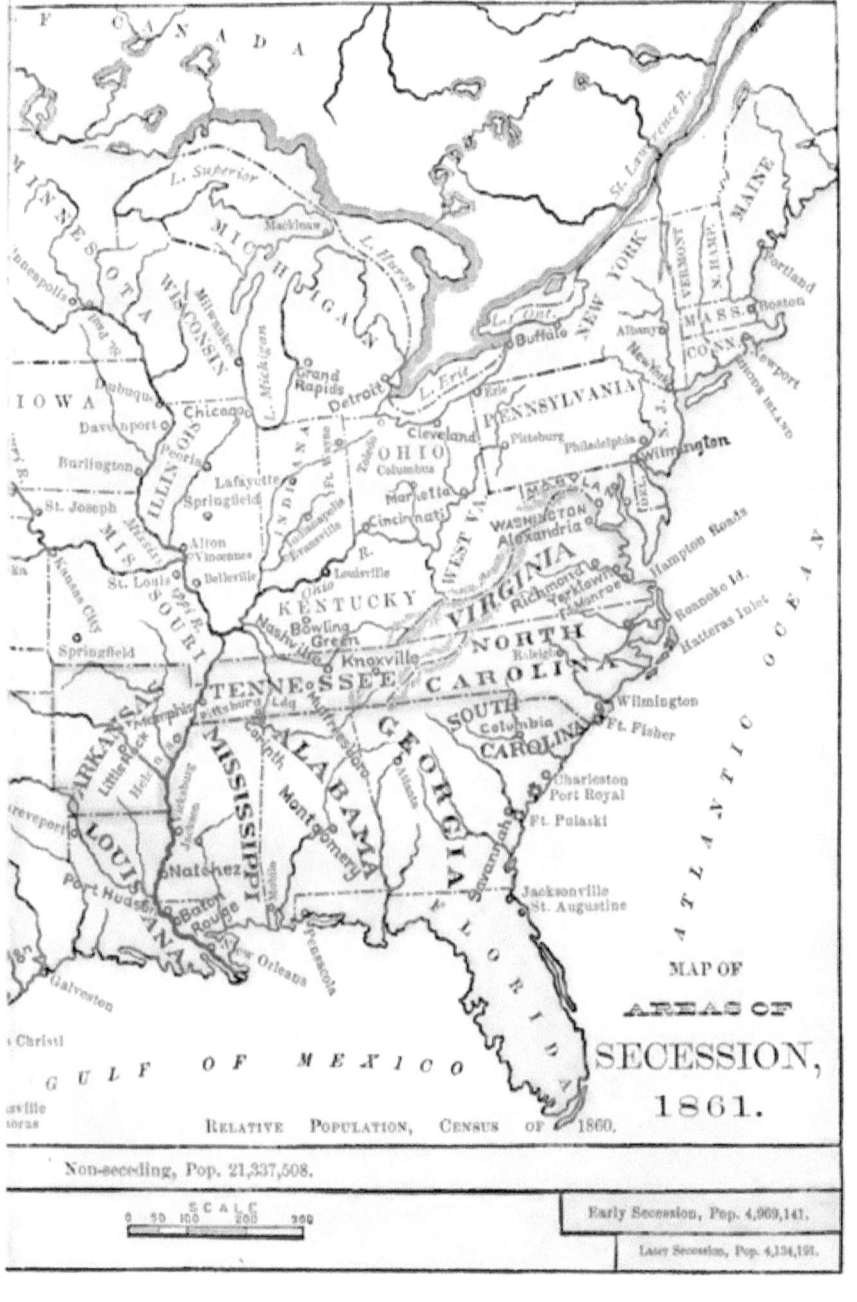

MAP OF AREAS OF SECESSION, 1861.

RELATIVE POPULATION, CENSUS OF 1860.

Non-seceding, Pop. 21,337,508.
Early Secession, Pop. 4,969,141.
Later Secession, Pop. 4,134,191.

graphed from Montgomery (585) to General G. P. T. Beauregard, in command of the Confederate batteries, to fire upon Sumter. Beauregard first called on Major Robert Anderson, the United States officer commanding, for the surrender of the fort. Anderson refused, and a heavy bombardment began on the morning of April twelfth, which was answered from Fort Sumter. By noon, April thirteenth, Anderson's ammunition was exhausted, his fort in flames, and he surrendered, marching out with the honors of war.

591. The Beginning of the War.—The civil war began with the bombardment of Fort Sumter. The flag had been fired on. The wavering spirit of the North was united in a storm of indignation. On April fifteenth the President called for 75,000 volunteer troops to serve for three months, to suppress rebellion, and four times the number offered themselves. Companies hurried from the North to protect the National Capital. On April nineteenth a Massachusetts regiment, passing through Baltimore, was attacked by a mob, and a few men were killed. Here was shed the first blood of the war. The South was equally excited and more united than the North. The Confederate Government called for 35,000 soldiers, and several times the number came forward. President Lincoln proclaimed a blockade of southern ports. The Confederate Government issued "letters of marque" against the United States. In May President Lincoln called for 42,000 volunteers, to serve for three years. Virginia, North Carolina, and Arkansas joined the Confederacy, and the seat of government was moved from Montgomery to Richmond, Virginia.

592. A General View of the War.—The Confederacy, claiming to be an independent nation, declared and waged war against the United States as a foreign power. The United States necessarily treated the people of the southern states as rebels against lawful authority. At the beginning no one on either side realized how great a conflict was at hand. The South looked for a divided North. The North did not expect the South to hold out. The South looked for help from northern Democrats, and to be recognized and aided by European nations. The war which came was a trial of actual strength and endurance between North and South. On each side there was the unflinching courage, steady determination, and faithful devotion of true Americans. It was a war between vast armies, in a civilized country where railroads permitted quick movements, telegraphs afforded instant communication, improved ordnance added to the destructiveness of conflict, and climate permitted almost continuous hostilities. The Union triumphed, and the South suffered a revolution in her whole life.

593. Foreign nations did not think that the Union would be preserved. England profited by trade with the southern states, and was, therefore, disposed to aid the South, but was deterred from really forming an alliance. She, however, in May, 1861, acknowledged the Confederacy as a belligerent power, and other nations followed her example. England claimed to be neutral, but allowed Confederate vessels the protection of her harbors, and secretly aided the Confederacy in fitting out war vessels and with stores of war. Several Confederate cruisers were built and equipped in British ship-yards, and partially manned by British seamen. France, also, was disposed to aid the Confederacy.

594. [**The Alabama** was the most noted of Confederate cruisers. She did vast damage to the commerce of the United States. In 1864 she was sunk in the harbor of Cherbourg, France, by the *Kearsarge*, Captain Winslow, after an hour's fight.]

595. [**The Affair of Mason and Slidell.**—In November, 1861, the *San Jacinto*, a United States war vessel, intercepted the British steamer *Trent*, in the West Indies, and took off two passengers, James M. Mason and John Slidell, Confederate envoys to Europe, who had taken passage at Havana. Great Britain immediately complained, and threatened

THE WAR OF SECESSION. 307

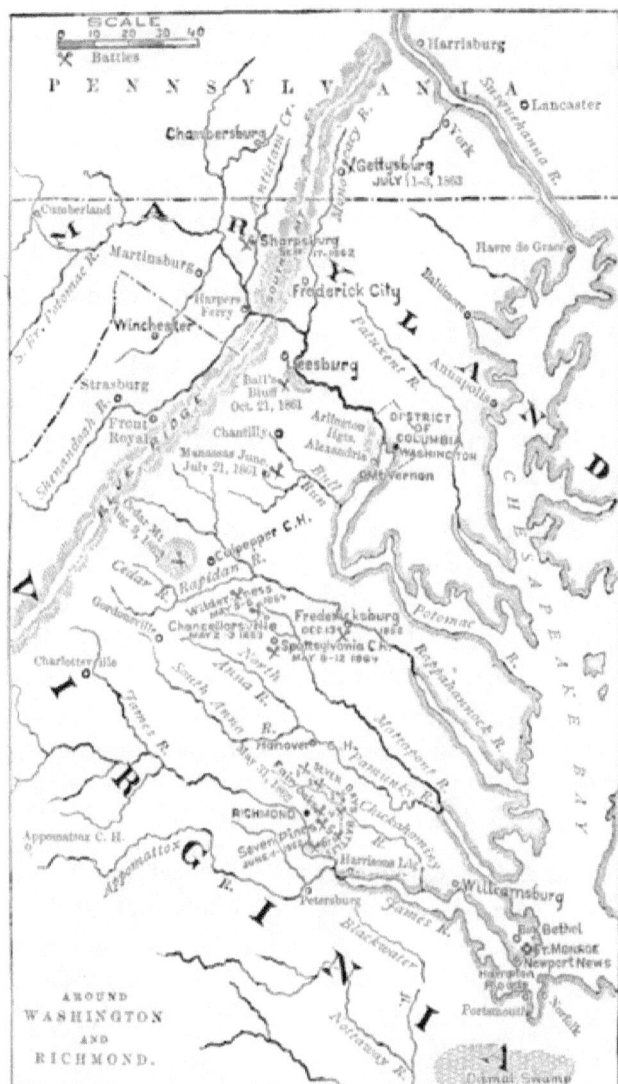

Map Questions.—Make a list of battles from the map in the order of their occurrence, giving date of each. About what is the distance from Washington to Richmond? How many rivers lie between? Did any other barriers to military movements exist? In what direction does the land slope on which these campaigns were conducted? How can you tell?

war. This right of search had been resisted by the United States in the war of 1812 **(431)**. The United States did not attempt to defend it now, but disavowed the act of Captain Wilkes of the *San Jacinto*, and surrendered the prisoners.]

1. AROUND WASHINGTON AND RICHMOND—1861-3.

596. Union troops gathered around Washington, under the command of General Winfield Scott **(535)**. Serious fighting began in West Virginia, where the Confederates were driven backwards by troops who had crossed over from Ohio, under the command of General George B. McClellan. The North felt encouraged, and called for an attack on Richmond. The Union army made ready for motion. The Confederates hurried their forces up from the South to defend their capital.

597. Battle of Bull Run (July 21st, 1861).—The Union force, under command of General Irwin McDowell, reached a little stream called Bull Run. A Confederate army, commanded by General Beauregard, was posted at Manassas Junction. McDowell crossed the stream and drove back a part of Beauregard's army. In the afternoon a fresh Confederate army, under General Joseph E. Johnston, reached the field. The undisciplined Union soldiers were struck with terror, and fled in wild disorder.

598. Army of the Potomac.—General McClellan was now put in command of the Union forces around Washington, General Scott being relieved at his own request. McClellan thoroughly organized and drilled his troops, who received the name of the Army of the Potomac. Washington was rapidly fortified.

599. Ball's Bluff (October 21st, 1861).—In October a detachment of Union troops was sent across the Potomac, at Ball's Bluff, to capture a Confederate force. Their information regarding the position of the enemy was faulty. The Union soldiers were cut off, and only a few got back across the river. This disaster at Ball's Bluff was almost as discouraging to the Union as that at Bull Run.

600. McClellan's plan was to transfer the army by water to Yorktown peninsula, and to advance on Richmond from the southeast. During the winter the Army of the Potomac had been increased to 200,000 men, all of them in good training. The government authorities wanted McClellan to march directly on Richmond. His objections were that there were many rivers to cross, and strong fortifications had been erected. In the spring of 1862 McClellan, with the principal army, was transferred to the vicinity of Yorktown; McDowell, with another army, was kept before Washington, and a force, under General N. P. Banks, was stationed in the Shenandoah Valley. The Confederate troops, commanded by General Joseph E. Johnston, hurried overland, and were ready to oppose McClellan on the peninsula. The latter spent a month in besieging Yorktown, and captured it May fourth, Johnston retiring northward. Union gunboats gained command of the James River to within eight miles of Richmond.

601. Battles of Fair Oaks and Seven Pines (May 31st, 1862).—McClellan gradually advanced his army, dividing it into two parts on either side of the Chickahominy River. His purpose was to stretch out his right wing, so as to communicate with McDowell, who was at Fredericksburg. Heavy rains deluged the army on the Chickahominy, and carried away the bridges. Johnston saw his opportunity, and attacked McClellan's weaker division at Seven Pines and Fair Oaks. Johnston was wounded, and the general result was favorable to McClellan.

602. Confederate Movements.—While Johnston was facing McClellan before Richmond, General T. J. Jackson, known to his men as "Stonewall Jackson," one of the bravest and most competent officers in the southern army, was sent into the Shenandoah Valley. Making a rush up the valley he drove Banks and his army across the Potomac. It was thought that Washington was in danger, and McDowell, who had been ordered to help McClellan, was recalled for the defense of the capital. In the middle of June, Colonel J. E. B. Stuart, with Confederate cavalry, crossed the Chickahominy above McClellan's right, rode completely around the Union army, cutting telegraph lines and tearing up railway tracks, recrossing the Chickahominy below McClellan's left, and rejoining the Confederate force with the loss of only one man.

603. **Seven Days' Battles (June 26th–July 1st, 1862).**—McClellan was now unsupported. The Confederate army was commanded by General Robert E. Lee, the defender of Richmond from this time until the end of the war. McClellan had the superior army, but the Confederate forces were concentrated against him. A series of fights, known as the Seven Days' Battles, began at Mechanicsville and ended at Malvern Hill. The Confederate army attacked the Union troops at Mechanicsville (June 26th), and were repulsed. The next day they were successful at Gaines's Mill, near Cold Harbor. McClellan was cut off from his supplies on York River, and resolved to fall back to the James River. This "change of base" would give him a new source of supplies. Lee's army followed him, and there was constant fighting. The principal battles were at Savage Station (June 29th), Frazier's Farm and Glendale (June 30th), and Malvern Hill (July 1st). At the end of the battle at Malvern Hill the Confederate army was demoralized and broken. McClellan was still strong. He withdrew, however, to Harrison's Landing. Here ended McClellan's peninsula campaign.

604. **Pope's Campaign, 1862.**—Just before the Seven Days' Battles all the Union troops around Washington

were placed under the command of General John Pope, who had gained some distinction in the West. General Henry W. Halleck was made General-in-Chief at Washington (611). Pope planned to march directly on Richmond, and he put his army in motion for that purpose. Lee sent Jackson to Gordonsville. The Confederate armies were recruited by conscription. Pope's advanced division, under General Banks, was met and defeated by a Confederate army under General Ewell, at Cedar Mountain (August 9th). Pope fell back to the Rappahannock. A midnight dash on his camp captured some of his staff officers and his dispatch book, revealing all his plans. A second battle at Groveton, or Bull Run No. 2 (August 30th), utterly defeated Pope's army. McClellan's army was ordered back to defend Washington.

605. Lee's First Invasion (September, 1862).—Lee now determined to carry the war into the North, hoping to receive help from Maryland. He crossed into Maryland and took Frederick City, but instead of increasing, his army fell off more and more the farther he went from Confederate territory. The Confederate armies fought fiercely when at home, but could not be held together for invasion. McClellan spread out his army for the defense of Washington and Baltimore. Lee was forced westward through the mountains. He made a stand at Sharpsburg, on Antietam Creek. Here was fought the great and decisive battle of Antietam (September 17th). Lee's army was seriously weakened, and retreated to Virginia.

606. McClellan Superseded.—McClellan's failure to capture Richmond had been a great disappointment to the Union. He had lost the confidence of the government by constantly demanding more men, and continually attributing his reverses to the weather or the authorities at Washington. After the battle of Antietam he did not seem disposed to follow up the success vigorously, and General Ambrose E. Burnside was put in his place. There were many people, however, who felt that McClellan was not treated justly.

607. Battle of Fredericksburg (December 13th, 1862).—Burnside was promoted against his own wish. He formed a plan of attacking Richmond by way of Fredericksburg, and put the army in motion. There was bad management and delay in crossing rivers. The Confederates gathered their forces at Fredericksburg, and strongly fortified the low hills on the bank of the Rappahannock. Burnside ordered an attack (December 13th). Brigade after brigade crossed the river and rushed to certain death before the Confederate intrenchments. The day's work was a terrible disaster to the Union side. Burnside was superseded by General Joseph E. Hooker, known to his men as "Fighting Joe."

608. Battle of Chancellorsville (May 23d, 1863).—Hooker's army spent the early part of 1863 on the north bank of the Rappahannock. In April it crossed the river above Fredericksburg, and became entangled in the Wilderness, the forest stretching from Fredericksburg to Richmond. Here it was attacked by the Confederates, and the great battle of Chancellorsville was fought. Hooker was rendered unconscious by a spent ball in the beginning of the fight. His army suffered heavy loss, and was driven back across the river. The Confederates lost "Stonewall Jackson," killed through mistake by his own men. Lee said that in Jackson he lost his right arm.

609. Lee's Second Invasion (June, 1863).—Lee again decided on invasion, and the two armies ran a race northward. Lee crossed the Potomac at Harper's Ferry and entered Pennsylvania. His advance troops nearly reached Harrisburg. In the North there was great alarm. Hooker gave place to General George G. Meade. The Union army kept between Lee and the cities of Washington and Baltimore, and the two forces met at Gettysburg.

610. Battle of Gettysburg (July 1st, 2d, and 3d, 1863).—The battle lasted three days. It was a tremendous struggle, the heaviest of the war, and one of the greatest in the world's history. The Union army occupied the line of a crest of hills called Cemetery Ridge; the Confederates were on an opposite ridge called Seminary Ridge. Between them lay a small valley in which was the town of Gettysburg. The Confederates had the advantage in the first day's fighting; they were defeated on the third. Lee led his shattered army back into Virginia, followed by the Union forces. Never again was Lee strong enough to attempt invasion.

2. THE WAR IN THE WEST—1861-3.

611. In Kentucky and Missouri a strong effort was made to carry the states into secession. Union troops came in quickly from the states on the north, and secession was prevented. In Missouri there was hard fighting in 1861. Confederate troops came into Missouri from Arkansas and Texas. The Union force under General Nathaniel Lyon was defeated at Wilson's Creek (August 10th), Lyon being killed. General John C. Fremont (537) was put in command of the Union forces; soon superseded by General Henry W. Halleck. Under Halleck's command the Confederates were driven out of Missouri and Kentucky.

612. Positions at the Beginning of 1862.—The Confederates held a line stretching through southern Kentucky. Their forces were under the general command of General Albert Sydney Johnston, who was considered one of the most brilliant officers of the war. In Kentucky were two Union armies, the larger under General Don Carlos Buell, in central Kentucky, the smaller under General U. S. Grant, at Cairo.

613. Battle of Mill Spring (January 19th, 1862).—The Confederate line was broken by General George H. Thomas, with a division of Buell's army, in a battle at Mill Spring. The Confederates were defeated and driven into Tennessee, their commander, General Zollicoffer, being killed.

614. Forts Henry and Donelson blocked the Cumberland and Tennessee Rivers. Both governments had built ironclad gunboats for service on the western rivers, sometimes covering over steamboats with iron rails. Grant's force advanced from Cairo up the Tennessee River. Union gunboats, commanded by Commodore Andrew H. Foote, captured Fort Henry (February 6th), a large part of the garrison escaping to Fort Donelson. Grant laid siege to Donelson, and by vigorous movements captured it (February 12th). Union troops were now advanced to Nashville, and President Lincoln appointed Andrew Johnson military governor of Tennessee.

[At Donelson, in answer to a request for an armistice in order to arrange terms of surrender, Grant replied: "No terms except unconditional and immediate surrender can be accepted." This gained him the nickname of "Unconditional Surrender."]

615. Battle of Shiloh (April 6th and 7th, 1862).—Grant's army, numbering about 40,000, was carried up the Tennessee on steamboats, and encamped at Pittsburg Landing. Buell's army was marching to unite with Grant's. Before its arrival Johnston gathered all his forces, and struck a sudden blow upon Grant's army, at Pittsburg Landing. The Union troops that received the heaviest attack were inexperienced, and were driven in confusion from their camp. Along the river they were protected by the gunboats, and during the afternoon and night some of Buell's army arrived. On the following day, Grant rallied the Union army and recovered the lost ground, the Confederates retreating hurriedly. General Johnston was killed. The

THE WAR OF SECESSION. 315

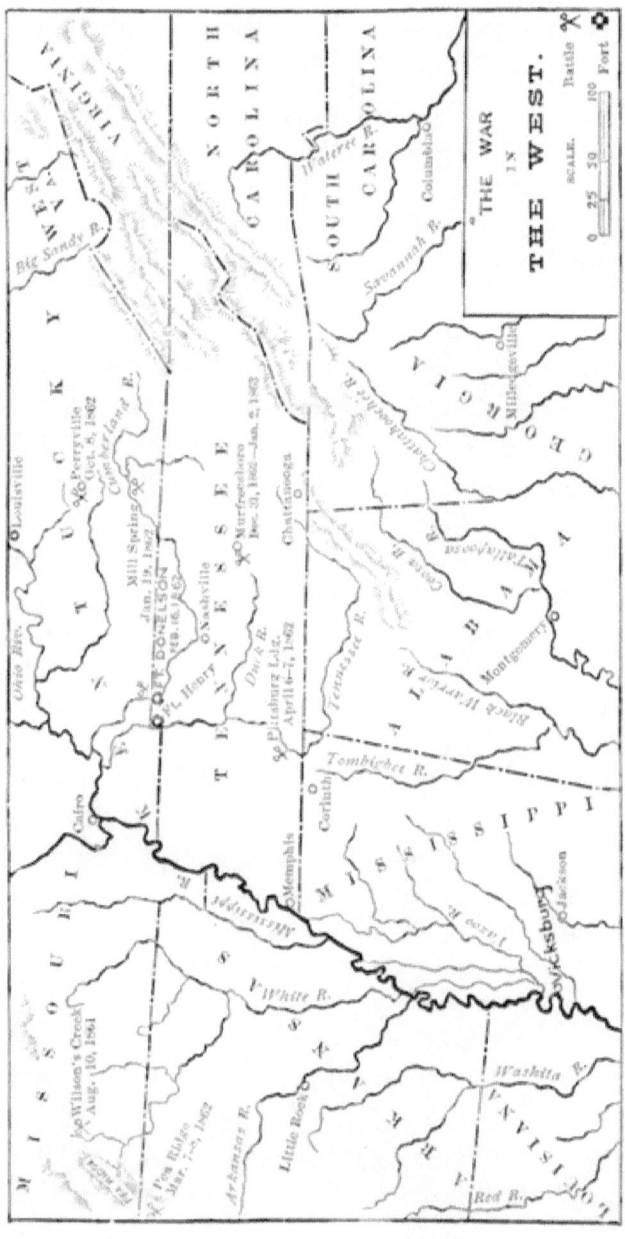

Map Questions.—What reasons can you give for the value of gunboat fleets in the West? State the advantage of Kentucky to either side. What advantages had the Confederates for the defense of Tennessee? Describe the battles in the order of date under the following heads: Date; Name and Locality; Union Commander (see text); Confederate Commander (see text); Result (see text).

battle is known as the battle of "Shiloh," from the name of a small church that stood on the battle field. It was the first great battle of the war.

616. Corinth was the next important position for the Union army to gain. General Halleck assumed command in the field in person. His army was advanced slowly upon Corinth in a sort of siege, a battle being avoided. General Beauregard, who had succeeded Johnston in command of the Confederates, abandoned Corinth, withdrawing his troops to the southward. Corinth was occupied by Halleck's army (May 30th). The Confederates were now driven from West Tennessee, Memphis was occupied, and Union arms controlled the Mississippi as far as Vicksburg.

617. Movements around Corinth.—Halleck having been called to Washington (604), Grant was placed in command at Corinth. His army was not strong enough for offensive operations, and had to depend on the country for supplies. There was considerable fighting, the Confederates trying to recapture Corinth and Nashville, but failing. Vicksburg was the next point toward the south for the Union army to gain.

618. West of the Mississippi there had been some severe fighting. In a battle at Pea Ridge, Arkansas, in March, a Confederate army, under General Price and General Earl Van Dorn, was defeated by a smaller Union army under General Samuel R. Curtis, in command in southern Missouri. All through the war there was bloody guerrilla fighting west of the Mississippi. The guerrillas were rough fellows, without any military control, banded together for war and robbery, fighting against Union soldiers or any Union men.

619. Invasion of Kentucky (September, 1862).—After the capture of Corinth, General Buell was sent eastward to attack Chattanooga. General Braxton Bragg, who had superseded Beauregard, instead of facing Buell, struck northward into Kentucky. Buell rushed north at the same time, and reached Louisville ahead of Bragg. Buell's army was strengthened from across the Ohio. As Lee in Maryland, so Bragg in Kentucky tried to gain the state for the Confederacy, but without success. Buell fought an indecisive battle at Perryville. After about a month in Kentucky, Bragg turned back into Tennessee, taking with him a long train of wagons, loaded with captured provisions and clothing, most valuable to the Confederacy. Buell was now superseded by General William S. Rosecrans.

620. **Battle of Murfreesboro (December 31st, 1862; January 1st and 2d, 1863).**—Having left his plunder at Chattanooga, Bragg led his army to Murfreesboro. General Rosecrans came on in December with about 40,000 men to attack Murfreesboro. The two armies met on the last day of December on Stone River, a small stream just outside of the town. The hotly contested battle that followed was one of the bloodiest of the war. The advantage of numbers, if any, was on the side of the Confederates. Both Bragg and Rosecrans showed fine military skill. After three days' fighting the Confederates withdrew, and a heavy storm prevented any further action. Of about 90,000 men engaged in the fight, one fourth were either killed or wounded.

3. Along the Coast—1861-2.

621. **The United States navy** could not enforce the blockade of southern ports, until it was strengthened by new vessels, which the government at once began to build. Naval excursions in 1861 captured a fort at Hatteras Inlet (August 29th), and another at Port Royal (November 7th). From Hatteras Inlet attacks were made on other points on the North Carolina coast, and from Port Royal on the islands between Charleston and Savannah.

622. The Merrimac.—In 1861 the Confederates had raised the *Merrimac*, a United States frigate, which had been scuttled in the navy yard at Norfolk. They covered her with iron, added a sloping roof of iron bars, gave her a heavy iron prow, and christened her the *Virginia*. She is better known, however, as the *Merrimac*. In March, 1862, she was ready for service, and steamed out of Norfolk to demolish the Union fleet at Hampton Roads (March 8th). In this fleet there were five large wooden war ships, and sev-

MONITOR AND MERRIMAC.

eral smaller ones. They poured their heavy cannon balls upon the *Merrimac*, but hardly dented her iron mail. Steaming at full speed toward the *Cumberland*, the *Merrimac* ran her iron prow through the wooden ship, beneath the water, at the same time sweeping her deck with shot. In three quarters of an hour the *Cumberland* sunk, carrying down the sick and wounded. Next the *Congress* was badly damaged, and finally blown up. The others escaped to shallow water, and the *Merrimac* retired to her moorings, expecting to finish her work of destruction the next day.

623. The Monitor was the name of a small sized, peculiarly constructed iron war vessel, invented by John Ericsson, which the United States had been building at New York. Almost entirely under water, she exposed only a cylindrical turret to the enemy's shot. She was armed with two heavy guns within the turret, which could be revolved for the guns to fire in any direction.

624. Fight between the Merrimac and Monitor (March 9th, 1862).—The *Monitor* arrived in Hampton Roads just after the *Merrimac* had retired. When the huge *Merrimac* steamed out the next morning to finish the Union fleet, she was confronted by the little *Monitor*, and a desperate contest ensued. The superiority of the *Monitor* for quickness was evident. She steamed around and around her antagonist, both firing at close range. Five times the *Merrimac* tried to run the *Monitor* down, but each time the little warrior glided out unharmed. For two hours the contest continued. Finally the *Merrimac*, disabled and discouraged, returned to Norfolk, where she was subsequently blown up by the Confederates.

[The battle between the *Merrimac* and *Monitor* showed the superiority of iron over wooden war ships. The United States built a number of monitors to guard the coast. European nations had already built ironclads for experiment, and after this fight wooden war ships were everywhere superseded by ironclads.]

625. Union Captures along the Coast, 1862.—In February a combined land and naval expedition captured a Confederate post on Roanoke Island. Later, St. Augustine was captured by Union troops, and a firm hold was gained in Florida. Fort Pulaski, at the mouth of the Savannah River, surrendered after a siege. The blockade (591) could now be enforced along the Atlantic shore. Wilmington and Charleston were the only Atlantic harbors in Confederate possession. These were closely watched by the blockaders.

[After one unsuccessful attack on Fort Fisher in Wilmington harbor

(December, 1864), it was captured in January, 1865. Wilmington soon after fell into Union hands.]

626. New Orleans was a very important place to the Confederates, and they built strong defenses for it. Forts Jackson and St. Phillip, about thirty miles from the mouth of the Mississippi, were armed with heavy guns. Between the forts was a raft of cypress logs, held in place by six heavy chains, so as to block the river. From the forts to the city there were gunboats and batteries along the banks.

627. The capture of New Orleans was accomplished in May, 1862, by Commodore David G. Farragut, commanding a Union fleet, accompanied by land troops under General B. F. Butler. After bombarding the fort for a week, Farragut decided to run his ships past them. A few daring men cut the chains under cover of night. The advance began about three o'clock on the morning of the twenty-fourth. Farragut's ships passed close to the forts, receiving and returning a heavy fire. Getting past the forts, they engaged the Confederate fleet, and destroyed it after one of the most desperate yet successful battles of the war. New Orleans surrendered (April 25th), and the forts soon afterwards. General Butler was placed in command of New Orleans.

[Union boats now had possession of all the Mississippi except the strip from Vicksburg to Port Hudson. Vicksburg enabled the Confederates to bring provisions from the southwest. They built an ironclad ram, the *Arkansas*, on the Yazoo River, in the hope of driving the Union fleet from the Mississippi. She was, however, destroyed by Union gunboats.]

628. [The Emancipation Proclamation.—During the first year of the war, President Lincoln checked attempts of Union commanders to free negro slaves. In 1862, however, the conclusion was forced upon him that the destruction of slavery was essential to the preservation of the nation. Therefore, on September twenty-second, just after the repulse of Lee at Antietam, the President issued a warning that on January 1st, 1863, he should declare that "all persons held as slaves, within any state or designated part of any state, the people whereof shall be in rebellion against the United States, shall be then, thence-

THE WAR OF SECESSION. 321

forward, and forever free." The Emancipation Proclamation was issued on the day stated. Thus ended slavery in the United States. The President recommended to Congress legislation offering compensation for the slaves of loyal citizens; but, on account of the opposition of Democratic congressmen who disapproved of emancipation, such legislation was never enacted.]

4. AROUND VICKSBURG—1863.

629. The Advantage of Vicksburg. — The possession of Vicksburg would give the Union forces the control of the Mississippi, and cut off the Confederate supplies from the southwest. Grant constantly aimed at Vicksburg after he was placed in command of the army at Corinth. General W. T. Sherman, who had been with Grant at Shiloh **(615)**, was his chief assistant. Sherman conducted operations against Vicksburg toward the end of 1862, which at that time could not be made successful. Early in 1863 he captured Fort Hindman, or Arkansas Post, and the way was open to

21-H

Vicksburg. General J. E. Johnston commanded all the Confederate forces confronting Grant. General J. C. Pemberton was intrusted with the defense of Vicksburg. This city is situated on low hills at the outside of a great bend in the river. The Confederates had built fortifications of the strongest kind, and believed the place impossible to capture.

630. Grant's Movement on Vicksburg, 1863.—The Union army moved down the west bank from near Memphis, and dug a great canal across the bend of the Mississippi, for the purpose of moving the gunboats below the city without having to pass the Vicksburg guns. The current of the river proved too strong to be turned, and after two months' work the attack from the west was given up. On the night of April sixteenth, the Union gunboats ran past the Vicksburg batteries without serious loss. Grant's troops marched to Grand Gulf, and there the gunboats ferried them across the river. Sherman's corps remained north of the city. Grant's troops swung around from the south. Marching to the northeast until he came to Jackson, Grant beat off Johnston in a series of five successful battles, and cut off Pemberton's supplies. Then uniting with Sherman, Grant, within twenty days from landing below the city, had Pemberton shut up within Vicksburg.

631. Assault, Siege, and Capture.—Grant first tried to take Vicksburg by assault, and a grand attack from all sides was made (May 22d), the gunboats having first bombarded the city. It proved unavailing, and assaults were given up. A siege of six weeks exhausted the food of Vicksburg, and on July fourth Pemberton surrendered with 37,000 men. The fall of Vicksburg and the blow to Lee's army at Gettysburg (**610**) weakened the Confederacy, and filled the North with rejoicing.

632. [**Port Hudson** surrendered five days after Vicksburg, to General

Banks, who had succeeded Butler (627) in Louisiana. Union forces now controlled the Mississippi throughout its whole length. Grant sent a force into Arkansas, which gained command of nearly the whole state.]

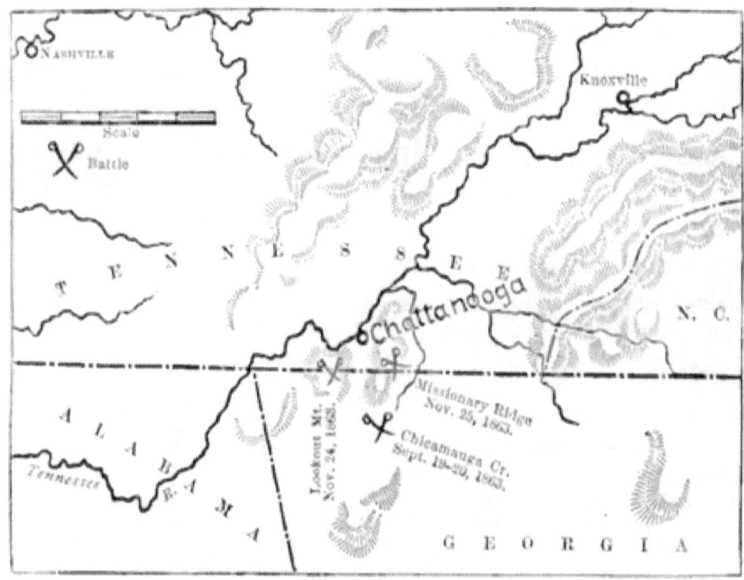

Map Questions.—Describe the country around Chattanooga. In what way was it suited for defensive fighting?

633. Destruction of property that might be useful to the enemy became common on both sides. The great losses were necessarily on the side of the South. It was the policy of Grant and Sherman to exhaust the country of the Confederacy, endeavoring however to protect private rights. Occasionally a Confederate cavalry raider dashed into Union territory. One of the boldest was the raid of the Confederate colonel, John Morgan, who, with 4,000 horsemen, dashed across Kentucky and into Indiana and Ohio (July, 1863). He was captured before he could get back to Kentucky.

5. AROUND CHATTANOOGA—1863.

634. Chattanooga.—In 1862 the Union forces had gained

western Tennessee; the mountains of the eastern section afforded strongholds for the Confederates. Chattanooga was an important point. Rosecrans's army, which had been resting, moved south from Murfreesboro in June, 1863. Bragg's army fell back to Chattanooga, but afterwards abandoned it, and took a strong position about twelve miles south, on Chickamauga Creek.

635. The Battle of Chickamauga was fought between the armies of Rosecrans and Bragg (September 19th and 20th). Bragg had been reinforced from Lee's army, and Rosecrans was defeated. A part of his army fell back to Chattanooga; a part, however, commanded by General George H. Thomas, aided by General James A. Garfield (706), made a stubborn fight, and prevented a terrible disaster. Bragg besieged the Union army in Chattanooga.

636. [**The Siege of Chattanooga** lasted about two months, and the Union army, under General Thomas, came near starving. Bragg was so sure that he would capture Chattanooga that he sent a corps, under General Longstreet, to besiege Knoxville, where General Burnside was stationed. Both places were held.]

637. Battles of Lookout Mountain and Missionary Ridge (November 24th and 25th).—After the capture of Vicksburg, Grant was recognized as the foremost of the Union commanders. He was placed in control of all the forces, from the Alleghanies to the Mississippi, and was sent to Chattanooga. Under his management the mountain strongholds of the Confederates were taken by storm. The principal assaults were upon Lookout Mountain (November 24th), and Missionary Ridge (November 25th), each a mountain about half a mile high. The Confederates were behind intrenchments on the summits, and thought themselves safe. General Hooker commanded the assault upon Lookout Mountain, and General Sherman that upon Missionary Ridge. All the Confederate troops were driven from Tennessee. Bragg's army took post at Dalton, and Johnston was put in command.

6. Sherman's Advance into Georgia—1864.

638. Positions January 1st, 1864.—The Confederates had two great armies. Lee's army of about 62,000 men was on the Rapidan, near Fredericksburg. Johnston's army of 75,000 held a strong position at Dalton, Georgia. Throughout the Confederacy weakness showed itself. The armies were recruited by conscription; soldiers were poorly fed and scantily clothed. The Union troops were well fed and clothed. The principal armies were the Army of the Potomac (**598**), numbering 122,000 men, and the army in Tennessee of about 100,000 men.

[In 1863 volunteering for the Union armies fell off, and some other way was needed to keep up the forces. Drafting was therefore resorted to. In the northern states lists of the names of able-bodied men were placed in a wheel, and a blindfolded man pulled out the names as chance directed. These men had to serve in the army, or hire substitutes. There was a great deal of opposition to the draft, and in New York city serious riots occurred.]

639. Change of Commanders.—In March, 1864, Grant was made Lieutenant-General, and placed in command of all the armies of the United States. He placed Sherman in command in Tennessee, with orders to advance upon Johnston, and to do as much damage as he could to the country of the enemy. Grant went to Virginia to superintend. Meade remained in immediate command of the Army of the Potomac (**609**).

640. Sherman and Johnston were wary and skillful generals. Sherman had the more powerful army, and he slowly drove his opponent back toward Atlanta. There was hard fighting, but both armies were skillfully preserved. The principal contests were at Resaca, Dallas, and Kenesaw Mountain.

641. Johnston Superseded.—Johnston was not willing to risk a decisive battle, for his army was not ready for it. Since Sherman drew his supplies by means of a single railroad in his rear, the further he followed Johnston the more he was obliged to weaken his army for the defense of his supplies. Johnston's retreat, though ably conducted, displeased the Confederate government, especially Jefferson Davis. General J. B. Hood was therefore put in command

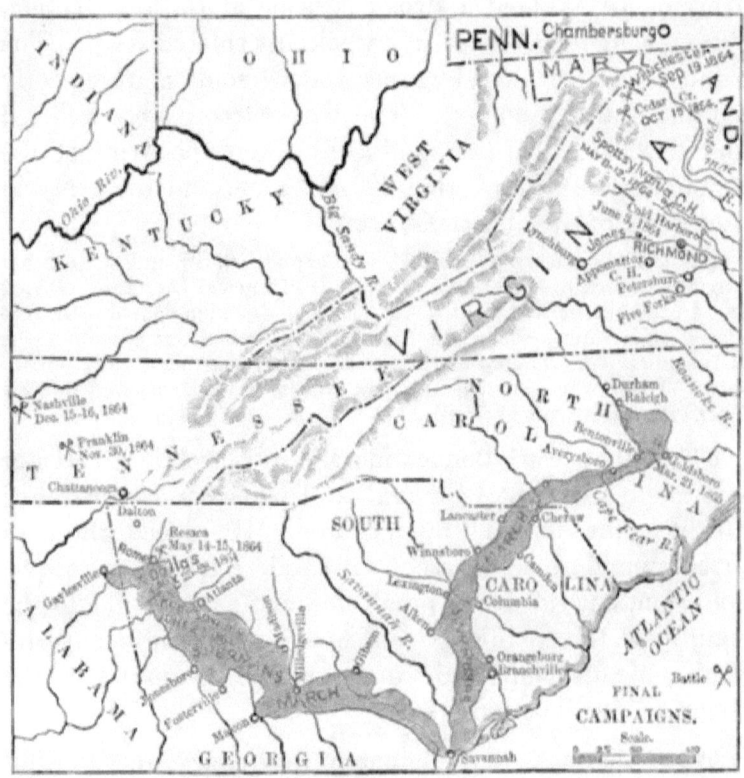

Map Study.—Describe the direction of Sherman's march. Make a list of the places touched by his army in the progress of his march. Which of these were places marked by prominent events in the Revolutionary War?

of Johnston's army. Hood's movements were vigorous, and, as they proved, fatal. He rushed his army upon Sherman's in several fights—the fiercest of which is known as the battle of Atlanta (July 22d). He was defeated, and fell back upon Atlanta. Early in September, Sherman gained a position toward the rear of Atlanta, and compelled Hood to leave the city. Sherman's army occupied Atlanta (September 2d). In October, Hood moved his army to the northwest, hoping that Sherman would follow him, and the war be transferred again into Tennessee. Sherman had already sent nearly half his army into Tennessee, and placed General Thomas in command there. Sherman soon gave up the pursuit of Hood, and leaving him to be dealt with by Thomas, turned back to Atlanta.

642. From Atlanta to the Sea.—Sherman had at Atlanta an army of 60,000 experienced soldiers. Around him lay the richest regions of the Confederacy, hitherto untouched by war and now defenseless, for Lee could not spare a man from Virginia, and Hood was in Tennessee. In November, Sherman burned Atlanta, and set his army moving toward Savannah in four parallel columns, covering a space of about sixty miles. Railroads were torn up, bridges burned, and the country made desolate. The army lived on plunder. A month was spent in the march through Georgia, and during this time no one at the North knew just what had become of Sherman and his army. Sherman reached the vicinity of Savannah the middle of December, and communicated with the Union fleet on the coast. The North then knew that Sherman was safe, and that the Confederacy was doomed to fall. Sherman captured Savannah after a siege of eight days, and remained there until February, 1865.

643. Thomas in Tennessee.—Thomas gathered at Nashville all the troops under his control, and was ready for Hood when he approached to regain Tennessee. A battle was fought at Franklin (November 30th), and Hood's army was badly damaged. He, however, laid siege to Nashville. Thomas routed the besiegers (December 15th and 16th), pursued them vigorously, and Hood's army was scattered forever.

7. FINAL CAMPAIGN IN VIRGINIA—1864-5.

644. The Army of the Potomac, which Grant came from the West to command (639), as fine a body of men as ever went to battle, was nearly double the opposing army of Lee. The Confederate army had the advantage of defensive warfare, and Lee had shown himself a commander of the highest skill. The North had come to trust Grant as a patient, tireless, and vigorous commander. His policy was to mass the whole strength of the Union against its foes, and to overcome them by "continuous hammering." This plan had brought success in the West; it brought success in Virginia, but at a fearful cost.

645. Grant's Movements on Richmond.—Grant decided to fight his way to Richmond by the overland route, but with auxiliary movements on either side. An army of 30,000 men, under General Butler, was sent by water to operate against Richmond from the south. Another army was sent up the Shenandoah to attack Lynchburg. Neither of these accomplished much. The main army was put in motion from the Rappahannock.

646. Fighting in the Wilderness (May 5th-7th, 1864.—Lee had made military surveys of the country that the Union army had to traverse, and was prepared to avail himself of every advantageous position. He had built defenses around Richmond of the strongest kind. As soon as the Union army entered the Wilderness, Lee flung his troops upon it in fierce attack (May 5th, 1864). For two weeks there raged the bloodiest fighting of the war. The first three days' fighting is known as the Battle of the Wilderness; the last eleven days made the Battle of Spottsylvania Court House. From behind fortifications Lee's army successfully resisted Grant's assaults, which had to be given up.

[The Union loss in these two weeks in killed, wounded, and captured, numbers 64,000 men. The Confederate loss was about 20,000.]

647. Grant's next plan was to keep Lee's smaller army busy in front, and by pushing out flanking parties force him to fall back upon Richmond. In this manner Grant worked his way to the Chickahominy. Once more an assault of the whole Union army upon the Confederate works proved terribly disastrous. The center of the assault was at Cold Harbor (**603**). This second battle of Cold Harbor lasted less than an hour. The assault was repulsed. The Union army was extended around to the south of Richmond, and without further loss, until it was confronted by the strong fortifications of Petersburg (June, 1864).

648. The Shenandoah Valley.—The Union forces sent against Lynchburg (**645**) were unsuccessful, and were driven into West Virginia. In July Lee sent a force under General Jubal A. Early to rush through the Shenandoah Valley, and thence upon Washington. Early passed into Maryland, found the defenses of Washington too strong for him, and returned into Virginia. Toward the end of July Early made a cavalry raid into Pennsylvania and burned Chambersburg. To stop these proceedings Grant appointed General Philip H. Sheridan, who had been one of his ablest commanders, to the control of all troops in Western Virginia and around Washington. Sheridan defeated Early at Winchester (September 19th). Later, Early surprised the Union army at Cedar Creek, twenty miles from Winchester. Sheridan was at Winchester. He rode to the scene of the defeat, rallied his men, and again defeated Early. Throughout this fertile valley of the Shenandoah Sheridan burned and destroyed, so that a Confederate army could not again live in it.

[The story of Sheridan's ride from Winchester is told in the poem, "Sheridan's Ride," by T. B. Read.]

649. The Siege of Petersburg occupied the army of the Potomac from July, 1864, to April, 1865. The Union army constantly increasing in numbers easily maintained a long circle around Richmond. Lee's diminishing numbers had

1. Sherman. 2. Sheridan. 3. Farragut.

harder and harder work to hold their lines within. One

attempt was made to storm the works at Petersburg. A mine was dug beneath one of the Confederate forts, and the fort was blown up with gunpowder (July 30th). Union troops attempted to rush through the breach upon Petersburg. They were thrown back with severe loss.

8. FALL OF THE CONFEDERACY—1865.

650. Final Movements.—By destroying Hood's army General Thomas (643) left Sherman free to march whithersoever he pleased. By devastating Georgia (642) Sherman destroyed the basis of Lee's support. From Savannah Sherman started northward (February 1st, 1865), continuing his work of damaging the Confederacy. General Johnston had been recalled to oppose him, and did all that was possible to gather a new army from the scattered fragments. Garrisons were removed from Confederate posts, and Johnston getting together about 40,000 men, fought Sherman furiously, near Goldsboro (March 19th). Sherman drove Johnston back, and the Union army rested at Goldsboro. With 10,000 cavalry Sheridan moved up the Shenandoah nearly to Lynchburg, scattering the forces that Early had collected. Then turning eastward, tearing up railways and cutting off Lee's supplies, Sheridan passed to the north of Richmond and joined the army of the Potomac.

651. Capture of Petersburg and Richmond (April 23d, 1865).—Sheridan made a dash to Five Forks (March 2d). Lee had to lengthen his line still further, and his 40,000 men could no longer protect it. Grant's army, 100,000 strong, burst through Lee's intrenchments (April 2d). Lee withdrew his troops to the westward. Jefferson Davis and other civil officers escaped into North Carolina. The Union army entered Petersburg and Richmond, and once more the flag of the Union floated over the capital of Virginia.

652. Lee's Surrender.—Lee's retreat was towards Lynchburg. From that point he hoped to unite with Johnston in

North Carolina. Sheridan pushed ahead of Lee and got between him and Lynchburg. Lee's men, worn out and

1. Lee.   2. T. J. Jackson.   3. J. E. Johnston.

without food, were surrounded. On April 9th, at Appomattox Court House, Lee surrendered his army. Grant's terms were generous. Lee's troops were sent to their homes upon oath never again to bear arms against the United States.

LIST OF GREAT BATTLES, WITH TABLE OF LOSSES ON EITHER SIDE.

Battle.	Date.		Killed.	Wounded.	Captured or Missing.	Total.
Bull Run No. 1	July 21, 1861	U.	481	1,011	1,216	2,708
		C.	387	1,582	13	1,982
Fair Oaks or Seven Pines	May 31–June 1 1862.	U.	790	3,594	647	5,031
		C.	—	—	—	7,997
Seven Days' Battles	June 25–July 1	U.	1,734	8,062	6,053	15,849
		C.	2,836	13,946	755	17,537
Pope's Campaign	Aug. 16–Sept. 2	U.	1,747	8,452	4,063	14,462
		C.	663	4,016	46	4,725
Antietam	September 17	U.	2,108	9,549	753	12,410
		C.	1,253	6,980	3,200	11,433
Fredericksburg	December 11–15	U.	1,284	9,600	1,769	12,653
		C.	595	4,074	653	5,322
Shiloh	April 6–7	U.	1,754	8,408	2,885	13,047
		C.	1,728	8,012	959	10,699
Murfreesboro	Dec. 31–Jan. 1–2 1863.	U.	1,717	7,794	3,665	13,176
		C.	1,272	7,694	1,070	10,206
Vicksburg Campaign	Jan.–July 4	U.	1,511	7,396	453	9,360
		C.	—	—	—	*
Chickamauga	September 19–20 1863.	U.	1,687	9,394	5,255	16,366
		C.	2,673	16,274	2,003	20,950
Lookout Mountain	November 23–25	U.	757	4,529	330	5,616
		C.	—	—	—	8,684
Chancellorsville	May 1–4. 1864.	U.	1,606	9,760	5,919	17,285
		C.	1,662	8,981	2,255	12,898
Gettysburg	July 1–3	U.	2,834	13,709	6,643	23,186
		C.	2,665	12,599	7,464	22,728
Battles of Wilderness	May 5–7	U.	2,265	10,220	2,902	15,387
		C.	2,000	6,000	3,400	11,400
Sherman's Atlanta Campaign	May 6–Sept. 15	U.	4,423	22,822	4,442	31,687
		C.	3,044	18,952	†12,983	34,979
Franklin and Nashville	Nov. 30–Dec. 16	U.	589	2,773	1,104	4,466
		C.	—	—	—	21,252
Siege of Petersburg	June 15–April 2	U.	3,219	12,344	3,872	19,435
		C.	—	—	—	—

* Total loss estimated at from 35,000 to 56,000 men, including those paroled.
† Captured.

653. General Surrender.—Johnston could do nothing after Lee's surrender, and yielded his army to Sherman, at Raleigh, April 26th. Union armies were in control of all parts of the Confederacy. There was no place again to raise the Confederate flag, even had there been hands strong enough to do it. All the Confederate troops east of the Mississippi surrendered early in May, and west of the Mississippi a little later in the month. Confederate soldiers returned to homes which civil war had desolated. The Union forces were reviewed at Washington, and gradually disbanded, returning to prosperous states and happy homes, save where the hand of death had left a never to be forgotten sorrow.

Finances of the War.

654. The expenses of the government for maintaining its vast armies were enormous for the whole period of the war, reaching the amazing sum of $1,000,000 a day toward the close. The cost of the war can not be counted. Besides what was paid out from the revenues collected during the period, the end found the national debt over $2,750,000,000 against about $65,000,000 at the beginning. Loyal states also were at vast expense, and churches, societies, and private persons had contributed for the care of sick and wounded. Moreover, in estimating the total cost of the war, the expenses of the Confederate states should also be added, and the losses from the destruction of public and private property make the sum too vast for computation.

655. War Taxes.—Every available means was employed for filling the national treasury. Loans were made from home and foreign capitalists, through the medium of interest-bearing bonds and notes. United States notes, commonly known as "greenbacks," payable on demand without interest, were issued in vast amounts, and were declared by law to be legal tender. As long, however, as the treasury of the United States contained no coin for their redemption, they circulated only at a discount as compared with coin. Duties on imports were greatly increased, and high internal taxes were levied.

[The interest-bearing notes were payable after short periods, as three years, the usual rate of interest being $7_{\frac{3}{10}}$ per cent per annum. The

THE WAR OF SECESSION. 335

bonds were payable after longer periods (twenty or forty years) with interest at 6 or 7 per cent per annum.]

656. National Banks and New States.—From the end of the Bank of United States (1836) (482), until 1863, banking business was entirely under state control. The need of an avenue through which government bonds might be sold brought about a national banking system in 1863. A Bureau of Currency was established in the Treasury Department, with a chief called the Comptroller of the Currency. Five or more persons could form a banking association, with capital not less than $50,000, deposited in government bonds with the Comptroller of the Currency. In exchange the banks thus incorporated would receive 90 per cent of the amount in the form of bills printed by the government, and after being signed by bank officers, to be loaned and circulated as money. No other banks of issue were allowed by law. During the war two new states were admitted; West Virginia, cut off from the original state of Virginia, in 1863, and Nevada in 1864.

657. [**The Presidential election of 1864** resulted in the reëlection of Abraham Lincoln as President, and the election with him on the Republican ticket of Andrew Johnson of Tennessee, as Vice-President. The Democratic nominees were George B. McClellan of New Jersey, for President, and George H. Pendleton of Ohio, for Vice-President. The Democratic nominees represented opposition to the war, as it had been conducted by the Republican administration, and a general belief that the attempt to bring back seceded states should be abandoned. Lincoln and Johnson received 212 electoral votes, against twenty-one for McClellan and Pendleton.]

THE FINAL TRAGEDY.

658. Assassination of President Lincoln.—The rejoicing of the loyal sections over the surrender of Confederate armies was cut short by the mournful news of the death of President Lincoln. A few rash spirits had formed a plan of assassinating the leading government officials, in the vain hope of giving fresh life to the Confederacy. President Lincoln was in the habit of occasionally visiting the theater, finding in the play some rest from his toil and cares. April 14th, 1865, John Wilkes Booth, an actor by profession, entered the President's private box, and shot him in the head from behind. The wounded man died the next day.

[Another assassin attacked Secretary Seward at his home, but failed to take his life. After shooting, Booth leaped to the stage, and made his escape from the building through a stage door, and from the city under cover of the night. Ten days later, he was found in a barn near Fredericksburg, Virginia, and on his refusal to surrender he was shot. Four other conspirators were condemned and hanged, and four more were imprisoned.]

659. Mourning for the murdered President draped the whole loyal land in shrouds of black. The remains were borne in slow procession to Springfield, Illinois. On leaving Springfield in 1861 Lincoln had said to gathered friends: "I now leave, not knowing when or whether ever I may return, with a task before me greater than that which rested upon Washington. Without the assistance of that Divine Being, who ever attended him, I cannot succeed. With that assistance, I cannot fail." And he did not.

REVIEW.

Make a list of the military events of the war, according to the form on pages 176, 177.

NOTE.—In the Army of the Potomac, as it entered the final campaign around Richmond, there were four infantry corps (with attached artillery), commanded by Major-Generals W. S. Hancock, G. K. Warren, John Sedgwick, and A. E. Burnside; and one cavalry corps, commanded by Major-General P. H. Sheridan. These five corps comprised eighteen divisions, commanded by one major-general and seventeen brigadier-generals; the divisions made up of fifty-one brigades, commanded by twenty brigadier-generals and thirty-one colonels, each brigade made up of regiments commanded by colonels, and each regiment made up of companies commanded by captains. Lee's army comprised three infantry corps under Lieutenant-General R. H. Anderson, Major-General Jubal A. Early, and Lieutenant-General A. P. Hill, and one cavalry corps under Lieutenant-General Wade Hampton. Each corps comprised three divisions, commanded by major-generals, each brigade being under a brigadier-general.

CHAPTER XXXII.
1865-1869.
THE CONSTITUTION AMENDED.

Andrew Johnson, *Tennessee, President and Vice-President.*

CABINET.

William H. Seward—State.
Hugh McCulloch—Treasury.
Edwin M. Stanton, } War.
John M. Schofield, }
Gideon Wells—Navy.

John P. Usher, }
James Harlan, } Interior.
O. H. Browning, }
William Dennison, } Postmaster-General.
Alex. W. Randall, }

James Speed, }
Henry Stanberry, } Attorney-General.
William M. Evarts, }

660. **To reconstruct governments** in the states that had seceded was perhaps the most difficult problem ever presented in our country's history. If men rebel against monarchy their punishment is usually death; but in a monarchy the government is above and not in the people. Monarchies rule through military power; republics can stand only upon the confidence of the people. The men who had carried slave states out of the Union were not to be trusted with the work of remodeling them for freedom. Yet they were almost the only men in the South who had the ability to manage public affairs.

661. [Andrew Johnson was born in North Carolina, in 1808. His family belonged to the class known at the South as "poor whites." **He** moved to Tennessee in 1826, gained an education after he had grown to manhood, and became a member of the House of Representatives (1843-1853), Governor of Tennessee (1853-1857), and United States Senator (1857-1862). He was the only Senator from a seceded state who remained in the Senate. He was always a strong Union man, but acted with the Republican party only while the war lasted. Before the war he was a Democrat, and as President he violently opposed the Republican measures for reconstruction. He was again elected to the Senate in 1875, but died the same year.]

662. **President Johnson** desired to punish the most prominent and wealthy of the Confederate leaders, for he

22-H

considered them to blame for the war; but he was not especially anxious to protect the "freedmen," as the ex-slaves were called. Temporary governors had been appointed by President Lincoln for Tennessee, Louisiana, Arkansas, and Virginia. President Johnson made appointments for the other seceded states. Conventions were called, which met and repealed the ordinances of secession, promised never to pay the debt of the Confederacy, and ratified the Thirteenth Amendment, proposed by Congress early in 1865. (Read Article XIII., Amendments to the Constitution.)

663. The Reorganized States.—After these conventions the white people—the former voters—elected legislatures, and a state government was under way before the end of 1865 in each of the states that had seceded. Ex-Confederate leaders were elected as members of Congress, and demanded their places.

[The thirteenth amendment having been duly ratified by three fourths of the states was declared adopted in 1865.]

664. The negroes in the southern states were utterly ignorant, and without ability or skill to work for themselves or to protect themselves. The majority of northern people desired to see their condition improved, but would have been contented to see them allowed to live where they were under the same laws as white men, with opportunities to work and learn, but without the right to vote. The new legislatures in the ex-Confederate states, however, immediately passed laws which, in some cases, amounted nearly to the reënslavement of the negroes. For crimes there was to be one penalty for a white man, and a severer one for a negro. The blacks were to be put under severe labor laws, and condemned as vagrants to forced labor if they were found idle.

665. Quarrel between the President and Congress.—Republicans had a two-thirds majority in both houses of

Congress, and were united in the determination not to readmit the seceded states into the Union until they gave full assurance that they would respect the rights of negroes. On the other hand, President Johnson claimed that Congress had no right to keep out these states after their state governments were reorganized. This quarrel ended only with the end of Johnson's term. He was supported by Democrats in Congress and by the southern states out of Congress. The Republican majority, however, enabled the Republicans to pass any measure upon which they agreed, despite the President's veto.

666. The Reconstruction Acts.—The Republicans in 1866-7 decided on a plan for admitting the states that were out of the Union. There were two main features. Negroes were to vote and the ex-Confederate leaders were to vote only when restored to political privileges by act of Congress. President Johnson vetoed these measures, but Congress passed them over the veto.

[The secession area was divided into five military districts. In each district a United States officer was stationed with a sufficient force to maintain authority. Voters were to be registered, conventions held to provide new constitutions, guaranteeing the right to vote to citizens of whatever color or previous condition. When these constitutions should be regularly adopted, the states were to be admitted to their membership in the Union.]

667. The plan of negro suffrage was adopted by Congress for the purpose of enabling the negroes to protect themselves. It was strongly opposed by white people in the South, for it made the despised blacks their political equals. The right to vote is of little use without proper intelligence and education. Negroes had been kept in utter ignorance and the poorer whites were in almost the same condition. The old state governments had been controlled by a narrow circle of leaders, many of whom were now disfranchised. Order was preserved by the troops of the

United States, but the work of establishing civil authority on the new foundation was extremely slow.

[The emancipation and enfranchisement of the negroes of the South at the close of the civil war forced at once and imperatively the question of their education upon the attention of the general and state governments. Normal schools for the training of colored teachers have been established in nearly every southern state, together with academies and colleges for the higher education of the negro. These, together with the common schools for colored children, derive their support mainly from state and national appropriations and the splendid donation of George Peabody, a native of Massachusetts, of over $5,000,000 for the encouragement of education in the South. Other considerable donations have been made, chief of which is that of $1,000,000 by John F. Slater of Connecticut.]

668. [**Readmitted States.**—Tennessee was readmitted in 1866. Alabama, Arkansas, Florida, Louisiana, North Carolina, and South Carolina came in with new constitutions in 1868. Georgia, Mississippi, Texas, and Virginia held out against the requirements of Congress, and were not admitted until 1870. A new state, Nebraska, was admitted in 1867.]

669. Amendments XIV. and XV. to the Constitution of the United States contain the permanent provisions of the Reconstruction Acts. States might exclude negroes from voting, but if they did so their representation in Congress was correspondingly diminished. The fourteenth amendment was proposed in 1866, and adopted in 1868. Its acceptance was the test for the admission of the reconstructed states. The question of negro suffrage was the special subject of the fifteenth amendment, which may be regarded as a supplement to the fourteenth. It was proposed in 1869, and adopted in 1870, under a new administration. Any state may require property or educational qualifications for voting. It must, however, treat all colors alike.

670. Tenure of Office Act.—The quarrel between the President and Congress over reconstruction extended to all the affairs of government. The President declared that

---

669. *Study Article XIV., Amendments to the Constitution. Make a list of its provisions in regard to negroes. State the steps made in Articles XIII., XIV., XV.*

Congress was an illegal body, since southern states were not represented. He sought to strengthen himself by removing Republicans from office, appointing men who would support him in his quarrel with Congress. To check the President, Congress passed the Tenure of Office Act (March, 1867). It took from the President the power of removal in the case of the higher offices, except upon the approval of the Senate. President Johnson claimed that the Act was unconstitutional, and refused to obey it.

[Read Article II., Section II., of the Constitution. The Tenure of Office Act was practically repealed after Grant became President.]

671. Impeachment of President Johnson.—The contest between Congress and the President resulted in a trial of impeachment. In February, 1868, the President attempted to remove Stanton, Secretary of War, without the consent of the Senate. The House of Representatives immediately adopted Articles of Impeachment, reciting acts by which it was charged that the President had violated his oath of office, and had been guilty of misdemeanors. The case was argued at great length before the Senate, and finally came to a vote. Of the fifty-four Senators thirty-five voted "guilty," nineteen "not guilty." The two-thirds vote required for conviction not having been cast, the President was acquitted.

672. [Affairs in Mexico.—While the United States was rent with civil war, France took the opportunity to overthrow the feeble republic of Mexico and establish Maximilian, an Austrian archduke, as Emperor of Mexico. He was for a time maintained upon his throne by the aid of French troops. At the close of the civil war our country demanded the withdrawal of the French troops, and France complied. Maximilian remained, attempting to rule a country that hated him. In 1867 he was shot by the Mexicans, and their government was reëstablished.]

673. The purchase of Alaska from Russia was completed in 1868, a preliminary treaty having been arranged the year before. At the time no one considered the acquisition very valuable. The wealth of Alaskan forests and fisheries is now recognized. The price paid was $7,200,000 in gold.

674. The presidential election in 1868 was decided on the question of approving or disapproving the Republican method of reconstruction. The Republicans nominated General U. S. Grant of Illinois and Schuyler Colfax of Indiana. The Democrats nominated Horatio Seymour of New York and Frank P. Blair of Missouri. Grant and Colfax were elected.

[Grant and Colfax received 214 electoral votes, Seymour and Blair seventy-one. Texas, Mississippi, and Virginia were not allowed to vote, being still out of the Union. Objection was made to counting the vote of Georgia, which sent in returns, although not readmitted to the Union at the time of the election. The House of Representatives sustained the objection, but the Senate did not. Counting Georgia, Seymour and Blair had eighty votes.]

REVIEW.

Amendments.
- XIII.
  1. Why proposed.
  2. Provisions.
  3. Left former slaves in what condition.
- XIV.
  1. The President's plan of reconstruction.
     1. Main features.
     2. How far carried out.
     3. Why unsatisfactory.
  2. Congress's plan of reconstruction.
     1. Main features.
     2. How enforced.
     3. Results.
  3. Provisions.
     1. (Sec. I.)
     2. (Sec. I.)
     3. (Sec. II.)
     4. (Sec. III.)
     5. (Sec. IV.)
- XV.
  1. Provisions.
  2. Left freedmen in what condition.

QUESTIONS.

Who are citizens of any state? What change in counting representation was made by the fourteenth amendment? What right had our country to demand the withdrawal of French troops from Mexico? How did the United States acquire Alaska?

CHAPTER XXXIII.

1869-1877.

THE NATION ONE.

Ulysses S. Grant, *Illinois, President.*
Schuyler **Colfax,** *Indiana,* } *Vice-President.*
Henry **Wilson,** *Massachusetts,*

CABINET.

Hamilton Fish—State.		Jacob D. Cox,	} Interior.
George S. Boutwell,	} Treasury.	Columbus Delano,	
William A. Richardson,		John A. J. Cresswell,	} Postmaster-General.
Benjamin H. Bristow,		Marshall Jewell,	
L. M. Morrill,		James N. Tyner,	
John A. Rawlings,	} War.	E. Rockwood Hoar,	} Attorney-General.
William W. Belknap,		Amos F. Akerman,	
James D. Cameron,		George H. Williams,	
Alphonso Taft,		Edwards Pierrepont,	
Adolph C. Borie,	} Navy.	Alphonso Taft,	
George M. Robeson,			

For Explanation.—Tribunal; arbitration.

To be Pronounced.—Staempfle (stĕm′fle); Sclŏp′is; Itajuba (ee-tä-hoo′bä).

675. **Our country** began its national life in the war for independence. Feeble at first, our national spirit strengthened with the years, and proved our right to be respected by the rest of the world. It kept its steady course, revealing to the world the new spectacle of a nation whose institutions were designed for the elevation of men. Its great trial came, not in dangers from abroad, but in disunion at home. The systems of slave and free labor had grown side by side until both could no longer live together. In the fires of civil war the slave system had perished. Through the sorrows of this war, we rose again one nation, indivisible forever. When our constitution was formed, in the minds of many Americans state citizenship stood before United States citizenship; when it was amended, the order was reversed. This change represents the constitutional growth

of eighty years. The states stand, the foundation of our Republic. The Union stands, the preserver of American nationality.

U. S. GRANT.

676. [**Ulysses S. Grant** was born in Ohio, in 1822. He was educated at West Point, graduating in 1843. He had no fondness for military life, and would have chosen to teach mathematics at West Point, rather than serve in the field, had the choice been given him. He was assigned to service with an infantry company, which entered the Mexican War under General Taylor (**529**). Later, he served under General Scott. Grant did brave service, but was not promoted above first lieutenant. In 1851 he was sent to the Pacific coast, where he was promoted to captain. He remained for three years on military duty, seeing a good deal of early California life, and forming the hope of some day making his home in this state. Not being able to provide for his family from his small salary, he resigned his commission in 1854 and became a farmer, living near St. Louis. In 1858 he was a real estate agent in St. Louis, and in 1860 he moved to Galena, Illinois, and became a clerk in his father's store. In 1861 he was commissioned a colonel, and placed in command of a regiment of Illinois volunteers, which went into service in Missouri (**611**). He soon became a brigadier-general. His further progress is told in the history of the Civil War. As lieutenant-general he continued in command of the United States army until his election as President.]

677. **The Treaty of Washington** is the name of a treaty between Great Britain and our country, arranged in 1871. There were several matters in dispute—our boundary line in the northwest corner, our right to fish off the coast of Canada, and damages to commerce during the civil war. The treaty provided for the appointment of tribunals of arbitration, to which should be submitted each question of

dispute. The northwest boundary was left to the Emperor of Germany, who decided in our favor, fixing the boundary through the Pacific inlets, as it now appears on our maps. The arbitrators appointed for the fishery dispute made their decision in 1877, and we paid $5,500,000 to Great Britain for the use that our fishermen had made of waters along the Canada shore.

678. [**The Fishery Question.**—The right to catch fish along the shore of British possessions was guaranteed to us at the close of the Revolution. By a treaty in 1818 our government agreed that American fishermen should not fish within three miles of inhabited portions of Canada. Disputes arose over the application of this rule, as to whether the distance should be measured from any point of the shore, or from headland to headland. The question of our right to use Canadian fisheries is still at issue (1887).]

679. **The Alabama Claims** were the estimated damages done to the commerce of the United States by the *Alabama* (594) and other cruisers fitted out in British ports during our civil war. The appointed arbitrators met at Geneva, Switzerland, examined claims, listened to arguments, and decided, in 1872, that Great Britain should pay to the United States $15,500,000, in full for all damages. This is known as the Geneva Award.

[The Geneva arbitrators were Sir Alexander Cockburn of Great Britain, Charles Francis Adams of the United States, ex-President Staempfle of Switzerland, Count Sclopis of Italy, and Baron Itajuba of Brazil. Citizens of Great Britain had claims against the United States for similar losses, and a separate board of arbitrators decided that the United States should pay Great Britain $1,928,819, in full for all claims.]

680. **The West Indies.**—Negroes occupying the western half of Hayti established the Republic of San Domingo in 1844. This government desired to be annexed to the United States. President Grant favored annexation, and a treaty was arranged. The Senate, however, refused to ratify the treaty, and the plan of annexation was abandoned. Cuba rebelled against Spain in 1868. In the United States there was much sympathy for Cuba, and in 1873 the *Virginius*,

an American vessel, was loaded with supplies for the Cubans. While on the open sea, and under the United States flag, she was captured by a Spanish war vessel. Spanish authorities condemned and shot several of the crew and passengers. President Grant indignantly protested, the Spaniards ceased their executions, returned the ship and the surviving prisoners, and made apologies that were accepted.

681. The first transcontinental railroad was completed in 1869. It had been planned before the civil war, and work was commenced while the war was in progress. The line from Omaha to San Francisco was constructed by two great companies, the Union Pacific from Omaha to Ogden, and the Central Pacific from Ogden to San Francisco. This line of railway brought the Atlantic and Pacific shores into close communication, while rapid travel and freighting quickened the development of the Pacific coast and added to the wealth of the whole country.

[The building of the Pacific railway was a vast undertaking, too great to be accomplished by private enterprise alone. The government therefore, in 1862 and 1864, gave subsidies, or help, to the companies undertaking the work. It became responsible for interest on bonds, and gave the companies every alternate section of public land for twenty miles each side of the railway so far as it should be constructed. The subsidy in land to the Central Pacific and Union Pacific amounted to 25,000,000 acres. In similar manner the government has since aided the construction of other great railways.]

682. [Great Fires at Chicago and Boston.—In October, 1871, the greatest fire of modern times occurred at Chicago. It lasted for three days. The burnt district included 3,000 acres and the loss of property amounted to $200,000,000. The same month there were terrible forest fires in Wisconsin, in which more than 1,500 persons were burned to death. A great fire occurred in Boston in November, 1872, which caused a loss of $70,000,000 in some of the best property of the city. The whole country sent aid to the sufferers by these fires. The burnt districts in the two cities were quickly rebuilt with larger and finer buildings.]

683. Troubles in the Southern States.—Negro suffrage

---

681. *Find a railroad map and learn how many railway lines now cross the continent of North America.*

proved to be a source of disorder rather than of good government in the South. The white people for the most part hated to see a ballot in the hands of a black man, and parties in the reconstructed states were divided on the "color line." The negroes had to look to white men for employment, and it was easy for white men to keep their laborers from the polls. Violence was used when threats failed. Corruption and bribery infested the local governments. Disorders were worst in South Carolina, Mississippi, Arkansas, and Louisiana. Some of the governments appealed to President Grant, and upon his order United States troops were sent into these states.

[The presence of troops was considered a grievance by many in the South. More hateful than the troops were men from the North, who settled in the South, and tried to get offices by negro votes. Such men were called "carpet-baggers," because they were said to come into the country with only a carpet-bag. A southern white who voted with the negroes was called a "scalawag."]

684. [**The Ku-Klux Klan** was a secret society, organized in the southern states after the war. It undertook to keep the negroes in subjection, or to prevent them from voting. Under its name negroes were intimidated, and whites were attacked who were disposed to defend the negroes. Murder became a sort of business. Congress in 1871 gave the President extreme powers to enforce the constitutional amendments, and stop these disorders. The better class of the southern people condemned the deeds of the Ku-Klux, and the society was suppressed.]

685. The presidential campaign of 1872 was contested chiefly upon the Republican management in the South. A number of Republicans disapproved the extreme measures resorted to in order to keep peace. Under the name of Liberal Republicans, they nominated Horace Greeley (**686**) of New York for President. The Democrats were unsettled in their policy, and decided to indorse the Liberal Republicans in platform and candidates. The regular Republicans renominated General Grant by acclamation, and Henry Wilson of Massachusetts for Vice-President. A part of the Democrats made other nominations. The regular Republican nominees were elected.

[Grant and Wilson received 286 out of 366 electoral votes. No vote was counted for Greeley. The returns of Arkansas and Louisiana were rejected as illegal; the vote of Georgia would have been counted for Greeley, had he been living when the returns were opened in Congress.]

686. [**Horace Greeley** was born in New Hampshire, in 1811. After varied experience in newspaper work, he began, in 1841, the publication of the *New York Tribune*, which became one of the most powerful newspapers of the country. No man has ever become more widely known or exerted more influence through the columns of a newspaper than Horace Greeley. He was by nature a reformer. He attacked slavery, called out sympathy for Ireland in time of famine, and demanded protection for plundered Indians. He firmly upheld the American System of Clay (**474**), and was necessarily objectionable to many Democrats. He died in 1872, soon after his defeat.]

687. **Serious political scandals** dishonored the Republican administration under President Grant. The "Credit Mobilier" was a corporation organized by stockholders of the Union Pacific Railroad for taking contracts in building their railway. Favorable legislation for the company was desired by Congress, and Credit Mobilier stock was given to Congressmen for the purpose of influencing their votes. An investigation in the House of Representatives, in 1872–73, resulted in a vote of censure against two members. The "Whisky Ring" was a conspiracy of distillers and revenue officers in the central states for defrauding the government out of the tax on distilled liquors. It was detected in 1875, and suppressed.

688. **The centennial anniversary** of our Declaration of Independence was celebrated with hearty spirit. The end of one hundred years found a nation cherishing the liberty fought for and won by its forefathers, and swiftly yet steadily advancing in power. As a part of the celebration, a grand International Exposition was held at Philadelphia. Nearly 10,000,000 people visited the Exposition. Colorado entered the Union in 1876, and is therefore often called the Centennial State.

689. **Manufacturing industries** advanced rapidly in New

England and the middle states, developing also in the South. Cloth manufacture, especially cotton, brought about

improved machinery, which has utilized the abundant water power of the New England states. Nothing shows better the contrast between this century and the preceding than a comparison of the old time

SPINNING JENNY IN SAN FRANCISCO FACTORY.

spinning wheel with a modern jenny; or the weaving room of a modern factory with the loom in which the cloth worn by the soldiers of the Revolution was woven by their wives and mothers.

690. [Indian Wars.—Modoc Indians living in the corner of California and Oregon refused to move to a reservation, and murdered the peace commissioners sent to them. For a year they defended themselves in the lava beds of the old volcanic region where they lived. They were subdued in 1873. Another Indian war was fought in 1876 with the Sioux tribe of Dakota Territory led by Sitting Bull. They were driven into southern Montana. General Custer with a cavalry regiment came upon the tribe encamped on the Big Horn River and rashly attacked. Custer and his men were surrounded and every one slaughtered. Fresh troops drove the Sioux warriors into British America.]

691. Financial Troubles.—There was prosperity throughout the land during Grant's first administration. The government debt (654), so large at the end of the war that many despaired of paying it, was reduced with a rapidity that astonished every one. Railroad building was active, and in every direction new agricultural land was brought into communication with the markets. In 1873 there was a reverse. Many railroads did not pay expenses. Crops were poor in some places. Money became scarce and a financial panic brought on many business failures.

692. The presidential election of 1876 was a close contest between the Republicans and Democrats. The Republicans nominated Rutherford B. Hayes (696) of Ohio, and William A. Wheeler of New York. The Democratic nominees were Samuel J. Tilden of New York, and Thomas A. Hendricks of Indiana. Democrats proclaimed Republican administration to be corrupt, and promised to carry out reforms. No great issues were brought before the people. When the ballots were counted throughout the country the result of the election was doubtful. In Florida, Louisiana, Oregon, and South Carolina both parties claimed the electoral vote. If the electoral votes of all these states were counted for Hayes he was elected; losing any one of them he was defeated.

[Florida and Louisiana were the ground of the chief dispute. There was evidence that in these states violence had been used to keep negroes from voting the Republican ticket. The reconstructed governments had established Returning Boards, whose duty it was to canvass election returns and to throw out the votes of districts where fraud and violence were proved. In Florida and Louisiana the returns, before inspection, gave the Democrats a majority; after correction by the Returning Boards, a Republican majority was declared.]

693. The Electoral Commission.—Never before had so serious a difficulty

WEAVING ROOM IN SAN FRANCISCO FACTORY.

occurred in the choice of a President. Congress was divided, the Republicans having control of the Senate, the Democrats of the House of Representatives. The danger was that no decision would be reached before the fourth of March, and civil war might follow. By a sort of compromise Congress established an Electoral Commission for the emergency, with power to settle all disputes. It was composed of fifteen members—five Supreme Court Justices, five Senators, and five Representatives. By its decision the disputed votes were counted for Hayes and Wheeler, and they were therefore declared elected.

[The electoral vote as finally counted was 185 for Hayes and Wheeler, and 184 for Tilden and Hendricks. It had been designed to elect on the commission seven Democrats and seven Republicans, with the fifteenth man a non-partisan. As matters turned the commission consisted of eight Republicans and seven Democrats. Every question was decided by a strictly partisan vote of eight to seven. The country had been greatly excited, and ill feeling at the result ran high among the Democrats. The decision, however, was legal, and therefore was accepted by the whole country.

REVIEW.

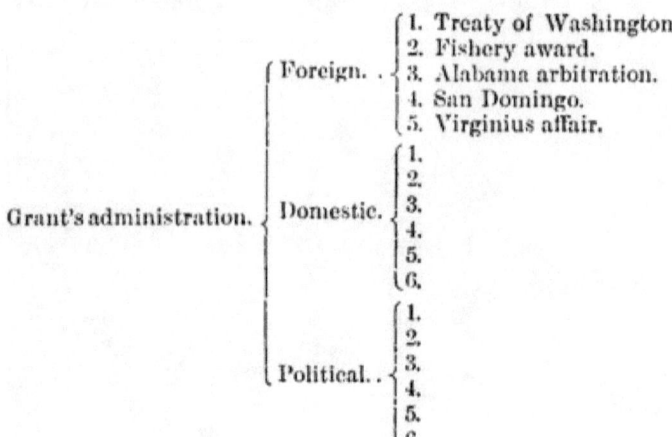

Grant's administration.
- Foreign.
  1. Treaty of Washington.
  2. Fishery award.
  3. Alabama arbitration.
  4. San Domingo.
  5. Virginius affair.
- Domestic.
  1.
  2.
  3.
  4.
  5.
  6.
- Political.
  1.
  2.
  3.
  4.
  5.
  6.

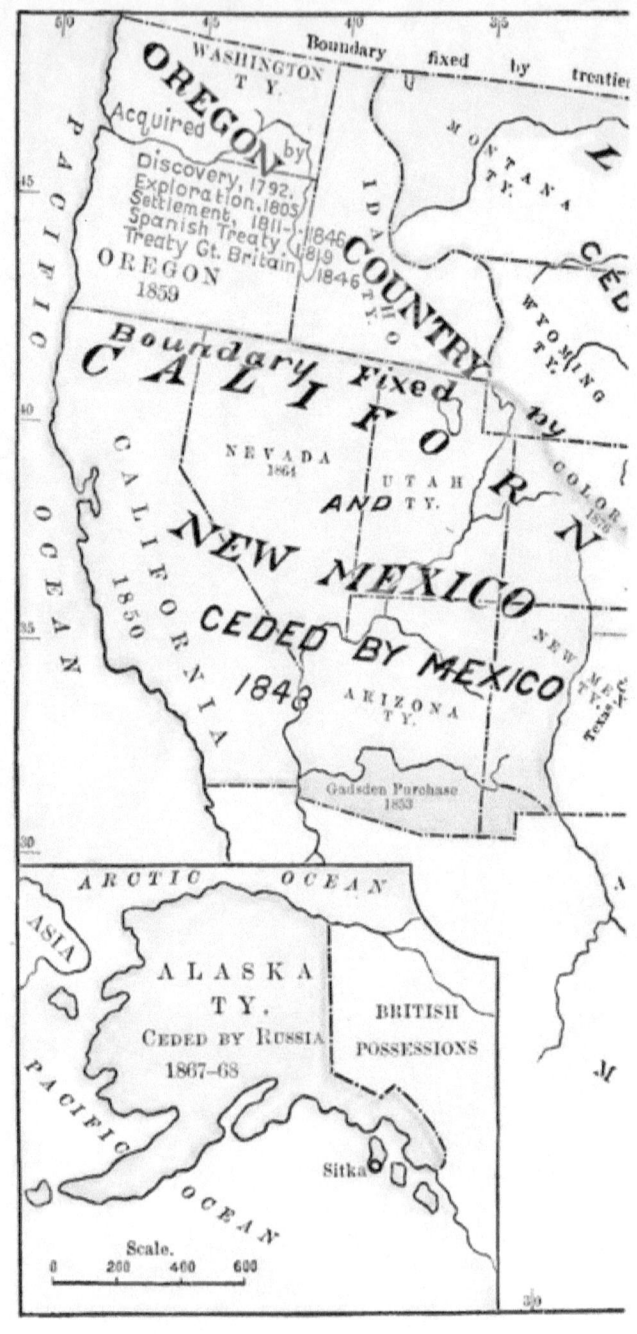

TERRITORIAL MAP
OF
1876.

CHAPTER XXXIV.
1877-1887.
THE BEGINNING OF A NEW AGE.

To be Pronounced.—Nez Perce (nay pĕr′cy); Ä-pä′che.

694. The second century of our national life can in no respect be a repetition of the first. Every age has its own work to do, and its own problem to solve. It must do its work, and solve its problems with whatever power it has. Happy the age that can call strength and wisdom its own; full of woe and trouble, if it be beset with weakness and folly. Very often men look upon the past as better than the present. Perhaps, because they cherish the memories of their youth, and never again see years so happy as their early ones. No one, however, can look back upon the first century of our nation and fail to see a constant progress, and a progress on the whole for good. It is for the youth of the present, understanding the work of the past, to be strong and wise to do the work of a new age, the beginning of which is now with us, but the end of which no man can see.

1.

Rutherford B. Hayes, *Ohio, President.*
William A. Wheeler, *New York, Vice-President.*   } 1877-81.

CABINET.

William L. Evarts—State.	Richard W. Thompson, } Navy.
John Sherman—Treasury.	Nathan Goff,
George W. McCrary, } War.	Carl Schurz—Interior.
Alexander Ramsay,	David M. Key, } Postmaster-General.
Charles Devens—Attorney-General.	Horace Maynard,

695. Hayes's administration began under the disfavor resulting from a disputed election. The country in general enjoyed quiet, and was not disturbed by exciting political contests. The President withdrew the remaining troops from the southern states, and military rule at the South came to an end. The Democratic party gained control in

Congress, and tried to repeal many of the laws that had been passed by the Republicans. President Hayes used the veto freely, and only a few measures were passed over the veto. There was important legislation in regard to finances and earnest discussion of Chinese immigration (712). The army was reorganized, and reduced to fit the needs of a peaceful country.

696. [**Rutherford Birchard Hayes** was born in Ohio in 1822. After graduating from Kenyon College, Ohio, he studied at Harvard Law School and became a lawyer. He joined the Union army in the Civil War and became a brigadier-general. He was a Representative in Congress (1865–7), and Governor of Ohio (1868–72 and 1876–7). As President, he endeavored to make appointments for the good of the public service, and to maintain purity in the government. After his presidency, he lived at his home at Fremont, Ohio, interesting himself in promoting the work of popular education.]

697. United States Coinage.—Gold coins, eagles, halves, and quarters, and silver coins, dollars, halves, quarters, dimes, and half dimes, were established by law in 1792. These coins were "lawful tender in all payments whatsoever." The silver dollar weighed 416 grains troy. In 1837 this weight was reduced to $412\frac{1}{2}$ grains, and small coins in proportion. In 1834 other gold coins—double eagles and three-dollar pieces—were authorized. In 1853 the weight of half dollars and smaller coins was still further diminished, and they were made legal tender only in sums not exceeding five dollars. In 1873 the coinage of silver dollars was stopped. A new silver dollar, called a "trade dollar," weighing 420 grains, was established, but in 1876 it was abolished as legal tender. Its coinage was continued in quantities sufficient for export. Gold was thus made the standard money of the United States, and silver was said to have been demonetized. A cry for silver money was again raised throughout the country, and in 1878 the silver dollar of 1837 ($412\frac{1}{2}$ grains) was reëstablished and made again legal tender for all payments except on contracts stipulating gold. This measure, known as the remonetization of silver, was passed over the veto of President Hayes. Other silver coins were made legal tender for payments not exceeding ten dollars.

698. [Money Standards.—If a country is very poor, copper answers for its money. When it gets richer, silver is better money, and with still greater wealth, gold money is needed. In a country like ours there is need of a great deal of gold money, considerable silver, and some copper. Our government, until 1853, tried to maintain what is called a double standard in money, gold and silver being coined in nearly equal amounts, and either legal tender for all payments. The difficulty in this plan is to regulate the relative weights between gold and silver coins so that both will circulate freely; for, from causes beyond control, the supply of either one metal or the other is bound to vary and drive the dearer out of circulation, since people will pay their debts in the cheaper coin, using the dearer metal for jewelry, etc. The various changes in weights were attempts to keep the ratio of weight between gold and silver dollars equal to the ratio of market value between the two metals—something no one has ever succeeded in doing.]

699. Resumption of Specie.—The paper currency, "greenbacks" (655), issued by the United States during the civil war, circulated as money, but at a depreciation as compared with coin. As people began to gain confidence that the government would eventually pay its debts, greenbacks rose in value. At length the treasury was in a condition to redeem its promises, and Congress ordered that after January 1st, 1879, the Treasurer of the United States should pay coin for greenbacks. This is known as the resumption of specie payments. Greenbacks at once became equal in value to gold.

700. Refunding the National Debt.—Where there is known to be risk a high rate of interest must always prevail. When the government was running into debt enormously every year, it could borrow money only by paying high rates of interest. The government bonds sold during the war bore interest at from 6 to $7\frac{3}{10}$ per cent. When the government was paying off its debts as fast as the terms of the loans would allow, it was easy to get money at lower rates, for there was no risk to the lender. The national debt was therefore *refunded*, that is, new bonds at lower rates of interest (3 to 4½ per cent) were sold, and the money received was used to pay off the former bonds.

701. The presidential election of 1880 resulted in favor of the Republican nominees, James A. Garfield (706) of Ohio, and Chester A. Arthur (708) of New York. The Democratic nominees were General Winfield S. Hancock of New York, and William H. English of Indiana. General Hancock had served with high distinction in the Union army, and was a popular candidate. The southern states had become Democratic, and supported Hancock. The chief political issue between the parties was the tariff, the Democratic platform calling for a "tariff for revenue only" (365), the Republicans standing for protection (366).

[Garfield and Arthur received 214 electoral votes against 155 for Hancock and English. The Republican nominating convention was very exciting. Ex-President Grant and James G. Blaine of Maine were the leading candidates. On the thirty-sixth ballot, when it became evident that neither Grant nor Blaine could be nominated, enough votes were transferred to nominate Garfield.]

702. [**Ex-President Grant** had recently returned from a tour around the world, in which he had spent most of his time since leaving the President's office. He had been the welcome guest of both European and Asiatic monarchs, receiving honors above any other American of his time.]

703. [**The Greenback Party** was called into existence through opposition to specie resumption. It favored the issue of irredeemable paper currency as the money of the country. Presidential **nominations** were made, but the candidates gained no electoral vote.]

2.

James A. Garfield, *Ohio, President, March to September 19, 1881.*
Chester A. Arthur, *New York, Vice-President.*

CABINET.

James G. Blaine—State.	William H. Hunt—Navy.
William Windom—Treasury.	Samuel J. Kirkwood—Interior.
Robert T. Lincoln—War.	Wayne McVeigh—Attorney-General.
Thomas L. James—Postmaster-General.	

704. Garfield's Administration.—A great deal was expected from President Garfield. A man of ability, purity of character, and experience in public affairs, the nation hoped for the correction of abuses in the government. Especially it was hoped that there would be honesty and reform in the civil service. Garfield was steady in his purpose to select suitable persons for office, and there arose ill feeling among politicians and a great deal of angry discussion in the newspapers.

705. Assassination of the President.—A half-demented wretch named Guiteau, who had been refused an appointment, resolved on murderous revenge. On July 2d, 1881, at a railroad depot in Washington, he shot the President in the back, wounding him, as it proved, mortally. For eighty days the strength of Garfield fought off death, but gave way at last. On September nineteenth he died at Elberon, near Long Branch, New Jersey, whither he had been taken for the benefit of the cool sea air. His patience and fortitude in that long struggle for life won him the love of a nation which had already respected and honored him. His remains were taken to Washington, and thence removed to their final resting place at Cleveland, Ohio. The whole nation mourned as for a friend, and foreign rulers sent many tokens of respect to the bereaved family.

706. [**James Abram Garfield** was born in Ohio, in 1831. After working his way through school and graduating from Williams College, Massachusetts, he became a professor at Hiram College, Ohio, where he had previously attended as an academic student. Later he studied and practiced law. He served in the Union army, rising to the rank of major-general. He was a Representative in Congress (1863–81), elected Senator in January, 1880, but raised to the chief magistracy before taking his seat. His career was that of a man ever faithful and earnest, rising from a low station to the highest.]

3.

Chester A. Arthur, New York, President—1881-5.

CABINET.

F. T. Frelinghuysen—State.
Charles J. Folger, } Treasury.
Hugh McCullough,
Robert T. Lincoln—War.

William E. Chandler—Navy.
Henry M. Teller—Interior.
Benj. H. Brewster—Attorney-General.

Timothy O. Howe,
Walter Q. Gresham, } Postmaster-General.
Frank Hatton,

707. Arthur's Administration was far more successful than that of any of the preceding Vice-Presidents who succeeded to the first position through a President's death. Soon after taking the oath of office he appointed a new Cabinet, retaining, however, Robert T. Lincoln, son of Abraham Lincoln, as Secretary of War.

708. [Chester Alan Arthur was born in Vermont, in 1830. He was educated at Union College, New York, and became a lawyer, gaining a lucrative practice. During the civil war he did good service on the staff of the Governor of New York. He was Collector of Customs at New York (1871-8), becoming an influential man in New York political circles. He died in 1886.]

709. The New South.—The whole country enjoyed prosperity during the years of Arthur's term. Nowhere, however, was prosperity more noticeable than in the Southern States. The energy of the southern people had been directed into new channels. With free labor agriculture became more varied, and manufactures were commenced. The establishment of public schools began the work of popular education, neglected at the South under the old rule.

[In the winter of 1884-5 a grand international exposition was held at New Orleans, the purpose of which was to show to the world the progress which the South had made under the rule of freedom. The results were surprising even to Southerners.]

710. Yorktown Centennial.—In 1881 the hundredth anniversary of the surrender of Cornwallis was celebrated at Yorktown (**338**). Besides the chief officers of the United

States, representatives were present from Great Britain, France, and Germany. To close the celebration, President Arthur had the flag of Great Britain raised, and a salute fired in its honor.

711. The Mormons.—The Mormons (510) gathered in Utah continued to practice polygamy, in spite of the prevailing sentiment of civilization condemning it. They sought to evade, and at times threatened to resist the authority of the United States. In 1882 Congress passed a strict law (Edmunds Act), designed to suppress polygamy, and the Mormons tried hard to prevent its enforcement. The national government opposed the formation of a state in Utah, because of the danger that Mormons would control it in the interest of polygamy.

712. Chinese Immigration.—The building of the transcontinental railways (681) required a great amount of unskilled labor, and Chinese were largely employed. China has almost a countless population, and her people have accustomed themselves to methods of labor and cheapness of living which Americans and Europeans cannot endure. On the Pacific Coast, and especially in California, the Chinese found abundant opportunities for labor and traffic far superior to any in their native land. Chinese immigration increased rapidly from year to year (about 3,500 in 1855; 19,000 in 1875). Their numbers in California alarmed and excited white laborers, who were forced out of employment by the cheaper labor of the Chinese. Serious riots resulted. Congress investigated, and attempted restrictive legislation. Our treaty with China (known as the Burlingame Treaty, obtained from China through the influence of Anson Burlingame, our Minister to China, 1861-7), however, allowed Chinese laborers to come into the country as those of any other nation. President Hayes appointed three envoys, who proceeded to China and concluded a new treaty, permitting restriction and suspension of immigration, but not absolute prohibition. This treaty was ratified, and proclaimed a law in 1881. In 1882 a law was passed suspending the immigration of Chinese laborers to the United States for a period of ten years.

[Chinese already in the country were free to go and come again, taking certificates with them at the time of departure from the United States.]

713. Tariff History.—The uniform *ad valorem* rates established by the compromise tariff of 1833 **(486)** did not provide adequate revenue for the government after 1842, and new regulations were attempted. Lack of harmony between Congress and President Tyler **(514)** prevented changes until 1846. In that year, the Democratic party being in control of the government, a new tariff law was established, founded mainly on principles of free trade (unrestricted commerce—manufacturers being left to sustain themselves). Protective rates were retained on some articles, but were somewhat reduced in 1857. Thus, from 1846 until 1860, our country had a system of tariffs not purely for revenue, but founded upon anti-protectionist principles. In 1860 began a series of changes which placed our country again under a distinctly protective system. A falling off of national revenue following the reductions of 1857 led to a new tariff (known as the Morrill tariff, from its author, Justin S. Morrill, of Vermont), which became a law in 1861, and considerably increased protective rates. The necessities of the government during the war led to enormous taxation in every way **(655)**, and under Republican management the tariffs became purely protective, with higher rates than ever before in our history, the average rate collected being forty-seven per cent of the value of the goods. The country accepted the high rates, as war measures, required by the needs of the government, but the protective system of these war tariffs gained so firm a hold that no attempt to lessen protective rates succeeded in making essential changes until 1883. On the other hand, protective rates on some articles, as wool and woolen goods, and steel rails, were raised even above the war rates, reaching in a complicated manner sixty, eighty, and 100 per cent.

714. Tariff Commission and Reform.—Congress, in 1882, provided for the appointment of a commission to examine into the tariffs and report a plan for revision. Some changes and reductions were recommended by the commission at the following session of Congress (1882-3). The recommendations were followed in part by Congress, but the tariffs of 1883 left the country still under a strongly protective system, with extremely high rates on many very important articles. In 1884 there was another unsuccessful attempt at tariff reduction. Both Democrats and Republicans were divided on the question of protection.

715. Civil Service Reform, 1883.—For regulating the appointment of officers in the civil service of the United States, a law was passed in January, 1883. It provided a system of competitive examinations for the selection of appointees, and non-competitive examinations to determine fitness for promotion. Competitive examinations were to be held in all states and territories, and appointments made in proportion to the population. A Civil Service Commission of three persons was provided to aid the President in making rules for the service, and to superintend examinations.

[The system of examinations does not apply to the higher offices for which confirmation by the Senate is necessary. The law also prohibited all officers from giving or receiving money for political purposes, and declared that no recommendation for appointments by members of Congress should be accepted, except as to character and residence.]

716. [**Floods and Winds.**—The Mississippi River and its larger tributaries have done great damage within recent years. A flood on the lower Mississippi, in 1882, drove 100,000 people from their homes. As the valley has been settled, forests have been cleared away, and the drainage of the land has been improved. This is no doubt a partial cause of the floods. In 1883 and afterwards peculiar wind storms, called *cyclones*, from their circular movement, were terribly destructive in sections of the upper Mississippi Valley.]

717. [**The United States Signal Service,** under the management of the War Department, has stations along the coast and through the interior. The telegraph enables warning of approaching storms to be sent to distant points.]

718. [**Arctic Exploration.**—The old desire for a sea passage from Europe to Asia, through the Arctic, was revived in the nineteenth century, stimulated by eagerness for geographical discovery and scientific research. There were numerous notable expeditions. Sir John Franklin, an English explorer, sailed with two ships in 1845, but did not return. Many attempts were made to rescue him, or to learn his fate. Dr. Elisha Kane, an American, conducted one of these expeditions in 1853. He became convinced that open water surrounds the pole, as a polar sea. In 1878-9 Nordenskjold, a Swedish explorer, passed through the Arctic, the first to accomplish a Northeast Passage. In 1879 the *Jeannette*, a steam vessel owned by James Gordon Bennett, publisher of the New York *Herald*, sailed from San Francisco to prosecute exploration in the far North. She was commanded by Lieutenant George W. De Long. The expedition was ill-fated, the vessel being crushed in the ice of the Arctic Ocean, and only one third of the company succeeding in reaching settlements in Siberia. In accordance with a plan adopted at an International Geographical Congress in 1879, the Signal Service Bureau, in 1881, sent Lieutenant A. W. Greely, U. S. A., with a party of twenty-four men, to maintain a station for scientific observation in the extreme North. The plan was to send provision ships each year, and in case these failed to reach the station the party was to return southward overland, after their two years' provisions should begin to give out. Relief expeditions of 1882 and 1883 failed. Greely held his station (named Fort Conger), prosecuting the work of exploration till August, 1883. Then he attempted to retreat, but was stopped by open water. A relief expedition in June, 1884, found and brought back Greely and six companions, all who had to that time fought off starvation.]

719. The presidential election of 1884 was closely contested. The Republicans nominated James G. Blaine of Maine, and John A. Logan of Illinois. The Democratic nominees were Grover Cleveland of New York, and Thomas A. Hendricks of Indiana. No great issues were brought out in the campaign. The contest was full of personalities touching the private character of the nominees. The state of New York gave the Democratic candidates a small plurality, and decided the election in favor of Cleveland and Hendricks.

[Cleveland and Hendricks had 219 electoral votes against 182 for Blaine and Logan. A considerable number of Republicans in the eastern states supported Cleveland on the ground that Republican administrations had not promoted purity in the civil service. These Independent Republicans supporting the Democratic nominees were nicknamed "Mugwumps." The Prohibition party, calling for the suppression by law of traffic in alcoholic liquors, nominated John P. St. John of Kansas. The Greenbackers, uniting with local parties favoring laws in the interest of the laboring classes, nominated Benjamin F. Butler of Massachusetts. Neither party gained any electoral vote.]

4.

Grover Cleveland, *New York, President— 1885.*
Thomas A. Hendricks, *Indiana, Vice-President (died November, 1885).*

CABINET.

Thomas F. Bayard—State.
Daniel Manning, }
C. F. Fairchild, } Treasury.
William C. Endicott—War.

William C. Whitney—Navy.
Lucius Q. C. Lamar, }
William F. Vilas, } Interior.
Augustus H. Garland—Attorney-General.

William F. Vilas, }
D. M. Dickinson, } Postmaster-General.

For Explanation.—Merchant marine.

720. **Cleveland's Administration.**—For the first time since Buchanan our country had a Democratic President. This fact is important simply in showing that the old questions of the Civil War were laid aside, and that new ones were demanding attention. As the old questions came to be settled and were laid away in the past, so the men who had settled them one by one went to their rest.

[General Grant died in July, 1885, after a long continued illness. At his death the nation honored him even more grandly than in life. General McClellan died three months later. General Hancock died in February, 1886, and General Logan in December. At the funeral of General Grant ex-Confederate soldiers joined with his Union comrades in the last sad honors. Other occasions gave opportunities for a grasping of hands by the Blue and the Gray.]

721. [**Grover Cleveland** was born in New Jersey in 1837. He received an education in common schools and in an academy. Having studied law he was admitted to practice at the age of twenty-two. He located at Buffalo, New York, gained some note as a lawyer and filled the positions of assistant district attorney and sheriff. He was mayor of Buffalo (1882), Governor of New York (1883-4), and President (1885-).]

722. [**The Grand Army of the Republic** is the name under which the volunteer Union soldiers kept alive the memory of their services. They grouped themselves in "posts," or associations in towns and cities, and maintaining their military organization, assembled in yearly national encampments. A braided hat on parade and a buttonhole badge in business dress designated the veterans of the Union. Through the association poor and needy comrades were cared for. Pensions were liberally bestowed by the government. There could be no pensions, however, for the Confederate veterans or for the widows and orphans of the South.]

723. New questions were before the people, growing out of the mutual relations of employers and the employed, the growth of monopolies, popular resistance against them, and plans for their control. Plans to guard against corruption in office holders and among electors, to extend government service in public telegraphs, to protect remaining public territory against "land grabbers," to preserve forests and fisheries, to give national aid to education, to suppress the liquor traffic, and to adjust the relation of a rapidly growing foreign population to a matured American nationality, were also subjects of discussion.

[Relations with foreign nations presented no new phases, save that the United States, from carrying on an independent commerce before the civil war, almost lost her merchant marine, sending exports and receiving imports almost entirely in foreign ships. Americans seemed to give up the sea, being contented with their wealth on land. Their navy, too, rotted away with age and fell behind the world in armor and equipment. The one great question received by the new age unsettled from the past was that of tariffs, for the experience of a century had not produced an unequivocal answer.]

724. The Indians continued to afford employment for United States troops, whenever the progress of settlements invaded their ancient lands or reservations once set apart for them. There was trouble in 1877 with the Nez Percé tribe in Idaho. Arizona tribes terrorized that country until 1874; then they were sent upon reservations. In 1885 and 1886 there was serious trouble from their leaving the reservations and attacking settlers. The Apaches were the most troublesome tribe. Peace came by the subjection of the savages and their return to the reservations. Some of the chiefs were held as prisoners.

725. Strikes and riots were common in the large cities in the years from 1877 to 1887. A strike is the refusal on the part of a number of workmen engaged in the same business to work except upon certain conditions. Throughout the land mechanics and laborers of all classes had formed

Unions—organizations for controlling hours of labor and daily pay, and for taking care of sick or unfortunate members. These organizations had been growing for many years. Trouble and riots began when striking laborers went beyond simple refusal to work and undertook to prevent other men from taking their places. Sometimes the strikes spread over large areas of the country. In a great strike of railroad employés in 1877 at least 100,000 men were at one time out of work, and every railway was affected from the Mississippi to the Atlantic.

726. [**A national organization** of trades unions, under the name of Knights of Labor, gained considerable notice in 1886 and 1887. The unions, in many cases controlled by men of foreign birth, frequently adopted methods of operation imported from the old world. Chief of these is the "Boycott," an attempt to make a man employ only men belonging to some one of the Unions, by trying to ruin his business in case he refuses.]

727. **Inventions** still kept pace with the growth of the nation. An energetic people, as ours has shown itself to be, finds a way for an improvement whenever the need of improvement is perceived. Engines, cars, street railways, printing presses, farming implements, and manufacturing appliances—all mechanical things—receive improvements from year to year. Most notable for these years was the application of electricity to the lighting of cities and buildings and to the transmission of mechanical power, as in electric railways.

728. [**Among great works of architecture** may be mentioned the Washington Monument, commenced in 1848 by voluntary subscription, and after a long interval, in which nothing was done, completed in 1884, chiefly through government aid. It is a lasting memorial to the foremost of Americans, the highest structure in the world, counting in total height 555 feet $5\frac{1}{2}$ inches. One of the great products of engineering skill is the Brooklyn suspension bridge. It joins New York City and Brooklyn, spanning East River at a height sufficient to clear the masts of the largest ships. It has five avenues, one for footmen, two for common vehicles, and two for street cars. The weight of the whole is supported by four immense wire cables, made by twisting wires into ropes and the ropes into cables. It was opened for use in May, 1883.]

729. The Centennial of the Constitution was appropriately noticed in September, 1887, by a celebration at Philadelphia, which aimed to present in visible form the vast material progress of the country in a hundred years. The century closed leaving the constitution essentially as its makers left it. The country for which it was designed had changed as no other portion of the earth ever changed in the same number of years. Why had the constitution stood? Because it was founded in wisdom and justice, and therefore nothing could prevail against it. So also if the work of the present age be done wisely, justly, honestly, it shall stand for the coming years, as the constitution has stood, a power for good, for the *elevation of men*.

Make a tabular review of the events of this chapter.

QUESTIONS.

Has the United States at the present time a "single" or a "double" standard in coinage? Do you know of any advantages of "paper money" over coin? How would the payment of all national debts affect the national banking system? What vice-presidents have succeeded to the first place by a president's death? By election? What vice-presidents have died in office? When did the United States begin protective tariffs? Have we ever had a free-trade system? Divide our history into periods with respect to our tariff laws. What reasons can you give why we require a system of appointing officers much more now than under the first administration? Read the signal service bulletin at your post office. What information does it give? Make a list of the political parties that made nominations at the last election and state what stand each takes in regard to questions now before the country. Write a paragraph about each of the "new questions" referred to in Article 723.

CHAPTER XXXV.

Education and Science.

It is by education that the man first becomes truly a man.—*Plato.*

The training of youth should be a concern of the state.—*Aristotle.*

Did I know the name of the legislator who first conceived and suggested the idea of the common schools, I should revere him as the greatest benefactor of the human race.—*Swift.*

1. Educational History.

730. National Schools.—While giving liberally to the states in aid of education, the United States has never undertaken the management or supervision of any system of public schools for the nation. In the District of Columbia, however,—a Federal district wholly under the control of Congress—excellent public schools have been established and fostered by the General Government. The subject of establishing a national University early attracted the attention of the founders. Pinckney **(426)** and Madison **(420)** sought to give, in the Constitution, express power to Congress to establish such a university. Adams and Jefferson proposed to secure it by "transplanting entire the members of the University of Geneva (Switzerland) to America." Washington, while doubting the wisdom of this policy, advocated the establishment of a "National Institution of General Learning," and as the motive to this he says: "At the juvenile period of life, when friendships are formed and habits established that will stick by one, the youth from different parts of the United States would be assembled together, and would by degrees discover that there was not cause for those jealousies which one part of the Union had imbibed against another part." Notwithstanding these early views, no national schools have been established save the military academy at West Point (437) and the naval academy at Annapolis (496).

731. National Land Grants in Aid of Education.—Congress was led in 1785, by public sentiment and by the example of Massachusetts, Connecticut, and Georgia, to make provision for public education in new states and territories by grants of land. This provision consisted at that time in setting apart in every township of government land, one section (640 acres) for the support of schools. The manner of disposing of these lands and investing the proceeds for public school purposes, was left to the several states and territories. At the same time two townships of land within each state thereafter to be admitted were donated for the purpose of establishing a university. Ohio, and all the western states admitted during the first half of the present century, received for the common school fund the sixteenth section of each township, and for university endowment, two full townships. States admitted since 1848 have received grants of two sections of land in each township for the support of common schools, and of two townships for the support of a university. In addition to this, Congress, in 1862, donated to each state, for the support of a college of agriculture, 30,000 acres of government land for each senator and representative from that state in Congress. Various other grants have at different times been made.

732. A National Bureau of Education was established by Congress in 1866, charged with the duty of collecting information from all parts of the Union and from foreign countries touching provision made for common schools, normal schools, colleges, universities, and technical schools,—the methods of instruction pursued, the progress made, and all facts that might aid in improving the means of general education. The information, when collected, was to be published and distributed throughout the country by a Commissioner of Education, to be appointed by the President, and who should have charge of the bureau. Henry Barnard, a man distinguished for his eminent services to education, was the first commissioner. Frequent publications from this bureau have done much to increase the general interest in education and improve the work done in its behalf.

733. State Provision.—Following the practice of the colonies from which they grew, the original states made various provisions for public schools. Nearly every state constitution declared it to be a high duty of the state to foster intelligence among the people by means of schools. The subject, however, received much more attention in some states than in others, but in none of them was our present system of free common schools fully established until a comparatively recent date. The appropriation of public funds was supplemented by a tuition fee called a "rate bill," a source of more or less annoyance for many years. Through the influence of many able and zealous friends of universal education, a public sentiment gradually grew up which demanded the complete equipment of the common schools at the public expense. Under this demand the "rate bill" has disappeared from every state in the Union, and the people of the United States now expend annually $100,000,000 for public education, or three times as much as England and six times as much as France.

734. [The character of the early schools was not high. Competent instructors were few and methods of instruction and discipline had not been touched by the refinements of later years. "A globe," says Edward Everett, "I believe I never saw at a public school, near enough to touch it." An academy that he attended had a small library, but the room was used as the whipping-room and the little fellows were afraid to go near it. The text-books were all foreign and all poor, the schoolhouse cheerless and uninviting, cold in winter, hot in summer, without ventilation or provision for comfort or health.]

735. Sources of Revenue.—The large sums expended by the states for common schools (733) are derived mainly from the interest on the proceeds of the sales of public lands

(731), from state and county taxes annually appropriated by the legislature, from local district and city taxes, from a per capita or poll tax, from fines and penalties collected for violation of certain laws. In some states, voluntary gifts like the Peabody (667) form a considerable portion of the revenue.

736. **State Universities.**—With the land endowment by Congress (731) as a foundation, free colleges or universities, under state control, have been established in most of the states of the Union, and annual appropriations for their support are made by the state legislatures. In some states, these appropriations are sufficient to give the institution a high place among the colleges of the country, while in others the state university takes a grade but little above that of a high school or academy. Among the most distinguished of the state institutions are the Michigan University, the Wisconsin University, Cornell University, partly established by the proceeds of the Agricultural College land grant (731), and the University of California.

737. **State Normal Schools.**—A much more general provision has been made for public normal schools than for state universities. This is probably owing to the fact that the immediate office of the normal school is to train teachers for the common schools. It is therefore naturally regarded as an institution affecting essentially the character of these schools, sharing with them, thereby, the just esteem in which the common school is held. The first normal school in the United States was established at Lexington, Massachusetts, in 1839. It has since been removed to Framingham. Edmund Dwight, of Massachusetts, donated $10,000 in aid of the enterprise, on condition of the appropriation of a similar sum by the state. In 1886 there were in operation in the United States 117 public normal schools, with more than 1,000 instructors and over 21,000 students.

738. Leaders in Education.—As in other departments of civil affairs public sentiment has been largely formed

1. Horace Mann. 2. Henry Barnard. 3. John Swett.

and led by men of commanding powers and devotion to

a cause, so, too, our educational systems have been founded and perfected through struggles led by great and wise and heroic men and women. In 1837 Horace Mann of Massachusetts, began a career of effort and discussion, which has given impulse and character to all succeeding achievements in education. Henry Barnard of Connecticut, in addition to distinguished services as an organizer of a model state system of schools for that state, began in 1855 the work of collecting and publishing information from the several states of the Union and of Europe respecting common schools, universities, normal, and other schools, and the methods of conducting them. This publication, consisting now of twenty-four huge volumes, issued largely at his own expense, is the most valuable repository of information on educational subjects in existence, and led to the establishment of the National Bureau of Education (732), of which Mr. Barnard was the distinguished first commissioner. J. P. Wickersham of Pennsylvania, Newton Bateman of Illinois, and John Swett of California are among those who have gained national distinction as founders and directors of state systems of public instruction. The names of Charles Brooks and David P. Page shine in the history of normal schools, while Mary Lyon and Emma Willard will never be forgotten in connection with early efforts to secure the higher education of women.

739. [**Horace Mann** was reared in the most straitened way on a small Massachusetts farm. In a letter to a friend he says: "I do not remember the time when I began to work." His father dying when Horace was thirteen years of age, he continued his life of severe toil and hardship till his twentieth year, when, having prepared for college by six months' study, he entered Brown University. Upon his graduation he studied law, and sprang rather than rose into eminence in his profession. As one of the Massachusetts House of Representatives and President of the Senate, he passed some years in political life, when he was elected Secretary of the Massachusetts State Board of Education. He immediately withdrew from all other business and professional engagements, and his splendid career as the foremost educationist in the country began. In so little estimation was educational work held at that time, that, with a single exception, his friends

sought to dissuade him from undertaking it. Dr. Channing, however, wrote him: "You could not find a nobler station. Government has no nobler one to give." His voice was now heard in all parts of his state. One writer says of him that he poured out everywhere upon little audiences in country school houses, streams of eloquence, wit, and sarcasm that would have delighted senates. His zeal and radical views led to heated and exhaustive controversies with politicians, teachers, clergymen, and others, through which better views respecting the work of education were gained. Mr. Mann retired from this post in 1848, to enter Congress as the successor of John Quincy Adams, but the impulse he gave to the work of educating the masses of the people is still felt throughout the country.]

740. [**Teachers' Institutes and Conventions.**—The voluntary gatherings of teachers and others in institutes and conventions for the discussion of questions connected with educational work, were greatly stimulated by Mann and Page, and have become almost universally recognized as an important agency in giving efficiency to the public schools. So strong is this recognition that in some states funds have been appropriated by the legislature for their support. These gatherings are both local and national. Nearly every county and state holds its annual convention of teachers, and the National Educational Association now draws to its yearly assembly from 7,000 to 12,000 of the foremost teachers of the country. The national convention for 1888 was held in San Francisco in July of that year. Educational journals, one or more of which are found in every state, some receiving legislative support, have also contributed much to the efficiency of the educational department of the government.]

741. **Higher Education.**—The seven colleges of Revolutionary days have grown to nearly 400 institutions for higher education sustained mainly by private endowment, though the old colleges of Harvard, Yale (100), and Columbia (160) (now styled Universities), have never lost their pre-eminence, steadily keeping at the front with the march of years. Among the great institutions of modern endowment are Girard College, Philadelphia, named for its founder, Stephen Girard; Vanderbilt University, Nashville, Tennessee, founded by Cornelius Vanderbilt, a New York capitalist; and Johns Hopkins University of Baltimore. Vassar College of Poughkeepsie, New York, Wellesley College, Wellesley, Massachusetts, and Smith College, Northampton,

Massachusetts, are institutions of high rank, admitting only women, but offering courses and giving degrees similar to those of colleges for men.

742. [Special Schools.—Schools for training in manual arts have also been established in considerable numbers. The most distinguished are the Chicago Manual Training School, and those in connection with Washington University, St. Louis, Boston School of Technology, and Rose Technological Institute at Terra Haute, Indiana. The subject of joining work schools with the common and normal schools has, in recent years, been much discussed, and the practice to some extent adopted. Kindergarten schools for the training of children of tender age have been established in many large cities, mostly by private munificence; but in some, notably in St. Louis, they are made a part of the public school system.]

2. PROGRESS IN SCIENCE.

743. Geology.—Investigations in America have largely increased our knowledge of this subject. Extensive geological surveys have been made by the states and by the general government. The more recent of these great surveys were made under the direction of J. W. Powell, in the cañon of the Colorado River, J. V. Hayden, and G. M. Wheeler. The demonstration of the existence of an ice sheet covering the earth at one time, as far south as latitude 38° or 40°, and of the theory that mountains are formed by being pressed together from the sides, instead of being pushed up from the center of the earth, are among the contributions to this science made by the scholars of the United States. Text-books on this subject, which are standard both in Europe and America, are by J. D. Dana of Yale College, and Joseph Le Conte of the University of California; and, in connection with this science as well as with Natural History, the name of Louis Agassiz, Professor of Geology and Zoölogy at Harvard University, is familiar to the whole civilized world.

744. Physics.—The forces of nature drive most of the machinery of the world, and do nearly all its work. American scholarship has added greatly to our knowledge of them. The discoveries of Franklin respecting the force that we call electricity, laid the early foundation of all that has been accomplished throughout the world by its aid.

The splendid researches of Joseph Henry, of the Smithsonian Institute, first established the fact that electricity may be sent along wires to act as power in the operation of machinery, and upon this Morse (524) has built the telegraph, and Bell and Edison have constructed the

AGASSIZ.

HENRY.

telephone. The genius of Brush and Edison has applied this property also in the production of electric light (727). What we know of tides, and ocean and atmospheric currents, has also been largely contributed by the scholars of our own country.

745. **The study of the stars** has received much attention in the United States, and progress in astronomical

science during the past century has been nowhere greater than here. In the eighteenth century Benjamin Franklin and David Rittenhouse of Philadelphia, and John Winthrop of Harvard College, made important observations of planetary movements. During the first half of the present century a great grandson of Franklin, A. D. Bache, and others in charge of the United States Coast Survey,

LE CONTE.

HOLDEN.

kept astronomy alive by their studies and observations. Government expeditions to South American countries for astronomical observations, under Lieutenant Gilliss of the United States Navy, and B. A. Gould, have also added much to this science. L. M. Rutherford and Henry Draper of New York, within the last few years have applied the methods of photography to the study of the heavenly bodies, which has placed many of the results of the most powerful telescopes directly before the eyes of the people, through pictures that can be effectively displayed by the magic lantern.

[The great observatories of the country are the Harvard College Observatory; the United States Naval Observatory at Washington; Ann Arbor Observatory; Dudley Observatory, Albany, New York; Washburn Observatory, Madison, Wisconsin; and Lick Observatory, on Mount Hamilton, California. The most distinguished directors in charge of these observatories have been G. P. Bond, and E. C. Pickering of Harvard, F. Bruennow of Ann Arbor, B. A. Gould of Dudley, J. C. Watson of Washburn, and E. S. Holden of Washburn and Lick. S. C. Walker, J. S. Hubbard, J. H. C. Coffin, S. Newcomb, and A. Hall, of the Naval Observatory, deserve a high place in the history of American Astronomy.]

CHAPTER XXXVI.
1520-1850.
SETTLEMENT OF CALIFORNIA.

For Explanation.—Padre; neophyte; peso; guerrilla; mesa; rancheros.

To be Pronounced.—Junipero Serra (hu-nip'e-ro sĕr'rä); pe'so; Perouse'; ran-che'ro; Sŭt'ter; mĕs'ä; Mäz-at-län; Sän Päs-quäl'; San Lu'is Obis'po; Do-lō'rĕs; San Juan (hoo'an); San Buenaventura (san-bwä-nä-vĕn-toó-rä); ä-yụn-tä-mī-en'to.

1.

746. California was planned by nature to be a vigorous and generous state. Other states may look upon broader lakes and greater rivers, but none view a wider variety of scenery in ocean, mountain, bay, river, and plain—all arranged on a grand, impressive plan. In geological history the Pacific slope is younger than the Atlantic, yet equally interesting in every feature of scientific study. Our state is young among the sisterhood, but already has a history that every citizen should appreciate.

747. Name and Early Exploration.—The name California originated in a popular Spanish romance, published as early as 1520, in which it was applied to a fabulous island "near the Indies, and also near the Terrestrial Paradise." Followers of Cortez probably applied the name to the peninsular of Lower California, with which they became acquainted. We have already noticed the visits of Spanish (31) and English (36) navigators to the California coast in the sixteenth century. The Spaniards made another exploring expedition in 1602–3. For a century and a half afterwards nothing was done toward the exploration of California.

748. The Franciscans.—Jesuits accompanied Spanish conquerors in Mexico and South America, as they did

French explorers in the Mississippi valley (176). In 1767, however, they were expelled from Spanish provinces, the Franciscans taking their places. Spain had considerable commerce with the East Indies, and desired a good harbor on the Pacific coast of America, as a stopping place for supplies and repairs. This desire, joined with the zeal of the Franciscans for the conversion of the natives, led to further exploration and the occupation of California.

749. First Settlement.—In 1769 four expeditions were dispatched from Mexico for San Diego Bay, two by land and two by sea. Either course was slow and difficult; the water expeditions having to work against adverse winds and currents, and suffering from scurvy; the land parties having neither road nor guide. The first arrival was by ship (April 11th, 1769). All four parties having arrived, the mission of San Diego was founded (July 16th, 1769), the beginning of our oldest city.

750. [**Leaders.**—These expeditions were military and ecclesiastical combined. The military forces were under the command of Gaspar de Portala, who had been appointed Governor of California, the first of the Spanish governors. The head of the ecclesiastics was Father Junipero Serra, whose name is famous in the early history of California. A priest of the most zealous determination, his perseverance against toil and suffering would not permit failure.]

751. Discovery of San Francisco Bay.—From San Diego an expedition under Portala set out northward to reach Monterey Bay, of which something had been learned from the early voyagers. The expedition went past Monterey Bay without knowing it, and finally reached the coast a little south of the Golden Gate. A detachment of soldiers while hunting, having climbed the hills, beheld the great bay, which by this discovery became known to Spaniards and the world, receiving the name San Francisco Bay in honor of the founder of the Franciscan order.

[The eastern shore of the bay was explored in 1772 and the San Joaquin River discovered the same year.]

JUNIPERO SERRA.

752. Missions.—The Franciscan plan for converting Indians included the building of churches, around which the Fathers lived, instructing the Indians in the faith and requiring them to labor and live in the ways of civilization. These establishments, called missions, are the chief feature of the colonization of California. The mission *padres* were earnest, devout men, devoting themselves to their work of superintendence with a singleness of purpose that insured success.

[By 1780 sixteen mission priests were the spiritual rulers of some 3,000 native converts. By the end of the century there were eighteen missions with forty *padres* and a neophyte population of 13,500. Crops of from 30,000 to 75,000 bushels per year were by this time produced in the territory, and there were 70,000 horses and cattle, while the mission buildings and other property were valued at a million *pesos*.]

753. [**Principal Missions.**—The missions founded by Father Serra were as follows: San Diego, 1769; San Carlos de Monterey, 1770; San Antonio (near Monterey), 1771; San Gabriel, 1771; San Luis Obispo, 1772; Dolores (San Francisco), 1776; San Juan Capistrano, 1776; Santa Clara, 1777; San Buenaventura, 1782. His followers in the work founded ten more: Santa Barbara, 1786; San Purissima (Lompoc Valley), 1787; Santa Cruz, 1791; Soledad, 1791; San José, 1797; San Juan Bautista, 1797; San Miguel, 1797; San Fernando Rey, 1797; San Luis Rey de Francia, 1798; Santa Inez, 1804.]

754. Pueblos.—The Spanish scheme of colonizing California included, besides the religious establishments, the foundation of towns as business and military centers. The arm of the government was extended over the early missions, and each one had a *presidio* or military station close by. Several towns, or pueblos, also were founded independent of the missions. The first of these was San José, founded in 1777. Los Angeles was second, founded in 1781.

755. [Government of Pueblos.—The pueblos were towns maintaining local civil government independent of church or military rule. Their chief officer was called an Alcalde. He was elected by the people annually, and it was his duty to maintain order and administer justice. Large towns had three alcaldes, and these with six or eight subordinate officers formed an ayuntamiento, or town council.]

756. [Visitors from Other Nations.—La Perouse, a Frenchman, visited California in 1786, and Vancouver, an English navigator, in 1792, and both gave descriptions of the land to Europeans. A Boston ship, the *Otter*, obtained wood and water at Monterey in 1796. The Russians extending exploration from the Pacific shore of Asia down the Pacific shore of America, established a colony at Sitka. In 1806 a Russian ship came down from Sitka, and obtained provisions at San Francisco. (Read Bret Harte's poem, "Concepcion de Arguello.")]

757. [Russian River Settlement.—In 1812 a company of Russians made a settlement on the coast a little north of the mouth of the Russian River. A fort was built, and a military settlement carrying on trade with the Indians was maintained until 1841. Although this lodgement was resented by the Spaniards, there was never any violence.]

758. The change to Mexican rule upon the independence of Mexico (**464**) in 1822 caused no commotion in California. A convention of California officers assembled at Monterey and assented to the new government of Mexico. In 1823 a provincial legislature, summoned by authority of Mexico, elected Don Luis Arguello first of Mexican **governors of California**.

SPANISH GOVERNORS OF CALIFORNIA.

Gaspar de Portala (Gäs-pär' dä Pōr-tä'lä).	1767–1771
Felipe de Barri (Fä-lī'pä dä Bär'rī)	1771–1774
Felipe de Neve (Fä-lī'pä dä Nā'vä.)	1774–1782
Pedro Fajes (Pä'dro Fä'hes.)	1782–1790
Jose Antonio Romea (Hō-sä' An-tō'ni-o Ro-mä'ä). . . .	1790–1792
Jose J. de Arrillaga (Hō-sä' J. dä Ä-rrīl-yä'). . . .	1792–1794
Diego de Borica (Dī-a'go dä Bō-rī'cä).	1794–1800
Jose J. de Arrillaga	1800–1814
Jose Arguello (Hō-sä' Ar-guäl-yō).	1814–1815
Pablo Vincent de Sola (Pä'blō Vī-cén-tä dä Sō'lä). . .	1815–1822

2.

UNDER MEXICAN RULE.

759. Government of California.—From 1822 till 1831 affairs in California went on quietly under the name of the Mexican government. Californians, however, did not feel dependent on Mexico, and, as Mexico grew into a republic, a spirit of independence was developed in California. This local spirit strengthened rapidly from 1831 to 1846. This period is distinguished by jealousy of Mexican government, and by political feuds between rival communities of Californians centered around Monterey in the north and Los Angeles in the south. The feuds were always settled without bloodshed.

760. Secularization of the Missions.—The mission *padres* exerted themselves to weaken Mexican power in California. Mexico retaliated by confiscating their property to the government and transferring their Indian wards to military care. This took place gradually from 1834 to 1837, and is known as the secularization of the missions. Many of the missions fell into decay. The Indian converts relapsed into their old ways of living, and only the mission buildings, or their ruins, now remain to tell us of the work of the Fathers.

<small>**761. California Life.**—The white population of California (in 1846 about 1,000) represented chiefly decendants of Spanish lineage. Many California families were of pure Castilian blood. The leading business of the country was cattle raising for hide and tallow, which were sold to American traders on the coast. Hides were the usual money of the country, passing at the uniform rate of two dollars apiece. Land was held in large tracts, called *ranchos*, not definitely bounded, but distinguished by name and located by natural landmarks. The *rancheros* lived an easy, unprogressive life, giving much time to festivities and much attention to gay and tasteful dress. All travel was on horseback. Without exception Californians were skillful riders, natural musicians, and graceful dancers. They were intelligent, quick witted, brilliant in conversation, but had no great endurance to maintain a cause or to resist moral temptation.]</small>

762. Americans in California before 1846.—American whaling ships appeared in the Pacific early in the century. Regular trade with California began in 1822 and grew rapidly. Hunters and trappers began to make their way overland into California as early as 1826. Between 1839 and 1846 a settlement of Americans grew up in the Sacramento Valley, of which Sutter's Fort was the nucleus.

763. [**Captain John A. Sutter** was of Swiss family and a native of Germany. Having come to the United States and become a citizen, he came to California in 1839. Two years later he gained title, through the Mexican government, to a large tract of land on the American and Sacramento Rivers. He raised grain, employing Indians as laborers, and prospered for a time.]

764. [**Thomas O. Larkin** was a native of Massachusetts, who came to California in 1832 and established himself as a trader at Monterey. In 1844 our government made him Consul, the first and last man to fill that office in California. He had considerable influence with Californians, which he used in preserving good will between them and Americans. His letters to home newspapers helped his countrymen to a knowledge of California.]

765. [**The Donner Party** is the name by which a company of some eighty persons is remembered, which set forth across the continent for California in 1846. They fell behind in crossing the great plateau, and winter came upon them in the midst of the Sierras. Their cattle were lost in a great snowstorm, and with only the shelter of huts a terrible struggle against cold and starvation followed. Twenty-two of the party tried to get through the snow to Sutter's Fort, but only seven succeeded. There were successive relief expeditions from the valley, but not until the snows were melting were the few survivors of the party rescued from the mountains.]

766. **John C. Fremont**, born in Georgia in 1813, and educated as an engineer, was commissioned in the United States army and employed in 1842 to explore the passes of the Rocky Mountains, with a view toward finding an overland route to the Pacific. He devoted several years to this enterprise, first exploring the region of Great Salt Lake, and entering California through the Sierras at the headwaters of the American River in the winter of 1843–4. Having returned with the results of his important work, Fremont

was again dispatched for California in 1845, to explore more thoroughly the region along the coast. He reached Sutter's Fort with about sixty men early in 1846, and obtained permission from José Castro, at the head of the California military department, and living at Monterey, to make explorations in the San Joaquin Valley. This permission was withdrawn after Fremont was already on his way southward; and rumors of intended attack caused Fremont to intrench his party upon a peak about thirty miles from Monterey. No attack being made, Fremont turned northward toward Oregon.

MEXICAN GOVERNORS OF CALIFORNIA.

Luis Arguello (Lu-ĭs' Ar-guäl'yō).	1823–1825
Jose Maria de Echeandia (Ma-rī'ä dā E-chän-dī'ä)	1825–1831
Manuel Victoria (Män-u-ĕl Vic-tō'rī-ä).	1831–1832
Pio Pico (Pī'ō Pī'cō)	1832–1833
Jose Figueroa (Hō-sā Fī-guä-rō'ä).	1833–1835
Jose Castro (Hō-sā' Cäs'trō).	1835–1836
Nicolas Gutierrez (Nĭ-co-läs' Gu-tĭ-ä'rres).	1836–1836
Mariano Chico (Ma-ri-ä'nō Chī'cō).	1836–1836
Nicolas Gutierrez	1836–1836
Juan B. Alvarado (Huän' B. Al-vä-rä'dō).	1836–1842
Manuel Micheltorena (Mĭ-chel-tō-rä'nō)	1842–1845
Pio Pico	1845–1846

3.

AMERICAN CONQUEST OF CALIFORNIA.

767. A desire on the part of the United States to acquire possession of New Mexico and California was well understood both in the United States and Mexico, after the annexation of Texas. At the outbreak of the Mexican war the United States was represented in California by a considerable number of resident citizens, by Fremont's exploring party, and, shortly after the declaration of war, by warships commanded by Commodore Sloat. Between these representatives there was no common plan of action, except the idea that California was foreign soil, which it

would be a great advantage to the United States to acquire.
All of these parties acted on their own responsibility, for
the most part, for Washington was a distant place from
which to receive orders in those days. As results, possession of California in the name of the United States was
easily gained. But the native people of California, though,
at the outset, nearly as cordial to Americans as to Mexicans,
were made to regard Americans as invaders and to hate
them as conquerors.

768. **The Bear Flag Affair.**—The trouble between Fremont and Castro (766) had created rumors of war and
intended conquest. Early in June a band of horses belonging to the California government was seized by the
Americans, and driven to Fremont's camp. A company of
Americans, without any clear plan or reason, went to Sonoma, took possession of the town, surrounded the house of
General Vallejo, and sent him with three other gentlemen
as prisoners to Sutter's Fort. The main party, remaining a
short time at Sonoma, amused themselves with some wild
proclamations about a new state, and with raising a new
flag of cotton cloth, on which was stained with berry juice
the rude figure of a bear. The affair has been dubbed
"The Bear Flag Revolution."

[Californians at once became alarmed and suspicious. Guerrilla warfare was imminent, but prevented by the news of hostilities between the
United States and Mexico.]

769. **Peaceful measures,** only, were intended by the
United States government. Commodore Sloat, commanding the fleet in the Pacific, was ordered, in case of hostilities
with Mexico, to gain possession of the ports, without a struggle, if possible. He arrived at Monterey July 1st, 1846, and
six days later, he raised the flag of the United States, and
took possession of the place, and the same thing was done
at Yerba Buena (774). Sloat had no intention of making

war. On the contrary, he said that he came as the best friend of California.

[Consul Larkin also was all the time active in trying to persuade eminent Californians to declare for independence, and then to come into the United States as Texas had done. These measures would doubtless have been more successful had not the doings in the north created suspicion and resentment.]

770. **Hostilities.**—Castro withdrew from Monterey, and laying aside personal differences, joined with Governor Pico at Los Angeles, for defense. Fremont joined Sloat at Monterey. On July 23d, Sloat gave up his command to Commodore Stockton. Stockton and Fremont began military operations on the assumed ground that Americans in California needed protection from the forces of Castro. Moving southward they entered Los Angeles (August 13th), without resistance, Pico and Castro, despairing of peaceful terms or successful resistance, having set out for Mexico. A proclamation from Stockton declared the country the property of the United States, and military officers were immediately stationed in the principal towns.

771. **Revolt and Subjugation.**—At Los Angeles was stationed Lieutenant Gillespie. His management exasperated the native population. An armed force was gathered, and Gillespie was compelled to give up his post and to retreat northward. All the southern country was regained by its native owners. Stockton and Fremont set out at once to recover possession, being soon after joined by General Kearny (537), who had arrived in California with a small escort. After an unsuccessful effort by Kearny in December, 1846, to dislodge the Californians at San Pasqual, San Diego County, the forces of Stockton and Kearny, on the ninth of January, 1847, attacked the Californians drawn up on the mesa north of the San Gabriel River. The Californians retreated northward and surrendered to General Fremont, receiving the most liberal terms. No further conflicts occurred.

772. [**A serious quarrel** ensued as to who had the right to govern the conquered land. Kearny had orders to enter California, and to act as military governor in case he should conquer it. Stockton would not recognize his authority, and appointed Fremont Governor. The title of General Kearny was in the end recognized by the government, but he did not long remain in the country.]

773. The Interregnum.—This interval between the American conquest and the treaty of Guadalupe Hidalgo (538), when California really became American, is a period that produced long-standing results. Many Americans of mixed classes came in during 1846 and 1847. Americans everywhere assumed control, the native population being content if not molested. Without regular civil government, with a quarrel between the military chiefs, in a new land where there was no clear distinction between what one might take for himself and what belonged to some one else, the new settlers had perplexing questions before them. There was wrong doing and discontent, but there was also solid work toward improvement, and a foundation for self-government.

774. [**San Francisco.**—"To the little cluster of houses that within about two years had grown up at Yerba Buena cove, was given, early in 1847, by the consent of all concerned, and by the decree of the alcalde, the name that was its proper due—the historic name of San Francisco—which the bay, the mission, and the presidio had all long since borne. . . . By the census of 1847 there were 459 persons in the village, which still excluded from its limits the mission settlement. The little cluster of houses stood for the most part a little back from the low, curving beach of Yerba Buena cove. Telegraph Hill loomed up close upon the village on the north side. Southward the distance was greater along the lowlands to Rincon Hill."]

MILITARY GOVERNORS OF CALIFORNIA.

Commodore John D. Sloat	1846.
Commodore Robert F. Stockton	1846–1847.
Colonel John C. Fremont } General Stephen W. Kearny }	1847.
Colonel Richard B. Mason	1847–1849.
General Bennet Riley	1849.

388 HISTORY OF THE UNITED STATES.

State Capitol.

CHAPTER XXXVII.
1850-1887.
Our State.

LIST OF GOVERNORS.

†Peter H. Burnett	1849-1851	Frederick F. Low		1863-1867
John McDougall	1851-1852	Henry H. Haight		1867-1871
John Bigler	1852-1856	†Newton Booth		1871-1875
J. Neely Johnson	1856-1858	Romualdo Pacheco		1875-1875
John B. Weller	1858-1860	William Irwin		1875-1880
†Milton S. Latham	1860-1860	George C. Perkins		1880-1883
John G. Downey	1860-1862	George Stoneman		1883-1887
Leland Stanford	1862-1863	*Washington Bartlett		1887
	Robert W. Waterman		1887-	

775. The Constitutional Convention, which, in response to the call of General Bennet Riley, military governor, assembled at Monterey (September 1st, 1849), was composed largely of men who had been residents of California previous to the gold discovery. Three-fourths of the forty-eight members were native Americans, representing all sections of the United States. Eleven were from New York,

†*Resigned.* *Died in office.* *Democrats.* Republicans. **Know-Nothing.**

and the constitution resembled that of New York in many features.

[There were eight merchants, eleven farmers, fourteen lawyers, and fifteen from other professions.]

776. Slavery and the state boundaries were the vital questions before the convention. The slave system was represented by a minority, skillfully led, however, by Wm. M. Gwin, recently come to California from Mississippi. As no favor was shown to the introduction of slavery at the time, a plan was formed to incorporate within the state Arizona, Nevada, and Utah, with the idea that so large a state would eventually afford an opportunity for division in the interest of slavery. The scheme failed, and the present state boundaries were adopted. With a natural boundary on the east, a magnificent frontage on the ocean, geographical unity, and free labor, California entered the Union, possessing extensive territory and natural resources that made sure the development of a great and powerful state.

777. [**The discovery of** gold has been already noticed (**544**). Previous to 1848 gold, in small quantities, had been found in California, but not much notice was taken of it. The discovery which led to the great excitement was made in January, 1848, near the site of the present town of Coloma, El Dorado County, where Captain Sutter was erecting a sawmill for getting out lumber from the forests on the mountains above. Sutter's foreman, John W. Marshall, tried to enlarge the mill race by sending artificial floods through it. A few shining particles washed out of the soil were picked up by Marshall, tested, and found to be genuine gold. Marshall reported the news to Sutter. With a few others they tried to keep the discovery a secret, but without success. By June, San Francisco and the other towns were almost deserted, every one having gone to the mines. During the summer authentic reports of the gold region were sent East, and the great migration to California began.]

778. The Gold Period.—Gold mining was necessarily the chief pursuit for a few years. The life of the state centered at San Francisco, which grew and spread marvelously. Sacramento, Marysville, and Stockton began their life as supply points for the miner and the gathering places of prospectors. The gold excitement brought together men from all parts of the world; and among them thieves, gamblers, and ruffians were swept into California in the general rush. The period is full of activity and of change, of romance, of heroism, and of wickedness, also. Laws, government, and society did not exist.

GOVERNOR BURNETT.

779. ["**Miner's Justice.**"—In the mining camps crime was frequent, and dissipation excessive. There was recklessness in one's own life, and carelessness for that of another. To carry small arms constantly and to settle disputes with pistols, seemed for a time in danger of becoming universal customs. The miners worked out principles for themselves in the matter of mining, land, and water titles; at first, however, their only mode of dealing with criminal offenders was to catch the first offender they could, give him a form of trial, and then to administer severe punishment. Regular courts, and jails for holding prisoners, were of slow growth. Meanwhile these spasmodic efforts of popular justice often confounded the innocent with the guilty, and failed to protect the peaceful and restrain the wicked, as true government should.]

780. [**Progress in Mining.**—The early miners came from other callings, and had to learn a new business by experience. The first mining was done along the lower courses of the present streams, but quickly pushed up into the high Sierras, where the gold-bearing gravel of former deposits was often found exposed far above the beds of the present watercourses. In the richest gravel the gold could be collected by shaking in a pan. Devices for washing gravel, as the "rocker," and the "long tom," led to "sluice" mining, which required a steady stream of water, considerable work in preparation, and afforded work for many in coöperation. With sluice mining came greater permanence in mining enterprises, and steadier habits on the part of miners.]

781. San Francisco, 1849-51.—In San Francisco occurred the great struggle of the early state for law and the protection of life and property. Municipal government in San Francisco fell into the hands of men of the weaker or baser sort. The ruffian population was so numerous as to be formidable to any power to suppress it. Mixture of races stirred up hatred that added to crime. A band of lawless men calling themselves "The Hounds," for a time maintained themselves by open violence, robbing whom they would, but making Spanish-Californians and Chilenos their most frequent victims. The buildings of the young city were the cheapest wooden and cloth structures, crowded together. Six times San Francisco was swept by disastrous fires. From 1851 onward, the business part of the city was more substantially built, and a vigorous fire department devoted itself successfully to prevention of conflagrations.

782. First Vigilance Committee, 1851.—Although lynch law never prevailed in San Francisco as it did at the mines, yet irregular tribunals and rough-and-ready justice were resorted to there on two notable occasions. Having lost confidence in their officials, the people of San Francisco, in 1851, formed what is remembered as the Vigilance Committee. In this organization the respectable citizens united against the criminal class, which for three years had reveled in robbery and murder. They acted promptly, yet with calmness and firmness, and, by hanging a few, taught other ruffians a lesson that was not forgotten.

783. Second Vigilance Committee, 1856.—San Francisco grew in wealth, but its politics fell into a bad condition. Elections were perverted by wholesale ballot-box stuffing, and the city government came under the control of rowdies. James King, editor of the *Bulletin* newspaper, boldly denounced the corruption of the city, and was shot and killed by a desperado named Casey. The people were wildly excited. The Vigilance Committee was reorganized, enrolling thousands of members. Casey was taken from jail and tried, and was hanged on the day of King's funeral. The committee maintained its organization for several months, devoting itself to the detection of election frauds, and the punishment of notorious criminals.

[The Vigilance Committees were composed chiefly of business men, many of them then and afterwards among the most prominent citizens. Opponents of the committee of 1856 demanded that the punishment of criminals should be left to the constituted authorities. They were known as "Law and Order Men." Wm. T. Coleman, afterwards a leading San Francisco merchant, was at the head of both committees.]

784. **Land Troubles.**—The early uncertainty with regard to land titles (773) was not removed by the formation of the state. Previous ownership did not cause the miners any serious annoyance. They demanded and maintained as a principle that mineral land should be yielded to those that discovered and brought forth its ores. Thus came the practice of locating "mining claims." Disputes arose when claims overlapped, but there was no contest with any original owners. The original land titles (known as Spanish or Mexican grants), applied chiefly to the more desirable valley lands, and here the land troubles began when men turned from mining to agriculture and the laying out of towns. A United States commission was appointed to examine and pass upon all titles, and years of litigation have hardly yet set them at rest.

785. [**Squatter Riot at Sacramento, 1851.**—There was serious trouble at Sacramento over land ownership. The site of Sacramento was a part of Sutter's ranch, acquired by him from the Mexican government (763). His title passed by sale to the founders of the city. A numerous party, however, in 1851, proposed to disregard Sutter's title, and to take and hold the land as theirs by right of American citizenship. This party, known as "squatters," actually organized for armed defense. In a collision with the county authorities, the Sheriff of Sacramento was killed. Excitement followed, during which the state militia was called upon, and firearms were shipped up from San Francisco. The squatters soon relinquished their pretensions.]

786. **State Politics.**—Personal intrigue and quarrels

occupy a large space in the early politics of the state. The first senators were John C. Fremont, who had returned to California in 1848, and William M. Gwin. Fremont drew by lot the short term (Constitution, Art. I., Sec. III.). John B. Weller, afterward Governor, succeeded him. As Gwin's term drew to a close, there arose a man fully his equal in political skill—David C. Broderick, born in Massachusetts, of Irish parents. The struggle between these two politicians came, later, to represent the struggle between North and South in national affairs. Broderick was a Democrat, but was opposed to southern aristocracy as represented in Gwin, and figured in California politics as the champion of free labor.

787. [**Broderick** gained the senatorship in 1857. Two years later he was killed in a duel by David S. Terry, Chief Justice of the State Supreme Court, the challenge having been given by Terry on account of certain utterances by Broderick in regard to the Lecompton Constitution.]

788. [**California's electoral vote** has been cast as follows: In 1852, for Pierce and Graham, four; in 1856, for Buchanan and Breckinridge, four; in 1860, for Lincoln and Hamlin, four; in 1864, for Lincoln and Johnson, five; in 1868, for Grant and Colfax, five; in 1872, for Grant and Wilson, six; in 1876, for Hayes and Wheeler, six; in 1880, for Hancock and English, five, for Garfield and Arthur, one; in 1884, for Blaine and Logan, eight.]

789. **The War Period.**—Though the sentiment in opposition to the Union was in a minority, it was strong and bitter, its representatives being mainly men of southern birth and feeling. For this reason doubt had been cast upon the loyalty of the state to the general government. When, however, the call for volunteers was made, her people responded with the full number required. No draft (**638**) was ever needed. Some few went from California to support the Confederacy, notably General Albert Sydney Johnston (**612**). California gold prevented the Union from ruin through the want of money, when excessive taxation (**655**) was making its fearful demands upon the business of the country.

790. New Mines.—San Francisco was a center for mining enterprises even outside the state. In 1863 there was fresh excitement over treasure in Oregon and Idaho, and much money was spent in trying to find gold where there was but little. Later, silver mines in Nevada proved to be wonderfully rich, and became the basis of vast mining operations. They formed the basis, also, of colossal stock operations, managed by brokers in San Francisco, resulting sometimes in the accumulation of large fortunes, and sometimes in their ruin. From 1875 onward rich mines were also developed in San Bernardino and San Diego counties.

791. ["**The Big Bonanza**" is the name by which is known a great body of rich silver ore, found in 1874 in mines of the Comstock Lode, Virginia City, Nevada. It gave a great impetus to mining stock speculation, which reached a crisis in 1875 with the temporary closing of the Bank of California, a leading San Francisco bank.]

792. Labor Agitation.—The presence of Chinese laborers in California caused labor agitation to take the form of opposition to Chinese immigration. There were serious riots in San Francisco in 1877, Chinese laundries being demolished, and a wharf used by the Pacific Mail Steamship Company being burned. The steamship company was attacked because by its vessels Chinese laborers were brought to California. The riots were suppressed by the organization of a Citizens' Safety Committee, similar to the Vigilance Committees. After the riots discontent took a political turn. Crowds of laboring men and idlers gathered on Sundays upon unoccupied ground in front of the San Francisco City Hall, known as the Sand Lot. Here would-be politicians delivered harangues, and a "Workingmen's Party" was developed, which spread its organization to all parts of the State, with the cry: "The Chinese must go."

793. A new constitution was decided upon, in order to correct some defects in the old document. The choice of members of the constitutional convention came at the time when the Workingmen's Party was at the height of its career, and many members were elected by it. The convention performed its work in the spring of 1879. Although warmly opposed, the new organic law was adopted by the people, and went into effect January 1st, 1880.

794. Railroads.—The first railroad in California, known as the Sacramento Valley Railroad, joined Sacramento and Folsom, and was opened January 1st, 1856. The great railroad enterprises of the state began, however, with the building of the Central Pacific (**681**), and have continued under the direction and control of the men who undertook and carried to completion that gigantic work. The manner in which these enterprises have been conducted has, at times, provoked much discussion. Questions arising out of the management of railroads have entered to a great extent into the later political movements of the state, and were controlling factors in the formation of the Constitution of 1879 (**793**). The railway service has steadily grown, however, and has exercised a powerful influence in the rapid development of the state.

795. Agriculture.—Early agriculture took, almost exclusively, the form of wheat raising, for which the great central valleys drained by the Sacramento and San Joaquin Rivers afforded inviting territory. With the increase of wealth, fruit raising, for which greater capital is required, came into prominence, and has steadily and rapidly advanced as facilities for irrigation have increased and profits have been shown. The leading fruits are grapes, oranges, peaches, apricots, cherries, prunes, and olives. Olives are mainly converted into oil, while grapes largely take the commercial forms of raisins, wines, and brandies.

796. Manufactures.—Early in the history of the state no attention was paid to the wool product, the hides and wool of slaughtered sheep being thrown away, and only the carcass used. In 1858 the first woolen mill was started. The industry grew in magnitude and its product improved in quality till California blankets came to lead all others in the markets of the eastern states. The manufacture of clothing has also grown to be a leading industry. The manufacture of leather is still more extensive, and its conversion into boots and shoes, belting, harness, and saddlery has reached vast proportions. Great iron works in San Francisco have achieved national distinction in building machinery and ships, and many other branches of manufacture have grown into importance.

797. Public Education.—The foundation of the State School Fund was laid when the convention that framed the first Constitution (775) determined that the 500,000 acres of land granted by Congress to new states for internal improvements should be set apart for the use of schools. The present state system, in its main features, was finally settled, and "rate bills" discontinued, during the administration of John Swett as State Superintendent from 1863 to 1867, and largely by his efforts. It consists in free schools for primary and grammar grades, supported by the interest on money received from the sale of lands granted by the government, and from general tax by state and county. The shortest school term is six months in each year. The great features that distinguish the system in California from that of other states, are: 1. The apportionment to every district with twenty pupils or more, of a sum not less than $500 for teachers' salaries and school library, and to every district with less than twenty pupils a sum not less than $400; 2. The compulsory use of ten per cent of this fund, not exceeding $50 per annum, in each district, for apparatus and library; 3. The support of teachers' institutes by public funds; 4. The preparation by the State Board of Education, consisting of the Governor, the State Superintendent, and the Principals of the State Normal Schools, of the text-books to be used in the state, their manufacture by the State Printing Office, and their sale at cost to pupils of the public schools. The last of these provisions was added to the Constitution in 1884.

798. [**John Swett**, whose good fortune it was to represent the educational interests of the state as Superintendent of Public Instruction during the years that settled our present system, came to California from New Hampshire in 1852, and soon after began teaching in San Francisco. During the early and formative period of the state, his activity was aggressive and incessant. He is the author of a history of the School System of California, of several school text-books, and of a standard work on "Methods of Teaching." (See portrait, p. 371.)

799. Normal Schools.—In 1862 the Legislature established a State Normal School in the City of San Francisco. In 1871 the school was removed to San José, where it still remains. Since 1873 it has been in charge of Mr. C. H. Allen, as Principal. In 1881 the Legislature established at Los Angeles a second State Normal School, of which Mr. Ira More was made Principal. A third State Normal School was provided for by the Legislature of 1887, and located at Chico, in Butte County. These schools have taken high rank among the institutions of the United States for the training of teachers.

800. State University.—In 1868 the state legislature, carrying out a provision of the Constitution of 1850, availed itself of the rich congressional grants in aid of higher education, and of the donation by the College of California located at Oakland, of its entire property, and by an additional appropriation of over $300,000, established at Oakland a State University, which was afterward removed to Berkeley. Appropriations for various improvements were made by each subsequent legislature, until 1887, when it was permanently endowed with one cent on each $100 of the property of the state. Dr. Henry Durant, the founder and President of the College of California, became the first President of the state institution. D. C. Gilman, John Le

Conte, W. T. Reid, E. S. Holden, and Horace Davis have successively filled the position. The University has six colleges, located in Berkeley, namely: The College of Let-

LIBRARY BUILDING—STATE UNIVERSITY.

ters, College of Agriculture, College of Mechanics, College of Mining, College of Civil Engineering, and College of Chemistry. The Colleges of Law, Medicine, Dentistry, and Pharmacy are located in San Francisco.

[Important donations have been made at different times by private individuals. A medical college has been endowed by H. H. Toland, a law college by S. C. Hastings, and a professorship of moral philosophy, by D. O. Mills, all capitalists of San Francisco. H. D. Bacon, a capitalist of Oakland, has also donated his art collection and library, and $25,000 towards the erection of the elegant library building that adorns the grounds. To this Michael Reese added $50,000 in aid of the library.

A. K. P. Harmon donated a gymnasium. The greatest of all its private gifts, however, is the sum of $700,000 bequeathed by James Lick of San Francisco, to build, equip, and support an astronomical observatory. This has been located upon Mount Hamilton, in Santa Clara County. It is the best located observatory in the world, and is furnished with the largest and best telescope yet constructed. E. S. Holden is director, and S. W. Burnham, principal assistant.]

801. Leland Stanford, Jr., University.—At Palo Alto, thirty miles south of San Francisco, the erection of buildings for the most richly endowed university in the world, by a single gift, is now (1888) going on.

LELAND STANFORD.

The gift was made in 1885 by Leland Stanford, and his wife, Jane Lathrop Stanford, in memory of their only son, Leland Stanford, Junior, who died March 13th, 1884. The endowment consists of 83,200 acres of highly improved land, valued at $20,000,000, and the management is vested in a board of twenty-four trustees. The university is to be open alike to young men and young women, with special attention given to preparing students for such occupations as they may select, and with provision for an advanced course of study for graduates of other colleges.

APPENDIX.

EXPLANATIONS.

[References are to paragraphs.]

A

abdicated (387). *vacated; gave up.*
accessible (296), *that could be reached.*
accession (178), *addition.*
admiral (11), *the commander-in-chief of a fleet.*
adventurer (25), *one who seeks bold and novel enterprises with great risk;* (102), *one moving anywhere on the chance of making a fortune.*
agile (191), *quick; nimble.*
alert (184), *keenly watchful.*
Alexander (5), *King of Macedon, and conqueror of the world; lived between 300 and 400 years before Christ.*
alien (405), *a foreign born resident of a country in which he is not a citizen.*
allegiance (78), *fidelity; loyalty.*
alternative (252), *choice between two things only.*
ambush (200), *a place where enemies have concealed themselves for the purpose of surprising a foe.*
anarchy (268), *political confusion; absence of government.*
arbitration (677), *the hearing and deciding between parties, by persons selected by the parties themselves.*
Aristotle (5), *a Greek philosopher, who lived between 300 and 400 years before Christ.*
armistice (536), *a temporary cessation of hostilities by agreement between the powers.*
artisans (159), *persons skilled in handcraft; mechanics.*
assumption (373), *undertaking to pay.*
astrolabe (5), *an instrument for noting the position of the stars—now disused.*
Austrian Succession (180), *relating to the question of the succession of Maria Theresa to the Austrian throne.*

B

bankrupt (124), *one who cannot pay his debts.*
Barbary States (419), *countries in the northern part of Africa, bordering on the Mediterranean Sea.*
barony (122), *the estate appertaining to an English nobleman of the rank of Baron.*
base (203), *bottom; foot, as base of the hill;* (281), *an area of country from which the movements of an army are made.*
belligerent power (593), *entitled to the rights of war, but not independent.*
besiege (256), *to hem in for the purpose of compelling a surrender.*
blazoned (6), *adorned, embellished.*
blockade (421), *to prevent entrance by stationing war ships in the way.*
borough (110), *a district incorporated for voting.*
burgess (110), *the inhabitant of a borough.*
brunt (77), *the greatest weight, or violence.*
burly (400), *of heavy figure.*

C

cabinet (219), *the select council or advisers of the king.*
Cæsar (224), *Roman General and Dictator, stabbed by Brutus and others, about 44 years before Christ.*

calumny (396), *false accusation; slander.*
cant (395), *insincerity.*
capital (240), *punishable by death.*
catastrophe (443), *disaster; calamity.*
caucus (466), *a meeting for the selection of candidates for a political office.*
cavalry (287), *troops on horseback.*
cede (349), *to give up.*
Celtic (3), *pertaining to the Celts, an ancient Asiatic race, formerly occupying a great part of Central and Western Europe, and whose descendants are now found in Ireland, Wales, the Highlands of Scotland, and on the northern shores of France.*
chamberlains (375), *officers having charge of the chambers of a nobleman or monarch.*
Chevy Chase (251), *an ancient ballad, celebrating the overthrow of an English Earl who had invaded the territory of Earl Douglas of Scotland.*
Cincinnati (345), *the name was taken from Cincinnatus, a Roman Emperor, called from his farm to the head of the Roman Government and retiring again to his farm, after conquering the enemies of Rome.*
cloth of gold (6), *cloth into which a fine gilt wire is woven, giving it the glittering appearance of gold.*
coinage (397), *money made by stamping pieces of metal, as gold and silver.*
commission (137), *to give authority to.*
commissioner (186), *a person to whom certain duties are committed by the person or government who employs him.*
common (223), *belonging alike to all.*
compete (54), *contend for place or possession.*
compromise (197), *a settlement of a disagreement by yielding or giving up something claimed by each party.*
concerted (407), *planned together.*
conciliation (248), *winning over to an agreement.*

conciliatory (261), *calculated or designed to win or pacify.*
conferred (56), *conveyed or gave.*
confiscating (341), *taking for the public use.*
Constantine (5), *a Roman emperor, who established Christianity as the religion of Rome, in the third century.*
controversy (71), *dispute.*
corsairs (419), *pirates.*
corral (332), *a yard for cattle.*
counter (187), *opposite.*
cowed (330), *made fearful; destroyed the courage of.*
coxswain (362), *the one who steers in a boat.*
craftsmen (61), *mechanics.*
cruiser (208), *a ship of war, sailing back and forth on the ocean, in search of an enemy.*
Crusades (5), *a military expedition undertaken by Christian governments in the eleventh, twelfth, and thirteenth centuries, for the recovery of the Holy Land from the Mohammedans.*
culmination (243), *coming to a head; the outcome.*

D

dead letter (91), *without force; not to be regarded.*
defalcation (367), *the taking of money for his own use by an officer having it in charge for others.*
De Medici (5), *the name of a ruling family of Italy in the fourteenth, fifteenth, and sixteenth centuries. Lorenzo, a prince of Florence and patron of Art, lived in the fifteenth century. (Read Lesson 113, Second Reader.)*
depreciation (342), *falling off in value.*
depredations (51), *robberies; plunderings.*
detachment (249), *a small body of troops taken from the main army.*
devastation (337), *wasting; plundering; ravaging.*
devised (157), *planned.*
dialect (18), *one of the branches of a language.*
dismantled (449), *rendered unfit for service; disabled; deprived of its equipment for service.*
dissensions (103), *disagreements of a violent character; strifes.*

dissolve (96) (223), *to discontinue the session of.*
dispelled (261), *drove away.*
disposed (326), *placed.*
diversified (458), *varied.*
drenched (252), *soaked.*
dubbed (466), *entitled.*
duties (216), *taxes on imported goods.*

E

embodied (230), *put into form or shape; given body.*
emigrant (61), *a person removing from a country.*
emissary (201), *an agent employed to do one thing while seeming to be engaged in something else.*
envoy (190), (391), *a messenger sent by the government to transact special business with a foreign power.*
epidemic (397), *any disease which affects numbers of persons at the same time.*
equipped (51), *fitted up with things needed.*
era (152), *a point of time from which succeeding years are numbered.*
ermine (6), *a white fur taken from an animal of the same name.*
evasion (131), *secret avoidance.*
executed (239), *performed; carried out.*
executive (278), *one who enforces laws or puts them into effect.*
expedient (233), *advisable; desirable.*
extortion (239), *wrongful or forcible taking.*
extradition (516), *the delivery by one nation to another of fugitives from justice.*

F

fabled (25), *unreal, fictitious.*
factions (74), *parties violently opposed.*
factious (73), *given to heated opposition to the government, or to the majority.*
fanatics (73), *those who indulge wild notions of religion.*
fashion (116), *sort, or kind.*
fatal compliance (231), *a yielding that would bring calamity.*
ferment (71), *tumult; disturbance.*
fervor (73), *heat; excitement.*

feudal (114), *pertaining to a system on which lands were to be granted on condition of military service to be rendered when called for.*
finances (219), *funds; moneys.*
flagship (443), *the ship that carries the commander of a squadron, and displays his flag.*
flank (187), *on the side of.*
flash in the pan (249), *old-fashioned muskets were fired by striking sparks with flint and steel into some loose powder in a little pan connected with the barrel. When it happened that this powder only flashed, and did not connect with that in the barrel, the discharge was said to "flash in the pan."*
flinch (47), *shrink; draw back from pain or danger.*
foraging (293), *roving about collecting food from the country wherever it can be taken.*
foray (202), *a sudden attack for war or plunder.*
forfeited (93), *lost the right to.*
franchise (58), *any special privilege granted by government, as the elective franchise—the privilege of voting for public officers.*
freeholders (240), *holders of lands.*
furlough (345), *leave of absence from military duty.*
futile (296), *failing of the intended effect.*

G

gentlemen (102), *Englishmen without a title of nobility, but with a coat of arms, and ranking next above the yeoman.*
Gibraltar of America (180), *the point which protects the entrance to the Gulf of St. Lawrence, as Gibraltar protects that to the Mediterranean.*
gorgeously (106), *splendidly.*
grievous (245), *hard to bear; painful; afflictive.*
guerrilla (618), *carried on by small parties under no general head.*

H

harassed (277), *disturbed; troubled.*
Hercules (5), *a Greek hero, son of the God, Jupiter, celebrated for his wonderful achievements of strength and endurance.*

EXPLANATIONS. 403

Hessians (287), *inhabitants of the German state of Hesse (hĕss).*
Hotspur (435), *a high-spirited, hot-headed fellow in Shakespeare's play* **of Henry IV** *and other plays.*
hulk (449), *the body of a ship* **no longer fit for** *service.*

I

identified (273), *united in* **interest** *so that their cause was the same.*
immigration (126), *the act of moving into a country; also the body of* **people who** *move into a country.*
immunity (58), *freedom from obligation.*
impediment (49), *obstruction; something in the way of.*
imperious (156), *haughty, overbearing.*
impetus (223), *motion or force of motion.*
impotent (307), *weak.*
incorporation (56), *the formation of a body by the union of individuals constituting in law one person.*
indecisive (286), *slow to decide; hesitating.*
indictment (231), *a* **formal accusation** *of crime.*
installment (417), *a payment, made at regular intervals, of a part of a total sum.*
instinct (84), **natural tendencies or** *impulses.*
insurrection (137), **a rebellion of the** *people against authority.*
intrepid (306), *bold; fearless.*
itinerant (138), *wandering; unsettled.*

J

Jaffa (5), *ancient Joppa, a city of* **Palestine, on** *the western coast of* **the Mediterranean.**
joint stock company (56), *a company of persons united for business, to which each contributes a sum of money called stock.*
judicial (85), *pertaining to the decision of cases at law.*

L

laconic (443), *brief.*
league (246), *an alliance or compact between states.*
levied (364), *collected* **by assessment.**

letter of marque (591), *a commission granted to the commander of a private ship to seize the vessels of another nation* **in** *retaliation for an injury.*
libertine (102), *one who* **leads a dissolute** *life.*
Lincolnshire (59), *a* **county in England** *(shire means* **county***).*
liveried (106), *dressed* **in a garb peculiar to the servant of a particular** *nobleman.*
lore (5), *learning.*

M

magnanimous (346), *honorable; liberal.*
malice (164), *hatred; ill will.*
malignant (329), *likely to* **produce death.**
maize (119), *Indian corn.*
maneuver (281), *a military* **movement to gain** *advantage* **of an enemy.**
manor (122), *such part of a nobleman's estate as was kept for his own and his servants' occupation.*
maritime (26), **having numerous seaports, and conducting commerce largely on the seas.**
martial law (258), **law imposed by** *military power.*
measures (215), *means employed to accomplish a particular purpose.*
mediator (450), **one who** *seeks to* **reconcile** *parties at variance.*
meditated (298), **intended;** *thought* **to** *accomplish.*
memorial (226), *a statement of facts accompanied by a petition; (   ), anything designed to preserve the memory of.*
menace (132), *threat; danger.*
men of war (236), *war ships.*
mercenary (307), *hired for money.*
merchant marine (723), *the body of a nation's shipping employed in commerce.*
mesa (770), table land.
metropolis (182), *the largest and* **most** *important town in a state or country.*
mileage (371), *an allowance per mile made to officers traveling on duty.*
ministry (221), *the persons who compose the council of the king, and conduct the government.*

Mohammedans (5), *followers of Mohammed, a religious prophet, who lived in Arabia in the sixth and seventh centuries.*
monastic orders (176), *living apart from the common concerns of life, and devoted to religious pursuits.*
monopoly (56), *an exclusive right or power, shutting out all other persons.*
mortgaging (60), *pledging.*
Moslem (419), *Mohammedan (see p. 9.)*
museum (20), *a collection of curiosities in nature or art.*
mysterious (98), *unexplained; not plain.*

N

national securities (372), *notes, bonds, or other obligations of the national government.*
naturalization law (405), *a law to give foreign born persons the rights of a native, or citizen.*
negotiations (340), *transactions of business.*
neophyte (752), *a new convert.*
Nestor (356), *a Grecian hero, distinguished for courage, wisdom, and eloquence.*
neutral (314), *being on neither side.*
nicotine (109), *an oily, colorless, poisonous liquid obtained from tobacco.*
niggardly (83), *stingy; applied to soil, it means unproductive.*
nominal (151), *in name only, not in reality.*
notable, *worthy of notice.*
nucleus (79), *central point about which a gathering is made.*

O

obnoxious (330), *offensive.*
official (230), *one who holds an office.*
on parchment (178), *merely in writing, not actually.*
onset (206), *sharp attack.*
ordeal (363), *trial; test.*
ordnance (306), *cannon.*
oriental (7), *pertaining to Persia and Eastern Asia.*
original (186), *first.*
ostentation (106), *extravagant or excessive display.*

outlaws (240), *persons not entitled to protection of law.*

P

Padre (752), *a priest or religious father in the Roman Catholic Church.*
pagans (3), *those who practice the worship of idols.*
panic (304), *sudden and violent fright without cause.*
parallel (184), *running in the same direction; side by side.*
paralytic (466), *one afflicted with palsy, or inability to control the movement of his muscles.*
paramount (459), *above all others.*
parapet (260), *a breastwork.*
paroles (328), *promises of prisoners of war, on condition of being liberated, not to bear arms against their captors.*
partisan (396), *showing unreasonable zeal for success of a party.*
patent (51), *an official paper granting rights and privileges.*
patrician (388), *above the common people.*
pawn (11), *to give as security.*
penal (172), *pertaining to punishment or penalty.*
pennant (443), *a long narrow piece of bunting, or flag cloth, worn at the masthead of war ships.*
per diem (371), *for a day.*
persecution (59), *state of being vexed or harassed.*
peso (752), *the Spanish dollar of exchange.*
pillaged (321), *robbed; stolen.*
platform (221), *statement of political principles.*
policy (248), *settled method.*
pompous (174), *boastful; big sounding.*
popular (94), *by the people.*
postal (173), *belonging to mail service.*
preamble (233), *introduction.*
press (220), *a term applied to the whole body of newspapers in a country taken together.*
pretensions (186), *claims.*
prevailingly (163), *mostly.*
prime minister (232), *the minister of highest rank in the council of the king.*

EXPLANATIONS.

privateers (208), *ships fitted out by private persons with the authority of government to cruise during war against the commerce of its enemy.*
profligate (324), *openly and shamelessly immoral.*
propagate (68), *spread; promote the growth of.*
property qualification (96), *the possession of property as a condition of voting.*
provincial (202), *pertaining to a province, or a region dependent on a distant government.*
provisional (538), *temporary; providing for present need.*
punctilious (363), *very nice or exact in forms of ceremony.*

Q

quarters (234), *lodging places.*
quorum (362), *the number necessary to transact business.*

R

raged (229), *were violent.*
raids (236), *sudden fierce attacks for murder or plunder.*
rancheros (760), *owners and occupants of ranches or large tracts of land.*
rancorous (521), *marked by hatred or extreme ill feeling.*
ranking (535), *of highest rank; also of rank higher than another.*
ratify (361), *confirm; give sanction to what has been done by an agent.*
ravages (264), *waste; havoc.*
redeem (343), *to purchase back.*
redress (235), *remedy; relief.*
redressed (245), *remedied; relieved.*
reference to a record (275), *looking to a record in books or papers for the facts needed.*
reflections (185), *incidents of.*
refugee (393), *one fleeing from a country to escape persecution.*
regulars (281), *soldiers enlisted for a permanent army, distinguished from militia, who are enlisted for a short time only.*
representative (243), *representing the people through persons chosen for the purpose.*
representative assembly (114), *one made up of persons who are elected by the people to represent them.*

reprieved (153), *delayed punishment of.*
republican (254), *in the form of a republic, or government in which the highest power is exercised by representatives elected by the people.*
resident councilors (58), *councilors residing in the colonies.*
retaliate (127), *to repay injury by injury.*
revealed (18), *made known.*
revenue cutter (217), *an armed vessel employed to prevent smuggling.*
revision (219), *amendment or change.*
rival (141), *one seeking to gain the same object as another.*
royalist (112), *a person in sympathy with the king as against Cromwell's party.*

S

sable (6), *a black fur from the sable.*
sail (436), *vessels; ships.*
sally (338), *a sudden attack made by besieged troops upon the besiegers outside the fortifications.*
Salzburgers (131), *Protestants from the Duchy of Salzburg, Austria, whither they were driven by the Catholics.*
San Salvador (13), *saint of rescue: Salvador, redeemer.*
satirized (70), *censured with severity; ridiculed.*
savannahs (178), *plains destitute of trees and covered with grass, differing from a prairie only in the zone they occupy.*
scale (206), *to climb as by steps.*
scruple (236), *to doubt the right.*
scrutiny (363), *inquiry; examination.*
sedition (405), *relating to those who stir up discontent against the government.*
seer (218), *a prophet.*
sentries (206), *soldiers placed on guard or watch.*
siege (137), *the placing of an army around a fortified place to compel it to surrender.*
signal (152), *a sign; a foreshadowing.*
signature (239), *name of a person signed with his own hand to some writing.*

smuggling (91), *importing or exporting goods secretly without paying the duties, or contrary to law.*
sound (363), *of strong mind and judgment.*
sovereign (90), *superior to all others; chief.*
Spanish succession (180), *relating to the question of who should be king of Spain.*
spare (191), *thin in flesh.*
squadron (180), *a part of a fleet of ships under the command of one officer.*
stages (176), *degrees of progress.*
stanch (404), *firm in principle.*
stand (283), *position.*
state (6), *condition.*
stealthily (249), *secretly.*
stickler (400), *one who contends for a trifling thing.*
struck root (63), *became established.*
stupendous (178), *immensely large.*
subsist (241), *support; feed.*
substantially (221), *in reality; really.*
subversion (243), *overturning.*
successively (11), *one after another.*
Sultan of Versailles (178), *an allusion to Louis XIV., king of France, whose seat of government was at Versailles, near Paris.*
superstitious (19), *full of idle fancies in regard to religion and the meaning of events.*
swooped (193), *came suddenly and fiercely.*

T

tactics (445), *the science and art of arranging troops in order for battle, and of performing military movements.*
tariffs (216), *charges or taxes on imported goods.*
Tarquin (224), *the last king of Rome, about 500 years B. C., driven from the throne by Lucius Junius Brutus.*
temerity (59), *boldness.*
threatened (286), *placed in danger.*
tide water (463), *water flowing from the ocean inland up the streams which empty into it.*
tinged (376), *impregnated; affected.*
tithing man (168), *a peace officer; an under Constable.*
title (348), *a right to hold in possession.*
toast (231), *a sentiment, usually honored by drinking.*
tradition (95), *that which is repeated from father to son for several generations, without being written.*
traversing (411), *crossing; traveling over.*
treason (319), *an attempt to betray or overthrow one's country.*
tribunals (677), *courts.*
tumults (235), *uproars; brawls.*
turbulent (73), *disposed to make disturbance.*
turnpike (397), *a road rounded up in the middle by scraping the dirt from the sides to the center.*
turquoise (6), *a bluish-green mineral brought from Persia, and much esteemed as a gem.*

U

unanimous (215), *without opposition; as one.*
upland (311), *occupying the higher land near the Alleghany mountains.*

V

vague (348), *not clear; uncertain in meaning.*
vain (307), *without result.*
vanguard (62), *those who march in front.*
Venetian (6), *belonging to Venice.*
veto (96), *to prevent enactment by withholding assent to.*
viceroy (11), *ruler in place of the king, and by his authority.*
vigilant, *keenly watchful.*

W

windrows (259), *hay raked up into a roll.*
wizard (98), *the masculine of witch; a man in league with evil spirits to do mischief.*
wreaked (325), *inflicted.*

Y

yeomanry (82), *in England a body of people owning land and farming it, next in rank below the gentry.*

Z

zigzag (259), *having short sharp turns this way and that.*

PRONUNCIATIONS.

Al-gŏn′quin.
Amerigo Vespucci (ah-mä-rē′go ves-poot′chee).
Ä-pä′chę.
Är-gall.
Är′is-tŏt-le.
Ar-kăn′săs.
Är′yan.
Asia (ā′she-a).
ăs′trō-labe.
Ayllon (il-yōn′).
Ä-yųn-tä-mĭ-ĕn′to.
Āz′ores.
Ba-hä′ma.
Bäl-bō′ä.
Beaufort (bū′fort).
Beausejour (bo-se-zhoor′).
Berkeley (bĕrk′le).
Bĕr′lin.
Bo-dę′gä.
Bon-hŏmme′.
Bŏs′pō-rus.
Bowdoin (bō′den).
Brä-zil′.
Bue′(bō)na Vis′ta.
Căb′ot.
Cä-brĭl′lo.
Cä′diz.
Cam-ba-lū′.
Cär-ri-bees′.
Cartier (kär-te-ā′).
Căs′si-mir.
Căs-tĭle′.
Ca-taw′ba.
Cath-ay′.
Chäl′co.
Chä-pųl′tä-pec.
Che′raw.
Chęs a-peake.

Chickahominy (chik-a-hŏm′e-ne).
Chi-hua-hua (che-wä′wä).
Chō-wän′.
Christendom (kris′n-dum).
Christina (kris-tee′nä).
Cipango (se-päng′o).
Col-o-rä′do.
Cŏn′stan-tine.
Con-trę′räs.
Côr-tę-rę-äl′.
Côr′tĕz.
Courant (koo-ränt′).
Dä Gä′mä.
Darien (da′re-en).
De Bienville (deh be-ăn′vĕl).
D'Estaing (dĕs′täng).
De (deh) Gourgues (goorj), Dŏm-i-nique′ (neek).
De Grässe.
De Kălb.
De Monts′ (mŏng).
Denys (deh-ne′).
Dę Sō′to.
Dieskau (dees′kow).
Din-wĭd′die.
Do-lō′rĕs.
Du Quesne (du käne).
Ēlbe.
Eū-ro-pē′an.
Fę-rę′lo.
Flŏr′en-tine.
Frŏb′ish-er.
Frŏn-te-năc′.
Fųl′ton.
Ġän′ġĕs.
Ġĕn′o-a.
Ġist.
Ġôr′ġĕs.

408 APPENDIX.

Gua(gau)da-lupe Hī-dāl′go.
Gus-tā′vus.
Hayti (hā′te).
Huguenots (hū′ḡe-nots).
Il-li-nois′
Iroquois (ir′o-quoy).
Itajuba (ee-tä-hoo′bä)
Jean (zhŏn) Nicot (ne-ko′).
Joliet (zho-le-ā′).
Juan de Fuca (hoo′an dā foo′kä).
Kanawha (ka-naw′wä).
Khän.
Kusciusko (kos-se-ŭs′ko), Thăd′de-us.
Koszta (kŏz′ta).
lām′ent-a-ble.
Laudonniere (lō-don-yāre′).
Le Boeuf (leh bŭf).
Leisler (līs′ler).
Leyden (lī′den).
Loy-ō′la.
Mä-drĭd′.
Mä-ĝĕl′lan.
Ma-hŏn′.
Marquette (mar-kĕt′).
Mäz-at-län′.
Medici (mĕd′e-chee).
Menendez (mä-nĕn′deth).
mĕs′a.
Mil′an.
Mo-hăm′me-dans.
Mo-lī′no del Rey′ (rā).
Nar-vä′ez (eth).
Navarre (na-vär′).
New Or′le-ans.
Nez Perce (nay pĕr′cy).
nic′o-tine.
Nu-e′çes.
O′gle-thorpe.
Pä′los.
Pän-a-mä′.
Pow-hat-ăn′.
Pavia (pä-vee′ä).
Pe-rouse′ (rōōz).

pe′so.
Pis-cät′a-qua.
Pī-zăr′ro.
Po-ka-nō′ket.
Ponce de Leon (pōn′thä dā lā-ón′).
prē′mi-er.
Ptolemy (tŏl′e-my).
Pueblo (pwĕb′lo).
Raleigh (raw′ly).
ran-che′ro.
Re-dīv′i-va.
Re-sä′cä de lä Päl′mä.
Rbaut (rē-bo′).
Rī′o Grän′de.
Ro-ber-väl′.
Rochambeau (ro-shong-bo′).
Russia (rŭsh′e-a).
Saint Augustine (sĕnt au-gŭs′tin).
Salzburgers (sạlts′bŭrg-ers).
San Buenaventura (san bwä-nä-vĕn-too′rä).
San Juan (hoo′an).
San-lū′is O-bīs′po.
Sän Päs-quäl′.
Sante Fe (sän′tä-fä).
Scarborough (skär′bŭr-eh).
Sclōp′is.
Se-rä′pis.
Sĕr′ra, Ju(hū)nīp′e-ro.
Shaftsbury (shafs′ber-re).
Slōugh′ter.
South-ämp′ton.
Staempfle (stĕm′fl).
Steū′ben.
Sŭt′ter.
Swansey (swon′ze).
Teū-tŏn′ic.
Trīp′o-li (le).
Trip-ŏl′i-tans.
Ve′ra Cruz (kroos).
Verrazzano (ver-rät-sä′no).
Versailles (ver-sälz′).
wĭg′wạm.
Wȳ-ō′ming.

BOOKS FOR SUPPLEMENTARY READING.

Colonial History.

Ashton, Adventures and Discoveries of Captain John Smith.
Ballantyne, Young Fur Traders.
Coffin, Old Times in the Colonies.
Cooper, Leather Stocking Tales.
Drake, Around the Hub (Boston).
Eggleston and Seelye, Famous American Indians.
Franklin, Autobiography.
Hale, Stories of Discovery.
Hawthorne, Grandfather's Chair.
    Legends of the Province House.
Helps, Life of Columbus.
Hemans, Landing of the Pilgrims (poem).
Higginson, History of American Explorers.
Holmes, Robinson of Leyden (poem).
Irving, Life of Columbus.
    Companions of Columbus.
    Knickerbocker History of New York.
Johnson, The French War.
Kellogg, Good Old Times.
Kingston, Notable Voyages, from Columbus to Parry.
Longfellow, Miles Standish, Evangeline, Hiawatha (poems).
Lowell, Chippewa Legend (poem).
Markham, Around the Yule Log.
    King Philip's War.
Marryat, Settlers in Canada.
Parkman, Conspiracy of Pontiac.
    Discovery of the Great West.
    Frontenac and New France.
    Jesuits in North America.
    Old Regime in Canada.
    Pioneers of France in the New World.
Payne, Voyages of Elizabethan Seamen.
Scudder, Boston Town.
    Men and Women in America One Hundred Years Ago.
Towle, Drake, the Sea-King of Devon.
    Magellan.
    Marco Polo.
    Pizarro and His Conquests.
    Raleigh.

Voyages and Adventures of Vasca da Gama.
Wallace, The Fair God (Aztecs).
Whittier, Bridal of Pennacook (poem).
    The Exiles (Quaker persecution).
    The King's Missive (Quaker persecution).

Revolutionary History.

Abbott, Revolutionary Times.
Bryant, Song of Marion's Men (poem).
    Seventy-Six (poem).
Brown, Life of Washington.
Campbell, Gertrude of Wyoming (poem).
Coffin, Boys of '76.
    Building the Nation.
    Story of Liberty.
Cooper, Lionel Lincoln (Siege of Boston).
Hawthorne, Twice-Told Tales.
Hoppus, A Great Treason (Arnold's).
Longfellow, Pulaski's Banner (poem).
Lossing, Field-Book of the Revolution.
Scudder, Bodley Books.

National History.

Adams, Our Standard Bearer (U. S. Grant).
Catlin, Life Among the Indians.
Champlin, Young Folks' History of the War for the Union.
Coffin, Boys of '61.
    Following the Flag (1861-5).
Custer, My Life on the Plains.
Dana, Two Years Before the Mast (California).
Ellis, Daniel Boone (Kentucky).
    David Crockett (Texas).
Hale, Man Without a Country.
    Philip Nolan's Friends (Louisiana Purchase).
    Stories of the War (1861-5).
Hughes, G. T. T. (Gone to Texas).
Irving, Astoria.
Johnson, War of 1812.
Ladd, War with Mexico.
Leland, Abraham Lincoln.
Lossing, Field-Book of the War of 1812.
    History of the Civil War.
    Story of the United States Navy.
Oliver Optic, Army and Navy Stories.
Parkman, Oregon Trail.
Penniman, Tanner Boy (U. S. Grant).

BOOKS FOR SUPPLEMENTARY READING. 411

PITTENGER, Capturing a Locomotive (Civil War).
STOWE, Uncle Tom's Cabin (Slavery).
TROWBRIDGE, Cudjo's Cave (Civil War).
    Three Scouts (Sequel to Cudjo's Cave).

IN GENERAL.

ABBOTT, Pioneers and Patriots.
ADAMS, History of the United States in Rhyme.
BONNER, Child's History of the United States.
BUTTERWORTH, America (Young Folks' Histories).
HIGGINSON, Young Folks' History of the United States.
NORDHOFF, Politics for Young Americans.
RICHARDSON, History of Our Country.

TEACHER'S REFERENCE.

AMERICAN Commonwealth Series.

California,	Massachusetts,	Pennsylvania,
Connecticut,	Michigan,	South Carolina,
Kansas,	Missouri,	Tennessee,
Kentucky,	New York,	Virginia.
Maryland,	Oregon,	

AMERICAN Statesmen Series.

Adams, John,	Jackson, Andrew,
Adams, John Q.,	Jefferson, Thomas,
Adams, Samuel,	Madison, James,
Benton, Thomas,	Marshall, John,
Calhoun, John C.,	Monroe, James,
Clay, Henry,	Randolph, John,
Gallatin, Albert,	Van Buren, Martin,
Hamilton, Alexander,	Webster, Daniel.
Henry, Patrick,	

BANCROFT, History of the United States (Centennial Edition).
BLAINE, Twenty Years in Congress (1861-1881).
BRYANT, Popular History of the United States (to 1865).
FROTHINGHAM, Rise of the Republic of the United States.
LODGE, English Colonies in America.
MCMASTER, History of the People of the United States.
SCHOULER, History of the United States (1789-).

THE DECLARATION OF INDEPENDENCE.

Adopted in Congress, July 4th, 1776.

When, in the course of human events, it becomes necessary for one people to dissolve the political bands which have connected them with another, and to assume, among the powers of the earth, the separate and equal station to which the laws of nature and of nature's God entitle them, a decent respect to the opinions of mankind requires that they should declare the causes which impel them to the separation.

We hold these truths to be self-evident: that all men are created equal; that they are endowed by their Creator with certain unalienable rights; that among these are life, liberty, and the pursuit of happiness; that, to secure these rights, governments are instituted among men, deriving their just powers from the consent of the governed; that, whenever any form of government becomes destructive of these ends, it is the right of the people to alter or to abolish it, and to institute a new government, laying its foundation on such principles, and organizing its powers in such form as to them shall seem most likely to effect their safety and happiness. Prudence, indeed, will dictate, that governments long established should not be changed for light and transient causes; and, accordingly, all experience hath shown that mankind are more disposed to suffer, while evils are sufferable, than to right themselves by abolishing the forms to which they are accustomed. But when a long train of abuses and usurpations, pursuing invariably the same object, evinces a design to reduce them under absolute despotism, it is their right, it is their duty, to throw off such a government, and to provide new guards for their future security. Such has been the patient sufferance of these colonies, and such is now the necessity which constrains them to alter their former systems of government. The history of the present King of Great Britain is a history of repeated injuries and usurpations, all having in direct object the establishment of an absolute tyranny over these states. To prove this, let facts be submitted to a candid world.

1. He has refused his assent to laws the most wholesome and necessary for the public good.

2. He has forbidden his governors to pass laws of immediate and pressing importance, unless suspended in their operations till his assent should be obtained; and when so suspended, he has utterly neglected to attend to them.

3. He has refused to pass other laws for the accommodation of large districts of people, unless those people would relinquish the right of representation in the legislature—a right inestimable to them, and formidable to tyrants only.

4. He has called together legislative bodies at places unusual, uncomfortable, and distant from the depository of their public records, for the sole purpose of fatiguing them into compliance with his measures.

5. He has dissolved representative houses repeatedly for opposing, with manly firmness, his invasions on the rights of the people.

6. He has refused, for a long time after such dissolutions, to cause others to be elected, whereby the legislative powers, incapable of annihilation, have returned to the people at large for their exercise; the state remaining, in the meantime, exposed to all the dangers of invasions from without and convulsions within.

7. He has endeavored to prevent the population of these states; for that purpose ob-

structing the laws for the naturalization of foreigners; refusing to pass others to encourage their migration hither, and raising the conditions of new appropriations of lands.

8. He has obstructed the administration of justice by refusing his assent to laws for establishing judiciary powers.

9. He has made judges dependent on his will alone for the tenure of their offices, and the amount and payment of their salaries.

10. He has erected a multitude of new offices, and sent hither swarms of officers to harass our people and eat out their substance.

11. He has kept among us, in times of peace, standing armies, without the consent of our legislatures.

12. He has affected to render the military independent of, and superior to, the civil power.

13. He has combined with others to subject us to a jurisdiction foreign to our constitution, and unacknowledged by our laws; giving his assent to their acts of pretended legislation:

14. For quartering large bodies of armed troops among us;

15. For protecting them, by a mock trial, from punishment for any murders which they should commit on the inhabitants of these states;

16. For cutting off our trade with all parts of the world;

17. For imposing taxes on us without our consent;

18. For depriving us, in many cases, of the benefits of trial by jury;

19. For transporting us beyond seas to be tried for pretended offenses;

20. For abolishing the free system of English laws in a neighboring province, establishing therein an arbitrary government, and enlarging its boundaries, so as to render it at once an example and fit instrument for introducing the same absolute rule into these colonies;

21. For taking away our charters, abolishing our most valuable laws, and altering, fundamentally, the forms of our governments;

22. For suspending our own legislatures, and declaring themselves invested with power to legislate for us in all cases whatsoever.

23. He has abdicated government here by declaring us out of his protection, and waging war against us.

24. He has plundered our seas, ravaged our coasts, burned our towns, and destroyed the lives of our people.

25. He is at this time transporting large armies of foreign mercenaries to complete the works of death, desolation, and tyranny, already begun with circumstances of cruelty and perfidy scarcely paralleled in the most barbarous ages, and totally unworthy the head of a civilized nation.

26. He has constrained our fellow citizens, taken captive on the high seas, to bear arms against their country, to become the executioners of their friends and brethren, or to fall themselves **by their hands.**

27. He has excited domestic insurrection among us, and has endeavored to bring on the inhabitants of our frontiers the merciless Indian savages, whose known rule of warfare is an undistinguished destruction of all ages, sexes, and conditions.

In every stage of these oppressions we have petitioned for redress in the most **humble terms; our repeated petitions have been** answered only by **repeated injury.** A prince whose character is thus marked by every act which may define a tyrant, is unfit to be the ruler of a free people.

Nor have we been wanting in attentions to our British brethren. We have warned **them, from** time to **time, of** attempts by their legislature to extend an unwarrantable jurisdiction over us. We have reminded them of the circumstances of our emigration and settlement here. We have appealed to their native justice and magnanimity, and we have conjured them, by the ties of our common kindred, to disavow these usurpations, which would inevitably interrupt our connections and correspondence. They, too, have been deaf to the voice of justice and of consanguinity. We must, therefore, acquiesce in the necessity which denounces our separation, and hold them as we hold the rest of mankind—enemies in war; in peace, friends.

We, therefore, the Representatives of the United States of America, in general Congress assembled, appealing to the Supreme Judge of the world for the rectitude of our intentions, do, in the name and by the authority of the good people of these colonies, solemnly publish and declare that these united colonies are, and of right ought to be, free and independent states; that they are absolved from all allegiance to the British crown, and that all political connection between them and the state of Great Britain is, and ought to be, totally dissolved, and that, as free and independent states, they have full power to levy war, conclude peace, contract alliances, establish commerce, and do all other acts and things which independent states may of right do. And for the support of this Declaration, with a firm reliance on the protection of Divine Providence, we mutually pledge to each other our lives, our fortunes, and our sacred honor.

The foregoing Declaration was, by order of Congress, engrossed, and signed by the following members:

JOHN HANCOCK.

New Hampshire.
JOSIAH BARTLETT,
WILLIAM WHIPPLE,
MATTHEW THORNTON.

Massachusetts Bay.
SAMUEL ADAMS,
JOHN ADAMS,
ROBERT TREAT PAINE,
ELBRIDGE GERRY.

Rhode Island.
STEPHEN HOPKINS,
WILLIAM ELLERY.

Connecticut.
ROGER SHERMAN,
SAMUEL HUNTINGTON,
WILLIAM WILLIAMS,
OLIVER WOLCOTT.

New York.
WILLIAM FLOYD,
PHILIP LIVINGSTON,
FRANCIS LEWIS,
LEWIS MORRIS.

New Jersey.
RICHARD STOCKTON,
JOHN WITHERSPOON,
FRANCIS HOPKINSON,
JOHN HART,
ABRAHAM CLARK.

Virginia.
GEORGE WYTHE,
RICHARD HENRY LEE,
THOMAS JEFFERSON,
BENJAMIN HARRISON,
THOMAS NELSON, JUN.,
FRANCIS LIGHTFOOT LEE,
CARTER BRAXTON.

Delaware.
CÆSAR RODNEY,
GEORGE READ,
THOMAS M'KEAN.

Maryland.
SAMUEL CHASE,
WILLIAM PACA,
THOMAS STONE,
CHARLES CARROLL, of Carrollton.

Pennsylvania.
ROBERT MORRIS,
BENJAMIN RUSH,
BENJAMIN FRANKLIN,
JOHN MORTON,
GEORGE CLYMER,
JAMES SMITH,
GEORGE TAYLOR,
JAMES WILSON,
GEORGE ROSS.

North Carolina.
WILLIAM HOOPER,
JOSEPH HEWES,
JOHN PENN.

South Carolina.
EDWARD RUTLEDGE,
THOMAS HEYWARD, JUN.,
THOMAS LYNCH, JUN.,
ARTHUR MIDDLETON.

Georgia.
BUTTON GWINNETT,
LYMAN HALL,
GEORGE WALTON.

CONSTITUTION OF THE UNITED STATES.

PREAMBLE.

We, the people of the United States, in order to form a more perfect Union, establish justice, insure domestic tranquillity, provide for the common defense, promote the general welfare, and secure the blessings of liberty to ourselves and our posterity, do ordain and establish this Constitution for the United States of America.

ARTICLE I.
LEGISLATIVE DEPARTMENT.
Section 1.

1. All legislative powers herein granted shall be vested in a Congress of the United States, which shall consist of a Senate and House of Representatives.

Section 2.

1. The House of Representatives shall be composed of members chosen every second year by the people of the several states, and the electors in each state shall have the qualifications requisite for electors of the most numerous branch of the state legislature.

2. No person shall be a Representative who shall not have attained the age of **twenty-five years and been seven years a citizen of the United States, and who shall not, when elected**, be an inhabitant of that state in which he shall be chosen.

3. [Representatives and direct taxes shall be apportioned among the several states which **may be included within** this Union, according to their respective numbers, which **shall be determined by adding** to the whole number of free persons, including those bound **to service for a term of years, and** excluding Indians not taxed, three fifths of all other persons. The actual enumeration shall be made within three years after the first meeting **of the Congress of the United States, and** within every subsequent term of ten years, in such manner as they shall by law direct. The number of Representatives shall not exceed one for every thirty thousand, but each state shall have at least one Representative; and until such enumeration shall be made, the state of New Hampshire shall be entitled **to choose** three, Massachusetts eight, Rhode Island and Providence Plantations one, Connecticut five, New York six, New Jersey four, Pennsylvania eight, Delaware one, **Maryland six,** Virginia ten, North Carolina five, South Carolina five, and Georgia three.]

This clause has been superseded, so far as it relates to representation, by section two of the Fourteenth Amendment to the Constitution.

4. When vacancies happen in the representation from any state, the executive authority thereof shall issue writs of election to fill such vacancies.

5. The House of Representatives shall choose their Speaker **and other officers, and shall have the sole power of impeachment.**

Section 3.

1. The Senate of the United States shall be composed of two Senators from each state, chosen by the Legislature thereof, for six years, and each Senator shall have one vote.

2. Immediately after they shall be assembled in consequence of the first election, they

shall be divided as equally as may be into three classes. The seats of the Senators of the first class shall be vacated at the expiration of the second year, of the second class at the expiration of the fourth year, and of the third class at the expiration of the sixth year so that one third may be chosen every second year; and if vacancies happen, by resignation or otherwise, during the recess of the legislature of any state, the Executive thereof may make temporary appointments until the next meeting of the legislature, which shall then fill such vacancies.

3. No person shall be a Senator who shall not have attained the age of thirty years, and been nine years a citizen of the United States, and who shall not, when elected, be an inhabitant of the state for which he shall be chosen.

4. The Vice-President of the United States shall be President of the Senate, but shall have no voice unless they shall be equally divided.

5. The Senate shall choose their officers and have a President pro tempore, in the absence of the Vice-President, or when he shall exercise the office of President of the United States.

6. The Senate shall have the sole power to try all impeachments; when sitting for that purpose, they shall be on oath or affirmation. When the President of the United States is tried, the Chief Justice shall preside; and no person shall be convicted without the concurrence of two thirds of the members present.

7. Judgment in cases of impeachment shall not extend further than to removal from office and disqualification to hold and enjoy any office of honor, trust, or profit under the United States; but the party convicted shall, nevertheless, be liable and subject to indictment, trial, judgment, and punishment according to law.

SECTION 4.

1. The times, places, and manner of holding elections for Senators and Representatives shall be prescribed in each state by the legislature thereof; but the Congress may at any time, by law, make or alter such regulations, except as to the places of choosing Senators.

2. The Congress shall assemble at least once in every year, and such meeting shall be on the first Monday in December, unless they shall, by law, appoint a different day.

SECTION 5.

1. Each house shall be the judge of the elections, returns, and qualifications of its own members, and a majority of each shall constitute a quorum to do business; but a smaller number may adjourn from day to day, and may be authorized to compel the attendance of absent members, in such manner and under such penalties as each house may provide.

2. Each house may determine the rules of its proceedings, punish its members for disorderly behavior, and, with the concurrence of two thirds, expel a member.

3. Each house shall keep a journal of its proceedings, and from time to time publish the same, excepting such parts as may, in their judgment, require secrecy; and the ayes and noes of the members of either house, on any question, shall, at the desire of one fifth of those present, be entered on the journal.

4. Neither house, during the session of Congress, shall, without the consent of the other, adjourn for more than three days, nor to any other place than that in which the two houses shall be sitting.

SECTION 6.

1. The Senators and Representatives shall receive a compensation for their services, to be ascertained by law, and paid out of the treasury of the United States. They shall, in all cases, except treason, felony, and breach of the peace, be privileged from arrest during their attendance at the session of their respective houses, and in going to and returning from the same; and for any speech or debate, in either house, they shall not be questioned in any other place.

2. No Senator or Representative shall, during the time for which he was elected, be appointed to any civil office under the authority of the United States, which shall have been created, or the emoluments whereof shall have been increased, during such time; and no person holding any office under the United States shall be a member of either house during his continuance in office.

Section 7.

1. All bills for raising revenue shall originate in the House of Representatives; but the Senate may propose or concur with amendments on other bills.

2. Every bill which shall have passed the House of Representatives and the Senate, shall, before it becomes a law, be presented to the President of the United States; if he approve, he shall sign it, but if not, he shall return it, with his objections, to that house in which it shall have originated, who shall enter the objections at large on their journal, and proceed to reconsider it. If, after such reconsideration, two thirds of that house shall agree to pass the bill, it shall be sent, together with the objections, to the other house, by which it shall likewise be reconsidered, and if approved by two thirds of that house it shall become a law. But in all such cases the votes of both houses shall be determined by ayes and noes; and the names of the persons voting for and against the bill shall be entered on the journal of each house respectively. If any bill shall not be returned by the President within ten days (Sundays excepted) after it shall have been presented to him, the same shall be a law, in like manner as if he had signed it, unless the Congress, by their adjournment, prevent its return, in which case it shall not be a law.

3. Every order, resolution, or vote, to which the concurrence of the Senate and the House of Representatives may be necessary (except on a question of adjournment), shall be presented to the President of the United States; and, before the same shall take effect, shall be approved by him, or being disapproved by him, shall be repassed by two thirds of the Senate and House of Representatives, according to the rules and limitations prescribed in the case of a bill.

Section 8.

1. The Congress shall have power to lay and collect taxes, duties, imposts, and excises, to pay the debts and provide for the common defense and general welfare of the United States; but all duties, imposts, and excises shall be uniform throughout the United States.

2. To borrow money on the credit of the United States.

3. To regulate commerce with foreign nations, and among the several States, and with the Indian tribes.

4. To establish an uniform rule of naturalization, and uniform laws on the subject of bankruptcies throughout the United States.

5. To coin money, regulate the value thereof, and of foreign coins, and fix the standard of weights and measures.

6. To provide for the punishment of counterfeiting the securities and current coin of the United States.

7. To establish post offices and post roads.

8. To promote the progress of science and useful arts, by securing, for limited times, to authors and inventors, the exclusive right to their respective writings and discoveries.

9. To constitute tribunals inferior to the Supreme Court.

10. To define and punish piracies and felonies committed on the high seas, and offenses against the laws of nations.

11. To declare war, grant letters of marque and reprisal, and make rules concerning captures on land and water.

12. To raise and support armies; but no appropriation of money for that use shall be for a longer term than two years.

13. To provide and maintain a navy.

14. To make rules for the government and regulation of the land and naval forces.

15. To provide for calling forth the militia to execute the laws of the Union, suppress insurrections, and repel invasions.

16. To provide for organizing, arming, and disciplining the militia, and for governing such part of them as may be employed in the service of the United States, reserving to the states, respectively, the appointment of the officers, and the authority of training the militia according to the discipline prescribed by Congress.

17. To exercise exclusive legislation, in all cases whatsoever, over such district (not exceeding ten miles square) as may, by cession of particular states, and the acceptance of Congress, become the seat of government of the United States, and to exercise like authority over all places purchased by the consent of the legislature of the state in which the same shall be, for the erection of forts, magazines, arsenals, dockyards, and other needful buildings.

18. To make all laws which shall be necessary and proper for carrying into execution the foregoing powers, and all other powers vested by this Constitution in the Government of the United States, or in any department or officer thereof.

Section 9.

1. The migration or importation of such persons as any of the states now existing shall think proper to admit shall not be prohibited by Congress prior to the year one thousand eight hundred and eight; but a tax or duty may be imposed on such importation, not exceeding ten dollars for each person.

2. The privilege of the writ of habeas corpus shall not be suspended, unless when, in cases of rebellion or invasion, the public safety may require it.

3. No bill of attainder or ex post facto law shall be passed.

4. No capitation or other direct tax shall be laid, unless in proportion to the census or enumeration hereinbefore directed to be taken.

5. No tax or duty shall be laid on articles exported from any state.

6. No preference shall be given, by any regulation of commerce or revenue, to the ports of one state over those of another; nor shall vessels bound to or from one state be obliged to enter, clear, or pay duties in another.

7. No money shall be drawn from the treasury, but in consequence of appropriations made by law; and a regular statement and account of the receipts and expenditures of all public money shall be published from time to time.

8. No title of nobility shall be granted by the United States; and no person holding any office of profit or trust under them shall, without the consent of the Congress, accept of any present, emolument, office, or title, of any kind whatever, from any king, prince, or foreign state.

Section 10.

1. No state shall enter into any treaty, alliance, or confederation; grant letters of marque and reprisal; coin money; emit bills of credit; make anything but gold and silver coin a tender in payment of debts; pass any bill of attainder, ex post facto law, or law impairing the obligation of contracts, or grant any title of nobility.

2. No state shall, without the consent of the Congress, lay any impost or duties on imports or exports, except what may be absolutely necessary for executing its inspection laws; and the net produce of all duties and imposts, laid by any state on imports or exports, shall be for the use of the treasury of the United States; and all such laws shall be subject to the revision and control of the Congress.

3. No state shall, without the consent of Congress, lay any duty of tonnage, keep troops or ships of war in time of peace, enter into any agreement or compact with another state

or with a foreign power, or engage in war, unless actually invaded or in such imminent danger as will not admit of delay.

ARTICLE II.

EXECUTIVE DEPARTMENT.

SECTION 1.

1. **The executive power** shall be vested in a President of the United States of **America**. He shall hold his office during the term of four years, and together with the Vice-President, **chosen for** the same term, be elected as follows:

2. Each state shall appoint, in such manner as the **legislature thereof may** direct, a **number** of Electors equal to the whole number of Senators and Representatives to which **the state may be entitled in** the Congress; but no Senator or **Representative, or** person holding an office of trust or profit under the United States, shall **be appointed an** Elector.

3. [The Electors shall meet in their respective states and vote by ballot for two persons, **of whom one at least shall not be an inhabitant of the same state with themselves. And they shall make a list of all the persons voted for, and of the number of votes for each; which list they shall sign and certify, and transmit sealed to the seat of the Government of the United States, directed to the President of the Senate. The President of the Senate shall, in the presence of the Senate and House of Representatives, open all the certificates, and the votes shall then be counted. The person** having the greatest number of **votes shall be the President, if such number be a majority of the** whole number **of** Electors appointed; and if there be more than one who have such majority, and have an equal number of votes, **then the House of Representatives shall immediately choose by ballot one of** them for President; **and if no person have** a majority, **then from the five highest on the list** the said house shall, in like manner, choose the President. But, **in choosing the** President, the vote shall be taken by states, the representation **from each state** having **one vote; a quorum for this purpose shall consist of a** member **or members** from two thirds of the states, and a majority of all the states shall be necessary **to a choice.** In every case **after the choice of the** President, the person having the greatest number of **votes of the Electors shall be the** Vice-President. **But** if there should remain two **or more who have equal votes, the** Senate shall choose from them, by ballot, the Vice-President.]

This clause has been superseded by the Twelfth Amendment to the Constitution.

4. The Congress may determine the time of choosing **the Electors, and the day on which** they shall give their votes, which day shall be the same throughout the United States.

5. No person except a natural-born citizen, or a citizen of the United States at the time **of the** adoption of this Constitution, shall be eligible to the office of President, neither **shall any person** be eligible to that office who shall not have attained the age of thirty-five **years, and been fourteen years a resident within the United States.**

6. In case of the removal of the President from office, or **of** his death, resignation, or **inability to discharge the** powers and duties of **the said** office, the same shall devolve on **the Vice-President, and the Congress may, by law,** provide for the case of removal, death, **resignation, or inability, both of** the President and Vice-President, declaring what officer **shall then act as President, and such** officer shall **act** accordingly, until the disability be removed, or a **President shall be elected.** (See note at bottom of p. 425.)

7. The President **shall, at** stated **times, receive for** his services a compensation, which shall neither be increased nor diminished during the period for which he shall have been elected, and he shall not receive within that period any other emolument from the United States or any of them.

8. Before he enters on **the execution of his office,** he shall take the following oath or affirmation: " I do solemnly swear (or affirm) **that** I will faithfully execute the office of

President of the United States, and will, to the best of my ability, preserve, protect, and defend the Constitution of the United States."

SECTION 2.

1. The President shall be Commander-in-Chief of the Army and Navy of the United States, and of the militia of the several states, when called into the actual service of the United States; he may require the opinion, in writing, of the principal officer in each of the executive departments, upon any subject relating to the duties of their respective offices, and he shall have power to grant reprieves and pardons for offenses against the United States, except in cases of impeachment.

2. He shall have power, by and with the advice and consent of the Senate, to make treaties, provided two thirds of the Senators present concur; and he shall nominate, and, by and with the advice and consent of the Senate, shall appoint Embassadors, other public Ministers and Consuls, Judges of the Supreme Court, and all other officers of the United States whose appointments are not herein otherwise provided for and which shall be established by law; but the Congress may, by law, vest the appointment of such inferior officers as they think proper in the President alone, in the courts of law, or in the heads of departments.

3. The President shall have power to fill up all vacancies that may happen during the recess of the Senate, by granting commissions, which shall expire at the end of their next session.

SECTION 3.

1. He shall, from time to time, give to the Congress information of the state of the Union, and recommend to their consideration such measures as he shall judge necessary and expedient; he may, on extraordinary occasions, convene both houses, or either of them, and in case of disagreement between them with respect to the time of adjournment, he may adjourn them to such time as he shall think proper; he shall receive Embassadors and other public Ministers; he shall take care that the laws be faithfully executed, and shall commission all the officers of the United States.

SECTION 4.

1. The President, Vice-President, and all civil officers of the United States shall be removed from office on impeachment for and conviction of treason, bribery, or other high crimes and misdemeanors.

ARTICLE III.
JUDICIAL DEPARTMENTS.
SECTION 1.

1. The judicial power of the United States shall be vested in one Supreme Court, and in such inferior Courts as the Congress may, from time to time, ordain and establish. The Judges, both of the Supreme and inferior Courts, shall hold their offices during good behavior, and shall, at stated times, receive for their services a compensation which shall not be diminished during their continuance in office.

SECTION 2.

1. The judicial power shall extend to all cases, in law and equity, arising under this Constitution, the laws of the United States, and treaties made, or which shall be made, under their authority; to all cases affecting Embassadors, other public Ministers and Consuls; to all cases of admiralty and maritime jurisdiction; to controversies to which the United States shall be a party; to controversies between two or more states; between a state and citizens of another state; between citizens of different states; between citizens of the same state claiming lands under grants of different states; and between a state, or the citizens thereof, and foreign states, citizens, or subjects.

2. In all cases affecting Embassadors, other public Ministers and Consuls, and those in which a state shall be a party, the Supreme Court shall have original jurisdiction. In all the other cases before mentioned the Supreme Court shall have appellate jurisdiction, both as to law and fact, with such exceptions and under such regulations as the Congress shall make.

3. The trial of all crimes, except in cases of impeachment, shall be by jury; and such

trial shall be held in the state where the said crimes shall have been committed; but when not committed within any state, the trial shall be put at such place or places as the Congress may, by law, have directed.

SECTION 3.

1. Treason against the United States shall consist only in levying war against them, or in adhering to their enemies, giving them aid and comfort.

2. No person shall be convicted of treason, unless on the testimony of two witnesses to the same overt act, or on confession in open court.

3. The Congress shall have power to declare the punishment of treason; but no attainder of treason shall work corruption of blood, or forfeiture, except during the life of the person attainted.

ARTICLE IV.
STATE ACTS.
SECTION 1.

1. Full faith and credit shall be given in each state to the public acts, records, and judicial proceedings of every other state. And the Congress may, by general laws, prescribe the manner in which such acts, records, and proceedings shall be proved, and the effect thereof.

SECTION 2.

1. The citizens of each state shall be entitled to all the privileges and immunities of citizens in the several states.

2. A person charged in any state with treason, felony, or other crime, who shall flee from justice, and be found in another state, shall, on demand of the executive authority of the state from which he fled, be delivered up, to be removed to the state having jurisdiction of the crime.

3. No person held to service or labor in one state, under the laws thereof, escaping into another, shall, in consequence of any law or regulation therein, be discharged from such service or labor, but shall be delivered up on claim of the party to whom such service or labor may be due.

SECTION 3.

1. New states may be admitted by the Congress into this Union; but no new state shall be formed or erected within the jurisdiction of any other state; nor any state be formed by the junction of two or more states, or parts of states, without the consent of the legislatures of the states concerned, as well as of Congress.

2. The Congress shall have power to dispose of and make all needful rules and regulations respecting the territory or other property belonging to the United States; and nothing in this Constitution shall be so construed as to prejudice any claims of the United States, or of any particular state.

SECTION 4.

1. The United States shall guarantee to every state in this Union a republican form of government, and shall protect each of them against invasion; and, on application of the legislature, or of the Executive (when the legislature cannot be convened), against domestic violence.

ARTICLE V.
AMENDMENTS.
SECTION 1.

1. The Congress, whenever two thirds of both houses shall deem it necessary, shall propose amendments to this Constitution, or, on the application of the legislatures of two thirds of the several states, shall call a convention for proposing amendments, which, in either case, shall be valid, to all intents and purposes, as part of this Constitution, when ratified by the legislatures of three fourths of the several states, or by conventions in three fourths thereof, as the one or the other mode of ratification may be proposed by the Congress; *provided*, that no amendment which may be made prior to the year one thousand eight hundred and eight shall, in any manner, affect the first and fourth clauses in the ninth section of the first article; and that no state, without its consent, shall be deprived of its equal suffrage in the Senate.

APPENDIX.

ARTICLE VI.
PROMISCUOUS PROVISIONS.
SECTION 1.

1. All debts contracted and engagements entered into, before the adoption of this Constitution, shall be as valid against the United States, under this Constitution, as under the Confederation.

2. This Constitution, and the laws of the United States which shall be made in pursuance thereof, and all treaties made, or which shall be made, under the authority of the United States, shall be the supreme law of the land; and the Judges in every state shall be bound thereby, anything in the Constitution or laws of any state to the contrary notwithstanding.

3. The Senators and Representatives before mentioned, and the members of the several state legislatures, and all executive and judicial officers, both of the United States and of the several states, shall be bound, by oath or affirmation, to support this Constitution; but no religious test shall ever be required as a qualification to any office or public trust under the United States.

ARTICLE VII.
RATIFICATION OF THE CONSTITUTION.
SECTION 1.

1. The ratification of the conventions of nine states shall be sufficient for the establishment of this Constitution between the states so ratifying the same.

Done in Convention, by the unanimous consent of the states present, the seventeenth day of September, in the year of our Lord one thousand seven hundred and eighty-seven, and of the Independence of the United States of America the twelfth. In witness whereof we have hereunto subscribed our names.

GEORGE WASHINGTON,
President and Deputy from Virginia.

NEW HAMPSHIRE.
JOHN LANGDON,
NICHOLAS GILMAN.

MASSACHUSETTS.
NATHANIEL GORHAM,
RUFUS KING.

CONNECTICUT.
WILLIAM SAMUEL JOHNSON,
ROGER SHERMAN.

NEW YORK.
ALEXANDER HAMILTON.

NEW JERSEY.
WILLIAM LIVINGSTON,
DAVID BREARLY,
WILLIAM PATTERSON,
JONATHAN DAYTON.

PENNSYLVANIA.
BENJAMIN FRANKLIN,
THOMAS MIFFLIN,
ROBERT MORRIS,
GEORGE CLYMER,
THOMAS FITZSIMONS,
JARED INGERSOLL,
JAMES WILSON,
GOUVERNEUR MORRIS.

DELAWARE.
GEORGE READ,
GUNNING BEDFORD, Jr.,
JOHN DICKINSON,
RICHARD BASSETT,
JACOB BROOM.

MARYLAND.
JAMES McHENRY,
DANIEL OF ST. TH. JENIFER,
DANIEL CARROLL.

VIRGINIA.
JOHN BLAIR,
JAMES MADISON, Jr.

NORTH CAROLINA.
WILLIAM BLOUNT,
RICHARD DOBBS SPAIGHT,
HUGH WILLIAMSON.

SOUTH CAROLINA.
JOHN RUTLEDGE,
CHARLES C. PINCKNEY,
CHARLES PINCKNEY,
PIERCE BUTLER.

GEORGIA.
WILLIAM FEW,
ABRAHAM BALDWIN.

Attest: WILLIAM JACKSON, Secretary.

AMENDMENTS.

ARTICLE I.

SECTION 1. Congress shall make no law respecting an establishment **of religion, or prohibiting the free exercise thereof, or** abridging the freedom of speech or **of** the press; or the right of **the people peaceably to assemble, and** to petition the government for a redress of grievances.—[*December 15, 1791.*]

ARTICLE II.

SECTION 1. A well regulated militia being necessary to the security of a free state, the right of the people to keep and bear arms shall not be infringed.—[*Id.*]

ARTICLE III

SECTION 1. No soldier shall, in time of peace, be quartered in any house, without the consent of the owner; nor in time of war, but in a manner to be prescribed by law.—[*Id.*]

ARTICLE IV.

SECTION 1. The right of the people to be secure in their persons, houses, papers, and effects, against unreasonable searches and seizures, shall not be violated, and no warrants shall issue but upon reasonable cause, supported by oath or affirmation, and particularly describing the place to be searched and the person or things to be seized.—[*Id.*]

ARTICLE V.

SECTION 1. No person shall be held to answer for a capital or otherwise infamous crime, unless on a presentment or indictment of a Grand Jury, except in **cases** arising in the land or naval forces, or in the militia, when in actual service, **in time of** war, or public danger; nor shall any person be subject **for the same offense to be twice put** in jeopardy of life **or limb; nor** shall be **compelled in** any criminal case to be **a** witness against **himself, nor be deprived** of life, liberty, or property, without due process of law; nor shall **private property be taken for public use** without just compensation.—[*Id.*]

ARTICLE VI.

SECTION 1. In all criminal prosecutions the accused shall enjoy the right to a **speedy** and public trial, by an **impartial jury of the state and district wherein the crime shall have** been committed, which district shall **have** been previously ascertained by law, and to be informed of the nature and cause of the accusation; to be confronted with the witnesses against him; to **have compulsory process for obtaining witnesses in his favor, and to have the assistance of counsel for his defense.**—[*Id.*]

ARTICLE VII.

SECTION 1. In suits at common law, where the value in controversy shall exceed twenty dollars, the right of trial by jury shall be preserved; and no fact, tried by jury, shall be otherwise reëxamined in any Court of the United States than according to the rules of common law.—[*Id.*]

ARTICLE VIII.

SECTION 1. Excessive bail shall not be required, nor excessive fines imposed, nor cruel and unusual punishments inflicted.—[*Id.*]

ARTICLE IX.

SECTION 1. The enumeration in the **Constitution of certain rights shall not be construed to deny or disparage others retained by the people.**—[*Id.*]

ARTICLE X.

SECTION 1. The powers not delegated to the United States by the Constitution, nor prohibited by it to the states, are reserved to the states, respectively, or to the people.—[*Id.*

ARTICLE XI.

SECTION 1. The judicial power of the United States shall not be construed to extend to any suit in law or equity, commenced or prosecuted against one of the United States by the citizens of another state, or by citizens or subjects of any foreign state.—[*January 8, 1798.*

ARTICLE XII.

SECTION 1. The Electors shall meet in their respective states, and vote by ballot for President and Vice-President, one of whom, at least, shall not be an inhabitant of the same state with themselves; they shall name in their ballots the person voted for as President, and in distinct ballots the person voted for as Vice-President; and they shall make distinct lists of all persons voted for as President, and of all persons voted for as Vice-President, and the number of votes for each, which list they shall sign and certify, and transmit, sealed, to the seat of the Government of the United States, directed to the President of the Senate. The President of the Senate shall, in the presence of the Senate and House of Representatives, open all the certificates, and the votes shall then be counted. The person having the greatest number of votes for President shall be the President, if such a number be a majority of the whole number of Electors appointed; and if no person have such a majority, then from the persons having the highest numbers, not exceeding three, on the list of those voted for as President, the House of Representatives shall choose immediately, by ballot, the President. But in choosing the President, the votes shall be taken by states, the representation from each state having one vote; a quorum for this purpose shall consist of a member or members from two thirds of the states, and a majority of all the states shall be necessary to a choice. And if the House of Representatives shall not choose a President, whenever the right of choice shall devolve upon them, before the fourth day of March next following, then the Vice-President shall act as President, as in case of the death or other constitutional disability of the President. The person having the greatest number of votes as Vice-President shall be the Vice-President, if such number be a majority of the whole number of Electors appointed; and if no person have a majority, then from the two highest numbers on the list the Senate shall choose the Vice-President; a quorum for the purpose shall consist of two thirds of the whole number of Senators, and a majority of the whole number shall be necessary to a choice. But no person constitutionally ineligible to the office of President shall be eligible to that of Vice-President of the United States.—[*Proposed December 12, 1803; ratified September 25, 1804.*

ARTICLE XIII.

SECTION 1. Neither slavery or involuntary servitude, except as a punishment for crime whereof the party shall have been duly convicted, shall exist within the United States, or any place subject to their jurisdiction.

SEC. 2. Congress shall have power to enforce this article by appropriate legislation.—[*December 18, 1865.*

ARTICLE XIV.

SECTION 1. All persons born or naturalized in the United States and subject to the jurisdiction thereof, are citizens of the United States and of the state wherein they reside. No state shall make or enforce any law which shall abridge the privileges or immunities of citizens of the United States; nor shall any state deprive any person of life, liberty, or property, without due process of law, nor deny to any person within its jurisdiction the equal protection of the laws.

Sec. 2. Representatives shall be apportioned among the several states, according to their respective numbers, counting the whole number of persons in **each state**, excluding Indians not taxed. But when the right to vote at any election for the choice of Electors for President and Vice-President of the United States, **Representatives in Congress, the** executive and judicial officers of a state, or the members of **the Legislature** thereof, is denied to any of the male inhabitants of such state, being twenty-one **years of age and citizens of the United States, or in any way** abridged, except for participation **in rebellion, or other crime, the basis of representation** therein shall be reduced in the proportion which the number of such male citizens shall bear to the whole number of male citizens twenty-one years of age in such state.

Sec. 3. No person shall be **a Senator or Representative in Congress, or Elector of President and Vice-President, or hold any office, civil or military, under the United States, or under any** state, who, having previously **taken an oath as a member of Congress, or as an** officer of the United States, or **as a member of any state legislature, or as an executive or judicial officer of any state, to support the Constitution of the United** States, shall **have engaged in insurrection or rebellion against the same, or given aid or** comfort **to the enemies thereof. But Congress may, by a vote of two thirds of each house, remove such disability.**

Sec. 4. **The validity of** the public **debt of the United States, authorized by law,** including debts incurred for payment of pensions and **bounties for services in suppressing** insurrection or rebellion, shall not be questioned. **But neither the** United States or any state shall assume or pay any debt or obligation incurred in aid of insurrection or rebellion against **the** United **States, or any claim for the loss or emancipation of any slave;** but all such debts, obligations, and **claims shall be held illegal and void.**

Sec. 5. The Congress shall **have power to enforce, by appropriate legislation,** the provisions of this article.—[Declared **ratified July 28th, 1868. (U. S. Statutes at** Large, **Vol.** 15, pp. 709–11.)

ARTICLE XV.

Section 1. **The right of** citizens of the United States to vote shall not be denied or **abridged by the United States, or by any state, on** account of race, color, or previous condition of servitude.

Sec. 2. **The Congress shall have power to enforce this** article by appropriate legislation.—[U. S. Statutes at Large, Vol. 15, p. 346.

Note.—Agreeably with the powers conferred by Clause 6, Section 1, Article II., of the Constitution (see p. 419), Congress in 1886 provided for the succession to the Presidency in case of the removal, death, resignation, or inability of the President or Vice-President **by directing** that the office devolve first upon the Secretary of State, and in case of his **inability,** for any reason, to perform its duties, it should pass, successively, upon similar **conditions, to** the Secretary of the Treasury, Secretary of War, Attorney-General, Postmaster-General, Secretary of the Navy, and Secretary of the Interior. If, however, any **one of these** officers should be of foreign birth, the Presidency passes to the next named in the list.

INDEX.

(For Reference and Topical Review.)

(Figures refer to paragraphs.)

Abolition, 492, 508.
Academy, United States Military, 437; naval, 496.
Acadia, settled, 45; becomes English possession, 180; inhabitants transported, 201.
Adams, John, 273, 295; vice-president, 361; president, 396; term, ch. xix; retirement, 410; death, 469.
Adams, John Quincy, elected president, 466; term, ch. xxiii; in House of Representatives, 509.
Adams, Samuel, 235.
Alabama, admitted, 459; Confederate cruiser, 594; claims for damage, 679.
Alaska, 673.
Albany Convention, 197.
America, name, 28.
"American System," 474.
Andre, Major John, 320.
Andros, Sir Edmund, 94, 95, 96.
Angles and Saxons, 3.
Arkansas, 523.
Army, American, during war for independence, 279; in war of 1812, 452; Mexican war, 539; in civil war, 592; note, p. 336.
Arnold, Benedict, 267, 320, 335, 336.
Arthur, Chester A., 708; elected vice-president, 701; term as president, ch. xxxiv, 3.
Ayllon, explorations of, 29.
Aztecs, civilization of, 22.
Bacon's Rebellion in Virginia, 137.
Balboa discovers Pacific ocean, 29.

Bank, United States, founded by Hamilton, 385; contest over, 482.
Banks, craze over, 502.
Banks, national, 656.
Barbary States, 419, 420.
Battles. *War for Independence.*—Bemis's Heights, 306; Bennington, 305; Brandywine, 291; Bunker Hill, 258; Camden, 327; Charleston, 271, 323; Cowpens, 332; Eutaw Springs, 334; Freeman's Farm, 306; Germantown, 292; Guilford Court House, 333; Hobkirk Hill, 334; King's Mountain, 330; Long Island, 280; Monmouth, 297.
War of 1812.—Chippewa Creek, 445; Erie, 442; New Orleans, 448; Plattsburg, 445; Queenstown Heights, 440; Raisin River, 441; Sackett's Harbor, 441; Thames, 444.
War with Mexico.—Buena Vista, 535; Cerro Gordo, 535; Chapultepec, 536; Churubusco, 536; Contreras, 536; Molino del Rey, 536; Monterey, 532; Palo Alto, 532; Resaca de la Palma, 532; San Gabriel River, 770; San Pasqual, 770; Vera Cruz, 535.
War of Secession.—Antietam, 605; Atlanta, 640; Ball's Bluff, 599; Bull Run, 597, 604; Cedar Mountain, 604; Chancellorsville, 608; Chickamauga, 635; Cold Harbor, 603; Corinth, 616; Dallas, 640; Donelson, 614; Fair Oaks,

601; Franklin, 643; Frazier's Farm, 603; Fredericksburg, 607; Gettysburg, 610; Goldsboro, 650; Groveton, 604; Kenesaw Mountain, 640; Lookout Mountain, 637; Malvern Hill, 603; Mechanicsville, 603; Mill Spring, 613; Missionary Ridge, 637; Murfreesboro, 620; Pea Ridge, 618; Perryville, 619; Resaca, 640; Savage's Station, 603; Seven Pines, 601; Shiloh, 615; Spottsylvania Court House, 646; Vicksburg, 631; Wilderness, 646; Wilson's Creek, 611; Winchester, 648.
Bear Flag Affair, 767.
Benton, Thomas H., 560.
Bonaparte, Napoleon, life, 387; in war of 1812, 431.
Boston, British troops in, 236; port closed, 243; siege, 262; capture, 264.
"Boston Massacre," 237.
"Boston Tea Party," 242.
Braddock's campaign, 200.
Bradford, William, 66.
Broderick, David C., 786, 787.
Brown, John, 578, 579.
Buchanan, James, elected president, 568; term, ch. xxx.
Bunker **Hill Monument,** 465.
Burr, Aaron, 409.
Cabot, John, discovers Cape Breton Island, 34.
Cabot, Sebastian, 35.
Calhoun, John C., early life, 435; ideas on states rights, 485.
California, ch. xxviii, xxxvi, xxxvii.
Calvert, Cecil, founder of Maryland, 114.
Calvert, George, Baron of Baltimore, 113.
Canada, settled, 45; ch. xiii; conquered 1760, 207; retained as British possession, 210; invaded 1775, 265. See also war of 1812.

Cartier, discovers St. Lawrence River, 33.
Carver, John, 66.
Champlain, Samuel de, explorer of Canada, 175; 45.
Charles II., king of England, government of New England, 92; in southern colonies, 134; in middle colonies, 152.
Charleston founded, 126; attacked 1776, 271; captured 1780, 323.
Cherokees raid in Tennessee 1776, 311; moved west, 498.
Chinese immigration, 712, 792.
Civil Service, spoils system, 480; reform, 704, 715.
Clay, Henry, early life, 434; presidential candidate, 466; final defeat, 521.
Clergymen, 167.
Cleveland, Grover, 721; elected president, 719; term, ch. xxxiv, 4.
Coinage of U. S., 697, 698.
Columbia, District of, 730.
Colorado, 688.
Columbus, Christopher, early life, 9; first voyage west, ch. ii; later voyages, 27; death, 27.
Commanders, military. *War for the Interior.*—Abercrombie, Braddock, Bradstreet, Dieskau, Forbes, Johnson, Loudon, Montcalm, Putnam, Rogers, Shirley, Wolfe.
War for Independence.—Allen, **Arnold,** Clinton, Cornwallis, D'Estaing, De Grasse, Gage, Gates, Greene, Herkimer, **Howe,** Knowlton, Lafayette, Lee (Charles), Lee (Henry), Lincoln, Marion, Montgomery, Morgan, Moultrie, Percy, Pickens, Pitcairn, Prescott, Putnam, Schuyler, **Stark,** Sullivan, Sumter, **Ward,** Washington, Wayne.

War of 1812.—Brock, Brown, Dearborn, Harrison, Hall, Hampton, Jackson, Proctor, Ross, Scott.

War with Mexico.—Doniphan, Fremont, Kearny, Taylor, Santa Anna, Scott, Wool.

War of Secession.—Banks, Beauregard, Bragg, Buell, Butler, Burnside, Custer, Early, Ewell, Fremont, Garfield, Grant, Halleck, Hood, Hooker, Jackson, Johnston (Albert S.), Johnston (Joseph E.), Lee, Lyon, McClellan, McDowell, Meade, Morgan, Pemberton, Pope, Price, Rosecrans, Scott, Sheridan, Sherman, Stuart, Thomas, Van Dorn, Zollicoffer.

Commanders, naval, Decatur, Farragut, Foote, Jones (John P.), MacDonough, Perry, Sloat, Stockton, Winslow.

Commerce in 1450, 5, 7; of colonies, 165; British regulations, 95, 216, 217; of United States, 422, 431, 723.

Concord skirmish, 250.
Confederacy, 585; ch. xxxi.
Confederation, articles of, 277, 347.
Congress, Stamp Act, 1765, 226.
Congress, Continental, I Session 1774, 244; II Session 1775, 253.
Congress of the Confederation, 277.
Congress under the Constitution, 363.
Connecticut, foundation, 75.
Constitution of United States—Convention 1787, 354, 356; adopted, 361; amendments, 370, 662, 669; centennial, 729.
Cortereal names Labrador, 37.
Cortez conquers Mexico, 29.
Courts, United States, 368; Supreme court and slavery, 573.
Dark Ages, 4.

Debt, United States, 372; assumption of state debts, 373; manner of payment, 381; end of civil war, 654; refunding, 700.
Delaware, settlement, 151.
De Soto discovers the Mississippi, 30.
Donner Party, 764.
Douglas, Stephen A., 557, 575, 576, 580, 582.
Drake, Sir Francis, visits California, 36.
Dred Scott case, 573.
Dutch in New York, 141.
Education, in New England, 99; in southern colonies, 138; in middle colonies, 160; general, 495; chapter xxxv.
Electoral commission, 693.
Emancipation proclamation, 628.
Embargo 1807, 423, 426.
Endicott, John, 66.
England, early, 3; sovereigns of, 41; government, 42.
Ericsson, John, 623.
Erie canal, 463.
Excise, 382.
Federalists, 388, 404, 405, 438, 451.
Filibusters, 565.
Fillmore, Millard, elected vice-president, 540; president, ch. xxviii.
Florida discovered, 29; settled, 48; becomes British possession 1763, 210; returned to Spain 1783, 210; purchased, 456; admitted, 523.
Franklin, Benjamin, early life, 158; plan of union, 198; in England, 244; in Congress, 273, 275; in France, 278; in constitutional convention, 357; death, 377.
Franciscans, 176; in California, 748.
Free Soil Party, 541, 554.
Fremont, John C., 568, 765, 767, 769, 770, 771.

INDEX. 429

French and Indian war, ch. xiv.
Fugitive Slave Law, 547, 549.
Fulton, Robert, 415, 446.
Gadsden purchase, 567.
Garfield, James A., 700; elected president, 701; term, ch. xxxiv, 2; death, 705.
Genet, French embassador, 390.
Geneva award. See Alabama claims.
George III., king of England, government, 215; policy toward colonies, 231.
Georgia, settlement, ch. x.
Gilbert, Sir Humphrey, explorations, 50, 51.
Gold in California, 775, 778, 780.
Government, colonial, 162; during war for independence, 268, 277; executive department, 367; salaries, 371; sub-treasury system, 506. See also **Congress, Reconstruction.**
Grant, Ulysses S., in civil war, ch. xxxi; elected president, 674; term, ch. xxxii; travels, 702; candidate for third term, 701; death, 720.
Greeley, Horace, 686.
Greenback Party, 703, 719.
Greenbacks, 655, 699.
Gwin, William M., 777, 786.
Hamilton, Alexander, early life, 353.
Hancock, John, 235.
Harrison, William Henry, 430, 441, 444; president, 511, 512; life, 513.
Hartford convention, 451.
Harvard College, 100.
Hayes, Rutherford B., 696; elected president, 692; term, ch. xxxiv, 1.
Henry, Patrick, 223, 224.
Higginson, Francis, 66, 68.
Huguenots. See Protestants.
Hutchinson, Mrs. Anna, 70, 73.
Illinois, 459.

Immigration, early, to U. S., 392; later, 490. See also Chinese Immigration.
Independence, war for, ch. xvi; declaration, 274; confirmed by France and Spain, 295.
Indiana, 459.
Indians, named by Columbus, 14; life, 18; character, 19; relics, 20; United States Indian policy, 380; outbreak in Indiana, 430; in Florida, 456, 498; in Illinois, 498; in Oregon and Montana, 690; in Idaho and Arizona, 724. See also names of tribes.
Indies, European commerce with, 7; a sea road to, 8.
Internal improvements, 462, 474.
Inventions, 414, 493, 566, 727. See also **Steamboat, Telegraph,** etc., and names of inventors.
Iowa, 523.
Iroquois, or Five Nations, 181; raid Wyoming valley 1778, 312; punished, 314.
Jackson, Andrew, defends New Orleans, 448; subdues Seminoles, 456; presidential candidate, 466, 477; term, ch. xxiv.
Jamestown, begun, 103; burned, 137.
Jay, John, 360, 369, 391.
Jefferson, Thomas, 275, 389, 400, 407; elected president, 409; term, ch. xx; death, 469.
Jesuits, in Canada, 176; in Mexico, 748.
Johnson, Andrew, elected vice-president, 657; president, ch. xxxii.
Kansas, slavery in, ch. xxix; Lecompton constitution, 575; admitted, 577.
Kentucky admitted a state, 378.
King, James, 783.
Ku Klux Klan, 684.
Lafayette, Marquis de, 289, 465.

430 INDEX.

Larkin, Thomas O., 763.
La Salle, Cavalier de, descends the Mississippi, 178.
Lewis and Clarke expedition, 418.
Lexington skirmish, 249.
Liberia, 461.
Lincoln, Abraham, 576; elected president, 582, 587; term, ch. xxxi; assassination, 658.
Literature, growth of, 497.
Locke, John, framer of the constitution for the Carolinas, 122.
Louisiana, French possession, 178; early growth, 182; divided 1763, 210; purchased, 417; explored, 418; admitted, 459.
Madison, James, 352; elected president, 426; term, ch. xxi.
Magellan crosses the Pacific, 29.
Maine, 460.
Maryland, settlement, ch. ix.
Massachusetts, settlement, ch. vi; under Charles II., 93; under James II., 94.
Mexico wins independence, 464; war with, ch. xxvii; Maximilian, 672; government in California, 758.
Michigan, 523.
Minnesota, 577.
Missions, 752, 753; secularization, 759.
Mississippi, 459.
Missouri, contest over admission, 460; admitted, 460.
Missouri Compromise, 460, 559.
Monitor, war vessel, 623.
Monroe, James, early life, 455; elected president, 453; term, ch. xxii.
Monroe Doctrine, 464.
Mormons, 510, 711.
Mound-builders, relics of, 21.
Narvaez attempts to conquer Florida, 29.
Navigation Acts, passed, 91; evaded, 216; enforcement commenced, 217.

Navy in war for independence, 269, 316; organized under Adams, 404; employed, 419; in war of 1812, 449; in Pacific in 1846, 768; in civil war, 621.
Nebraska, 668.
Negro suffrage, 667.
Nevada, 656.
New England, land, 83; towns, 84; counties and states, 85; confederacy, 86.
Newfoundland, visited by French fishermen, 32.
New Hampshire, foundation, 80.
New Jersey, settlement, 143, 144.
New Mexico explored, 31; settlement at Santa Fe, 48; comes under power of United States, 537.
Newspapers, 220, 497.
New York, settlement, 141, 142.
New York city founded, 141; captured by British 1776, 281.
North Carolina, settlement, ch. x.
Northmen visit America, 23.
Northwest Territory, 350.
Nullification, 407, 485.
Oglethorpe, James, founder of Georgia, 129.
Ohio, 459.
Ohio Company, 189.
Omnibus Bill, 547.
Oregon, disputed ownership, 518; state admitted, 577.
Otis, James, 218.
Panama Congress, 470.
Parliament, origin, 3; composition, 42.
Parties, Political, growth of, 388, 475, 487, 554, 561.
Pennsylvania, settlement, ch. xi.
Penn, William, founder of Pennsylvania, 145; treaty with Indians, 149.
Philadelphia, founded, 147, 148; captured 1777, 291; abandoned, 296.

Pierce, **Franklin**, elected president, 553; term, ch. **xxix.**
Pirates subdued, 154.
Pitt, William (Earl of Chatham), prime minister, 204; on American war, 307; death, 309.
Pizarro conquers Peru, 29.
Plymouth, settlement, 62.
Pocahontas, 108.
Polo, Marco, 5; wonders related by, 6.
Ponce de Leon discovers Florida, 29.
Pontiac, chief of Ottawas, 200.
Prohibition, 552, 719.
Protestants, French, settle in South Carolina, 46; destroyed by Spaniards, 47.
Protestantism, origin, 39.
Pueblos, 754.
Puritans, origin of, 40; colonize Massachusetts, 59 *et seq.*
Quakers, in Massachusetts, 97; in Pennsylvania, 145; doctrines, 146; in war for independence, 286.
Quebec, founded, 45; captured 1759, 206; assaulted 1775, 267.
Railroads, beginning of, 494; transcontinental, 681; in California, 794.
Raleigh, Sir Walter, first colony, 52; second colony, 53.
Reconstruction Acts, 666.
Republicans, 561.
Republicans—**Democratic,** 389, 406.
Revolution. See War for Independence, ch. **xvi.**
Rhode Island, foundation, ch. **vii.**
Sacramento, squatter riot, 785.
St. Lawrence, gulf of, discovered, 32; river discovered, 33; explored, 44.
Salem witchcraft, 98.

San Diego, 749.
San Domingo, purposed annexation, 680.
San Francisco, bay, 751.
San Francisco, city, 773, 781.
Seminoles, 456.
Serra, Father Junipero, 750.
Shays' Rebellion in Massachusetts, 355.
Silver coinage, 697.
Slavery in colonies, 164; growth of, 379; in politics, 457, 458; ended, 628.
Smith, John, hero of Jamestown, 104.
Sons of Liberty, 221, 225.
South Carolina, settlement, 126, 127; resist the tariff, 484, 486.
Stamp Act passed, 219; resisted, 220; repealed, 229.
Standish, Miles, 64.
State rights, 406, 476.
Steamboat, 415, 416.
Strikes, 725.
Sutter, John A., 762.
Tariff, First, law for, 364; for revenue, 365; for protection, 366, 471; sectional opposition, 472; compromise, 486; later history, 713, 714.
Taylor, Zachary, General, 529; elected president, 540; life, 543.
Telegraph, 524.
Temperance, reform, 491. See also Prohibition.
Tennessee, 459.
Territories, the Northwest, 350; general provision for, 370.
Texas, annexation, 517, 522.
Ticonderoga, 202, 256.
Tobacco in Virginia, 109.
Tories, or Loyalists, 221.
Town government, 84.
Townshend taxes, passed, 232; repealed, except on tea, 538.

Treaties, of Paris (1763), 210; of Paris (1783), 340; Jay's, 391; of Ghent, 450; Webster-Ashburton, 516; on Oregon boundary, 528; of Guadalupe-Hidalgo, 538; of Washington, 677; with China, 712.
Trent affair, 595.
Tyler, John, vice-president, 511; president, ch. xxvi; life, 515.
Valley Forge, winter quarters 1777-8, 293.
Van Buren, Martin, vice-president, 483; president, 489; ch. xxv; life, 500.
Vermont, settlers, 255; admitted a state, 378.
Verrazzano, explorations of, 33.
Vespucci, Amerigo, gives name to America, 28.
Vigilance committee, 782, 783, 792.
Virginia, settlement, ch. ix.
Walpole, Sir Robert, ministry of, 101, 156.
Wars, Pequod, 77; King Philip's, 89; Bacon's Rebellion, 137; between French and English colonists, 180; between France and England for America, ch. xiv; for independence, ch. xvi; of 1812, ch. xxi; with Mexico, ch. xxvii; of Secession, ch. xxxi. See also Indian.
Washington, George, early life, 191; fights the French, 194; commander of American army, 256; retreat across New Jersey, 284; recovers New Jersey, 287; plot against, 294; elected president, 361; inaugurated, 362; methods in office, 375; retirement, 395; death, 408.
Washington, capital of United States, 374; sacked 1814, 417.
Webster, Daniel, 465, 473; debate with Hayne, 488; secretary of state, 516.
West Virginia, 656.
Whigs, or Patriots, 221.
Whigs, a political party, 487, 514.
Whitney, Eli, 399.
Whisky insurrection, 383.
Williams, Roger, 70, 72.
Wilmot Proviso, 534.
Wisconsin, 523.
Wolfe, James, captures Quebec, 206.
Workingman's Party, 792, 793.
Writs of assistance, 217.
Yorktown, siege (1781), 338; capture, 339; siege (1861), 600; centennial, 710.

www.ingramcontent.com/pod-product-compliance
Lightning Source LLC
Chambersburg PA
CBHW032000300426
44117CB00008B/846